THE OLD TESTAMENT PROPHETS

An Outline

Homer Heater, Jr., Ph.D.

Hesed Publications
245 Prather Road
Somerset KY 42503

2015

Preface

I have been teaching the Old Testament for many years, both at Capital Bible Seminary and Dallas Theological Seminary. I am very grateful for the opportunity of interacting with hundreds of students during that time, striving to get them excited about this vital area of the Bible.

This is an outline rather than a commentary. Consequently, many will be disappointed that there are not more details. However, my intent is to provide a general outline that will assist the student as he or she works through the biblical text. I hope it will prove helpful.

I have arranged the books in chronological not canonical order. I am strongly committed to the thesis that knowledge of contemporary history is a prerequisite to understanding the prophets. Consequently, I have placed the prophets in the era of their ministry. There are a couple of books that are hard to situate historically, but I believe the study of each century (eighth through the fifth) will assist in the comprehension of what these prophets are saying.

Homer Heater, Jr., Ph.D.
Professor emeritus
Capital Bible Seminary
October 2015

TABLE OF CONTENTS

Interpreting Prophecy

There are a number of difficulties in interpreting Old Testament prophecy. The reasons for this are several. The first is the question of the type of literature. Much of the prophetic literature is in poetic form, and one is always struggling to sort out what is to be taken literally (normal, expected meaning) and what is figurative. We will try to stay as literal as possible in the interpretative process. Even where symbols, metaphors, and parables are employed, there is not too much difficulty understanding the literal meaning behind the figure.

An even larger difficulty is ascertaining when the prophecy will be fulfilled. As a rule of thumb, we should look back into history to see if an event has happened. If so it may well be that was the fulfillment. If the language of the prophecy is such that it has never been fulfilled, we should look to the eschatological future for its fulfillment. (Cf. Chapter 20 of Isaiah which is a prophecy concerning Egypt. The first part was no doubt fulfilled in the attack and conquering of Assyria. The language of the second part is stereotypical and eschatological. A similar pattern is found in Luke 10 (see also Matt. 10). There Jesus sends out the apostles and the seventy. The first part of the chapter pertains to that time, but the second part is eschatological.)

Historical Background of the Eighth Century

Five writing prophets ministered during this important century: Jonah, Amos, Hosea, Isaiah and Micah. This century was dominated politically by the Assyrians, but the far-reaching spiritual impact came from little known men from fairly obscure kingdoms called Israel and Judah.

Historical background is essential for a proper understanding of the setting and message of these prophets. There are times when that background cannot be ascertained, but to the extent that it can be known, the understanding of the prophet's message is enhanced. Amos is the first writing prophet who directs his message to Israel. Hosea follows on his heels; then the great statesman-prophet Isaiah and his contemporary, Micah.

The upper Euphrates valley has a very complex history. Many different peoples over many centuries intruded, settled, mixed and fought with whoever preceded them. These people came to have a very important influence on God's covenant people. To better understand the events affecting the Old Testament people and the prophets who spoke to them for God, two major groups will be discussed: the Arameans and the Assyrians.

The period of the transition from judges to kings in the history of Israel (c. 1100 B.C.) was a significant period in the entire Mediterranean area. Smith says of this period:

"The last two centuries of the second millennium B.C. [1200-1000] had witnessed in western Asia and the Levant ubiquitous disturbances which caused a new distribution of political power. The Egyptian empire had declined, the Hittite had collapsed. Troy had fallen, the days of Cnossus and of Mycenae were over. When things have settled down and the scene-shifting is complete, we find Assyria (which had relapsed into obscurity after a brief emergence) occupying the centre of the stage. Phrygia, and Lydia, and Greek Ionia become the important powers in western Asia Minor. In European Greece the Achaeans have ceased to be the principal power; they have been replaced by the Dorians. In Syria and Palestine we meet with a number of minor peoples and states—Phoenicia, Damascus, Israel, Judah, Moab, Edom, and others."[1]

The new Assyrian power that came to "occupy center stage" arose again about 1000 BC. This new kingdom period of Assyrian history (900-600) dramatically affected the eighth century Israel/Judah and the message of the prophets.

---

[1]S. Smith, "The Foundation of the Assyrian Empire," *CAH* 3:1.

Before going on with Assyrian history, it is necessary to examine a group that began to show up in the North West about this same period of time. These people were called Arameans by Semites but the Greeks referred to them as Syrians (perhaps from the Semitic word for Tyre, Tsur, hence Tsuria). (Likewise the languages will be referred to as Aramaic and Syriac.)

The presence of Aramaic names for rivers and mountains argues for their presence north of Syria from early times. Sometime at the beginning of the first millennium, they began to move in large numbers into the North West area of the Euphrates and even made their way down to the Persian Gulf. This was not a cohesive movement, but a drifting of nomadic tribes with a similar dialect and religion. They posed a large threat to the Assyrians and probably should be credited with bringing the Middle Assyrian period to a close. They settled around the Khabur River, as far south as the border of Babylonia, and the Chaldean tribes (Bit Yakin), who are also Aramean, settled in the marsh lands north of the Persian Gulf. (See map on p. 12.) These Chaldeans eventually infiltrated the Babylonian peoples and founded the Neo-Babylonian Empire in 625 B.C.

One group of Arameans consolidated their power and made Damascus their capital. These are the ever-present Syrians in the Bible. David conquered the Aramean coalition that came against him, placed garrisons in Damascus, and probably thereby unwittingly contributed to the ability of Assyria to rise again. The Aramaic language became the *lingua franca* (trade language) from about the eighth century because the people were so widely spread throughout the area (cf. Isa. 36:11). Even during the Indo-European Persian period, Aramaic was the official language of the empire (hence, sections of Daniel and Ezra are Aramaic, and the *script* used for the Hebrew Bible is Aramaic).

As the Aramaic groups settled down and formed solid political entities, the Assyrians began to reassert their control of the west. During the ninth century, they conducted almost yearly campaigns over a period of sixty years and established dominance around the Khabur and Balikh rivers.

Biblical contact with the Assyrians came in the ninth century when a coalition of kings (Arameans and others) which Ahab joined fought Assyria. This coalition was an effort to assert independence in the west from the Assyrian over lordship. The account of this battle is found in Shalmaneser III's annals and is dated at 853 B.C. The Assyrians claimed victory, but they did not return for some time and it took several battles before they were completely triumphant. This happened in 841 B.C. and Jehu, king of Israel, and other kings were forced to come to Nahr el-Kelb to pay tribute. This event was recorded on Shalmaneser's black obelisk.[2]

Assyria declined somewhat at the end of the ninth century, but Adad Nirari III (810-783 B.C.) marched west in his fifth year and defeated Damascus.[3] This removed for a time the pressure of Syria on Israel. Later, the Assyrians were too occupied to keep up the pressure, but Damascus and Hamath were battling for control of their area allowing Israel and Judah a respite for new growth.[4]

The mighty Tiglath-Pileser III (745-727) brought his country back to great heights. He campaigned in the west from 743-738. There he encountered a certain Azariah in Syria, defeated him and destroyed much of his territory.[5]

---

[2] S. Smith, "The Foundation of the Assyrian Empire," *CAH* 3:13-14.

[3] *ANET*, pp. 281-282: "In the fifth year (of my official rule) I sat down solemnly on my royal throne and called up the country (for war). I ordered the numerous army of Assyria to march against Palestine. I crossed the Euphrates at its flood. As to the numerous hostile kings who had rebelled in the time of my father Shamshi-Adad (V) and had wi[th held] their regular (tributes)....I received all the tributes [...] which they brought to Assyria. I (then) ordered [to march] against the country Damascus. I invested Mari' in Damascus [and he surrendered]. One hundred talents of gold (corresponding to) one thousand talents of [silver], 60 talents...[I received as his tribute]."

[4] See Hans Wolff, "Joel and Amos" in *Hermeneia, a Critical and Historical Commentary on the Bible,* p. 89.

[5] *ANET*, p. 282: Tiglath-Pileser says "[In] the (subsequent) course of my campaign [I received] the tribute of the kin[gs...A]zriau from Iuda in...countless, (reaching) sky high...eyes, like from heaven...by means of an attack with foot

Some scholars have a problem accepting Azariah as the biblical one, but Bright says that it would be exceptional to have two kings and two territories with the same name in the same period of time.[6] The devastation spoken of in Isaiah 1 is therefore possibly the result of this attack from Assyria, and so, early on, Judah came under the shadow of this eastern scourge.[7]

---

soldiers...He heard [about the approach of the] massed [armies of] Ashur and was afraid.... I tore down, destroyed and burnt [down...for Azr]iau they had annexed, they (thus) had reinforced him...like vine/trunks...was very difficult...was barred and high...was situated and its exit...I made deep...I surrounded his garrisons [with earthwork], against....I made them carry [the corvee-basket] and...his great...like a pot [I did crush...] (lacuna of three lines)...Azriau...a royal palace of my own [I built in his city...] tribute like that [for Assyrian citizens I imposed upon them...] the city Kul[lani...] his ally...the cities...19 districts belonging to Hamath and the cities in their vicinity which are (situated) at the coast of the Western Sea and which they had (unlawfully) taken away for Azariau, I restored to the territory of Assyria. An officer of mine I installed as governor over them. [I deported] 30,300 inhabitants from their cities and settled them in the province of the town Ku[...]; 1,223 inhabitants I settled in the province of the Ullaba country."

[6]Bright, *History of Israel*, 252.

[7]For a defense of the idea that Azariah of Judah headed up an anti-Assyrian coalition, see Tadmor, "Azarijau of Yaudi" *Scripta Hierosolymitana* 8 (1961): 232-271. However, *Israelite and Judaean History*, Old Testament Library. Edited by John H. Hayes and J. Maxwell Miller. London: SCM Press, 1977 says, "Recently, Na'aman [Nadav Na'aman. "Sennacherib's 'Letter to God' on His Campaign to Judah," BASOR CCXIV (1974) 25-39] has shown conclusively that the fragment presumably mentioning Azriau king of Yaudi actually belongs to the time of Sennacherib and refers not to Azariah but to Hezekiah. In Tiglath-Pileser's annals there are two references to an Azariah (in line 123 as Az-ri-a-[u] and in line 131 as Az-r-ja-a-í) but neither of these make any reference to his country. Thus the Azriau of Tiglath-pileser's annals and Azariah of the Bible should be regarded as two different individuals. Azriau's country cannot, at the present, be determined." Na'aman separates the country (Yaudi) from the name Azriau (p. 36). Also p. 28 on line 5 where the original transcription was "[I]zri-ja-u *mat* Ja-u-di" he reads "*ina birit misrija u mat Jaudi*" However, Kitchen, *On the Reliability of the Old Testament (OROT)*, p. 18, is less dogmatic. He says "Hence we cannot certainly assert that this Azriau (without a named territory!) is Azariah of Judah; the matter remains open and

Tiglath-Pileser III put pressure on the northern kingdom of Israel as well. Of King Menahem, the Bible says, "There came against the land Pul [Tiglath-Pileser, Pul was his Babylonian name],[8] the King of Assyria, and Menahem gave Pul a thousand talents of silver, that his hand be with him to confirm the kingdom in his hand" (2 Kings 15:19). Tiglath-Pileser III's annals say, "[As for Menahem, I ov]erwhelmed him [like a snowstorm] and he . . . fled like a bird, alone, [and bowed to my feet(?)]. I returned him to his place [and imposed tribute upon him, to wit:] gold, silver, etc. Israel [Omri land], all its inhabitants (and) their possessions I led to Assyria."[9] When Pekah allied himself with Rezin, King of Syria, against Ahaz of Judah, Ahaz sent to Tiglath-Pileser for help (2 Kings 16:5-8). Another deportation of Israel is mentioned in 1 Chron. 5:5, 6. Apparently a number of incursions were made against Samaria and people were carried off each time.

Tiglath-Pileser had put Hoshea on the throne,[10] but Shalmaneser V (726-722 B.C.) "found conspiracy in Hoshea; for he had sent messengers to So king of Egypt, and offered no present to the king of Assyria, as he had done year by year" (2 Kings 17:3-4). "And it came to pass...that Shalmaneser king of Assyria came up against Samaria, and besieged it. And at the end of three years they took it...and the king of Assyria carried Israel away unto Assyria, and put them in Halah...and in the cities of the Medes" (2 Kings 18:9-11).

Sargon II (722-705 B.C.), in his inscriptions at Khorsabad, claims to have captured Samaria and led off the captives of Israel. "I besieged and conquered Samaria, led away as booty 27,290 inhabitants of it. I formed from among

---

undecided for the present and probably unlikely." See Also S. Smith, "The Foundation of the Assyrian Empire," *CAH* 3:35-36.

[8]See J. A. Brinkman, "Merodach-Baladan II," p. 12.

[9]*ANET,* pp. 283, 84.

[10]*ANET*, pp. 284.

them a contingent of 50 chariots and made remaining [inhabitants] assume their [social] positions. I installed over them an officer of mine and imposed upon them the tribute of the former king."[11] This does not agree either with the biblical data or Shalmaneser V's annals quoted above. As Finegan suggests, Sargon may have come to the throne on the heels of the defeat of Samaria and carried out the deportation begun by Shalmaneser.[12]

Sennacherib (705-681 B.C.) came west and conquered the fortified cities of Judah and besieged Jerusalem (2 Kings 18). Hezekiah paid him tribute. It was in preparation for this kind of attack that Hezekiah had the tunnel dug which bears the famous Siloam inscription (2 Chron. 32:1-8). "As to Hezekiah, the Jew, he did not submit to my yoke, I laid siege to 46 of his strong cities, walled forts and to the countless small villages in their vicinity, and conquered [them] by means of well-stamped [earth]-ramps, and bat-tering-rams . . . Himself I made a prisoner in Jerusalem, his royal residence, like a bird in a cage. I surrounded him with earthwork in order to molest those who were leaving his city's gate. His towns which I had plundered, I took away from his country and gave them [over] to Mitinti, king of Ashdod."[13] This is part of an extended account found on a prism inscription. Sennacherib fails to note that he did not conquer Jerusalem. Hezekiah entertained ambassadors from the newly arising neo-Babylonian empire as part of an anti-Assyrian conspiracy.

The decline of Assyria was swift and decisive. The Babylonians, under Nabopolassar, joined with the Medes and Scythians. After a series of victories, they invested Nineveh, the great capital, and it fell in 612 B.C. The Assyrians fled to Haran in the west where the Egyptians joined them in an effort to prop them up against the Babylonians. The Babylonians won this battle under Nebuchadnezzar in 609 and began to take over the southern half of the Assyrian empire.

---

[11]*ANET*, p. 285.

[12]Jack Finegan, *Light from the Ancient Past*, p. 210.

[13]*ANET*, p. 288.

Historical Summary

Adad-Nirari III (805 B.C.) defeated Damascus.

Jeroboam II; Uzziah (Azariah)

Tiglath-Pileser III (732) defeated Damascus (Isaiah 7; Ahaz).

Shalmaneser V (722 B.C.) defeated and began to deport Samaria.

Sargon II (722 B.C.) completed the deportation of Samaria.
      (711 B.C.) fought Ashdod (Isaiah 20).

Sennacherib (701 B.C.) defeated Lachish and threatened Jerusalem (Isaiah 36-37; Hezekiah). (689 B.C.) defeated and destroyed Babylon.

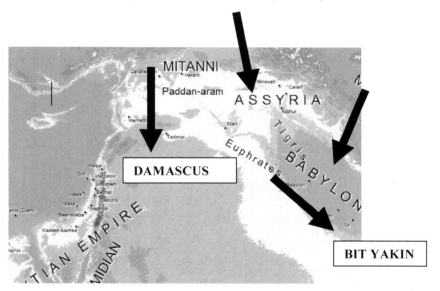

ASSYRIAN EMPIRE AND ARAMEAN GROUPINGS

Map from Bible Works

EIGHTH CENTURY PROPHETS AND THEIR WORLD

DECADE	PROPHETS	JUDAH	ISRAEL	ASSYRIA
800				Adad-Nirari III 810-783
790		Uzziah 792-40	Jero. II 793-753	
780	A M O S	J O N A H		Shalmaneser IV 783-772
770	H O S E A			Ashur-Dan III 772-754
760				
750		I S A I A H	Jotham 751-32	Zech. 753 Shallum 752 Menahem 752-742 Pekahiah 742-740 Pekah 752-31	Ashur-nirari V 754-746 Tiglath-pileser III 745-727
740			Ahaz 735-15	Hoshea 731-722	
730			Hezekiah 728-687		Shalmaneser V 727-722
720		M I C A H			Sargon II 722-705
710					
700					Sennacherib 705-681

Notes on the Book of Amos

The Prophet:

Little is known about Amos. He has a rural background and comes from Judah (hence is viewed as an interloper by the priests of Bethel). He was not a member of the "prophetic guild" but was a prophet nevertheless.

The Time:

The general time frame is given in 1:1 as the reigns of Jeroboam II (793-753) in the north and Uzziah in the south (792-740), hence a period of some 50 years. However, Amos' message was probably preached over a fairly short time (perhaps one year?). Consequently, it is difficult to place him in the longer period.

The Kings:

Israel—Jeroboam II (793-753)
Judah—Uzziah (792-740)
Assyria—Adad Nirari III (810-783)
Syria—Hazael

Events:

Adad Nirari sacked Damascus in 805. This took the previously relentless pressure of the Syrians off the Israelites. Consequently, there is a time of unprecedented prosperity in the north as the boundaries (both north and south) are restored to that which David and Solomon held (2 Kings 14:21-29).

Synthesis

Amos' primary message is to the covenant people of God. When he preaches to Damascus, Philistia, Tyre, Edom, Ammon and Moab, he deals primarily in horizontal sins: unjust actions against others. But when he turns to Judah and Israel, the indictment is that they have rejected the Torah of Yahweh (2:4).

The keeping of this law is indeed worked out in social justice, but the basis for the action is the holiness of God. Israel has apostatized from the living and true God (4:4-5), their ritual is empty (5:21-27), they have become dissolute in their daily conduct (6:1-7), and they oppress the needy (8:4-6). Because of this a holy God must discipline them (4:11-13). In spite of a series of messages full of doom, however, God's covenant with His people cannot be broken. The last section of the book (9:7-15) is a message of hope. The "booth of David" is in the process of falling (participle). It is not yet down (that will happen in 586 B.C. when Jerusalem falls). God will raise up the "booth" when He restores Israel and Judah.

Structure

Rhetorical indictment of eight nations (1-2).

Oracle #1 (Hear) seven questions—judgment (3:1-11).
Oracle #2 (Hear) cows of Bashan—judgment (4:1-13).
Oracle #3 (Hear) call to repentance in midst of sin (5:1-17).

Woe #1 to those longing for the Day of Yahweh (5:18-27).
Woe #2 to those who are at ease in Zion (6:1-14).
Woe #3 to those who put off the day of doom (6:3)

       Vision #1 Locust swarm (7:1-3).
       Vision #2 Fire (7:4-6).
       Vision #3 Plumb line (7:7-9).

[Historical interlude—Amaziah the priest confronts Amos and orders him to return to the south (7:10-17)]

Vision #4 Summer fruit (kaytz/ketz) (8:1-3).

Oracle #4 (Hear) you who trample the needy (8:4-14).

Vision #5 the Lord by the Altar (9:1-6).

Concluding section of hope (9:7-15).

I.   Historical Background.

Amos ministered for a period of time (perhaps a short period) during the reigns of two powerful and long-lived monarchs.[14] Jeroboam II ruled in Israel from 793 to 753 B.C. or forty-one years.[15] Uzziah (Azariah) ruled in Judah from 792 to 740 B.C.[16]

The Assyrian King, Adad Nirari III (810-783 B.C.) marched west in his fifth year (805 B.C.) and defeated Damascus.[17] This removed for a time the pressure of Syria on Israel.[18] Later, the Assyrians were too occupied to

---

[14]See Simon Cohen, "The Political Background of the Words of Amos," *HUCA* 36 (1965): 153-160. "Two years before the earthquake (1:1)." K. Kitchen, *OROT*, p. 53, says Hazor was destroyed by an earthquake in the 8th century.

[15]Fourteen of these years must have been as co-regent; otherwise the synchronism does not work (see Thiele, *MNHK*, 106-7).

[16]Again there must have been a co-regency of twenty-five years—Thiele, *MNHK*, 111.

[17]*ANET*, pp. 281-282.

[18]2 Kings 13:7 indicates the desperate straits in which Israel found herself because of Syrian pressure.

keep up the pressure, but Damascus and Hamath were battling for control of their area.[19] As a result Israel was able to extend her borders apparently to the original boundaries of David and Solomon (2 Kings 14:25). Jonah was used to prophesy regarding the extended borders of Israel. Judah likewise conquered the Philistines, the Arabians, and the Ammonites. Elath at the Gulf of Aqaba was restored by Uzziah's father (2 Chron. 26:2).[20]

The vacuum created by the political situation and the filling of that vacuum by Israel brought great prosperity. With the increase in wealth came an increase in religious apostasy. The poor were oppressed, and the rich languished in large houses in a perpetual party atmosphere (Amos 4:6-8; 5:10-13; 6:4-7). The cult center established by Jeroboam I fifty years earlier was in full swing, and Amos inveighed against it (7:10-17).[21]

II.   The Prophet Amos.

Amos had the difficult task of leaving his country and going to Israel. Consequently, his message was unpopular not only because of its content, but because it was being delivered by a "foreigner." Amos' village was located a few miles southeast of Bethlehem. A good view of the area can be had from the heights of the Herodium. The area is fairly barren, and the Bedouin graze their sheep there.[22] Amos was a shepherd (1:1) as well as a

---

[19]LaSor, *et al.*, Old Testament *Survey*, 321 and J. Bright, *History of Israel*, 238-240.

[20]See Schedl, *History of the OT,* 4:133-149, for a good, fairly conservative discussion by a Roman Catholic scholar.

[21]See T. E. McComiskey, "Amos," *EBC*, 7:269-331. See S. Cohen, "The Political Background of the Words of Amos," *HUCA* 36 (1965): 153-160, for a different perspective. He argues that chapters 1-2 indicate a tailing off of the prosperity.

[22]There is a modern Jewish town called Tekoa, an Arab village called El Tuk, and a ruin that was probably Amos' town.

tender of sycamore figs (7:14). The word for shepherd is *noqed* (נֹקֵד)
which refers to a type of spotted sheep and then the caretaker of such
sheep. The word translated sycamore figs is from *shiqmim* (שִׁקְמִים).[23] The
work of Amos in connection with the fig trees was to prick the figs, "a
fruit that must be punctured or slit shortly before ripening to be edible."[24]

Thus we can see that Amos was of humble origins and probably a fairly
poor farmer.[25] Whereas his later contemporary, Isaiah, seems to be at
home in upper class circles, Amos came into the wealthy community of
Israel as an interloper.

Amos' statement about not being a prophet has provoked a lot of
discussion (7:14). Is he saying that he is not a prophet? The verbless clause
("I not a prophet") can only be given a time from the context. It should
probably be translated in the past: "I was not a prophet nor the son of a
prophet." The latter phrase does not mean that his father was not a prophet,
but that he did not belong to a guild of prophets called "sons of prophets"
(בְּנֵי הַנְּבִיאִים *bene hanevi'im*) (2 Kings 2:3ff). Amos is most assuredly a
prophet at the time. He himself says: "The Lord has spoken! Who can but
prophesy?" (3:8).

III. The Outline of Amos.

A. Amos gives an introduction and the theme of his repeated message (1:1-2).

---

[23]"Sycamore" is Greek for "black fig." I am not sure why the American sycamore is
called that since our sycamore is quite different from the Middle Eastern sycamore.

[24]LaSor, *et al.*, *Old Testament Survey*, 319.

[25]But see Wolff, "Joel and Amos," p. 90, who argues that he was a sheep breeder
and hence better off than a lowly shepherd.

Amos was apparently a peripatetic prophet who kept repeating a basic message, the summary for which is given by Amaziah in 7:10-11. Jonah's preaching in Nineveh must have been similar.

Amos must have subsequently returned to Tekoa where he assembled and edited his messages as we now see them in the book. The final chapter of hope was probably written at that time (note the reference to the booth of David which represents Judah).

The introduction likens Yahweh to a lion who roars with devastating results. He roars from Jerusalem to the northern kingdom.[26] The Carmel range was very fertile, and a judgment resulting in its drying up would be very severe.[27]

B. Amos speaks of God's judgment of all the nations surrounding Israel and Israel herself (1:3—2:16).

The pedagogical device is to condemn other nations before coming to Israel. He begins with Damascus, crosses south to Gaza, goes back north to Tyre, crosses southeast to Edom, north to Ammon, back south to Moab, westward to Judah and finally comes to Israel. Each message is introduced with the phrase "Thus says Yahweh" (כֹּה אָמַר יהוה *koh amar Yahweh*).

1. Yahweh indicts Damascus (1:3-5).

The Hebrew idiom "for three + one" is a way of saying "enough is enough."[28] The Arameans were enemies of Israel most of the time.

[26.] See McComiskey, "Amos," *EBC*.

[27] For a continuation of the roaring lion theme, see 3:8.

[28] Numerical parallelism. Parallelism in which a number is used in one line, then the next higher number in the second line. (As Watson explains, "Since no number can have a synonym the only way to provide a corresponding component is to use a digit which is higher in value than the original" [*Classical Hebrew Poetry*, p. 144]).

Because of their abuse of Gilead (northeast section of Israel, cf. 2 Kings 13:1-9), God is going to judge Damascus (their capital) and send them into the Assyrian exile to the city of Kir (2 Kings 16:9).

2. Yahweh indicts Philistia (1:6-8).

Gaza was instrumental in sending a complete captivity into Edom where they would be sold as slaves. This represents border raids on Judah when the captives would be sold into slavery. Ashdod, Ashkelon, and Ekron are mentioned as three other cities in the Philistine grouping.[29]

3. Yahweh indicts Tyre (1:9-10).

Tyre, the great maritime merchant power, was also involved in the slave trade. The covenant of brotherhood may hearken back to the relationship between David and Hiram.

4. Yahweh indicts Edom (1:11-12).

The Edomites were "brothers" to Israel and Judah, yet they were implacable enemies. They are condemned by most of the prophets. The little prophecy of Obadiah is devoted exclusively to the Edomites.

5. Yahweh indicts Ammon (1:13-15).

The Ammonites were also distant relatives of Israel, through Lot, living on the east side of the Jordan. The modern capital of Amman retains the ancient designation. Because of Ammon's attack on Gilead (Israelite territory), God would send them into exile.

---

[29]M. Haran, "Observations on the Historical Background of Amos 1:2--2:6," *IEJ* 18 (1968): 201-212, argues for "Aram" rather than "Edom." The mistake between "d" and "r" in Hebrew (ד ר) is easily made, but we should stick with Edom since they could have sold the slaves to the Arabians.

6. Yahweh indicts Moab (2:1-3).

   Moab apparently defeated Edom at some point and burned the king into lime. This heinous deed (among others, no doubt) brings the judgment of God upon Moab.

7. Yahweh indicts Judah (2:4-5).

   The edict of judgment is circling ever closer and now alights on Judah. Judah's sin is in rejecting the law of God and failure to keep His statutes. As noted earlier, Judah and Israel hold unique positions as God's chosen people. They are more accountable than other nations as a result.

8. Yahweh indicts Israel (2:6-16).

   The circle has now closed on the object of Amos' message: Israel. Up to this point, the Israelite could say, "Amen!" Now, however, the shoe is being placed on their foot, and Amaziah's reaction was probably typical (7:10-15).

   This sin is threefold (2:6-8). They oppress the poor, commit sexually lewd acts, and sleep on pledged garments by pagan altars and drink wine. Pusey says, "By a sort of economy in the toil of sinning, they blended many sins into one."[30]

   God reminds them that they are in the land by His grace (2:9-16). Because He is lord and His lordship has been flouted, He will judge them. God raised up prophets and Nazirites, but the people abused them.

C. Three messages are delivered against Israel (3:1—6:14). The key phrase is "hear this word."

---

[30]Pusey, *Minor Prophets*, 1:262.

1. Judgment is coming on the chosen people of Israel (Oracle #1) (3:1-15).

   Israel is God's chosen people, and yet she has sinned against her Lord. Other nations do not enjoy that position, and therefore Israel's judgment is harsher (3:1-2).

   Through a series of five proverbs (two men, lions, bird, trap, trumpets, and finally a calamity caused by God), pointing to the certainty that God has spoken, God says that He has spoken through His servants, and they must prophesy (3:3-8).

   God calls on surrounding pagans to witness Israel's sin and proclaims her devastation (3:9-15).

   Judgment will come through "an adversary." We know this is Assyria. They will plunder their land and their buildings. Through a beautiful, but violent, metaphor, he compares Israel's destruction to a shepherd, tearing a lamb from a lion's mouth, only to find a few pieces left. So God will deal with Israel. The idolatry of Bethel and the luxury of fine homes will disappear.

2. Judgment is coming on the "cows of Bashan" (Oracle #2) (4:1-13).

   Women are involved in the same sinful practices as the men, and they will go into judgment (4:1-3).[31] You will go out through breeches in the wall, each one straight before her (4:3). (Cf. Josh. 6:5, 20).[32]

---

[31]Freedman and Anderson, "Harmon in Amos 4:3," *BASOR* 198 (1970):41 connect Harmon with Ugaritic *hrnm* in northern Syria. One hundred fifty years later Zedekiah was brought to Riblah to be sentenced by Nebuchadnezzar. This is only a few miles from Harnam/Harmon.

[32]Cf. Wolff, "Joel and Amos," p. 207.

The idolatrous, futile practices of the northern kingdom are set out next. Bethel is the cult center with ancient connections, but was made the southern religious cult center in Jeroboam I's day. The Israelites are bringing tithes, sacrifices and offerings, but they are insincere as they bring them (4:4-5).

God sent a series of five judgments to try to turn them to Himself, "yet you have not turned to Me, declares the Lord" (4:6-11).

Famine (4:6).
Drought (4:7-8).
Crop failure (4:9).
Plague (4:10).
Judgment (4:11).

Consequently, even more severe punishment awaits them as He tells them to "prepare to meet your God, O Israel…the Lord of Hosts is His name" (4:6-13).

3. God predicts defeat and captivity for Israel and urges her to turn to Him (Oracle #3) (5:1-6:14).

Gilgal and Bethel were cult centers and Beersheba may have been the object of pilgrimages. Only Yahweh can bring salvation because He is the creator of the universe (5:1-9).

Israel's transgressions are obvious in their social sins, and God admonishes them to seek good (5:10-15).

Hate good judges (5:10)
Tread down the poor (5:11)
Afflicting the just; taking bribes (5:12)

God promises them judgment and tells them the Day of the Lord will be disastrous for them (Woe #1) (5:16-20).[33]

Amos condemns their empty religious activity. He wants instead obedient lives. Amos is not against sacrifice or the priesthood, he is against hypocrisy. Even in the wilderness, Israel was disobedient. Her history was one of disobedience. Therefore, God will send them into exile beyond Damascus (5:21-27).[34]

He pronounces woe on their luxurious and sinful lifestyle (6:1-3), first by saying that they are no better than other cities God has judged (Calneh, Hamath and Gath—Gath is missing from the Philistine pentapolis in the judgment promised in 1:6-8) (Woe #2).[35]

They hope to postpone the Day of the Lord (calamity), but they practice violence themselves (6:1-3).[36] The second reason God

---

[33]The Day of the Lord was looked upon as good because it is a time when God makes all things right. However, in the process of rectifying all things, judgment must come on sinners. Therefore, they are told not to look forward to it. For an excellent technical discussion on this topic, see Weiss, "The Origin of the 'Day of the Lord' Reconsidered," *HUCA* 37 (1966): 29-71. Cf. also Wolff, "Joel and Amos," pp. 255-56 for an excellent discussion of this passage.

[34]Verse 25 is a contrast: "For forty years in the wilderness you brought sacrifices and grain offerings, but you carried Sikkuth, etc." In other words, they offered sacrifice in the wilderness but still sinned, and thus it was not really to God (so Acts 7:42). They are doing the same thing in Amos' day. See Wolff for a discussion of the view that Israel did not offer sacrifice in the wilderness.

[35]On one of his expeditions, Adad Nirari III says that the Medians, Persians, Hittites, Tyre, Sidon, Israel, and Edom, Palestine submitted to him. One must wonder if the mention of these cities in Amos might not represent one of those Assyrian forays to the west.

[36]B. K. Smith and Frank Page, *Amos Obadiah and Jonah, loc. cit.,* says, "'Violence' is the usual word selected to render into English the idea in the term

pronounces woe on the Samarians is that their immoral practices will cause them to go first into the exile (6:4-7). Exile (*golah*, גּוֹלָה or גָּלָה) appears nine times in Amos (1:5; 5:5, 5, 27; 6:7; 7:11, 11, -17,17). The exile of 722 B.C. is in view, but it has not yet taken place as the critics would have it.

The suffering from the siege is depicted in 6:8-11. People die from the plague, but no one calls on God's name. This may be out of superstition, fear, or a sense of futility.[37]

Because of Israel's perverse rejection of God, He promises to bring Assyria (not mentioned by name) on them (6:12-14). Hamath to Arabah are the areas recovered by Jeroboam II.[38]

D. Amos predicts God's judgment on Israel through a series of visions (7:1—9:6).

The prophecy began with "For three transgressions, yea upon four." Perhaps a link is being made with the opening three plus one indictment

---

translated 'terror'…The word rendered 'reign'…means "sitting" or "seat." To dismiss the concept of punishment for evil tends to promote the practice of violence. Israel's leaders precipitated and accelerated 'the very misfortune that they claim will never overtake them.'"

[37]Cf. the siege of Samaria—2 Kings 6:24ff.

[38]Smith, *Amos, Obadiah and Jonah, loc. cit.,* says, "The two rhetorical questions expect negative answers. No one in their right mind runs horses on rocky crags. The second question is literally, "Does he plow with oxen?" Either the object is understood to be the 'rocky crags' mentioned in the first question or the word translated 'with oxen' (בבקרים *b^eqarim*) may be divided into two words (ים בבקר *b^eqar yam*), which would mean 'with oxen the sea.' The prophet's audience would have understood the absurdity of either scenario. What Israel had done in turning justice into poison and the fruit of righteousness into bitterness was equally absurd (see 5:7). Such perversion of right relationships and of justice in the courts was self-destructive."

with these visions. There are three visions of judgment interrupted by
Amaziah's criticism as an example of religious Israel's refusal to hear the
Word of God, followed by the fourth vision. (There is another vision at
9:1-6. It has a different introductory formula, but it may be the fifth
vision.)

1. Vision #1: Yahweh God shows Amos a locust horde (7:1-3).

    The locusts eat the spring crop. Amos pleads for clemency, and
    Yahweh listens to him (7:2-3).[39]

2. Vision #2: Yahweh God shows Amos a devastating fire (7:4-6).

    It consumes the deep and the farmland. Amos pleads again and
    Yahweh relents.[40]

3. Vision #3: Yahweh God shows Amos a plumb line (7:7-9).

    The plumb line is a builder's tool to show what is straight and, here,
    morally right. Israel is "crooked" because of idolatry. As a result,
    judgment is going to come. In this vision, Amos does not plead for
    mercy and so none is given.

4. Interlude: Amos' messages are interrupted by the priest of Bethel
    (7:10-17).

    Amaziah charges Amos with disturbing the peace (7:10-13).

    He argues that Amos has conspired against Jeroboam and that the land
    cannot hold all his words. (Cf. 7:9: "sword . . ."). The treason charge

---

[39]The king's mowing was probably the royal portion taken first.

[40]The great deep (תְּהוֹם רַבָּה *t'hom rabbah*) refers to the sea and is used here as a
symbol of the extent of God's judgment. The "farmland" is the Hebrew word "portion"
(הַחֵלֶק *haḥeleq*) and refers more probably to the people as God's "portion."

comes because Amos predicts Jeroboam's death and the exile of the people (7:10-11).

Amaziah demands that Amos go back to his own country and earn his bread from his own people. In the process he indicates that Bethel is a royal sanctuary (מִקְדַּשׁ מֶלֶךְ *miqdash melek*) and a royal residence (בֵּית מַמְלָכָה *beth mamlakah*) (7:12-13).

Amos responds by saying that he is there by God's appointment (7:14-17).

His own origins are humble, and he was not a part of the official prophetic movement (7:14-15).

He prophesies against Amaziah, his family and his land. Amaziah will go into exile as will all Israel.

5.   Vision #4 (3 + 1): Yahweh God shows Amos a basket of summer fruit (8:1-14).

He shows Amos the fruit: *qayitz* (קַיִץ). He gives its meaning: the end *qetz*, (קֵץ) has come for Israel.

By a pun he indicates that judgment will come on the palace as in other places.

He shows the reason for the judgment (8:4-14).

They cheat with shekel size and scales and thus take advantage of the poor (8:4-6).

Because of this God will judge Israel (8:7-10).[41]

---

[41]See Smith, *Amos, Obadiah, and Jonah, loc. cit.,* for dates of solar eclipses.

God's word will be withheld from those who refuse to hear it (8:11-14).

6. Vision #5: Amos sees Yahweh standing beside the altar (9:1-6).

The religious system will be broken, and the people will be judged and sent into exile (9:1-4).

Yahweh shows his sovereignty and power in creation (9:5-6).[42]

E. A final covenantal promise is made to restore Israel (9:7-15).[43]

1. God shows His sovereign control over the nations of the world (9:1-7).

Israel, boasting that she was God's chosen nation, was really no better than far off Cush because of her disobedience.

2. Israel judged but not destroyed (9:8-12).

Scattered as grain through a sieve
Sown not scattered
Sinners judged
Tabernacle restored[44]

3. There will be a time of great prosperity (9:13-15).

---

[42]Cf. Psalm 139.

[43]See LaSor, *et al.*, Old Testament *Survey*, 319-329 for an excellent discussion of this passage and a rebuttal of the position that it does not belong to Amos.

[44]James seems to be using the *idea* of Gentile inclusion, not the time frame. R. Longenecker (*Acts, loc. Cit.*) argues that James is saying in the Eschaton Gentiles will be included without losing their identity. Thus in the church, the same thing should prevail. Cf. also, H. Heater, "Amos," in *The Case for Premillennialism*, pp.148ff. The interpretation of a previous prophecy even using a different text is sanctioned by the Holy Spirit.

Historical Recap

Assyria (Adad-Nirari III) attacked Syria—805 B.C.

This took pressure off Israel

Assyria then fell into decline (Jonah's preaching?)

Israel/Judah expanded

Jonah prophesied in the north (2 Kings 14)
Jeroboam II 793-53 (40 years)
Uzziah 792-40 (52 years)

Assyria becomes strong again

Tiglath-Pileser III 743-38 campaigned in west (contact with Judah?)
 He defeated Damascus in 732
 He put Hoshea on the throne 732
 Shalmaneser V, Sargon II defeat Samaria 722
 Sargon II against Philistia 711
 Sennacherib against Hezekiah 701

Notes on the Book of Hosea

Synthesis

God uses Hosea's marriage to Gomer as an extended metaphor representing Israel and her relationship to God. Israel has broken God's covenant as Gomer broke her marriage covenant with Hosea. Israel's sin is idolatry which comes from a lack of knowledge of God and results in inane acts such as seeking direction from a stick. Israel's idolatry is Baalism, the fertility cult. They believed that their worship of Baal was repaid in productivity in crops, animals and children. Because of the idolatrous practice, God promised judgment. The most significant judgment took place in 722 when Samaria was defeated and the people deported. However, God's covenant with Israel was unconditional. Therefore, in the eschatological future, Israel will be restored. This is stated in the extended metaphor and especially in chapters 11 and 14.

Structure

Seed Bed (1-3)   Development (4-14)

Woman

1:2 Go, marry a woman
2:2 Contend with mother >>>>>>>>>>>>>>>>>>>>>> Israel's idolatry (4-7)
3:1 Go, love a woman

Children

1:4 Jezreel
1:6 Lo-ruhamah 2:4 no compassion
1:9 Lo-ammi   children of harlotry >>>>>>>>>>> Israel's judgment (8-10)
2:6 Hedge in 3:3-4 separation
2:8-13 end fasts

Restoration

1:10-11 Jezreel/Ammi
2:14-23 Baali/Ishi
Jezreel/Ruhamah/Ammi >>>>> Israel's Restoration (11-14)
3:5 Return and seek Lord

I.   Historical Background.

Elisha had commissioned Jehu to avenge the house of Ahab (2 Kings 9:1-10:36). He carried out the deed with relish and hundreds of people were killed. However, he did not learn from the past and is indicted with the statement that "Jehu was not careful to walk in the law of the Lord, the God of Israel, with all his heart; he did not depart from the sins of Jeroboam, which he made Israel sin" (2 Kings 10:32). For some reason, God was not pleased with his deed and promised judgment on his house (Hosea 1:4). This promised judgment on the house of Jehu leads to the conclusion that the dynasty of Jehu was still on the throne in Hosea's day. Jehu ruled from 841 to 814, Jehoahaz from 814 to 798, Joash from 798-782, Jeroboam from (793) 782 to 753 (add 14 more years for co-regency). Shallum murdered Jeroboam's son Zechariah after the latter had ruled six months. The real but of the Jehu indictment, however, is Jeroboam II, who rules during Hosea's time and is the last significant of Jehu's dynasty.

Assuming that Hosea's ministry began toward the latter end of Jeroboam II's reign, it would have extended over the reigns of Menahem (752-742), Pekah (740-732) and Hoshea (732-722) (This statement is made because of the southern kings mentioned in 1:1. Hezekiah would take us past the captivity of the northern kingdom).[45] During this time, the optimism of the

---

[45]B. K. Smith, "Amos, Obadiah and Jonah," *loc. cit.* says, "The strange thing about the chronology that v. 1 provides is that the reigns of the kings do not fully overlap. That is, the dates for the reign of Jeroboam II of Israel are approximately 793–753 B.C. This does overlap with the first king of Judah mentioned, Uzziah (792–740 B.C.). However, the verse also mentions three subsequent kings of Judah (Jotham, Ahaz, and Hezekiah) whose reigns go from approximately 750 to 686 B.C.

previous decades vanished. If Cohen is right about the first two chapters of Amos reflecting the beginning of the decline of Israel's fortunes, the decline would have become a slide after Jeroboam's death with the Assyrians encroaching more and more on Israel, demanding tribute, and finally defeating Samaria and deporting the people to other cities in fulfillment of the prophecy of Amos.[46]

Assyria is mentioned eight times in the book and Egypt thirteen (although five of these refer to past events). The nemesis of Israel is the Neo-Assyrian Empire which increasingly takes control of the west and pushes out any opposition daring to rear its head. The speech of Rab Shakeh to Hezekiah in Isaiah 36 is instructive.[47]

---

without any mention of the kings of Israel that reigned at the same time (Zechariah, Shallum, Menahem, Pekahiah, Pekah, and Hoshea, going from 753 to 722 B.C.). This might not be surprising if Hosea had been a prophet to the kingdom of Judah, but his message was for the Northern Kingdom.

"At the very outset of this disorienting book, therefore, we find ourselves confronting a riddle. Why did Hosea neglect to mention the rest of the kings of Israel? The reason appears to be twofold. First, he regarded Jeroboam II as the last king of Israel with any shred of legitimacy. Those after him were a pack of assassins and ambitious climbers who had no right to the title 'king.' Hosea's assessment of the kings of Israel appears in texts like 7:1–7. Second, he hoped for better things from Judah. At times he criticized the south as heavily as the north (5:5, 12), but he also prayed that they not follow Israel's lead (4:15). Most importantly, he looked for salvation and reunification in the line of David (3:5).

"The superscript of the book is therefore extraordinary. It has given us in cryptic form something of the theology of the prophet. It has also warned us that the interpretive task ahead will not be easy."

[46]See L. Wood, *Hosea* in *EBC*, for more background.

[47]References to Assyria, Egypt and Judah:

Assyria

5:13	Then Ephraim went to Assyria and sent to King Jareb
7:11	They called to Egypt, they go after Assyria
8:9	For they are gone up to Assyria
9:3	They shall eat unclean things in Assyria
10:6	It shall be also carried unto Assyria
11:5	But Assyria—he will be their king
11:11	As a dove out of the land of Assyria
12:1	Moreover, he makes a covenant with Assyria

Egypt

2:15	As in the day when she came up from the land of Egypt
7:11	They call to Egypt, they go to Assyria
7:16	This will be their derision in the land of Egypt
8:13	They will return to Egypt
9:3	But Ephraim will return to Egypt (and in Assyria)
9:6	Egypt will gather them up, Memphis will bury them
11:1	And out of Egypt I called My son
11:5	They will not return to the land of Egypt (but Assyria . . .)
11:11	They will come trembling like birds from Egypt (doves from Assyria)
12:1	Makes a covenant with Assyria; and oil is carried to Egypt
12:9	LORD since the land of Egypt
12:13	By a prophet the LORD brought Israel from Egypt
13:4	Yet I have been the LORD since the land of Egypt

Judah

1:1	Kings of
1:7	But I will have compassion on the house of Judah
1:11	And the sons of Judah and the sons of Israel will be gathered together
4:15	Do not let Judah become guilty
5:5	Judah also has stumbled with them
5:10	The princes of Judah have become like those who remove boundaries
5:12	Like rottenness to the house of Judah
5:13	Judah (saw) his wound
5:14	Like a young lion to the house of Judah
6:4	What shall I do with you, O Judah
6:11	Also, O Judah, there is a harvest appointed for you
8:14	Judah has multiplied fortified cities

The Kings

Israel—Jeroboam II (793-753).

Jeroboam was the last major king of the Jehu (841-814) dynasty. Jehu was anointed to attack Baalism and the house of Ahab (2 Kings 9-10). Because of his faithfulness in carrying out God's commands, God promised him sons to the fourth generation to sit on the throne: (1) Jehoahaz (814-798), (2) Joash (798-782), (3) Jeroboam II (793-753), and (4) Zechariah (six months). The thrust of the book is at Jeroboam II. While the historical allusions hint at the later kings of Israel, they are not mentioned (Shallum [753], Menahem [753-742], Pekahiah [742-740], Pekah [740-732], Hoshea [732-722]).

Judah—Uzziah (791-740); Jotham (751-732); Ahaz (735-716); Hezekiah (728-687).

Assyria—Tiglath-Pileser III (745-727); Shalmaneser V (727-722); Sargon II (722-705); Sennacherib (705-681).

Events

The latter part of Jeroboam II's rule saw great prosperity, but his death brought in an era of chaos. Jeroboam, Zechariah, Shallum and Menahem were all kings during the year of 753. Tiglath-Pileser attacked Menahem and forced his submission. Pekah was defeated by the same king who put Hoshea on the throne. When Hoshea rebelled, Shalmaneser V defeated Samaria and deported the people. Sargon II was also involved in the deportation in 722. Sargon also attacked Philistia in 711 B.C. (Isaiah 20).

10:11   Judah will plow, Jacob will harrow for himself
11:12   Judah is also unruly against God
12:2   The LORD also has a dispute with Judah

Assyria - 8
Egypt - 13 (5 refer to the past)
Judah - 15

II. The Prophet Hosea.

We know virtually nothing about Hosea beyond the fact that he was the son of Beeri, that he was married to a woman of questionable repute, and that three children were born to her. The biographical data in chapters two and three is designed to teach about Israel; therefore, little more can be learned about Hosea from that section. Whether he is an Israelite or a Judean is not stated. Whether he is a priest as were other prophets (e.g., Jeremiah) is not stated. Hosea is a later contemporary of Amos. The only northern king mentioned is Jeroboam II. The last southern king listed is Hezekiah who ruled from 728 to 687. This would mean that Hosea lived far beyond the fall of Samaria in 722 and no doubt spent his later years in Judah.

The prophet's marriage has provoked as much debate and discussion as almost any other Old Testament prophetic passage. H. H. Rowley, in a definitive article on the issue,[48] opts for an old accepted view: Hosea was divinely instructed to marry an immoral woman. The first child, Jezreel, was Hosea's, but some would argue that the other two were not his (this depends on how one interprets 2:4). She left Hosea and consorted with paramours, but God instructed Hosea to go bring her back to him. She had apparently become enslaved for debt, and he was forced to pay a price to bring her back to him.

Because of the ethical issue of God asking Hosea to marry an immoral woman and then later to take her back after she had committed adultery, some try to avoid the idea that she was an immoral woman when Hosea married her. The problem is not obviated by saying that she was not immoral when Hosea married her since God still told him to marry her knowing that she would later become immoral. We should probably accept the fact that God often asked His prophets to do difficult things such as

---

[48]H. H. Rowley, "The Marriage of Hosea," *BJRL* 39 (1956-57): 220-33.

going naked and barefoot (Isaiah) and eating dung and having his wife die (Ezekiel).

III. The Message of Hosea.

Some would argue that Amos' message is one of harsh justice while Hosea preaches love. G. Farr, however, argues that Hosea is not different from Amos (since he talks about the vengeance of God for the blood of Jezreel); rather, he says, Hosea goes beyond Amos.[49] He can only say this by removing the closing section of Amos in which good is promised to Israel. Even so, his discussion shows that the disastrous marriage into which God asked Hosea to enter taught him about love and grace and as such became a marvelous picture of God's love and grace toward His people. His discussion of that important Hebrew word *hesed* (חֶסֶד) shows that "for Hosea [it] is, first of all, that undeserved forgiving love of God, which for no better reason than the impulse of its own nature, pardons and restores." The word *hesed* appears at 2:19; 4:1; 6:4, 6; 10:12; 12:6.[50]

Hosea puts great stress on knowledge: "My people are destroyed for lack of knowledge. Because you have rejected knowledge, I also will reject you from being My priest. Since you have forgotten the law of your God, I also will forget your children" (3:6). Knowledge is not mere intellectual comprehension; it is tied in with a right relationship with Yahweh. The last verse in the book summarizes this truth: "Whoever is wise, let him understand these things; whoever is discerning, let him know them. For the ways of the Lord are right, and the righteous will walk in them, But transgressors will stumble in them."

---

[49]G. Farr, "The Concept of Grace in the Book of Hosea," *ZAW* 70 (1958): 98-107.

[50]See also D. Stuart, *Hosea—Jonah*, xxxii-xlii, for a development of the idea that Leviticus and Deuteronomy show up in Hosea as the covenant.

Like Amos, Hosea says that God hates their empty religious ritual: "As for My sacrificial gifts, they sacrifice the flesh and eat it, But the Lord has taken no delight in them. Now He will remember their iniquity and punish them for their sins; they will return to Egypt."

IV. Outline of Hosea.

A. God demonstrates His divine love for Israel through the marriage of Hosea to Gomer (1:1—3:5).

   1. Hosea marries an immoral woman, and a child is born to the union who is named Jezreel at God's direction (1:2-5).

       The name Gomer is otherwise known only as one of the groupings of the Japheth descendants (Genesis 10; Ezekiel 38). The meaning for the name is not obvious. The root means "to complete" or "to accomplish" (cf. Gemariah). The name Jezreel on the other hand is the well-known fertile valley running diagonally through the northern part of Israel. The word means "God sows" and probably refers to the fertility of the valley. The usage of the name as a message to the people (cf. Isaiah's sons) was first of all negative: the dynasty of Jehu who carried out his bloody purge in Jezreel must be punished. Jeroboam II was the last important king of that dynasty (his son Zechariah lasted only six months).[51]

   2. Gomer has a second child (a girl) who is named Lo-ruhamah at Yahweh's direction (1:6-7).

       Lo-ruhamah (לֹא רֻחָמָה) means "No-mercy." This little girl had to bear the name "Merciless." The merciful God ("showing loving kindness *ḥesed* [חֶסֶד] to thousands, to those who love Me and keep

---

[51]See Smith, *Amos, Obadiah, and Jonah, loc. cit.* The bloodshed caused by Jehu will come upon his descendants because they commit the same sins as Jezebel and Ahab.

My commandments" Exod. 20:6) will now show no mercy. As a parenthesis, Yahweh says that He will have compassion *reḥem* (רָחֵם) on Judah. He may be referring to the defense of Judah against Sennacherib in 701 B.C.

3. Gomer has a third child (a boy) whom Yahweh names Lo-ammi (לֹא עַמִּי) (1:9).

   This little boy was called "Not-my-people." He became a walking symbol of God's rejection of Israel.[52]

4. Yahweh gives a pericope of hope in the midst of promise of judgment (1:10-2:1).

   The Hebrew text closes chapter 1 with verse nine. This section should be treated as a unit. In spite of the fact that God is disowning Israel, the act is temporary and the time will come in which they will be as the sand of the sea, and instead of being called Lo-ammi, they will be called sons of the living God. Furthermore Judah and Israel will be together again with one leader. Now Jezreel becomes a promise of glory as Yahweh again sows the fields with His people. Then they can say to their brothers "Ammi" and to their sisters "Ruhamah."

---

[52]Paronomasia in Hosea

English	Hebrew	Meaning/Sign
Jezreel	יִזְרְעֶאל	Place of blood/Yahweh sows
Lo-Ruhamah	לֹא רֻחָמָה	No mercy/mercy
Lo-Ammi	לֹא עַמִּי	Not my people/my people
Baali	בַּעְלִי	My husband/my baal
Ishi	אִישִׁי	My husband/my man
Gomer	גֹּמֶר	??

   Cf. 1:4 with 2:22. 1:6 with 2:1, 23. 1:9 with 2:1, 23.

5. Yahweh applies Hosea's marriage to His own relationship with Israel (2:2-23).

The imagery slips back and forth between Yahweh and Hosea. I personally would take the entire chapter as a metaphor of God and Israel, but some of it may refer to Hosea and Gomer as well. Israel has committed adultery. Adultery is a picture throughout the Old Testament of idolatry. At the same time the Canaanite religion was so bound up with sex that adultery/idolatry can almost be considered one thing. Her lovers who give her wool and flax (2:5) are the Canaanite fertility deities who they believed gave them produce. Yahweh promises to "hedge her in" so that she will finally say, "I will go back to my first husband, for it was better for me then than now!" (2:2-7).

Yahweh shows the perennial conflict between Him and Baal as to who is the Lord of creation.[53] Since Israel believed Baal brought her crops, Yahweh would remove them so that she would have to acknowledge His lordship (2:8-13).

Yahweh promises a day in which He will woo Israel back to Himself, provide her with riches after which she will sing His praises. She will not say "Baali" but "Ishi." *Baal* is a perfectly good Hebrew word meaning lord or master, and then husband. It could at one time have been used of Yahweh as the lord/husband of Israel. However the ambivalence of the word allowed it to be used of Yahweh and the Canaanite deity. Therefore, Yahweh says, in that day of restoration, Israel will not use it to refer to Yahweh as her husband, but she will use the generic word *Ish* (אִישׁ) meaning simply man, and *Ishi* means "my man" or "my husband" (2:14-20).

In that day the negative messages of the three children will be turned into positive ones. Jezreel will take on its primary meaning: "I will

---

[53]Cf. Elijah on Mt. Carmel in 1 Kings 18.

sow her for Myself in the land." His compassion (*ruḥamah*) will be restored, and the people will now be called "My people" (*Ammi*) (2:23).

6. The intensity of Yahweh's love for His people is shown in asking Hosea to take Gomer back after she has left him and lived with other men (3:1-5).

    Hosea has to pay a price to redeem her from slavery (probably for indebtedness, not to get her from her paramour). He takes her home and "quarantines" her from men (probably including him). This is an illustration of God's great love for Israel that will result in "quarantine" without king, prince, sacrifice or idolatrous devices. In the last days Israel will come trembling to Yahweh and return to David their king.[54] I take these references to be typologically referring to the Messiah.

Recurring Themes in Chapters 1-3

Idolatry: 1:2 Take a wife	2:1 Contend with mother	3:1 Love a woman
Judgment: 1:4-9 Names	2:4 No compassion	3:2 Bought her
	2:6 Hedge her in	3:3-4 Sit without king
	2:8-13 End of feasts	
Restoration: 1:10-11 Names	2:14-23 Names	3:5 Return seek Lord

B. Hosea inveighs against Israel for her idolatry (4:1—7:16).[55]

    The messages of Hosea are not as clearly structured as they are in Amos. They are full of poetry, symbolism, analogies and graphic descriptions of

---

[54]Cf Ezekiel 37:25 "and David My servant shall be their prince forever."

[55]In Ugaritic religion, Mot kills Baal (everything dies); Anath (Baal's wife/sister) kills mot; Baal revives, embraces Anath and a calf is born. Vegetation flourishes.

Israel's hypocrisy. The following structure is generally: 4-7 = idolatry; 8-10 = judgment; 11-14 = restoration.[56]

1. The importance of knowing Yahweh is stressed (4:1-19).

    Yahweh has a court case (רִיב *riv*) against Israel because "there is no faithfulness (אֱמֶת *emeth*), kindness (חֶסֶד *ḥesed*) nor knowledge (דַעַת

---

[56]Analogies in Hosea:

4:4	Those who contend with a priest
4:9	Like people like priest
4:16	Stubborn heifer
4:16	Like a lamb
5:10	Like those removing a boundary (Judah)
5:12	God is like a moth/rottenness
5:14	God is like a lion (11:10; 13:7,8)
6:4	Loyalty is like morning cloud/dew (13:3)
6:5	God is like light
6:7	Like Adam
7:4,6	Like an oven
7:8	Like an unturned cake
7:11	Like a silly dove
7:16	Like a slack bow
8:8	Like vessels in which no one delights
9:4	Bread like mourner's bread
9:10	Like grapes
9:10	Like early fruit
9:11	Glory like a bird
9:13	Like Tyre
10:1	Like a Luxuriant vine
10:4	Judgment is like poisonous weeds
10:11	Like a trained heifer
11:8	Like Admah/Zeboim
11:11	Like birds/doves
13:3	Like chaff/smoke
14:5	Like cedars, lily, olive tree
14:7,8	God is like wine of Lebanon/luxuriant Cyprus

See also Wolff, *Hosea*, p. xxiv.

daath) in the land."[57] Kindness, sometimes translated loyalty, is the word *ḥesed* (חֶסֶד). It refers to God's acts of kindness, grace and mercy toward His people. Eventually (as in Psalm 16) the recipient of that kindness will be referred to as the *ḥasid* (חָסִיד) from which we get the modern term *Hasidim*. Because Yahweh has lavished His grace on His people, He expects a horizontal expression of that grace to others. To know God, then, is to be aware of His wonderful grace toward us and to share that same forgiving grace with others (cf. Jesus' parable of the bad steward). No wonder he says "My people are destroyed for lack of knowledge" (4:1-3).

Because of the references to priests in 1-6, the next section refers to God's judgment of the priesthood. "They feed on the sin (offering) of my people" refers to the priests. The priests are no better than the people, and therefore "like people, like priest" means that both will go into judgment (4:4-10).

The issue of knowledge (now understanding, לֵב *leb*, the heart as the seat of understanding) is taken up again. Harlotry, wine and new wine take away understanding and as a result Israel consults lifeless idols and divination instead of going to God for guidance. This idolatry/-adultery takes gross forms. Even the brides commit adultery (probably some sort of sacred prostitution). However, Yahweh will not single out the brides for punishment since the men are more involved in leading them astray. "So the people without understanding (לֹא יָבִין *lo yabin*) are ruined" (4:11-14).

Judah is urged not to follow Israel in her harlotry. Gilgal and Beth-aven are cult centers. Yahweh says there is no hope of expecting

---

[57]See Farr, "The concept of Grace in the book of Hosea" for an important discussion of these three terms.

Israel to return to Him (4:15-19). Hosea is following Amos here (Amos 5:4) where Bethel will come to trouble (*aven* אָוֶן = sin).

2. Yahweh chides both Israel and Judah and promises judgment on both houses (5:1-15).

For the first time in the book, Judah comes under denunciation as well as Israel. Ephraim is criticized for her idolatry, but Judah also has stumbled (5:5). "The new moon will devour the land" (5:7) is difficult. With Keil it may be part for the whole: new moon represents the sacrifices which instead of helping Israel will prove their downfall (5:1-7).[58]

Both Israel and Judah at different times went to Assyria for help. In the Syro-Ephraimite war against Ahaz which figured so largely in Isaiah's ministry (Isaiah 7), Judah went to Assyria for help. Tiglath-Pileser gladly responded, attacked Samaria and carried away captives (2 Kings 16,17). Judah was told by Isaiah, however, that this same people would come back to judge them. For Hosea this is the "young lion in the house of Judah." Israel, in a later time, paid tribute to Shalmaneser to postpone the inevitable; this too would prove futile because Assyria could not "cure your wound" (5:8-15).

3. Hosea delivers a plea to Israel and a complaint against her (6:1-11).

This first section seems to be a prayer of repentance on the part of Israel. Wolff argues that this prayer mentioning rain is part of the Canaanite cult.[59] In other words, they are mixing their worship of Yahweh and Baal and praying for Yahweh to heal them (6:1-3).

---

[58]F. C. Keil, *The Twelve Minor Prophets* 2:89.

[59]Wolff, *Hosea*, 120-121.

Yahweh, however, rejects their superficial repentance. Their loyalty (*hesed* חֶסֶד) disappears like a morning cloud or the dew when the sun dries it out (6:4). Yahweh has condemned them through the prophets and promises judgment upon them. The reason is that He wants loyalty (*hesed* חֶסֶד) rather than sacrifice, and the knowledge of God rather than burnt offerings. This of course does not mean that God was against the sacrificial system, only that he opposed the hypocritical use of it (6:4-7).

The conduct of the people bears out the charge made against them. There is murder in Gilead. Priests murder on the way to Shechem. Yet there is hope for Judah when God restores the fortunes of His people (6:8-11).

4. Chaos and strife come from rebelling against Yahweh (7:1-16).

Chapter 7 is tied in with the preceding by the word "heal." The prayer of 1-3 was that Yahweh, having torn them like a lion, would heal them. Yahweh says in 7:1 that when He sets out to heal the people, all He sees is iniquity (7:1-2).

The next section may reflect the chaos of the last days of Israel. After Jeroboam II's death, there were two assassinations in one year (753 B.C.). The same was true after Menahem's death (742 B.C.). Intrigue and plotting characterize the princes who are hot like an oven to carry out their deeds and "they consume rulers; all their kings have fallen and none calls on me" (7:3-7).[60]

Ephraim has sought a solution to her problem by going to the nations. They are being pillaged by other nations, but they refuse to turn to the

---

[60]D. A. Garrett, *Hosea, loc. cit.* "The princes incapacitate our king with poisoned wine."

Lord. As a result she goes back and forth with indecision like a silly dove—first to Egypt then to Assyria (7:8-11).

Therefore God will cast a net over her and bring her down. When they assemble (in a cultic situation) to seek rain (Baal/Yahweh) He will not answer them (7:12-16).

C. Hosea preaches messages emphasizing judgment (8:1—10:15.

1. Yahweh's judgment comes because they have forsaken his *torah* and turned to idolatry (8:1-14).

Yahweh issues a cry for battle preparation because the enemy is coming against the house of the Lord.[61] The reason for the judgment is that they have transgressed God's covenant and rebelled against His law or instruction (8:1-3).

Does v. 4 refer to Hoshea coming to the throne via assassination (2 Kings 15:30,31)? They have also become even more religious, but God has rejected their "calf" (8:4-7). One calf may be mentioned instead of two because Galilee where Dan was situated was cut off by Tiglath-Pileser III (2 Kings 15:29). Tiglath-Pileser says of this campaign: "[As for Menahem I ov]er whelmed him [like a snowstorm] and he . . . fled like a bird, alone, [and bowed to my feet(?)]. I returned him to his place [and imposed tribute upon him, to wit:] gold, silver, linen garments with multicolored trimmings, . . . great . . . [I re]ceived from him. Israel (lit.: 'Omri-Land' *Bit Humria*) . . . all its inhabitants (and) their possessions I led to Assyria. They overthrew their king Pekah (Pa-qa-ha) and I placed Hoshea (A-u-si-') as king over them. I

---

[61]This cannot refer to a temple. Assyria refers to Israel as the House of Omri (Bit Umri). This phrase may be a counterpoint—Israel is the House of Yahweh (see Wolff, *Hosea*, 138, and *TDOT*, 503 on Arad ostraca).

received from them 10 talents of gold, 1,000(?) talents of silver as their [tri]bute and brought them to Assyria."[62]

Israel has been severely damaged (swallowed up). They are sending ambassadors to various nations for help, but no one is interested. Even if they can get response, God will frustrate their plans. The "burden of the king of princes" may refer to the tribute paid to Shalmaneser (2 Kings 17:3) (8:8-10).

Israel has multiplied altars and in the process has multiplied sin. God on the other hand has 10,000 statutes which they have ignored. The religious practice of Israel brings no delight to Yahweh (8:11-14).

2. Israel is warned not to rejoice because God will judge her (9:1-17).

The setting of this chapter should be tied in with the previous one (note the mention of going to Egypt: 8:13; 9:3, 6), yet the attitude of verse 1 is one of rejoicing. Perhaps they have successfully survived the ravishing attacks of 732 B.C. when Damascus was defeated and deported, and a good crop is bringing a sense of optimism not found in the previous chapter.

A charge is made in the second person (9:1), and the threat is carried on in the third person (9:2-4). Wolff sees a public confrontation where verse 1 may be addressed to the priests and then Hosea turns to others to make the threat.[63] The "harlots' earnings" would be especially apropos.

If someone answered Hosea to the effect that the blessing of Yahweh was evident in the abundance of the grain crop, his answer is that the wine press will not feed them and the new wine will fail them. Not

[62]*ANET*, pp. 283, 284.

[63]Wolff, *Hosea*, 153.

only so, but they will return to Egypt, the place from which God originally redeemed them and brought them to the land of Canaan.[64] Others will be deported to Assyria where they will be unable to offer sacrifices pleasing to the Lord (9:2-6).

The people seem to respond to Hosea by calling him a fool (אֱוִיל *awil*) and a madman. Thus Hosea joins the ranks of Elisha's prophets (מְשֻׁגָּה *meshugah*) 2 Kings 9:11) and Jeremiah (29:26). Hosea says that this seems to be true only because of their sin. Verse 8 is very difficult, but the following paraphrase is probably the intent of the passage: "A watchman of Ephraim with my God [am I and] a prophet. Yet [Ephraim] is the snare of a bird catcher in all his ways [against me], and there is only hostility in God's territory (house of his God)." He closes the section by saying that the sin of Israel in Hosea's day was like that of the Benjamites when they abused the concubine of the Levite, and the result was a horrible civil war that decimated the Benjamite tribe (Judges 19) (9:7-9).

Yahweh again reminds Israel of her condition in which He found her. She was like wild, worthless grapes in the wilderness. In spite of His grace in redeeming her from Egypt, she went to Baal-Peor and devoted herself (וַיִּנָּזְרוּ *wayinazeru* as in Nazirite) to shame. This is one of those references to "first" events in Hosea. Num. 25:1-5 recounts this unsavory event when the Israelites committed fornication with the people who worshipped Baal. That same kind of fornication with religious implications was yet being carried on in Israel. God will therefore judge them in the very area they are trusting Baal to care for them: conception, pregnancy, and childbearing (9:10-14).

As Gibeah represented the depths of depravity in the era of the Judges (9:9) and Baal-Peor in that of the Exodus (9:10), Gilgal represents Saul's rejection of the lordship of Yahweh in the initial stages of the

---

[64]This may speak of emigration to Egypt under the coming threat of Assyria.

monarchy. Gilgal was also apparently a cult center (4:15; 12:11; Amos 4:4; 5:5). His judgment is that He will drive them out of His house (i.e., His country) (9:15-17).

3. Under two similes, God threatens Israel with impending judgment (10:1-15).

Israel is a luxuriant vine (10:1-10).

Under Jeroboam II Israel had prospered greatly. Unfortunately, she had taken her material blessings as indications of a response to her pagan worship; she multiplied her altars to match her prosperity. However, God will break down her altars and sacred pillars (10:1-2).

Hosea hopes that Israel will repent and acknowledge that they have not feared Yahweh. The human king, (Hoshea?) they realize, cannot help them. They are trying to enter into covenants (international pacts?) to no avail. Justice is turned into poison (Amos 5:7; 6:12). Heavy tribute imposed by Assyria is indicated by reference to the calf of Beth-aven.[65] Samaria and her king will be cut off (by Assyria). They will be defeated in Gibeah as poetic justice for the history of their wickedness which in some sense began in Judges 19 (10:3-10).

Ephraim is a trained heifer (10:11-15).

Yahweh speaks first of the election of Ephraim. She was viewed by Him to be a "trained heifer," i.e., she was to serve Him. Threshing is a light task: the animal was permitted to move around freely and to eat of the grain. However, God had higher duties for Ephraim, namely to plow and harrow. These activities are said by Hosea to represent living a life of righteousness and loving kindness (צְדָקָה *tsedakah*, חֶסֶד

---

[65]Beth-aven, בֵּית אָוֶן, is a word used by Hosea to refer to the cult center at Bethel, 4:15; 5:8; 10:5-8 to describe it as the "Temple of Sin."

ḥesed). Instead they have plowed wickedness and reaped injustice (10:11-13).

Because of this life of rebellion, God is going to judge them. Neither Shalman nor Beth-abel have been identified with any certainty. Some have suggested that Shalman is an abbreviation for Shalmaneser others identify it with a Moabite king Shalamanu mentioned by Tiglath-Pileser.[66] We will have to be content to know that there was a devastating battle at one time to which the coming one will be compared. The king of Israel, says Hosea, will be completely cut off (10:14-15).

D. Hosea preaches messages emphasizing restoration (11:1—14:9.

1. Yahweh gives a historical account of His love for Israel and a promise of her restoration (11:1-11). See Wolff for a helpful discussion.[67] He maintains the unity of the chapter by showing the first person addresses in both parts and linking up the love of Yahweh for Israel in verse 1 with His compassion for them in 8-10.

    Yahweh brought Israel from Egypt as His loved one. He called them out as His son, yet, the call of the prophets to repentance went unheeded. God's tender affection for Israel brought no response. In view of their sin, though they will not be sent back to Egypt, they will be sent to Assyria and God will judge the city (11:1-7).

    Yahweh gives a tender lament, addressing Israel in the second person. He is moved with great compassion over her suffering and declares that He cannot wipe her out as He did Admah and Zeboim. Furthermore, He will roar like a lion and bring her sons from the west, from Egypt, from Assyria and settle them in their own houses (11:8-11).

---

[66]Wolff, *Hosea*, 188.

[67]Ibid., 193.

2. Yahweh's indictment continues through the reference to the historical past (11:12— 12:14).[68]

Ephraim is mentioned four times: Ephraim surrounds me with lies (11:12); Ephraim feeds on wind (12:1); Ephraim said, "Surely I have become rich" (12:8); Ephraim has provoked to bitter anger (12:14). An indictment is given in 11:12-12:1 in the third person. An indictment of Judah (included in Jacob) is given in 12:2-5 in the third person. A plea is made to repent in the second person (12:6). A further indictment is given in 12:7-8. God speaks in the first person to Israel in 12:9-11. A final historical reference is made tying in Moses the prophet with the prophets of Hosea's day and a final statement of judgment (12:12-14).

Yahweh indicts Ephraim, Israel and Judah with being deceitful (11:12). Ephraim is particularly singled out as "feeding on the wind" because she practices lies and violence and is trying to create alliances with Assyria and Egypt to protect herself (12:1).

Yahweh's further dispute is with Judah as part of the elect people and as being one with Israel in God's sight. Jacob's life is given as a sort of a parable for Israel. He struggled long and hard until he finally came to know the God who reveals Himself. So Israel has struggled against God, but now is urged to return to Him. The shift to the second person in 12:6 is part of the plea pattern followed in this book (12:2-6).[69]

Yahweh speaks in the first person to appeal to Israel to repent. Ephraim is cheating but bragging about being rich (this may reflect an earlier time when Israel was prosperous). Yahweh reminds them that He was their God who brought them from Egypt. He says He has

---

[68] The Hebrew begins chapter 12 with 11:12 which is clearly correct.

[69] See Wolff, *Hosea* for a discussion.

revealed Himself to them through the prophets, visions and parables, but they have not responded. Idolatry is everywhere (12:7-14).

3. A final indictment is made against Ephraim for her idolatry (13:1-16).

Ephraim was blessed of God (the fruitful bough), but in turning to idolatry and to Baalism in particular, they have lost their wisdom (13:1-3).

Yahweh reminds them again of the youthful days in the wilderness in which He cared for them so graciously. Yet they forgot Him so that He will turn into a lion and devour them (13:4-8).

The king in whom they put their hope is apparently no longer there to help them (does this refer to Pekah or Pekahiah who were assassinated?). God says that He took the king away in His wrath (13:9-11).

Yahweh seems to indicate that the sin of Israel has become full to the point where it of necessity must be judged. There will be no deliverance from Sheol; as a matter of fact He calls upon Death and Sheol to wreak disaster upon them (13:12-14).[70]

In terse, graphic statements, Yahweh promises the destruction of the northern kingdom. How sad that this nation with such an auspicious beginning under the caring, guiding hand of God has come to such a disastrous end. So is the end of all those who forsake the Lord (13:15-16).

4. A final plea is made for Israel to return to her God (14:1-9).

Yahweh pleads with Israel to return to Him. He gives them a sample prayer of confession: "forgive, receive, so that we may praise. We will

---

[70]Paul uses this verse to show that death has been defeated. He understands it in the sense that God is in control of Death and Sheol.

not worship idols nor go to other nations for help. You are the one who gives mercy" (14:1-3).

Yahweh speaks in the first person again to give a wonderful promise if they will repent. He will heal their apostasy and make them fruitful (14:4-7).

He turns (second person) directly to Ephraim and poignantly pleads for them to recognize that He is like a luxuriant Cyprus (remember the luxuriant vine of 10:1). Since He is the fruit producer, why should they resort to idols (14:8)?

A final general request is made (third person) for understanding and discernment. The righteous will walk in the ways of Yahweh, but the transgressors will stumble (14:9).

The Book of Jonah

Authorship. The only reference to Jonah in a historical context is found in 2 Kings 14:25 where Jonah prophesies the restoration of Israel's borders. This places the prophet in the eighth century. However, the Book of Jonah is presented in a "non-historical" setting. Certainly the book is historical and the events historical, but their presentation demands a question as to the purpose of the book. I am setting out these theses in the form of sermons I preached in Irving TX several years ago.

"Thesis #1: The Gospel Belongs in the Market Place"

This opening sermon on a series in the Book of Jonah is designed to encourage believers to look beyond the limiting horizons of our present situation to God's design for the world. It is also designed to challenge believers to become involved in personal evangelism and foreign missions.

Dallas Morning News of January 15, 1992 had four major religious news stories. Even though three were from the religious section, this many columns devoted to religion and much of it to the evangelical faith indicates a high degree of interest in the subject. We are told by various polling services that a very large number of people claim to be "born again." Church attendance continues to be higher in the US than perhaps any other country. Here in Dallas alone, we boast of two seminaries which combined make up probably the largest seminary student body in the world. We have a large number of Bible churches and others who identify themselves as evangelical. Surely, one might legitimately ask, with this number of people claiming to be Christians, there will be a large impact on the life style of an urban area. What we see instead is a rising tide of violence, an epidemic of sexually transmitted disease (usually biblically illicit sexual activity), and hatred and bitterness between peoples. Both newspapers and television feature ads and columns pertaining to psychics and astrologers. Furthermore, the conduct of those who claim to be Christians does not seem to be much different from that of those who do not so claim. It is surely symptomatic that several leaders of the "Bible believing" movement have come under intense criticism for conduct that is either outright immoral or at least unexpected of those who claim to be following the lowly Jesus.

Evangelical Christians are increasingly finding themselves a subculture. Like other religious subcultures, the primary goal is to maintain the status quo. We develop mores and practices which we share in common with other evangelical groups and with which we are very comfortable. I attended one of the most "high tech" and professional Christmas cantatas in California three years ago I have ever seen. One had to have tickets even to get into the performance, it was so popular. It was very entertaining, and while I am sure it had an evangelistic purpose, I came away wondering what kind of an impact it ultimately had. I attended a "Fourth of July" program at a Christian retreat center some years ago that left me feeling entertained, but very spiritually empty. As Greek Orthodox people tend to want to preserve their traditions and are not interested in turning others into Greek Orthodox (just to take one example), so Evangelicals are increasingly working "in house" rather than making an impact on the pagan community around them.

It is with this situation in mind that I want us to approach the book of Jonah. Because Jonah is such a striking story, it is easy to get caught up in the story line and overlook the purpose of the book. The account of Jonah's call and disobedience is unparalleled in the Old Testament. No other prophet is called to go to a foreign city. No other prophet disobeys by taking a ship to the Phoenician west. No other prophet encounters an experience with sailors that results in his being thrown into the sea. And above all, no other prophet was swallowed by a great fish and subsequently was vomited up to the shore. In fine, the story is unique.

But why did God put this story in the canon? Was it to teach that disobedience suffers punishment? Was it to teach that God is able to create great things? Was it to teach missionary principles? Certainly, the historical aspects are very important, but these are obviously not the reason the book was written. I believe that the concept of God's compassion on the pagan world is the theme of the book. This shows the universalistic theology of the Jews, but it also indicates a reluctant reception of that theology on the part of some.

The book of Jonah is also unique among the Old Testament books. We believe it should be taken as an historical account: that Jonah was indeed a prophet; that he was swallowed by a large fish; and that he preached to the historical city of Nineveh. Nonetheless, the account is given in marvelous story telling fashion, containing literary devices to make the point of the message even sharper.

What can we know about the historical context of the book of Jonah? There is nothing internal to tell us anything about dates. We know that Nineveh as the capital of Assyria dominated the area of Syria and Palestine off and on from 900-600 B.C. We know that they were a powerful and cruel people. They showed no mercy (an important word in Jonah) to those they conquered and even less to those who rebelled against them after they had taken an oath of allegiance to the Assyrians. But into what period does Jonah fit?

During the ninth century B.C., Israel had suffered terribly at the hands of the Syrians or Arameans. Their army was reduced to virtually nothing. We read in 2 Kings 13:7, "For he left to Jehoahaz of the army not more than fifty horsemen and ten chariots and 10,000 footmen, for the king of Aram had destroyed them and made them like the dust at threshing." But God had mercy on them and 2 Kings 14:25 tells us that God allowed Israel and Judah to restore their borders to the same extent as that in the days of Solomon. This was prophesied, says the author of Kings, by Jonah ben Amittai from Gath Hepher. The kings of Israel and Judah during this time were Jeroboam II and Uzziah (Amaziah). We know that these two kings had long contemporaneous rules early in the eighth century. Thus we can place Jonah's time in this period, but we cannot pinpoint it in the fifty year era involved. He had to be early in Uzziah and Jeroboam's rule because he prophesied the expansion.

What was happening in Assyria during this time? We know that an Assyrian ruler (Adad Nirari III) had come west and defeated the Syrians. This of course took pressure off Israel and Judah and allowed them to rise from their previous century of decline. After this, however, the Assyrians themselves, under the pressure of mountain invaders and internal disasters, also declined. This decline was so serious that the Simon Cohen says "Assyria lay nearly prostrate before its northern foe; it was impoverished and dispirited. Well might a prophet be believed who would proclaim: 'Yet forty days, and Nineveh shall be overthrown!'"[71] There are other contacts which caused Jonah's message to be received which we will take up later.

The Jews of the Old Testament much as the Jews of our time considered themselves a unique people with little or no spiritual obligation to those around them. Proselytes came to Judaism, but they were seldom sought. In a recent Public Television program on intermarriage among Jews, one rabbi said quite explicitly, we are not interested in converting people to Judaism. They are interested in preserving their ethnic (and for some, religious) purity. In the second part of Isaiah are some of the loftiest and most sublime statements of the Lord's concern for all people, but it probably never filtered down very far. The book of Jonah, therefore, is a statement made through the wonderful medium of the story of Jonah of God's compassion even for a pagan people like the Ninevites who were enemies of the Jews. Jonah's reluctance to bring that message mirrors the Israelites' equally stubborn disinterest in the relation of the Assyrians to God. My hope is that we as believers will be challenged anew by the book of Jonah to show compassion on the pagan world around us—not just in theory but in consecrated practice. I am using the book as a springboard for discussion about the mission of the church in the world, and to interact with some of the ideas of the book in that direction.

---

[71]S. Cohen, "The Political Background of the Words of Amos," HUCA 36 (1965) 158.

Jonah the prophet encounters two pagan groups: the Phoenicians in chapter 1 and the Assyrians in chapter 3. We will discover a number of similarities between the two encounters. First, I want us to go through chapter 1 to see the issues confronting Jonah and us as God seeks to reach a lost world through those who own him as lord.

1. Jonah was given a very clear commission. The church likewise has a mandate: to preach the good news and to disciple. Everything else the church does is secondary, but this is clearly and unequivocally stated in the Bible. We have no more choice in the matter than Jonah had.

2. Jonah tried to flee from the Lord's presence (*milpene Yahweh* מִלִּפְנֵי יהוה). This phrase occurs twice. It means at least to leave the land of Israel and the temple where God would address him directly. In 2:4 he says "I have been expelled from Thy sight" (*nigrashti mineged 'eneka* נִגְרַשְׁתִּי מִנֶּגֶד עֵינֶיךָ). This is a deliberate effort to escape his response-bility. Dare we hide from God in a "sub cultural enclave" and miss what God has ordered us to do?

3. The name of God revealed to Israel (Yahweh) appears 12 times in chapter 1. This personal name representing God's covenant relationship with his people was unknown outside Israel. The Phoenician sailors worshipped many Gods. Baal was only one name they called upon. Jonah had the name of God to reveal. God in our time has revealed himself in the person of Jesus Christ. It is through his name that we have access to God, and it is that name we are to preach to a needy world.

4. The Phoenician sailors were in desperate need. The world in which we live could not be more desperate. Jonah was not even conscious of their need, let alone concerned. He went below and fell into a "deep sleep" of no concern.

5. God forced Jonah's hand both with the Phoenicians and with the Assyrians. He bore clear testimony to both groups with marvelous

results. A missionary in France said to me, "Everyone talks about the French people being agnostic, but I am able to talk with them freely every day and they listen and interact with me." May God do whatever He must do to get us more involved in this glorious task of reaching the world of Texas and the world beyond.

"Thesis #2: 'The Great City' is the Target of God's Program"

I grew up in a little hollow in West Virginia called Riffle Run. There were no more than a dozen families who lived along the two branches of the creek. We walked to our one room country school with a population of around 20. We walked to church with a similar population. Town was three miles away, which meant a six mile walk if we needed something from the grocery store or walked home from high school. We had hills all around us. We could climb the rock-faced mountains, explore caves, trap fur, fish and swim in the Little Kanawha River—in fine, it was a glorious experience growing up in the country. Cities then and now were disdained. Only those who grew up in the Big Apple or the Windy City enjoy the taste. We tend to speak of San Francisco, Los Angeles, Chicago and above all New York as awful places which we would be better off without. We don't like cities.

The vast majority of early missionaries were from rural areas in this country. It was unusual to meet a missionary from a large city. Consequently, they tended to go to rural areas when they went to Africa, South America or India. The twentieth century, however, has thrust the populations of the world into cities. From Nairobi, Kenya to Mexico City, innumerable multitudes have crowded into cities little prepared to handle the influx. Poverty, crime and family disintegration have replaced the quiet stability of the rural areas from which these people come. The poor of Rio de Janeiro build flimsy huts up the side of the mountain of the Christ of the Corcovado, a tourist attraction, and when the rains come, their "houses" are washed down the side of the mountain. Mexico City may be the largest city in the world with 18,535,000 in 1978. The annual growth rate at that time was said to be 2.9%. At that rate there would now be 26,877,000 in that vast city.

The Book of Jonah was not written to tell us about urbanization of the world, nor about strategies for reaching those vast urban areas, but it does say something about the great city of Nineveh and says it in such a way as to draw attention to it. I want us to look at the four occurrences of this phrase to see whether they are instructive for us.

Nineveh, that great city, was wicked (1:1).

There are numerous occurrences of the word "great" in Jonah: 1:1, 4, 4, 10, 12, 15; 2:1, 3:2, 3; 4:1,7, 11. Only "great city" has the definite article. God has singled out this city to give it emphasis, and as we read the book, we must ask why that emphasis was placed there.

Cities are "great" because of the civilization there. City, citizen, and civilization are from the same Latin root. Art, music and education flourish in a city. Unfortunately, these same things tend to have the seed of destruction within them, because the leisure to follow such pursuits tends to self-indulgence and sin. Then judgment must follow. Gen. 18:20-21 speaks of the end result of Sodom and Gomorrah's civilization and the judgment that came upon it.

Cities are "great" because of the sheer number of people there to be reached. The ministry of missionaries is essentially the same in Sao Paulo, Brazil as it is in the States. Vast numbers of people are to be reached in the city dwellings. Missionaries are working with the large numbers of apartment dwellers and others in Caracas. Paul's great desire to go to Asia (and Ephesus in particular) was no doubt because of the size.

Cities are "great" because they become a "melting pot" of peoples and nationalities. People can be reached when they are out of their rural culture and brought to the cities where their horizons are pushed back. They thereby become more open to new ideas, including the Gospel.

Nineveh was a "great city" because God wanted his message to be proclaimed to it.

It is important to note the difference between 1:2 and 3:2. "Arise, go to Nineveh the great city, and cry *against* it (1:1), but "Arise, go to Nineveh the great city and cry out *to* it" (3:2). There is only one letter difference in the Hebrew, but the difference is great. Chapter 1:2 is judgmental "against it" (*'aleha* עָלֶיהָ); 3:2 is gracious "to it" (*'eleha* אֵלֶיהָ). Before judging the city, God gave it an opportunity to repent.

We are not in a large city in terms of today's standards. However, we are in a city and in a metroplex. The international character of Dallas is outstanding. The Hispanic population is large and the black community is fairly large. "Little Asia" is also significant. We dare not turn our backs on a city to which God has sent us to proclaim a message. Our Tarshish may be our little building on Texas Street. Our vision must include reaching out to a city that ranges from Los Colinas to south Irving.

Nineveh was a great city because it belonged to God (3:2)

The phrase "exceedingly" in 3:2 is literally "to" or "for God." Because the word for God in Hebrew has to do with might or power, it is sometimes used to modify a noun. This is how the NASB has taken it. It could also mean the city was great "to or for the gods," that is the gods of Assyria, and would refer to the many temples and deities in the city. However, I believe the literal translation is the better one: the city of Nineveh belonged to God. The three days' journey describes the physical size (some 1800 acres), but the book of Jonah is talking about more than physical greatness. This city belonged to God.

Could we have a vision that Irving belongs to God? Indeed it, as any city, is full of rebellion against the holy God, but he loves it none the less, and wants us to share that love. May he help us go a "day's journey" and proclaim that love.

Nineveh was a great city because it was full of people in great spiritual need (4:11)

Jesus was moved with compassion when he saw the multitude because they were as sheep having no shepherd. God's compassion was evident over this city, but Jonah was unwilling to participate in that compassion. He was willing to preach a message of judgment, but not one of salvation. It is easy to hate criminals, perverts, and violent people, but God's message is one of grace to just such people. Those closest to God's heart share his love for such people.

"Thesis #3: The Message is Everything"

The word "call" is very important in the English language. My dictionary has 15 meanings for the verb, 15 for the noun and another 13 when it is used with other words such as "call in, up, out, etc.' NASB has translated this word in Jonah with "cry," "call," and "proclaim." The use of this word in Jonah includes proclamation of a message. We also have something to say to our society and we must say it clearly.

Pagan condemnation (1:2)

God has made it clear that the world system in which we live is hostile to God and *vice versa*. John 15:18 "If the world hates you, you know that it has hated Me before it hated you." As a result, God has judged the world: "He has appointed a day in which he will judge the world" (Acts 17:31). This situation means that "friendship with the world is enmity with God" (James 4:4). But God has redeemed us from this world system: "Who gave Himself for our sins, that He might deliver us out of this present evil age, according to the will of our God and Father" (Gal 1:4). Redeemed people are admonished to recognize this situation and avoid entanglement with the world (1 John 2:15-17). Have we become too friendly with that which God hates? When Christians are falling right and left to adultery, divorce, sexual immorality, lying, and cheating, is it any wonder the Church is weak? Jonah was to deliver a message of condemnation against a wicked city.

Pagan compassion (3:2)

We have already indicated the difference in prepositions in 1:2 and 3:2 ("against," "to"). There is a slight nuance here that I believe indicates a change of emphasis. In spite of God's promise of judgment against Nineveh, He promises compassion if the city repents. God says the same thing through Jeremiah in the famous potter chapter (18). The only hope for the desperation felt in this world is "that God so loved the world that he gave his only begotten son . . ." The same compassion awaits you. "For God sent not his son into the world to condemn the world, but that the world through him might be saved."

Pagan religion (2:5, 6; 3:5)

The problem with the world is not the lack of religion, but too much religion. Jerusalem is full of black robed Christian priests, orthodox Jews, and white robed Muslims, yet hatred and injustice are the rule of the day. In Jonah's day the religious attitude of the Phoenicians is illustrated in their prayers of desperation (ch 1). Likewise, the Assyrians called a fast as part of their effort to avoid the judgment proclaimed by Jonah. There is plenty of religion today, but the truth of the gospel of simple faith in Christ's redemptive work must be preached and believed.

Pagan repentance (1:14,16; 3:8)

The nature of this repentance is not clear; nor is the long term result. However, there was a response to the preaching of the message. Large numbers of people are coming to the Lord in Eastern Europe and Africa. We must not grow discouraged with the proclamation. It is God's responsibility to deal with results. We should use all available means to get out the Word.

Personal conviction (2:3; 4:4)

Jonah had to accept God's purposes in the world. This learning experience was thrust upon him by his presence in the fish. This psalm of Jonah is a collage of theological ideas from the Psalms (which Jonah had no doubt memorized). By calling out to God in the midst of affliction, he came to conviction of the person of God. As a result, he was able to call out the message God gave him (4:4) with conviction. Likewise, we need to have solid conviction of our relationship with God in order to have conviction about our preaching. What does it mean to have the "call" of God in our lives?

"Thesis #4: The Content of the Message is Everything"

We live in an ecumenical age in which it is popular to reduce our messages to the least common denominator. It is not happily accepted when we insist on the uniqueness of Christianity. Jonah had to stand for the truth in a time of hostility. We need to examine the message we proclaim and make sure we do not dilute it.

Our God is the great creator (Jonah 1:9)

Jonah's confession exalted God as the God of the universe. Pagan religion held to local gods. When one left the territory of one god, he sought out the god of the next territory. The king of Syria miscalculated when he believed that Yahweh was the God of the mountains or the God of the valleys (1 Kings 20:23). The idea of only one God, who controlled the elements because He had created them, was foreign to the pagan world. When Elijah confronted the prophets of Baal in 1 Kings 18, the issue was "who can bring rain." Elijah argued that only Yahweh, not the storm god, Baal, could bring rain—and He did.

"I am a Hebrew," he confessed, and as such acknowledged that he was a member of the people of God—chosen by God to be a witness of God's grace in that choosing. He goes on to say, "I fear Yahweh Elohim of Heaven," the one who revealed himself to Moses as Yahweh, the covenant keeping God, but also the powerful God who is able to execute all His will. Furthermore, he does not dwell in tents or temples, nor is he carried about as a talisman; He dwells in Heaven.

This God "made the sea and the dry land." The Canaanites (of whom the Phoenicians were a part), worshipped many gods, including Yam (the Sea) and Baal (the god of fertility). Jonah is confessing that his God is the creator of all. We read in Exodus 20:11 that in six days Yahweh made the heavens and the earth. Nehemiah 9:6 has become a creedal statement: "Thou alone art the Lord. Thou hast made the heavens, the heaven of heavens with all their host, the earth and all that is on it, the seas and all that is in them. Thou doest give life to all of them. And the heavenly host bows down before Thee." This creatorship is assigned to Jesus in John 1 and in Mark 4:41, the disciples say, "Even the wind and the sea obey him." The creedal statement of Nehemiah becomes a bulwark in times of adversity for the disciples (Acts 4:24). Our faith in God's authority and power, demonstrated through creating and sustaining the world provides us with confidence in the shifting circumstances of our time and gives us courage.

This God is also sovereign (Jonah 1:14). The Phoenician sailors call upon Jonah's God, even calling Him Yahweh. Just before tossing Jonah overboard they pray, "Do not let us perish on account of this man's life and do not put innocent blood on us; for You, O Yahweh have done as you pleased." These pagans recognized that God the creator had caused the seas to be roiled as a punishment of Jonah, and they recognized that He had every right to do so. Can we accept God's work in our lives and in the world around us? Can we accept the wonderful teaching of Romans 8:28-30?

Our God is just (Jonah 3:4)

"Yet forty days and Nineveh will be overthrown"—Nineveh was a wicked city and had to be judged.

The Assyrians, like all people in the ancient east, were idolaters with all that implies. They especially worshipped the astral deities (sun, moon, and stars). While not atypical, they were a cruel people. The pictures of the siege of Lachish on the walls of Ashurbanipal's palace depict extremely cruel acts against the Jews of that city. Consequently, the God of love must deal with them. His love is not maudlin; his love is disciplined and firm. It will not tolerate rebellion.

Jesus makes it clear that the judgment of God must come upon the world of unbelief (John 3:16-21). In our post-modern age, it is not politically correct to talk about particularism in faith, but the alternative to faith in Christ for eternal redemption is eternal judgment. Our hearts need to be moved with compassion as we see the vast multitudes of people roaming through life as sheep without a shepherd. In this post 9-11 atmosphere, it is easy to hate. May God give us love!

Our God is gracious (Jonah 3:10)

God takes no pleasure in the death of the wicked.

The pagan deities of the ancient world were harsh and unforgiving. They were also capricious and unpredictable. Consequently, people lived in fear of them. The God of Israel, however, is a consistent God. He hates sin, but he loves the sinner. One gets the feeling that the God of Islam, while referred to as the all compassionate one, is nonetheless harsh and unforgiving.

Willingness to receive God's grace brings forgiveness.

God's predictability is shown also in his willingness to forgive. Like the father of the prodigal son, the father is always waiting with open arms. Just as the older brother could not comprehend such grace, so much of the world today cannot comprehend the grace of God that allows the worst sinner to be forgiven.

God's message through Jonah is much like that of Jeremiah. Even if God has predicted judgment on a people or a nation, if that nation will repent, God will change His mind. It is not possible to comprehend the enigma of this action. Philosophically it is a contradiction, but with God it is not. He will open his heart even after pronouncing judgment if the people will only repent. Jonah could not comprehend such grace. Neither could Israel as a people.

"Thesis #5: The Message Will Have an Impact (Jonah 1 and 3)"

The generation prior to Jonah found the Israelites in the North prostrate before the Arameans or Syrians (2 Kings 13:1-7). Relief for both Israel and Judah came when the great Assyrian general Adad-Nirari III defeated the Arameans at Damascus in 805 B.C. This allowed Israel and Judah to expand their territories in an unprecedented way. (Jonah prophesied this expansion, 2 Kings 14:23-25). This was early in the 8th century (Jeroboam II, 793-753 B.C.). The Assyrians, however, declined rapidly after Adad-Nirari III. From 782-745 (the time of Jonah) they were in serious trouble. The people from Mt. Ararat defeated the Assyrians. Their western colonies revolted. There were revolts against the king in the Assyrian cities themselves. The country was left an impoverished and disordered land with restricted borders. A now prosperous country (Israel) has a message of the one true god (Yahweh) and a prophet to preach it (Jonah) to a now desperate international power. Is there an analogy today? Impotent Assyria is comparable to impotent Russia and Eastern Europe. The Christians in the United States have a message of salvation and hope. We also have the personnel to take it. Will we respond like Jonah or will we have a vision of the grace of God for the whole world?

The tendency of the evangelical church today is to become insular. We are developing a sub culture of schools, churches, and societies that effectively cut us off from the market place. God calls upon the church to be salt and light and that include the requirement to reach out to the lost in our own country and cross culturally.

The Phoenicians repented (1:6)

They feared. This word includes the semantic range of awe and worship. They were absolutely convinced of the existence of Yahweh the God of Israel and of His ability to control all the forces of nature. This kind of fear always produces a response.

They offered sacrifices. The Old Testament system required animal sacrifice as a symbol of devotion and reverence. It was substitutionary as well as symbolic.

The physical gesture of sacrificing indicated the level of their faith in the God of Israel.

They made vows. Making vows was an evidence of the depth of the devotion to God. They no doubt involved promises to do certain things when they returned to dry land. We often scoff at "foxhole conversions," but they are often times genuine.

Desperation led to a response. It is unfortunate that the state of the human condition often requires us to be brought to the point of desperation prior to our willingness to humble ourselves before God. Naaman, for example, had to have leprosy before coming to the God of Israel (2 Kings 5). Faced with the inevitability of death, the Phoenicians repented. Perhaps as our world is hurtling toward self-destruction, we may see repentance in our time.

The Ninevites repented (3:7-9)

The King of Nineveh was sufficiently astute to recognize an opportunity when he saw it. Devastation was being predicted by Jonah, and the king was determined to avert it. He thus decreed a series of actions. He first proclaimed a fast of both food and water. Then he required that all (humans and animals) wear sackcloth, a sign of mourning and repentance. Thirdly, they were ordered to call on God. This would no doubt be understood by most to refer to Assyrian gods, but the king may well be referring to Jonah's God, Yahweh, the God of Israel. Finally, he orders all to "turn from their wicked way and from the violence in their hands."

The hurts of the world are so profound that it is difficult for us to even think about them. The suffering in Darfur, Syria, or Iraq, for example, is overwhelming to our sensitivities. We feel we must look away. The violence in our cities as well as in our suburbs is so frightening, that we would rather pretend it does not exist. All the efforts of the UN, however well intentioned, will not solve the problems of violence, hatred, and disfunctionality that characterize the world in which we live. Only the Gospel will change that.

What is our responsibility?

The old three-fold opportunity still presents itself. Christians should be Praying (2 Thes. 3:1-2), Giving (3 John 5-8), and Going (2 Kings 7). These three are not necessarily separate. You may be required by God to do all three. Are you willing?

"Thesis #6: Jonah the Worm vs. God's Compassion"

"Compassion" means to feel similarly to someone else. Lack of compassion is illustrated by the way criminals can shoot people and feel no remorse. A major characteristic of God throughout the Old Testament is that he is compassionate. Think of Sodom and Gomorrah and Abraham's intercession. A delightful line in the movie Yentl occurs when her father closes the blinds lest the neighbors see a woman reading the Talmud. (God understands more than the neighbors.) Often times we are less compassionate than God. On the other hand God is not compassionate unless there is repentance.

God changed his mind when he saw repentance (3:10)

A century after Jonah, God revealed himself through Jeremiah to Israel as a compassionate God (Jeremiah 18). As a matter of fact, He is bold to say that even if he has determined judgment against His people, if they will repent, He will change His mind. There is much discussion today about what these two passages mean theologically. Does the immutable God actually change? Or is this merely an anthropomorphism (accommodation of God's thinking to man's). From a missiological point of view, it does not matter: God is a compassionate God, and He will forgive those who have genuinely repented even if they deserve judgment.

Jonah Resented God's Compassion (4:2)

It may seem strange that Jonah was unhappy that God wanted to forgive the Assyrians until we remember what an enemy Assyria was to Israel. They were a vicious and violent people (as were most nations in those days). The Jewish people hated, loathed, and feared them.

He tried to stop it by fleeing (Ch. 1). Perhaps he feared God would leave him looking foolish by changing his mind. Subordinates never like it when their superior overturns their decision to deal harshly with a customer!

He knew that God is compassionate (Exod. 20:6). God is truly compassionate, and that has been his revealed characteristic from the beginning. He delights in showing mercy to thousands—when those thousands have chosen to obey Him.

He knew that God changes his mind about calamity as judgment (4:2). This theology is the same mentioned above in Jeremiah 18. God will change His mind if people will only repent. Jonah knew this and resented it in the case of the Ninevites. May God give us His mind concerning our enemies! May he encourage us to love our Moslem neighbors in spite of the hostility that religion shows to Chri stianity.

He wanted to die (4:3). This is a cry of self-pity and echoes Elijah's moan years earlier when he was fleeing Jezebel (1 Kings 19:4). However, God kept Jonah alive in the whale, and He would keep him alive in Nineveh. He has a job to do.

God chided him (4:4). God delightfully interacts with Jonah by asking him a question. "Is this kind of attitude justifiable"? The answer is obvious to all but Jonah who will continue to protest to the end. "O would the gift that God would give us to see ourselves as others see us."

Jonah and the Worm Serve the Same Function (4:5-11)

God made a shade (His mercy) to protect Jonah from his discomfort (calamity or evil *mera'atho* מֵרָעָתוֹ) (4:6) See my discussion below on the literary uses of *ra'ah* (רָעָהThe little bush gave a measure of respite in a part of the world that becomes unbearably hot. Jonah appreciated that compassion on God's part but resented His compassion in the larger arena of sin and forgiveness. Jonah's discomfort is a micro example of the spiritual "discomfort" the Assyrians had.

To dramatize His parable, God made a worm to attack the tree. The bush represents God's compassion on the Assyrians. The worm represents Jonah who attacks God's compassion. The worm does turn. Who would have thought that Jonah would be the worm, but he is. To fight against God's compassion is to be a worm indeed.

Then God made an east wind to beat on Jonah (4:8). Not only is there scorching heat, now the fiercely hot east wind blows unrelentingly on his head. The wind represents God's judgment. The bush protected Jonah from the judgment, but now the worm has destroyed the bush. So God wants Jonah to feel the pressure he in turn wanted applied to the Assyrians.

Jonah pled to die (4:8). Once again Jonah falls into his self-pity. He begs God to let him die. He believes the judgment (east wind) is so harsh, that his only option is to die. Is he beginning to get the message?

God chided him (4:9-11). Once more God gently asks Jonah if his attitude is appropriate and Jonah insists that it is. Well, says God, if you are upset over the loss of one little bush (you had compassion it), why should I not be upset over the loss of a great city full of people who are groping spiritually.

And so the story ends—or does it? The message of Jonah is both universal and timeless. The only question is whether we will be upset over a bush or a city full of people.

▼▼▼▼▼▼▼▼▼▼▼▼▼▼▼▼▼▼▼▼▼▼▼▼▼▼▼

From Sasson, *Jonah* in AB, p. 317 (word count is from the Hebrew text).

A Jonah's monologue—39 words (vv. 2-3)

B God's query (unanswered)—3 words (v. 4)
B' Jonah's query (sotto voice) — 3 words (v. 8)

C Dialogue: God— 5 words (v. 9)
C' Dialogue: Jonah—5 words

A' God's monologue—39 words (vv. 10-11)

וַיִּתְפַּלֵּל אֶל־יְהֹוָה וַיֹּאמַר ² וַיֵּרַע אֶל־יוֹנָה רָעָה גְדוֹלָה וַיִּחַר לוֹ:

Jonah's monologue 39 words

אָנָּה יְהֹוָה הֲלוֹא־זֶה דְבָרִי עַד־הֱיוֹתִי עַל־אַדְמָתִי עַל־כֵּן קִדַּמְתִּי לִבְרֹחַ תַּרְשִׁישָׁה
כִּי יָדַעְתִּי כִּי אַתָּה אֵל־חַנּוּן וְרַחוּם אֶרֶךְ אַפַּיִם וְרַב־חֶסֶד וְנִחָם עַל־הָרָעָה:
³ וְעַתָּה יְהֹוָה קַח־נָא אֶת־נַפְשִׁי מִמֶּנִּי כִּי טוֹב מוֹתִי מֵחַיָּי: ס

⁴ וַיֹּאמֶר יְהֹוָה

God's query 3 words

הַהֵיטֵב חָרָה לָךְ:

⁵ וַיֵּצֵא יוֹנָה
מִן־הָעִיר וַיֵּשֶׁב מִקֶּדֶם לָעִיר וַיַּעַשׂ לוֹ שָׁם סֻכָּה וַיֵּשֶׁב תַּחְתֶּיהָ בַּצֵּל עַד אֲשֶׁר
יִרְאֶה מַה־יִּהְיֶה בָּעִיר: ⁶ וַיְמַן יְהֹוָה־אֱלֹהִים קִיקָיוֹן וַיַּעַל מֵעַל לְיוֹנָה לִהְיוֹת צֵל
עַל־רֹאשׁוֹ לְהַצִּיל לוֹ מֵרָעָתוֹ וַיִּשְׂמַח יוֹנָה עַל־הַקִּיקָיוֹן שִׂמְחָה גְדוֹלָה:
⁷ וַיְמַן הָאֱלֹהִים תּוֹלַעַת בַּעֲלוֹת הַשַּׁחַר לַמָּחֳרָת וַתַּךְ אֶת־הַקִּיקָיוֹן וַיִּיבָשׁ:

⁸ וַיְהִי כִּזְרֹחַ הַשֶּׁמֶשׁ וַיְמַן אֱלֹהִים רוּחַ קָדִים חֲרִישִׁית וַתַּךְ הַשֶּׁמֶשׁ עַל־רֹאשׁ יוֹנָה
וַיִּתְעַלָּף וַיִּשְׁאַל אֶת־נַפְשׁוֹ לָמוּת וַיֹּאמֶר

Jonah's query (sotto voice) 3 words

טוֹב מוֹתִי מֵחַיָּי:

וַיֹּאמֶר אֱלֹהִים אֶל־יוֹנָה ⁹

Dialogue: God 5 words

הַהֵיטֵב חָרָה־לְךָ עַל־הַקִּיקָיוֹן

וַיֹּאמֶר

Dialogue: Jonah 5 words

הֵיטֵב חָרָה־לִי עַד־מָוֶת:

וַיֹּאמֶר יְהֹוָה ¹⁰

God's monologue 39 words

אַתָּה חַסְתָּ עַל־הַקִּיקָיוֹן אֲשֶׁר לֹא־עָמַלְתָּ בּוֹ וְלֹא גִדַּלְתּוֹ שֶׁבִּן־לַיְלָה הָיָה וּבִן־לַיְלָה אָבָד:

¹¹ וַאֲנִי לֹא אָחוּס עַל־נִינְוֵה הָעִיר הַגְּדוֹלָה אֲשֶׁר יֶשׁ־בָּהּ הַרְבֵּה מִשְׁתֵּים־עֶשְׂרֵה רִבּוֹ אָדָם אֲשֶׁר לֹא־יָדַע בֵּין־יְמִינוֹ לִשְׂמֹאלוֹ וּבְהֵמָה רַבָּה:

Some Literary Aspects in Jonah

Repetitive phrases generally beg for interpretation. Watch for the word "call" (*qara* קָרָא) "Arise call against Nineveh," 1:2); "Arise, call on your god," 1:6; "They called on Yahweh," 1:14; the word "fear" (*yare'* יָרֵא) "The sailors were afraid," 1:5; "I fear Yahweh," 1:9; "They feared," 1:10; "They greatly feared Yahweh," 1:16; and the word "hurled" (*hetil* הֵטִיל) "Yahweh hurled a storm," 1:4; "They hurled cargo," 1:5; "Hurl me overboard," 1:12; "They hurled him overboard," 1:15. There are patterns in the book of Jonah around these words.

There are two contacts with the "pagans" in the book: Chapter 1 (Phoenicians) and Chs. 3-4 (Assyrians). There is a striking parallel in the interaction between Jonah and the two groups. The parallelism can be expressed in the following way.

Phoenicians

A   Call against (*'al* עַל) Nineveh (1:2)—Pagan condemnation

    B   Call on your god (1:6)—Pagan religion

      C   They called on Yahweh (1:14)—Pagan repentance

Jonah

       D I called from my affliction (2:3)—Personal conviction

       D' He called "within 40 days . . ." (4:4)—Personal conviction

Assyrians

      C'   They called on God (4:8)—Pagan repentance

    B'   They called a fast (3:5)—Pagan religion

A'   Call to (*'el* אֶל) Nineveh (3:2)—Pagan condemnation

The A, A' units provide the object of the call. Nineveh is called a great city four times. In 1:2 the word "great" conjures for us its importance as the capital of the Assyrian Empire that dominated the Middle East for about three centuries. Key words are "call," "against," "wickedness," "before me." Thus A is repeated in A' with one difference. The Hebrew word for "against" *'al* עַל) is used in 1:2 but the word "to" (*'el* אֶל) is used in 3:2. A speaks of pagan condemnation: Assyria's wickedness has "come up before God." But is there a softening indicated in 3:2? There is often little distinction between these two prepositions in Hebrew (particularly to be observed in Jeremiah), but it may be that the author wants us to recognize a changing in God's attitude in A'.

The phrase "great city" in 3:2 means the same as it did in 1:1, but the same phrase in 3:3 ("a great city to God") means something else.[72] The ambiguity introduced by the author is displayed in the fact that the city is great to God, taking three days to go through it. Now we have physical as well as metaphorical usage, and that is intended. It is a "great city" in terms of empire and in terms of size, but it is also "great" in spiritual importance to God. Finally, in 4:11 the city is referred to in terms of God's compassion. The city is full of spiritually unlettered people. Should God not be concerned with it?

Another polysemantic word occurring frequently in Jonah is *ra'ah* (רָעָה). Sometimes the word is physical, referring to calamity (e.g., Isa 45:7 "I create *ra'ah*") (1:7, 8; 4:2, 6). At other times it is used metaphorically of "evil" (1:2; 3:8, 10). The failure of God to judge the Ninevites was "evil" to Jonah (4:1). Nineveh is an "evil" city that deserves the "punishment" (*ra'ah*) of God. He also sends "calamity" against the sailors in order to punish Jonah for his disobedience.

A genuine paronomasia is found in Ch. 4, and therein lies at least one key to the meaning of the book. The purpose of the *qiqayon* bush was to "ease his discomfort." Literally this phrase is "to deliver him from his discomfort" (*ra'ah*). The *qiqayon* bush becomes a symbol of grace. As God was going to protect Nineveh upon her repentance, so he was protecting Jonah. Jonah delighted in the bush as God delights in grace. Furthermore, the worm (God's creation also) quite happily, though obliviously, destroyed the bush (God's grace to Jonah). Jonah, on the other hand, was a prophet. He should have understood God's grace. Instead, like the worm, he was willing to destroy the shade of God's mercy over the Ninevites.

The B, B' units indicate the religious practices of the pagans. The sailors were praying desperately when their ship was about to be swamped. The ship's

---

[72] All versions say something like "exceedingly great," but Jack Sasson (*Jonah* in the AB) agrees with me.

captain demanded of Jonah that he likewise pray to his god. They were not concerned about particularism; they simply wanted deliverance from their angry gods. Likewise, the Assyrians called a fast. Jonah's era was a period of trying times for the Assyrians.[73] Consequently, when Jonah preached, "within 40 days Nineveh will be overturned,"[74] they believed in god (note "god" not "Yahweh"). This is a nuance, but one wonders if there is a distinction between the normal turning to pagan deities in sackcloth and a thorough-going repentance of the king's command.

The C unit of 1:14 says that the Phoenician sailors actually feared Yahweh with a great fear.[75] This means that they have accepted Jonah's confession of faith in Yahweh, the God of Heaven who created the sea and the dry land (1:9). Thus, he claims for Yahweh universal rule and ownership. This is no local deity Jonah worships.[76]

In the C' unit, the Assyrians at the King's command wear sack cloth, fast and above all "turn from their wicked way."

---

[73]S. Cohen, "The Political Background of the Words of Amos," *HUCA* 36 (1965) 53-160, says, "Assyria lay nearly prostrate before its northern foe; it was impoverished and dispirited. Well might a prophet be believed who would proclaim: 'Yet forty days, and Nineveh shall be overthrown!'" He goes on to say, "Although the book is a piece of didactic fiction, it is based on a sound historical reminiscence, for the prophet Jonah ben Amittai (II Kings 14:25) could very well have lived about the time when Nineveh was threatened with capture and destruction."

[74]The word "overthrown" (*nehpaketh* (נֶהְפָּכֶת)) is so often used of Sodom and Gomorrah that it is probably designed to evoke that image.

[75]Elliger in BHS suggests that "Yahweh" (אֶת יהוה) is added, but in light of Jonah's great confession in 1:9, the object of their fear does not seem misplaced.

[76]For the Canaanites the deities would be Yam (Sea) and perhaps Dry Land.

Jonah —Page 78

Notes on the Book of Micah

Four prophets ministered somewhat contemporaneously:

Amos——Uzziah	(Jeroboam)
Hosea——Uzziah, Jotham, Ahaz, Hezekiah	(Jeroboam)
Isaiah——Uzziah, Jotham, Ahaz, Hezekiah	
Micah——Jotham, Ahaz, Hezekiah	

I. Historical Background.

Both Hosea and Amos mention Jeroboam II as the king of Israel under whom they ministered. Micah talks about Samaria, but does not list a northern king in his opening statements. He does mention "decrees of Omri" and "works of the dynasty of Ahab" (6:16). This would indicate, along with other things (such as references to Assyria), that part of his ministry was prior to the fall of Samaria in 722 B.C.

II. The Man, Micah.

Not much is known about Micah. His name is the shortened form of the older Micayahu (מִכָיְהוּ) "Who is like Yahweh?" He was from Moresheth which may be the same town as Moresheth-Gath in 1:14. This would be a rural town not far from Jerusalem. Isaiah was apparently a more urbane prophet, personally acquainted with kings and leaders. Micah, like Amos, may not have been part of the official prophets' guild. His trips to Jerusalem as a "country" prophet no doubt confirmed what he had heard from a distance. He shared with Isaiah, however, an unswerving commitment to the covenant of Yahweh and an abhorrence of the sin so prevalent in his day.

III. The Structure of the Book.

Hear—1:2   **Hear—3:1   Hear—6:1**

GOD'S CASE AGAINST ISRAEL & SENTENCE PRO-NOUNCED BY THE JUDGE. 1:1-7 (Cf . Isa 1)	GOD'S CASE DETAILED AND MORE SENTEN-CING. 2:1-5	GOD'S FURTHER INDICT-MENT. 3:1-4	GOD'S CASE AGAINST ISRAEL. 6:1-5	GOD'S INDICT-MENT. 6:9-16 STATUTES OF OMRI, WORKS OF AHAB
MICAH'S LAMENT TEN CITIES OF JUDAH. 1:8-16	MICAH'S LAMENT AND DEFENSE. Cf. PAUL 2:6-11	MICAH'S DIATRIBE AGAINST FALSE PROPHETS . 3:5-12	MICAH'S CONFES-SION OF WHAT GOD REQUIRES . 6:6-8	MICAH'S LAMENT OF LACK OF GODLI-NESS. 7:1-6
	HOPEFUL PROMISE FOR ISRAEL 2:12-13	HOPE IN LAST DAYS (ZION). 4:1-8		HOPE FOR ISRAEL IN THE FUTURE. 7:7-20
		BABYL-ONIAN EXILE AND RETURN. 4:9-5:1		
		MORE HOPE OF FUTURE DELIVER-ANCE. 5:2-15		

IV.   The Message.

Micah decries the abuses of the rich carried out against the poor as does Isaiah (5:8-12 "Woe") and Amos (2:6-8). Isaiah (1:10-15), Hosea (6:6), Amos (5:21-24) and Micah (6:6-8) all decry the emptiness of sacrifice without obedience. Micah also shares with Isaiah one of the most beautiful passages in the Old Testament referring to the messianic kingdom (Isaiah 2:1-4, Micah 4:1-5). Micah adds the verses about dwelling under vine and fig tree and walking in the name of the Lord.

V. The Milieu

The historical background has been discussed in connection with the previous prophets. Suffice it to say here that Assyria is looming yet large so that some of the prophecies are prior to 722 B.C. The list of towns in chapter one may refer to Sennacherib's invasion in 701 B.C. Babylon is on the horizon and the Babylonian captivity is referred to (4:10-11). The latter, as in the case of Isaiah, would be prophetic, but the Babylonians were on the scene in the days of Hezekiah as we learn from Isaiah 38-39.[77]

VI. Outline of the Book.

A. Two indictments are brought against the people, two laments by Micah and a slight ray of hope (Hear!) (1:1—2:13).

1.   God's case against Israel and the sentence pronounced by the judge (1:1-7).

---

[77]C. H. Bullock, *An Introduction to the Old Testament Prophetic Books*, says that this reference to the Babylonians is irony: Hezekiah is looking to Babylon (Isaiah 39), but Judah will go to Babylon.

The time frame is the eighth century as discussed above. The message
is directed toward both Samaria, the capital of the north, and
Jerusalem, the capital of the south (1:1).

God begins with a description of his judgment of the whole world and
then, like Amos, moves to Israel.[78] He calls the witness to hear his case
against Israel (cf. Isaiah 1 for the *Riv* argument). In dramatic terms, He
speaks of coming down to the earth to set things right. "High places of
the earth" (*bamoth* בָּמוֹת) in this context should refer to hills or mountains. Since it is also used (usually) of pagan cult centers, there may be
a play on the word since it seems to be used in the sense of idolatry in
1:5-7 (1:2-4).[79]

The reason for this is given as the rebellion of Jacob/Israel (*pesha'*
פֶּשַׁע a word used when a subordinate king throws off the yoke of his
master). Samaria was the symbol of the rebellion in the north and
Jerusalem was looked upon as the high place in the south. God will
judge Samaria and smash her idols. "Harlot's earnings" refers to the
fact that she served Baal as part of her agriculture cycle. Her wealth
was then poured into idolatry (cf. with Hosea 9:1). Samaria received
the brunt of the judgment at this time because her turn was coming
first (722 B.C.). Jerusalem managed to survive by the grace of God for
another century (1:5-7).

2.   Micah laments over the suffering that will take place and mentions ten
cities in Judah (1:8-16).

Micah laments as he walks about barefoot and naked (cf. Isaiah 20:2
where Isaiah prophesied judgment with the same dramatic action). The
reason for the lament is that the sin of Israel has reached and
influenced Judah so that she also will be judged (1:8-9).

---

[78]L. Allen, *Joel, Obadiah, Jonah, and Micah,* p. 269.

[79]See McComiskey, *Micah* in EBC, 404.

The coming judgment on Judah is so severe her enemies will rejoice over her. Therefore, the admonition is to not let the Philistine city of Gath know about the judgment (the phrase comes from David's prayer in 2 Sam. 1:20 in connection with the death of Saul).

Micah then lists ten cities that are warned of coming suffering. He apparently makes a word play on the names of the towns located in the Shephelah region around Jerusalem.[80]

Beth-le-aphrah (Dust City) "roll yourself in the dust."
Shaphir (Bellvue, or Buenavista, "Pretty City") "you will go away in nakedness."
    Zaanan (צַאֲנָן "Exit City") "she does escape" (יָצְאָה *yatse'ah*).
    Beth-ezel ("Neighbor Village") "He will take from you its support." The pun is not clear. Perhaps the nearness of this town was viewed as protection to Jerusalem.
    Maroth ("Bitterville") will suffer bitterly because God will judge Jerusalem.
Lachish sounds like "harness to the chariot" רֶכֶשׁ *rakish*. Lachish was apparently early involved in the apostasy of Israel.
Moresheth-gath (was this Micah's hometown?) is admonished to give going away   presents. This may be a play on the word "betrothed" and hence the leaving of the bride.
Achzib means "deception."
Mareshah is enough like Hebrew *yoresh* "to possess" to allow a pun on it.
Adullam the last of the ten cities is the one to which David fled from Saul. This is enough of a historical connection to remind the people that as David fled so they will flee.

The time element in this lament over the Shephelah is probably Sennacherib's invasion in 701. Lachish was attacked and defeated as were many other towns in the area.[81]

---

[80]See the beautiful *Atlas of the Bible* edited by John Rogerson, 85.

[81]See my notes on Isaiah 36 for the text from Sennacherib.

3. Through a "woe" oracle, God details their social sins and promises more judgment (2:1-5).

   Reminiscent of his contemporary, Isaiah, Micah condemns those who scheme to rob people of their possessions. Because of this God plans a calamity against "this family." Because they have robbed people of their inheritance of land, God will remove their portion, and there will be no one to "stretch a measuring line for them in the assembly of the Lord," i.e., no one will represent them in the dividing of land portions.

4. Micah strikes out in defense of his prophetic ministry against the false prophets (cf. Paul's defense in 2 Corinthians) (2:6-11).

   Verse six is difficult because it is the account of an emotional, heated encounter between Micah and the prophets who opposed his message. The word for "speak" in the verse mean literally "to drip" (נָטַף *nataph*) and is used almost exclusively of prophetic speech. The false prophets are telling Micah not to rock the boat (Amaziah told Amos a similar thing, Amos 7:10ff). The difference between the translation of *NIV* and *NASB* is rather striking. The *NASB* is more literal, but the sense is better captured by *NIV*. To get what *NIV* has, the verb must be made impersonal: "Let them (Micah and others) not prophesy." The next phrase is equally difficult. It should probably be better understood as the words of the false prophets: "Calamities will not overtake *us*" (2:6).[82]

   Israel is questioning Micah's message. God is surely not angry is He? Micah says that his message will be good to those who do good, but those who treat God as an enemy and God's people as easy prey can expect to be expelled from the land (2:7-10).

---

[82]This requires reading יַשֵּׂג (*yasag* with sin) instead of יַסֵּג (*yasag* with a samek).

On the other hand, false prophets who are windy liars and talk about wine and liquor would fit in nicely with these people (2:11).[83]

5. Yahweh speaks to Israel for the first time in the second person singular (כֻּלָּךְ *kullak*) in a vignette of hope (2:12-13).

Yahweh will lead the sheep out of the confining fold into which he has assembled them. He goes before them to lead them. The idea is clearly to lead them to peace or rest or some positive idea.

B. Another indictment is brought against the people of God, a diatribe against false prophets and a marvelous prophesy of hope (Hear!) (3:1—5:15).

1. The indictment is given (3:1-4).

The phrase Jacob/Israel should refer to the northern kingdom. Yet verses 8-10 tie it to Zion and Judah, and the rest of the section on hope is really related to Jerusalem. This seems to indicate that Micah, like Hosea and Amos, views the people of Israel/Judah as one people—that the blessing of one comes on the other and vice versa. The indictment refers once again to the mistreatment of the poor. But even the poor will not be heard in the day of his cry because he has rejected the Lord.

2. The Lord through Micah gives a diatribe against the false prophets who are forever in the service of self (3:5-12).

The prophets cry "Peace" if they get paid for it, but declare holy war against those who do not pay them. Because of this sinful practice, God calls for judgment upon them when vision, divination and prophecy will be gone (3:5-7).

---

[83]Speak/spokesman are again from *nataph* "to drop (words), to prophesy."

On the other hand Micah is confident and assured that he speaks in the name of Yahweh and that he is filled with the spirit and power of Yahweh, with justice and courage. May God give all his servants this confidence! Because of this confidence of his call, he will continue to declare to Jacob/Israel their sin. These people are building Zion with bloodshed and Jerusalem with injustice. The leaders, priests and prophets are all hirelings who do not care for the people. They religiously lean on Yahweh and say "Is not Yahweh in our midst? Calamity will not come upon us."

Because of this dreadful attitude, God promises that Zion (the place where Yahweh dwells) will become a plowed field.[84]

3. A message of hope is given to Zion for the last days (4:1-8).

Zion will be turned into a plowed field as God's judgment, but her latter end will be glorious.

This little section on Zion's future (verses 1-3 are found in Isaiah 2) is one of the most beautiful in the entire Bible. It is inscribed on the UN building. The Israelis set it up on a rock at the "good fence," but it will never come to pass until the prince of peace comes. The components are: Zion will be exalted, peoples will come there, they will seek God and ask Him to teach them His Torah, the law will go forth from Zion, God will act as the judge (shophet), warfare will cease, great prosperity will be the rule, and people will walk in the name of the Lord. Hallelujah! (4:1-5).

God's restoration will involve bringing the remnant back from the distant places and making them into a strong kingdom with the Lord over them (4:6-8).

---

[84]This situation is cited by the elders in Jer. 26:18 when king Jehoiakim and his ilk would have killed Jeremiah for his negative prophecy.

4. Before that marvelous restoration takes place, Zion must suffer the ignominy of the exile, but she will triumph over her enemies (4:9—5:1).

The key to this section is the word "Now" which introduces calamity in 4:9, 11 and 5:1.

The first unit speaks of Zion being taken to Babylon as captives. Merodach Baladan made overtures to Hezekiah who was roundly criticized by Isaiah. These events caused both Isaiah and Micah to predict a Babylonian captivity for Judah. At the same time, God promises that those nations who have gloated at the troubles of Zion will be "threshed" by Zion on God's threshing floor (4:9-13).

Before victory however, there must be shame. 5:1 says "Now" Israel is to muster herself in troops in defense of her besieged city. The king will be treated shamefully.[85]

5. Ultimate victory for Zion will come through a divinely sent ruler who will come from Bethlehem (5:2-15).

The king of Zion will be mistreated in the capture of Jerusalem,[86] but God will provide a king who will bring permanent victory and peace to her. The ruler to come has an ancient background (cf. Isaiah 9:6).[87] God will turn Zion over to a time of captivity until this one will be born (of Israel as the woman in travail and as in Revelation 12) who will shepherd Israel. Verse 3b seems to refer to the joining of the people of Israel as in the two sticks of Ezekiel 37:15ff. This one will

---

[85]The king is called judge (*shophet* שֹׁפֵט) perhaps to rhyme with rod (*shebet* שֵׁבֶט).

[86]L. Allen, *Joel, Obadiah, Jonah, and Micah*, p. 341, thinks this refers to 701 B.C.

[87]See also H. Heater, "Matthew 2:6 and Its Old Testament Sources," *JETS* 26 (1983) 395-397.

bring peace to Israel (the chastisement that produced our peace was upon him [Isaiah 53:5]) (5:2-5b).

Zion will have victory over their enemies at that time. Assyria probably refers to whoever the enemy will be in that day. The nemesis of Israel/Judah in Micah's day was Assyria.[88] Notice the motif of seven/eight for emphasis (5:5b-6).

The remnant of Jacob will not sit passively among her captors. She will be a mighty force under God's hand against her enemies (5:7-9).

The final statement of blessing refers to the complete removal of any vestiges of idolatry from the people of God. There will be no need for armies, fortifications or horses. He will also bring vengeance on those who have not obeyed (5:10-15).

C.   A final round of indictment/lament/hope is given by the Lord (Hear!) (6:1—7:20).

1. Yahweh gives his court case (רִיב *riv*) against Israel (6:1-5).

Yahweh returns to His indictment because the message of hope delivered in the middle section might leave people with the impression that it does not matter what they do.

Yahweh addresses the court (nature) and tells them He has a case against His people (6:1-2).

He now addresses His people in the second/singular to plead with them to listen to Him. He reminds them of all His redemptive work in their behalf and asks them to explain how He has failed them (6:3-5).

---

[88]See McComiskey, *Micah*, for a discussion of Assyria as a type. Allen, *Joel, Obadiah, Jonah, and Micah*, sees 5-6 as a war chant that Micah has turned into a messianic promise. The people thought they could win, but only Messiah will bring victory.

2. Micah confesses that bringing sacrifices to God alone is not what He requires (6:6-8).

   The greatness of God requires more than mere ritual. Sacrifices even of one's firstborn are inadequate to please the Lord. What Yahweh requires is justice (מִשְׁפָּט *mishpat*), loving kindness (אַהֲבַת חֶסֶד *'ahabath ḥesed*) and a humble walk before Him.

3. A final major indictment is handed down against Israel (6:9-16).

   The people are first admonished to pay attention when the Lord speaks. Verses 6:9 and 10a are difficult and have some textual problems. The word "tribe" and "rod" are the same in Hebrew. Perhaps we should read: "Listen to the Rod, who has fixed its time" (that is Yahweh has fixed the time for judgment). For "are there yet" (הַאֵשׁ *ha'esh*), NIV adds two letters to the Hebrew word to get "shall I forget" (הַאֶשְׁכָּח *ha'eshkah*). I believe they are correct (6:9-10).

   The wickedness of the people in becoming dishonestly rich will result in God's judgment upon them. They have been following the wicked practices of former kings (Omri and the dynasty of Ahab). Therefore God will judge them (6:11-16).

4. Micah laments the lack of godliness in Israel (7:1-6).

   Micah says that godly people are as scarce as grapes after the harvesters have picked them. Everyone, including the princes and the judges, are dishonest and take unfair advantage of people. However the watchmen (prophets) will proclaim judgment and punishment will come. It will be a time of internecine strife of the worst sort.

5. The book closes with a final message of hope and expectation of God's vindication of His people (7:7-20).

Micah gives a delightful testimony of his willingness to wait for Yahweh because He is his light (7:7-8).

Micah identifies with the people and says that in spite of the fact that they have sinned against Yahweh, He will plead his case and bring forth justice. Israel will be regathered, the city will be rebuilt and God will judge the sinful world (7:9-13).

The prophet calls upon Yahweh to shepherd His people, the flock of His possession. The idea of shepherding goes back to the divine shepherd of 5:2. God responds in 7:15 to say that He will show them miracles such as when He brought them from Egypt. Nations will be brought into submission to God.

A final word of praise is given to the God who pardons iniquities, passes over rebellious acts, does not retain anger forever, delights in *ḥesed*, casts sins into the depths of the sea, gives truth to Jacob and *ḥesed* to Abraham. What a great God is this!!!

Notes on the Book of Isaiah

I. The Man

Isaiah prophesied during the reigns of Uzziah, Jotham, Ahaz and Hezekiah. Depending on the interpretation of chapter 6 (is it Isaiah's call to the ministry?) the termini of his work would be 745 and 680 (death of Sennacherib—Isa. 37:38). 1 Chron. 26:22 (Now the rest of the acts of Uzziah first to last, the prophet Isaiah, the son of Amoz, has written) indicate some activity prior to Uzziah s death in 740 B.C. "The period of his activity is thus the last four and a half decades of the eighth century, the reigns of the Judean kings Jotham (…) Ahaz (…) and Hezekiah (…), decades which were filled with the most momentous events, more so than almost any other period of Israelite history."[89] Isaiah was married to a prophetess (8:3) and had at least two children (Shear jashub, "a remnant will return" and Maher shalal hash baz, "hurry spoil, hasten booty"). Little more is known about Isaiah's personal life (contrast Jeremiah's many references to himself).

II. The Milieu

Uzziah (Azariah) (792-740) had a long reign of 52 years in Jerusalem. Gershon Brin[90] shows that the roots *'azar* and *'azaz* (עָזַז עָזַר) converged and thus explains the two names. (Both mean "to help.") It was during Uzziah's reign that Tiglath-Pileser III began to make inroads to the west

---

[89]Eissfeldt, *The Old Testament, an Introduction*, 305.

[90]Gershon Brin, " *'azar* and *'azaz*," *Leshonenu* 24 (1960): 8-14.

and confronted Israel, forcing them to pay tribute (Menahem, Pekah, 2 Kings 15:29; Assyrian annals). Uzziah intruded into the priest's office and God struck him with leprosy, and Jotham his son began to rule as co-regent (2 Kings 15:7, 2 Chron. 26:21). The setting for chapter 6 of Isaiah is the year that King Uzziah died (6:1). One must wonder what relationship if any Isaiah had with this king who was generally sympathetic with spiritual things, but died a leper.[91]

Jotham (750/40-732) was a spiritual man (2 Kings 15:34), but he saw the beginning of the decline of Judah as the initial attacks of Israel/Syria were in his time.

Ahaz (735-716) was not a spiritual man (2 Kings 16:1-3). During his rule, Jerusalem suffered a devastating attack from the combined armies of Israel and Syria (2 Kings 16:5,6; 2 Chron. 28:5-15). Ahaz sent to Tiglath Pileser for help (2 Kings 16:7-9) who gladly obliged for a price, and Israel/Syria withdrew their pressure from Judah. It was at this critical juncture that Isaiah met Ahaz and challenged him to trust in God for deliverance, but Ahaz refused (Isaiah 7:1-19).

Hezekiah (716-687), along with his later descendent Josiah, is known for his spiritual fervor and reform (2 Chron. 29:1—31:21). However, during his time, the Assyrian threat became stronger, culminating in Senna-cherib's attack of the fortified cities of Judah, including Jerusalem, and Hezekiah's payment of tribute. It is poetic justice that the Rab Shakeh stands in the very spot Isaiah had met Ahaz and warned him to trust in Yahweh rather than in Assyria and hurls insults at Hezekiah (2 Chron. 32:1-23). Isaiah uses these two events as bookends for the structure of the book. Hezekiah received ambassadors from a newly emerging political

---

[91]For an excellent discussion of the historical setting of Isaiah (with some different conclusions) see J. H. Hayes and S. A. Irvine, *Isaiah, the Eighth Century Prophet; His Times and His Preaching*, pp. 17-49.

group in Babylon. Their purpose was probably to stir up revolt in the west against Assyria.[92]

The second part of Isaiah (40-66) focuses on the period of the exile. The historical background for that epoch will be discussed in the notes at that point.

III. The Message

There is a distinctive difference in perspective between the first 39 chapters and the last 27 of Isaiah. (We will ignore 36-39 as a unit at this time). This difference, above all other issues, has led critical scholars to argue for at least two different authors and perhaps three or four. The emphasis in the first half of the book is on judgment while the last half is clearly an encouraging word of comfort: "Comfort ye, comfort ye my people (40:1)." The setting of most of the second half is certainly the exile (from a prophetic point of view). It is designed to encourage the exiled Jews with the promise of restoration and messianic blessing.

The most unusual component of Isaiah is the magnificent individual Servant of the Lord passages (*'eved Yahweh* יהוה עֶבֶד). The passages are Chs. 42, 49, 50, 52-53.[93]

IV. The Structure of Isaiah

The macro-structure of Isaiah is, of course, 1-35 (36-39) and 40-66.

---

[92]This period (Uzziah—Hezekiah) is one of the most difficult chronologically in the entire monarchial period—see the literature for discussions. We are using dates from Thiele, *Mysterious Numbers of the Hebrew Kings.* For a survey of the dating issues, see Provan, Longman, and Long, *A Biblical History of Israel*, Westminster John Knox Press, Louisville, 2003.

[93]For a discussion of this very important theme see E. J. Young, *Studies in Isaiah* and Christopher North, *The Suffering Servant in Deutero-Isaiah.*

Chapters 1-39 have two historical centers: the Syro-Ephraimite war in chapter 7 where Ahaz is urged to trust the Lord (the implication is that Ahaz should not go to Assyria for help), and the Assyrian attack in 36-37. Isaiah meets Ahaz at the "conduit of the upper pool, on the highway to the fuller's field," the precise place the Rab Shakeh hurled insults and threats at Hezekiah who trusted Yahweh and was delivered. This section of Isaiah should be considered the "Assyrian" section. It should probably be understood as a response to the Assyrian threat in which Judah is urged to repent of her sins and trust Yahweh for deliverance.

Chapters 36-37 are a statement of the devastating results of apostate Ahaz' refusal to trust Yahweh (the help for Ahaz, Assyria, becomes his son's enemy). They also show Yahweh's grace to a repentant Hezekiah as the Assyrians are supernaturally routed.

Chapters 38-39, on the other hand, look toward Babylon and the Babylonian captivity, the major subject of the second half of the book. (These chapters should precede chronologically the events of chapters 36-37 since Merodach Baladan had fled Babylon in 702/1. Thus his ambassadors to Judah must have been sent in 703 B.C.).[94]

Chapters 40-66 are a response to the Babylonian captivity (in prophecy), urging Judah to recognize the uniqueness of Yahweh and to rejoice in His work of bringing His people and His world back to Himself through the Servant.

Assyrian Threat	**Babylonian Threat**

Ahaz seeks Assyria's help➔ Result: Judah becomes a tributary to Assyria.
      7-35   36-37

Hezekiah seeks Babylonia's help➔ Result: Judah goes into captivity.
      38-39   40-66

---

[94]Hayes and Irving, *Isaiah*, pp. 13-14, place these chapters in 712-711.

V. Relevance

Before any discussion can be held on contemporary relevance, the importance of Isaiah in his own time and context must be determined. This is a major task in itself. But the fact that Isaiah is quoted so extensively in the New Testament (as many as 411 times) should alert us to the fact that the meaning of Isaiah is greater than its own historical milieu. While the Old Testament must always be studied in its *sitz im Leben* it has a larger meaning as well. Therefore, we study the book of Isaiah in its historical, cultural context to ascertain first its meaning for the people of that time. At the same time, we are asking whether some of its messages are being stated prophetically with a fulfillment in later time. We cannot with McKenzie say that while Isaiah 53 speaks of vicarious suffering, it cannot refer to Jesus Christ except as the later church made it do.[95] We believe that the one and only meaning of Isaiah 53 is the death of Jesus Christ. Consequently, there are parts of Isaiah that are fulfilled in the NT, parts to be fulfilled in the eschatological future, and part that can only be secondarily applied by application to our day. This latter requires us to ask, "In what sense are we like Israel so that the words of God to them should be directed to us?"

VI. Outline Notes

Part I: Judgment (Chs. 1—39)

Working on the Assyrian construct, we can split off the indictment unit (1-6) and show its Assyrian connection. The introductory *riv* chapter calling Judah into court for her sinfulness, informs us that "Your [Judah's] land is desolate, your cities are burned with fire, your fields—strangers are devouring them in your presence; it is desolation, as overthrown by strangers. And the daughter of Zion is left like a shelter in a vineyard, like a watchman's hut in a cucumber field, like a besieged city. Unless the Lord

---

[95]McKenzie, *Second Isaiah*, XXXIX, XLIX.

of hosts had left us a few survivors, we would be like Sodom, we would be like Gomorrah" (1:7-9).

The devastation spoken of in Isaiah 1 could be the result of the attack from Assyria during Tiglath-Pileser III's campaign of 743-738.[96] Whether it was this or some other attack, Yahweh has used it to punish Judah for her sins and to focus her attention on Him. In His grace He has left a "few survivors."

Azariah (Uzziah), old and leprous, died a year or two after this attack (740/39). Isaiah received his vision in that same year. The vision may be placed in chapter 6 rather than in chapter 1, as would be expected, because it represents a climax of the judgment section in 1-5. Chapter six judicially seals Judah in her sins.

A. Yahweh demonstrates that Judah has violated His covenant and is therefore worthy of judgment (1:1—6:13).

Chapters 1-6 are a unit. It begins with a court case against Judah, moves to explicit statements about Judah's sin, speaks of the unfruitful vineyard Yahweh planted, and culminates in Isaiah's vision telling him to preach a message of hardening because of Judah's sin.

1. Yahweh's court case against Judah (1:1-31).

The Hebrew word *riv* (רִיב) as in 1:23 is used to describe the type of literature we have in chapter 1. It is God's court case with his people.

The introduction (1:1).

The author—Isaiah (*yesha'yahu* יְשַׁעְיָהוּ or *yesha'yah* יְשַׁעְיָה) means Yahweh is salvation.

---

[96]*ANET*, p. 282. For the text, see my notes at "Historical Background of the Eighth Century" and footnote 5. For a full discussion, see footnote 7.

The time—Spanning parts of the reign of four kings.

The medium—*ḥezon* (חֲזוֹן). This word pertains to divine communication (cf. 1 Sam. 3:1).

The stupidity of Judah (1:2-3).

In God's court case he calls as witness Heaven and Earth to testify to Judah's conduct. The natural realm (animals) acts in an expected fashion, but Judah goes contrary to nature in forgetting God. (Note the parallelism in v. 3).

The sinfulness of Judah (1:4).

Yahweh delineates the sad state of affairs in which Judah finds herself. The children who have abandoned their father in v. 2 have become children of corruption.[97]

The suffering of Judah (1:5-9).

Judah's suffering is described first in metaphor as that of a sick man who receives no treatment (5-6). Then a more literal description is given of the desolation of the land (7). Finally he refers metaphorically to Judah as a shelter in a vineyard or a watchman's hut in a cucumber field or a besieged city. Except for God's grace, Judah would have been wiped out like Sodom and Gomorrah (8-9). This situation refers to some period in Judah's history during which she was invaded and suffered terribly. As indicated above this might be the result of Tiglath-Pileser III's invasion under Uzziah.[98]

---

[97]Note the use of the "Holy One of Israel" to describe God. The phrase occurs thirty times in Isaiah.

[98]But see Hayes and Irvine, *Isaiah*, pp. 69-73, who argue that the devastation was caused by an earthquake, not an invasion. Most now question the Tiglath-Pileser III contact with Judah. See Historical Background section (p.5).

The futile sacrifice of Judah (1:10-15).

Some have taken this section to show an antipathy to the sacrificial system on the part of (second) Isaiah. These kinds of statements however are known from other prophets (Jeremiah, Amos, Micah) who decry the empty formalism of sacrifice that does not acknowledge a personal relationship with Yahweh.

The admonition to Judah (1:16-20).

God first gives Judah specific areas that must be rectified: Ceasing to do evil, learning to do good, justice, reproving the ruthless, defending the orphan and pleading for the widow. The second part (18-20) is a promise of blessing for obedience and judgment for disobedience.

The lament over Zion and hope for Zion (1:21-26).

Yahweh's faithful city has become a harlot. Everything God desires in a people is missing from this city. Consequently, God through judgment will purge away Zion's sins until she will be called the faithful city. (Note the chiasmus in "faithful city.")

The promise of blessing for Zion and judgment for idolaters (1:27-31).

This early prediction of redemption for Zion should be noted carefully. The promise of redemption is similar to the second half of the book; the idolatry to the first half. Watts argues that the whole book was assembled in the middle of the fifth century and that there is a literary unity.[99] Hayes and Irvine argue that chapters 1-33 are essentially from the eighth century prophet.[100]

2. Jerusalem: Yahweh's and Israel's contrasted (Ch. 2-4).

---

[99]Watts, *Isaiah 1-33, loc cit.*

[100]Hayes and Irvine, *Isaiah,* 13.

Zion in the last days (2:1-4).

This beautiful passage (parallel in Micah 4:1-3) speaks of a time when all things will be made right and people will flow to Zion as the center of the universe where they will be taught the torah of God. This messianic age spoken of often by Isaiah will be fulfilled in the Millennium. The purpose in this unit is to show the great difference between the sinfulness of Jerusalem in Isaiah's day and the purity of Jerusalem in the time to come.

Zion in Isaiah's day (2:5-11).

This section depicts Judah enthralled with idolatry, a system she has learned from the nations around her. God promises to judge this conduct.

Zion to be judged and purged (2:12—4:1).

The sins of Judah will be judged by God in that day of reckoning. The great sin here is pride. God will humble all the proud ones. In chapter 3 God speaks of a time when he will judge Zion and leave her leaderless and in shambles (3:1-12). He speaks of his court case again against the leaders (3:13-15). Finally he indicts the women who are preoccupied with their physical appearance (3:16—4:1).

The Branch of the Lord (4:2-6).

This unit speaks of the purification of Zion and uses the imagery of the Exodus (cloud by day, flame by night) to speak of God's blessing on Jerusalem.[101]

---

[101]The word Branch (צֶמַח *tsemah*) will later be developed into a symbol of the Messiah (cf. Isaiah 11, Jeremiah 23, Zechariah 3,6). Here it may be a general symbol of fruitfulness (because of the parallel line: "the fruit of the earth . . ."), but one has to wonder if it is a seminal allusion to the Messiah. Hayes and Irvine, *Isaiah*, p. 96, believe it may refer to a Davidic prince.

3. The song of the vineyard (Judah's sinful state) (5:1-30).

    Yahweh indicts Judah with the parable of the vineyard (5:1-7).

    The vine dresser prepared the vineyard in the best possible way and yet it produced stinking grapes rather than good grapes. So, says Yahweh, is Judah: He has done everything possible for her, but she has turned away from Him. In beautiful paronomasia, he says that "He waited for justice (*mishpat)* and behold bloodshed (*mishpaḥ)*; for righteousness (*tsedekah*) and instead a cry (*tseakah*) of the oppressed ones."

    Yahweh sets out a bill of particulars as to the sinful state of Judah (5:8-12).

    The sins of that day were in the area of greed (real estate expansion), drunkenness and debauchery.

    Yahweh promises judgment on Judah in the form of exile (5:13-17).

    Note the pattern: "Woe" (5:8) followed by judgment (5:13); "Woe" (5:18) followed by judgment (5:24). Then the judgment is amplified in 5:26. What exile is this? It could refer to the Syro-Ephraimite war, perhaps to Sennacherib's expedition against Lachish in 701, or even to the exile of 605, 597, 586. The time is deliberately kept vague.

    Yahweh delineates further sins of Judah (5:18-23).

    Judah is indicted for mocking Yahweh. They are heavily involved in sin (like construction workers dragging stones with ropes) yet they mock God by asking Him what his plans are. They call evil good and good evil. They reverse everything God does.

Yahweh states his judgment on those sins (5:24-30).

The promise is of devastating judgment (24-25). The threat is expanded by referring to the coming of a distant nation who will dominate the land (26-30).

4. Yahweh reveals to Isaiah by a vision the reason for His judgment of Judah (6:1-12).

The setting of the vision (the glory of Yahweh) (6:1-4).

If this is Isaiah's inaugural vision, it has been placed to make a point in the argument of the book: it is the culmination of the indictment of Judah because of her sins. God will harden those who have hardened themselves.[102]

The problem with Judah (Isaiah is representative) (6:5).

This verse shows that all people stand guilty before a holy and glorious God. Isaiah represents all people and Judah in particular in his uncleanness.

The need for cleansing by Judah (6:6-7).

God in His grace cleanses those who come contritely to Him as Isaiah does.

The response of service (Isaiah's message is given to him) (6:8-13).

Isaiah volunteers to go to serve Yahweh and is then given a dismal message to preach. His message is one of judgment. This same message is used by Jesus (Matt. 13:14-15) and Paul (Acts 28:26-27).[103]

---

[102]See Hayes and Irving, *Isaiah*, p. 109, who argue that Ch. 6 is used by Isaiah to justify his political stance in subsequent chapters.

[103]Note that it is *preaching* that hardens hearts. The people reject the preaching by

The message is so hard that Isaiah cries out asking how long he must preach it. The answer comes back that he will preach it until devastating judgment is wrought in Judah. At the same time a ray of hope shows in v. 13 where a stump (the holy seed or faithful remnant) is promised to Israel.[104]

B. Yahweh promises deliverance and predicts a divine son (7:1—12:6).

Chapters 1-7 are set in the time of Uzziah's declining years. The era of 7—12 follows chronologically in the days of Ahaz. The "Book of Immanuel" (7-12) is designed to show the futility of trusting in human help and the blessing from trusting in Yahweh. The hired deliverer (Assyria) will indeed break the back of the Syro-Ephraimite coalition, but the deliverer will become the devastator (Ch. 8). Hope must come from Yahweh (the divine child, Chapter 9), and even though Assyria will cut down trees, they themselves will be cut down. However, out of the stump of Jesse, Yahweh will raise up the righteous deliverer who will usher in the Kingdom (Ch. 11). Chapter 12 is a psalm, giving praise to Yahweh for His deliverance.

1. The Syro-Ephraimite war (7:1-25).

The situation (7:1-2).

Pekah of Israel and Rezin of Syria (Aram) have decided to join forces to attack a weakened Judah ruled by King Ahaz and set up a puppet

---

hardening their hearts. This is also how Jesus interprets the words (Matthew 13:15). The fault lies with the people entirely.

[104]G. K. Beale, *We Become What We Worship—a Biblical Theology of Idolatry*. I like what Beale does with Isaiah 6. The "making blind and deaf" are allusions to idolatry and therefore God is sealing them in the judgment they have brought on themselves by becoming blind and deaf (Isa 45). He has a more controversial position on the "remnant" and "stump" and "holy seed." These represent unbelieving Israel (holy seed is their position not their practice as in Nehemiah). Burning the terebinth in Isaiah is judgment for idolatry. So even the tenth who will be saved will be judged because of their idolatry (Chapter 2).

king, Tabeel.[105] One attack has already been carried out and the Syrians are "resting" on Israel (that is they have encamped there instead of returning home). This latter action creates the fear that another attack will take place and Ahaz and his advisors are greatly frightened.[106] Most scholars argue that the Syro-Ephraimite war was to force Judah into a coalition against Assyria, but see B. Oded[107] who argues against that position.

God sends Isaiah to promise deliverance to Ahaz (7:3-9).

Isaiah is instructed to go to the upper pool (location unknown, but perhaps near Gihon or 'Ayin Rogel). He is to take with him his son with a prophetic name Shear Jashub (שְׁאָר יָשׁוּב) meaning "a remnant will return." This name has both negative and positive connotations. It is negative, because judgment will take place and only a remnant will return; positive, because in spite of judgment, a remnant will return. Isaiah tells Ahaz not to fear—that God will take care of the situation. As a matter of fact a specific time period is given (65 years) within which Israel will be shattered and judgment will come on Syria. Because of the difficulty in chronology it is difficult to relate these dates, but we know that Damascus was defeated by Assyria in 732 B.C. and Samaria in 722 B.C. Events of chapter 7 should have

---

[105]The MT points the name as if it were טָב אַל *tab al* "no good," i.e., they are punning on the word to say that whoever this person was he was no good. See W. F. Albright (*"The Son of Tabeel [Isa. 7:6]" BASOR* 140 [1955]: 34-35). He discusses a letter from a "Tab'elite" to Tiglath-Pileser III toward the end of his reign. Hence, this is a prince (possibly a son of Uzziah or Jotham) with a Tabelite mother.

[106]For a harmony of this account with that of Kings and Chronicles, see E. J. Young *Studies in Isaiah* or his three volume commentary in NICOT. Hayes and Irving (*Isaiah*, pp. 120-121) believe that Syria controlled Gilead and Galilee and now through the puppet, Pekah, virtually controlled Ephraim.

[107]B. Oded, "The Historical Background of the Syro-Ephraimite War Reconsidered," *CBQ* 34 (1972): 153-65.

transpired about 735 B.C. Hence there are only about twelve years between Isaiah's prediction and the fall of Israel in 722 B.C. Some believe the 65 year terminus is 670/69 when final deportations were made (Ezra 4:2, 10.) Ahaz is told that if he will not believe, that he will not last: *ki lo' te'amenu 'im lo' te'aminu* כִּי לֹא תַאֲמֵנוּ אִם לֹא תַאֲמִינוּ.

God gives a sign to the whole house of Israel for all time (7:10-16).[108]

Isaiah then instructs Ahaz to ask for a sign from God to confirm the fact that God will deliver him from the Syro-Ephraimite hostility. Ahaz, not known for his spiritual integrity, refuses to ask for a sign under the pretext of not tempting God. The fact is that he intends to go to Assyria for help and does not want anything to interfere with this (2 Kings 16:7-9). I find it hard to understand Watt's argument[109] that Isaiah is urging Ahaz to remain faithful to Assyria. It seems to me that Isaiah wants Ahaz to trust in God and not in human deliverance, namely, Assyria.

Because Ahaz refuses the sign, Isaiah turns to the whole house of Israel (plural in Hebrew) and gives them a sign. The sign is that a virgin ('*almah* עַלְמָה) will conceive and bear a child and call his name Immanuel (עִמָּנוּאֵל, God with us). This is one of the most controversial passages in the Old Testament. Knowing how Matthew uses the Old Testament it is not impossible to view this prophecy as a reference to a young woman (virgin at that time as all '*almahs* are presumed to be) who later married and had a child. However, I believe the prophecy to be a reference to the virgin birth of Christ. It is as if Isaiah peered into

---

[108]Hayes and Irving, *Isaiah*, p. 117, agree that the message is one of hope for the Davidic dynasty, but they argue that Isaiah encouraged Ahaz and later editorial placement of 17-25 caused it to be taken negatively.

[109]Watts, *Isaiah 1-33.*

the future and said, "I see a boy being born, and before he is old enough to choose good and evil . . . ." In answer to the question, "how is it a sign to that generation?," we must turn to chapter eight where a second son of Isaiah, Maher shalal hash baz , is said to be a sign and a similar time frame is assigned to him. With E. J. Young, I believe that Ahaz's refusal of God's promise causes God to give a sign to the whole house of Israel that refers to God's ultimate deliverance of Israel through a savior. The time frame is important here—before the child knows . . . In order to give a sign to the people of that generation as well as to predict the birth of Christ, God uses Isaiah's son Maher shalal hash baz to provide the *ad interim* sign[110] of the short time before God would judge Israel/Syria.[111]

---

[110]See J. A. Motyer, *The Prophecy of Isaiah*, p. 135 for a discussion of *ad interim* prophecies in another context.

[111]Some reasons why I believe Isa. 7:14 refers only to Christ.

1. Cited in connection with Christ's birth—Mary was a virgin before, during and after conception.
2. The word *'almah* is used seven times in the Bible and is not used of a married woman (Prov. 31 does not necessarily involve sex). (The word *bethulah*, often argued to be the better word if Isaiah really meant virgin, is used of a married woman in Joel 1:8).
3. *'Almah* does not fit Ahaz's wife or Isaiah's wife (must not be married and assumed to be a virgin).
4. There is no one on the scene to fit this description.
5. For a woman or women in general to give birth and say "Immanuel" is not much of a sign.
6. Isaiah's son is not the same one: different name; different mother, who is not a virgin, so he must be taking the place of Immanuel.
7. The unit of Isaiah 7-12 is to be viewed as a whole. This section is teaching that God will deliver His people through His own means—a special son (7:14; 9:6; 11:1). IT IS NOT NECESSARY FOR A PROPHECY TO BE FULFILLED AT A GIVEN TIME IN ORDER TO BE RELEVANT.

God promises judgment from the very people to whom Ahaz has gone for help (7:16-25).

It is clear that Assyria is going to come against Judah for God will supernaturally cause it to happen. This judgment will bring great difficulty on the Judeans. There were several Assyrian contacts with Judah, the most severe being in 701 B.C. when Sennacherib attacked the fortified cities. 2 Chron. 27:16-21 shows that Ahaz's attempt to bribe Assyria failed to prevent Assyrian oppression.

1. God's deliverance as shown by Isaiah's sons (8:1-22). The prophecy through Maher shalal hash baz (8:1-4).

Since the fulfillment of the coming of Immanuel will not be for seven centuries, God provides a son for Isaiah who will serve a similar function: his early childhood will represent the time lapse before the captivity of Damascus. Isaiah writes a large sign that says "Maher shalal hash baz" or "hasten spoil, hurry booty." Then he approaches his wife who conceives. The boy will then be called "Maher shalal hash baz." This strange name will mean that Assyria will quickly carry off Damascus as booty.[112]

---

[112]Note the way John the Baptist serves as the interim for Elijah in the Elijah prophecy, and the "little horn" for Antichrist:

Malachi 4:5	Matt. 17:12	Matt. 17:11
Coming one	John Baptist	Elijah
Isaiah 7:14	Isaiah 8	Matt. 1:23
Immanuel	Maher Shalal Hash Baz	Jesus
Daniel 7	Daniel 8	Revelation
Little Horn	Antiochus	Antichrist
Antichrist		

The prophecy of the invasion of Assyria (8:5-8).

Under the imagery of water, God explains why Assyria will not only damage Damascus, but also Judah. The gently flowing waters of Shiloah probably refer to the waters coming from the spring Gihon and flowing through the water channel. (Hezekiah will later cut a new tunnel under the city through which these same waters will flow.) The gently flowing waters represent God's protection of Judah—a protection being set aside in favor of Assyria's arm. The phrase "rejoice in Rezin and the son of Remaliah" is difficult. It must mean that Judah is rejoicing because they expect to defeat them through the Assyrians. Next the king of Assyria is depicted as a flood of water inundating all the land as he overflows the banks of the river. The phrase Immanuel occurs again. It should be related to the son to be born in 7:14. To him belongs the land of Israel. With this confidence, Isaiah can now challenge the nations of the world and say that regardless of what they plan, it will be frustrated because of the fact that "God is with us."

God challenges Isaiah to trust His authority (8:11-15).

Isaiah is warned not to follow the patterns of the people of Judah. His desire to trust God rather than Assyria is viewed as conspiracy by these people who refuse to trust God (cf. 7:9). Those who trust in Yahweh will find Him a rock, but those who refuse to do so will stumble over him (cf. 1 Pet. 2:8; Luke 2:34; Matt. 21:44; Rom. 9:33).

God predicts a time when His testimony will be rejected and a time of difficulty for Judah (8:16-22).

The words of verse 16 should be understood as coming from God. "My disciples," therefore, refers to God's disciples, not Isaiah's. These are the people who trust in the Lord and believe His word. In a secondary sense they are Isaiah's disciples in whose hearts the word of God is being imbedded. The section beginning with v. 19 speaks of a people who are rejecting the revealed word of God and going to the occult for information. The result is that God will bring judgment upon them.

3. God's deliverance is shown by the coming victorious Deliverer (9:1-7).

The judgment God has promised will one day be lifted (9:1).

Matthew quotes this passage during Jesus' Galilean ministry (Matt. 4:15,16).

Victory will come through the Deliverer (9:2-7).

The people who have been walking in the darkness of judgment will see great light.[113] The yoke will be taken from their shoulder. This will come about through the son whose name will be called Wonderful Counselor (*pele' yo'etz* פֶּלֶא יוֹעֵץ), Mighty God (*'el gibbor* אֵל גִּבּוֹר),[114] Eternal Father (*'bi'ad* אֲבִיעַד), and Prince of Peace (*sar shalom* שַׂר שָׁלוֹם). These epithets have divine implications. God will establish an eternal government which shall be centered in the throne

---

[113]"The area between the Sea of Chinnereth and the Mediterranean north of the Jezreel Valley had always been something of a melting pot, with Hebrews, Canaanites, Arameans, Hittites, and Mesopotamians all contributing to the mix. It was in this region, through which the various inland powers reached westward and southward toward the seacoast, that Israel commonly encountered the rest of the world (hence the name). But the area was destined to see an even more intense mixing after 735, for this was the first part of Israel to be stripped away by Tiglath-pileser, with the inhabitants resettled in Mesopotamia and new settlers from the area brought in. (See 2 Kings 15:29; cf. also the annals of Tiglath-pileser III [ANET, pp. 283-84.])" Oswalt, *The Book of Isaiah 1-39*, p. 239.

[114]See Isa 10:21; Deut 10:17; Jer 32:18 where this phrase is used of God.

of David. God's zeal will effect this program which will result in justice and equity for all.[115]

4. Before that victory comes, God will judge His people (9:8—10:4).

This judgment will come through Rezin and others (9:8-12).

Refrain: His anger does not turn away, and His hand is still stretched out (9:12).

This judgment will take place because of the stubborn rebellion of the people (9:13-17).

Refrain: (9:17).

God's judgment even takes the form of civil war (9:18-21).

Refrain: (9:21).

Sins of social neglect will result in exile (10:1-4).

Refrain: (10:4).

5. God predicts judgment on his instrument Assyria (10:5-34).

God pronounces a "woe" on Assyria (10:5-11).

The theology of judgment in the Old Testament is that God uses kings and empires to execute His will against His people. As a result, He refers to Nebuchadnezzar as his servant (Jer. 25:9) who will later be

---

[115]See E. J. Young (*Isaiah* in *NICOT* 1:324-43) for a thorough defense of the divine aspects of this child. See also A. Cohen (*Every Man's Talmud,* pp. 52-53) for a discussion of the Talmudic references to "metatron," an angel that is almost worshiped. See J. H. Charlesworth, *The Old Testament Pseudepigrapha,* 2:243: "By far the most significant angel in 3 Enoch is Metatron. Metatron's position in the heavenly world is briefly and accurately summed up in the title 'The lesser YHWH' (3 En 10:3-6). Like the Holy One himself, he has a throne and presides over a celestial law court (3En 16:1). See also Oswalt, *The Book of Isaiah 1-39,* pp. 244-48.

punished (Jer. 25:12). Likewise, Cyrus is even called "My anointed" (Isa. 45:1). However, when that "instrument" arrogates to itself the accomplishment, God in turn punishes it. Chapter 10 is God's declaration of judgment against Assyria.

God gives the reason for judgment against Assyria (10:12-19).

The time element is "when Yahweh finishes all His work on Mount Zion and on Jerusalem." The word "finishes" is Hebrew *batsa* (בָּצַע). It usually has violent connotations, to break off, to plunder. Here it has the idea of fulfillment, but probably in a violent sense: "When Yahweh has finished punishing Zion."

The reason for the punishment of Assyria is her arrogance. She boasted in herself and did not give credit to Yahweh. (Cf. Rab Shakeh's boast to Hezekiah in Isa. 36:13-20). The axe (instrument) is boasting against the hewer (God). Therefore, God is going to destroy Assyria. The city of Nineveh was defeated by the Babylonians, Medes, and Scythians in 612 B.C. The army fled west and was twice defeated by the Babylonians. Note the emphasis on trees in verses 18-19.

God promises deliverance for His people (10:20-34).

The doctrine of the remnant is prominent in Isaiah. It begins in chapter 1, is developed in chapter 6 and here is spelled out in even more detail. Isaiah's son, Shear Jashub (שְׁאָר יָשׁוּב) was an early promise of a returning remnant. Here God says a remnant will return that will trust in Yahweh and not in Assyria.

In light of this promise Judah need not fear Assyria. The description of vv. 28-32 is that of an advancing army striking fear in the hearts of God's people. Yet God says not to fear because he will defeat Assyria and all her glorious trees will be lopped off.

6. God predicts victory through the coming Deliverer (11:1-16).[116]

There will be a root out of Jesse's stump (11:1).

Though the trees of Assyria will be cut down and Judah's trees will also have been cut down, the stump of Jesse still exists, and God will cause a branch to grow from it.

The root will rule by the power of God (11:2-5).

This person will be anointed by the Spirit of the Lord, and because of his relation to Yahweh, he will be able to judge with equity. He will also destroy the wicked with the breath of his mouth (2 Thess. 2:8).

The Kingdom will be ushered in (11:6-10).

There will be also an unprecedented period of peace and tranquility. This is the glorious Kingdom age spoken of often in the Old Testament and referred to as the one thousand year (Millennium) reign in Revelation 20. The nations will come to the center of God's enterprise at Jerusalem to this "root" of Jesse.

There will be a restoration of Israel (11:11-16).

See the following section for a discussion of the future identity of these various nations mentioned in this chapter. The language of this section takes us beyond the return of Israel in 538 B.C. It is being

---

[116]See J. J. Roberts, "The Old Testament's Contribution to Messianic Expectations," in *The Messiah*, ed. Charlesworth *The Messiah: Developments in Earliest Judaism and Christianity*, pp. 39-51: "Hillers has suggested a similar background for Micah 5:1-5. The reference to the seven shepherds and eight princes is most easily explained against the background of the south Syrian league active in the late eighth century and in which Judah apparently played a leading role prior to the battle of Kullani. Isa 11:1-9 would also fit this period as a statement of Isaiah's hope in the context of the Syro-Ephraimitic war." p. 45.

treated as the "second exodus" (11:16) and is universal in scope. See p. 119 for a discussion of Egypt.

7.   The result of this great deliverance will be a people praising God (12:1-6).

First there is an acknowledgement that deliverance comes from Yahweh. In light of this they will be able to "draw waters from the springs of salvation." Out of that attitude will come a desire to share the good news with the whole world.

C.   Yahweh urges Judah to trust Him because He is going to judge the very nations they hope to join for protection against Assyria (Chs. 13—23).

The unit dealing with God's deliverance of His people through the Messiah has concluded. The following section "Oracles against the Nations" (OAN) forms a unit. S. Erlandsson[117] I believe is on to something when he argues that the section on the nations is a response to those who are trying to form an anti-Assyrian coalition. The section cannot represent a general group of prophecies against the enemies of Judah (as in Jeremiah), for Judah herself is included in the oracles (Ch. 22). Erlandsson points out that the conquests of Tiglath-Pileser III created problems for the Elamites in the east (cut off trade routes) and the Egyptians in the west (cut off Phoenician trade). Consequently, it was in the interest of these two nations to foment rebellion against Assyria at every opportunity. Elam supported the Chaldean sheiks (from around the Persian Gulf) and Egypt stirred up trouble in the Levant. (Listen to Sennacherib: "The officials, the patricians and the [common] people of Ekron—who had thrown Padi, their king, into fetters [because he was] loyal to [his] solemn oath [sworn] by the god Ashur, and had handed him over to Hezekiah, the Jew—[and] he [Hezekiah] held him in prison, unlawfully, as if he [Padi] be an enemy— had become afraid and had called [for help] upon the kings of

---

[117]Seth Erlandsson, *Burden of Babylon* (Lund, Sweden: CWK Gleerup, n.d.), 65-108.

Egypt . . . land of the king of Ethiopia, an army beyond counting—and they actually had come to their assistance").[118]

It is interesting that each nation mentioned in the OAN occurs in the Assyrian annals. Damascus and Samaria were defeated by Tiglath-Pileser III (732). Moab, Ethiopia, Egypt, Ashdod, Edom and Tyre are all mentioned in Sennacherib's campaign of 701. The "Valley of Vision" (Ch. 22) seems to refer to the preparation for a siege in Hezekiah's time (the Siloam tunnel was probably dug at this time [2 Chron. 32:2-4,30]).

Ahaz had probably refused to join the anti-Assyrian coalition headed up by Rezin of Syria, but he also refused to trust Yahweh and turned to Assyria for help. Hezekiah trusted Yahweh for victory over the Assyrians but listened to Babylonia's overtures for an anti-Assyrian coalition. The purpose of the OAN unit, therefore, is to say that this anti-Assyrian coalition is futile. All the nations who become part of it will suffer defeat. On the other hand the Assyrians will be defeated, but it will be by Yahweh (14:24-27).

1.   Babylon (Chs. 13—14:23).

The word used to describe the message against a nation is *massa* (מַשָּׂא). It probably comes from the root meaning "to lift up" or "to bear" and therefore means a burden. It usually is associated with doom and judgment.

It is strange that the prophecy headed "the burden of Babylon" does not mention Babylon until v. 19. The description of the "Day of Yahweh" is classic.[119] There are astronomical changes (10, 13), He is

---

[118]*ANET*, p. 287.

[119]See Weiss, "The Origin of the 'Day of the Lord' Reconsidered," *HUCA* 37 (1966): 29-71, for a discussion.

dealing with the whole world (Hebrew: *tebel* תֵּבֵל) (11); in fine, the destruction wreaked seems to be universal and eschatological.

Without going into the use of the phrase "Day of Yahweh" (which at times refers to local events), I would suggest that this introduction is placed here at the beginning of the Oracles against the Nations (OAN) to say that Yahweh has promised to destroy the nations. What follows is a catalog of oracles against those people who wished to conspire against the Assyrians as though they in their own strength could deliver themselves. The purpose is to show Judah that it is futile to trust them for deliverance. The opening statement on the Day of Yahweh, therefore, applies to the entire group of nations. Since the New Testament is still looking for an eschatological "Day of the Lord," we should not see the fulfillment of this promise in Babylon. The fact that God will ultimately bring the nations into judgment and destruction is an argument that He will judge those nations with whom Judah is trying to ally herself in Isaiah's time.

The section beginning with 13:17, becomes very specific referring to the Medes and Babylonians. I believe Erlandsson is probably correct when he argues that the "to them" (v. 2) and "against them" (v. 17) are general references.[120] The latter probably referring to the wicked in v. 11. It is more probable that the pronoun "them" is the beginning reference to Babylon made specific in v. 19. The Medes were enemies of Assyria in the eighth century, but these "Medes" may be mercenary troops in the Assyrian Army.[121] (Sennacherib defeated them completely and tore down the city for the first time in 689 B.C.). (Note Isa. 23:13 where the destruction of Babylon is attributed to Assyria, not Persia in 539 B.C.) It is to this destruction that Isaiah is referring, and

---

[120]Erlandsson, *The Burden of Babylon,* 116-117. So Hayes and Irving, *Isaiah, loc.cit.*

[121]Hayes and Irvine, *Isaiah,* p. 222. Note also the use of Elam as part of the attack on Jerusalem perhaps in 701.

with this oracle God is warning Hezekiah and Judah not to put their trust in Babylon because she will be destroyed.[122]

Sennacherib speaks of his destruction of Babylon (689 B.C.) in these words:

"The city and its houses,—foundation and walls, I destroyed, I devastated, I burned with fire. The wall and the outer-wall, temples and gods, temple-towers of brick and earth, as many as there were, I razed and dumped them into the Arahtu canal. Through the midst of that city I dug canals, I flooded its site with water, and the very foundation thereof I destroyed. I made its destruction more complete than that by a flood. That in days to come, the site of that city, and its temples and gods, might not be remembered, I completely blotted it out with floods of water and made it like a meadow. . . . . After I had destroyed Babylon, had smashed the gods thereof, and had struck down its people with the sword,—that the ground of that city might be carried off, I removed its ground and had it carried to the Euphrates (and on) to the sea. Its dirt reached (was carried) unto Dilmun..."[123]

Chapter 14 gives a vivid description of God's judgment on the king of Babylon. This chapter is often said to describe the fall of Satan. However, the heading and all that follows are said to be descriptions of the king of Babylon. Indeed Satan is the arch enemy of God. As such every ruler who opposes God and God's people is a servant of Satan. In some sense, the king of Babylon may be a "type" of Satan much as Antiochus IV is a type of Antichrist in Daniel 11. It is difficult to identify any one Babylonian king by this description. Consequently, he may be a personification of all Babylonian kings. Some would

---

[122]See H. Heater, "Do the Prophets Teach that Babylonia will be rebuilt in the *Eschaton?" JETS* 41 (1998) 23-43.

[123]D. D. Luckenbill, *Annals of Sennacherib*, p. 17.

argue for an Assyrian king ruling from Babylon, as indeed was the case at times, but the eschatological significance of the passage takes us beyond the eighth century.[124]

The introduction to chapter 14 refers to Israel's return in glowing terms. As a matter of fact, Isaiah 40-66 is anticipated in these verses, and the same questions arise here as in that section: were these events fulfilled in 538 B.C. when the Jews returned, and if so how is the language to be understood? Certainly, the Jews returned under Zerubbabel in fulfillment of God's promises (particularly Jeremiah 29). However, the return was rather pathetic in comparison to this language. Only a relatively small number of Jews returned. They were living among the ruins of Jerusalem, and their efforts to rebuild the temple were met with staunch resistance by the Gentiles (whereas this verse says the Gentiles will be servants). The language of the passage forces the interpreter who is trying to take the language seriously to see a future for Israel that far exceeds what happened when Cyrus permitted the Jews to return to Jerusalem (as in 11:11ff). The same will be said of chapters 40-66.[125]

The message conveyed by Isaiah in chapter 14 is threefold: (1) Babylon, to whom Hezekiah was appealing, would one day be an

[124]J. A. Motyer, *The Prophecy of Isaiah*, p. 142, "…so here the general idea of a hostile world power is personalized into the imaginative portrayal of the end of the world king and this, in turn, receives intermediate realization in the end of the imperial dynasty of Babylon (22-23). The more we think of chapters 13-27 as a study of the principles of world history merging forward into eschatology, the easier it becomes to see that from the start Babylon carries overtones of the 'city of emptiness' (24:10) whose fall is the end of all that opposes the Lord's rule."

[125]Ibid., p. 141: "Just as Babylon, by providing mini-illustrations of the punitive aspects of the day, gave notice that the day was on its way, so the return foreshadowed some beneficent aspects of the day and provided an 'earnest' that the full promise would yet be kept."

oppressor as in chapter 39 (the first reason for not going to them for help); (2) Assyria will defeat Babylon in 689 B.C. and thus they would not be of any help (14:22-23 with 23:13); (3) God himself will judge Assyria (14:24-27). 14:28-32 is an example of the futility of alliances.

At 14:24, the subject switches from Babylon to Assyria to show that this mighty threat to God's people will be broken by God. Judah thought she needed help from other nations, but God tells her to trust Him. Assyria's swift demise sounds much like this verse, I will "break Assyria in My land, and I will trample him on My mountains." Philistia is warned not to expect relief because the "rod that struck her is broken." It sounds as though the rod is Ahaz, but Erlandsson argues (with some difficulty because of the chronology) that it is Assyria.[126] 2 Chron. 28:18 says that the Philistines had attacked Ahaz and taken six of his towns. "How then will one answer the messengers of the nations?" indicates that the Philistines were trying to forge an alliance. Therefore, the Philistine passage continues the warning not to expect deliverance from Assyria until Yahweh brings it.[127]

2. Moab (Chs. 15-16).

Two chapters are devoted to the destruction of Moab. Certainly Moab has been destroyed and no longer exists. The emphasis on pride is a warning to Judah. The last verse in Chapter 16 was probably added to the prophecy later by Isaiah when the time was imminent.

---

[126]Erlandson, *The Burden of Babylon, pp. 68-69.*

[127]See *ANET*, p. 286 for the attack by Sargon II on Ashdod in 711. Hayes and Irvine, *Isaiah*, p. 236, argue for a date of 720 B.C.

3. Damascus (Chs. 17:1-3).

    Damascus likewise comes into God's judgment. Assyria defeated Damascus in 732 B.C. This is a fulfillment of chapters 7-8 and is here to prove Yahweh's prophecies to be authentic.

4. Ephraim (Chs. 17:4-14).

    The mention of Damascus brings Isaiah to discuss Ephraim because she was contiguous to Damascus. The glory of Jacob will fade under this judgment. Apparently many will look to the Lord in that day of judgment.[128] The reason for the judgment is because they have forsaken the Lord. Because people will plunder Israel (12-14) they will in turn be judged by God.

5. Land of whirring wings (Ch. 18).

    The description refers to the Nubian Cushite dynasty ruling in Egypt. This country sends envoys (to plan for defense against Assyria?). Are they sending messengers to the Medes? Whatever, the message will come to them that God will nip Assyria in the bud (4-5). Then that nation will bring a tribute to Jerusalem. The language of this prediction indicates an eschatological future. It is part of that great picture of the future when nations will flow together to Jerusalem.

6. Egypt (Chs. 19-20).

    The section covered by verses 1-15 seems to be a prophecy of the near future when Assyria will attack Egypt. Yahweh will frustrate Egypt's strategy and cause them to be defeated in battle. We know that Assyria was able to garrison upper Egypt,[129] but Ashurbanipal allowed Egypt

---

[128]Young, *Isaiah*, 1:470, sees this fulfilled in the movement south by some of Israel after 732, 22 B.C.

[129]See *ANET*, p, 290 for Esarhaddon's campaign (680-669) "its king, Tirhaka, I

to slip away from Assyrian control—an important move since Egypt became an ally of Assyria, but in the earlier days, Assyria was a "mighty king" (19:4).[130]

Verses 6-10 predict a devastated land. It sounds like a period of drought as known in Joseph's day.

Verses 11-15 castigate the alleged wisdom of the princes of the delta who have led Egypt astray, probably in the matter of military strategy, but also in that they lead them into idolatry.

A marvelous messianic section begins at v.16 and goes to v. 24. It is nothing less than the conversion of Egypt. The first 15 verses of the chapter refer to God's judgment on Egypt, but this section refers to

---

wounded five times with arrowshots and ruled over his entire country."

[130]Kitchen says that Shebitku (702-690 B.C.) was the son of Shabako (a Nubian) and nephew of Piankhy. He brought his sons to Thebes and to the Delta. Among them was Taharqa (690-664) who was then twenty years old. In 702/1 Hezekiah and others opened negotiations with the new Nubian king to rebel against Assyria. Sennacherib came west in 701 to put down the rebellion. He defeated the allies, including the first force of Taharqa, at Eltekah, proceeded to demolish the fortified cities of Judah and sent his officer to demand the surrender of Jerusalem by Hezekiah. However, upon hearing a report that Taharqa was going to attack with his second force, he withdrew Jerusalem to reunite his forces. The Egyptians withdrew, but God miraculously destroyed most of the Assyrian army. Taharqa was not pharaoh at this time, but was referred to as such in 681 when the account was written. Thus it is used proleptically and is not a dual account of Sennacherib's invasion. Kitchen, *The Third Intermediate Period* (p. 384-85) and in *Ancient Orient and the Old Testament* (pp. 82-83). See also an earlier discussion by D. D. Luckenbill, *Annals of Sennacherib*, pp. 11-14.

Esarhaddon of Assyria perceived Egypt to be the reason for rebellion among his western provinces. Consequently, he invaded Egypt in 674 but was defeated. He invaded again in 671 and defeated Taharqa. He set out again in 669 to attack Egypt but died on the way.

Under Ashurbanipal the Assyrians ruled Egypt. Taharqa fled to Thebes and then to Napata. The Assyrians appointed Necho I of Sais as a subordinate king.

God's blessings on them. Should we expect that the very same nations mentioned in the Old Testament as having a place in the future will indeed exist at that time? Especially for those nations whose Old Testament identity has been lost, e.g., Moab, Ammon, Edom, Philistia, etc., I would look to the continued work of God with at least the *geographical* areas. In this case Egypt still exists although she has been greatly influenced by other nations and ethnic groups, now speaks Arabic, and is largely Islamic although a large contingent of Orthodox Christians continues there.

The events predicted for Egypt are (1) terror on them from Judah (that is, Judah will dominate), (2) five cities will speak the language of Canaan—that is the language of the people of God. It means what we mean when we say: "I speak your language," that is, I agree with what you are saying and doing. One city will be for destruction; but the word destruction with a slight change (as in 1QIsa[a]) means sun, and so he may be talking about "sun city" or Heliopolis.

Traditional enmity existed between Assyria and Egypt both of whom overran Judah, but in that day there will be a divine triangle of the three worshipping the Lord.

What a prophecy! Egypt today stands as an enemy of Israel in spite of the breakthrough under Sadat. Egypt today is essentially Muslim and unregenerate. But God is going to do a great work in the last days in her behalf. Today we must pray for the salvation of contemporary Egyptians; and in the future there is assurance that God will do a great work of salvation.

Sargon II (722-705 B.C.) came to the throne in time to lead off some of the captives of Israel. We know that there was a rebellion against Assyria, and Egypt was probably involved in it.[131] Isaiah has been

---

[131]*ANET*, p. 287.

preaching against going to Egypt for help against Assyria. Now God tells him to loosen his garments to say symbolically that Egypt will be defeated by Assyria. For three years Isaiah went about in the state of undress (the addition of "barefoot" should indicate that he was not totally naked, but wearing an undergarment). This symbolic act was to warn everyone that there was no hope in opposing Assyria (20:5-6).[132]

7. Wilderness of the sea (21:1-10).

This oracle refers apparently to Babylon (21:9). The Chaldeans who ruled Babylon after 625 B.C. had their origins at the head of the Persian Gulf. Perhaps this is why they are referred to as the wilderness by the sea. Erlandsson argues that the mention of Elam and Media, countries near Babylon, are being called on to join a coalition against Assyria.[133] This prophecy (in light of the discussion above) is given here because of Hezekiah's move to join with Merodach Baladan against Assyria as recorded in Isaiah 39.

8. Edom (21:11-12).

This is a short oracle predicting the destruction of Edom. When this destruction will take place is unknown. It may be tied in with the overall Assyrian activity.

9. Arabia (21:13-17).

The same words could be said about Arabia.

---

[132]Motyer, *The Prophecy of Isaiah*, p. 163 calls this chapter an interim fulfillment (19:1-15 is a long range prophecy). See Herschel Shanks, "Assyrian Palace Discovered in Ashdod," *BAR* 33:1 (2006) 56-60.

[133]Erlandson, *The Burden of Babylon*, pp. 81ff.

10. Valley of Vision (Jerusalem) (Ch. 22).

It may seem strange that Judah is mentioned in this section containing God's oracles against the nations. The point is to indicate that, though Judah is God's chosen people, she is one of the nations when it comes to God vindicating himself among them.

The attack on Judah (22:1-11).

The time of this attack seems to be in Hezekiah's day (note especially 22:11 and 2 Chron 32:1-7). This would be Sennacherib's attack in 701. There are problems with this, and Young decides that the prophecy is generic, that is referring to the general idea that Judah will suffer from invading forces.[134] The final and most significant one will be Babylon in 586 B.C.

The revelry of Judah (22:12-14).

God had called upon Judah to fast and repent, but for some reason they are having a high old time. Some link this with the withdrawal of Sennacherib in 701.

The rebuke of Shebna and the investment of Eliakim (22:15-25).

The steward over the house was a powerful office (see E. J. Young for a discussion). Shebna has abused his office for self-aggrandizement. His powerful office causes him to hold a symbolic position, and he has misused it (was he part of an anti-Assyrian move?). As a result God promises to remove him. Eliakim will be appointed in his place and as such becomes a type of the Messiah (Rev. 3:7). Leadership is so important to the Old Testament prophet (who is always looking to that perfect leader), that human leaders come under chastisement for failing to measure up. Even Eliakim will be removed because he

---

[134]Young, *Isaiah,* 2:85-104.

apparently will yield to the same temptations that befell Shebna (22:25).

11. Tyre (Ch. 23).

The city of Tyre located on the Phoenician coast was the younger of two Phoenician cities: Sidon being the older. Tyre became almost a byword for trade and merchandizing. She controlled the Mediterranean and established colonies in North Africa and Spain. The destruction of Tyre mentioned here probably took place in the time of Nebuchadnezzar who besieged it for thirteen years. From 700 to 630 B.C. the Assyrians kept Tyre in check, but with her decline beginning in 630, her hold loosened. This may be what the seventy years refer to. God will allow restored Tyrian trade to flow to Judah.

D. Yahweh shows his sovereignty in salvation and judgment (Chs. 24—27).

This unit is often referred to as "the little apocalypse" and is considered by some to be an early form of apocalyptic literature,[135] but the tendency today is to move away from that identification, since there are a number of generally accepted facets of apocalypticism that are not present.[136] There is also a general consensus that 24—27 must be understood in connection with 13—23.[137] The questions are, how does the section relate to 13—23, and how are we to understand the contents of the unit.

---

[135]See W. R. Millar, *Isaiah 24-27 and the Origin of Apocalyptic*, 1976.

[136]J. Jensen, *Isaiah 1-39*, 8:190.

[137]J. N. Oswalt, *Isaiah 1-39*, p. 441. J. Jenson, *Isaiah*: "This collection...is neither haphazard nor purposeless. It provides a framework within which to understand those other oracles, which are seen now not simply as God's dealing with individual nations but as steps on the way to the final age."

1.   Yahweh promises judgment on the *earth* (chapter 24).

There is a general agreement that chapter 24 refers to the destruction
of the nations and generalizes what was specific in 13-23.[138] However,
I am going to launch out on my own and argue that 24:1-13 refers to
Israel. I do this on the basis of the mention of "priest" in 24:2, the
ruined city in 24:10,12, the apparent remnant in 24:13 (who rejoice in
14-16b) but especially the reference (v. 5) to laws (*toroth* תּוֹרֹת),
statute(s) (*hoq* חֹק), and everlasting covenant: *berith 'olam* בְּרִית עוֹלָם).
The latter phrase in particular is difficult to apply to the Gentile world.
Further, the language of the verse (including the idea that the people
have polluted the land) sounds much like prophetic language applied
to Israel. It is usually taken to refer to the Noahic covenant or to God's
covenant with the world (Calvin). It is instructive to replace "land"
with "Israel": "Behold, the LORD lays Israel waste, devastates it,
distorts its surface, and scatters its inhabitants" (24:1). "Israel will be
completely laid waste and completely despoiled, for the LORD has
spoken this word" (24:3). "Israel is polluted by its inhabitants, for they
transgressed laws, violated statutes, broke the everlasting covenant"
(24:5). "Jerusalem is broken down" (24:10). "Jerusalem is left desolate
and the gate is battered to ruins" (24:12). "For thus it will be [for
Israel] in the midst of the earth among the peoples. As the shaking of
an olive tree, as the gleanings when the grape harvest is over"
(24:13).[139]

There are two things that argue against this position: (1) the use of
"world" (*tebel,* תֵּבֵל) in 24:4 which seems usually to refer to the

[138]So, e.g., Young, *Isaiah,* 2:146ff; J. Jensen, *Isaiah;* J.H. Oswalt, *Isaiah 1-39*; F.
Delitzsch, 1:421ff.

[139]M. Kline ("Death, Leviathan, and Martyrs: Isaiah 24:1--27:1," pp. 228-249) argues
that this entire section has to do with death and resurrection. Certainly those two
themes are throughout this passage, but I believe the tribulation period is also in view.

inhabited earth; (2) the use of the idea of "city" in 25:2 to refer to the enemies of Israel ("For thou hast made a city into a heap, a fortified city into a ruin, a palace of strangers is a city no more, it will never be rebuilt."). In 13:11 this word is used in a clearly universal sense. However, if "earth" (*eretz,* אֶרֶץ) is used in a limited sense then perhaps its parallel member "world" (*tebel* תֵּבֵל) can also be so used. Perhaps also the ruined city "Israel" is being compared with the ruined city "enemies of Israel."

If indeed 24:1-13 is specific, referring to Israel, it is the scattered Israelites who cry out in exultation over their preservation in 24:14-16a. But why do they cry out? They are still alive after the judgment Yahweh has brought upon His people and are anticipating a return to their land. However, Isaiah responds negatively, saying that judgment is coming on the whole world. Now the message becomes universal, and the language more apocalyptic. The consummation will be the Lord of hosts reigning on Mount Zion and in Jerusalem.

This is a fitting conclusion to 13—23. Israel (Judah) is urged not to go to Babylon, Tyre, Sidon, etc., for help against Assyria for two reasons: (1) These nations will all fall before Assyria and therefore will be of no help and (2) God Himself will defeat the Assyrians and establish His eternal rule in Jerusalem. Israel's failure to trust Him (epitomized by Ahaz and later Hezekiah) will result in destruction of the "land" (Israel). In the exile they will rejoice in their preservation and anticipate God's deliverance. Before that can happen, however, God's judgment will be poured out on the entire world. Finally, God will restore His people and rule over them.

The following chart shows the structure of 13-23. The relationship of the two units is shown by the Day of the Lord motif in both chapters 13 and 24. There is even a chiasm in the structure as shown below.

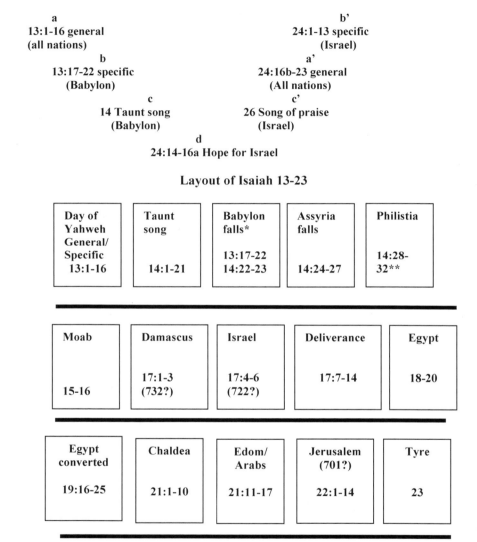

```
                a                              b'
        13:1-16 general                24:1-13 specific
        (all nations)                    (Israel)
                b                              a'
        13:17-22 specific              24:16b-23 general
        (Babylon)                      (All nations)
                        c                      c'
                14 Taunt song          26 Song of praise
                (Babylon)              (Israel)
                        d
                24:14-16a Hope for Israel
```

Layout of Isaiah 13-23

Day of Yahweh General/ Specific 13:1-16	Taunt song 14:1-21	Babylon falls* 13:17-22 14:22-23	Assyria falls 14:24-27	Philistia 14:28-32**

Moab 15-16	Damascus 17:1-3 (732?)	Israel 17:4-6 (722?)	Deliverance 17:7-14	Egypt 18-20

Egypt converted 19:16-25	Chaldea 21:1-10	Edom/ Arabs 21:11-17	Jerusalem (701?) 22:1-14	Tyre 23

*By Assyria (23:13)

**Sargon 711

2. The believer praises Yahweh and hears about a future time of bliss (Ch. 25).

This chapter consists of a psalm of praise (25:1-5), a banquet for resurrected saints (25:6-8), and a promise of defeat for Moab (as Edom, an archetype of evil against Israel). The millennial promises of Isaiah seem to merge into eternity (cf. New Heavens and New Earth of chapter 65). There will be a resurrection of believers, but we know from Revelation that death will not be removed for all time until Rev. 21 where this verse is cited (21:4).

3. The believer sings of God's goodness and is told that a time of judgment is coming (Ch. 26).

This song seems to answer to the taunt song of chapter 14. There it was sung against Babylon in the day of Israel's restoration. The second stanza of that song celebrates God's victory in Israel's behalf (including Leviathan and the Dragon, 27:1). The wicked will be judged and will not be a part of the saint's resurrection (26:14), but the saints will rise and shout for joy (26:19).

Finally, Isaiah exhorts his people to hide until the tribulation and trouble caused her passes, and God will have vindicated them (26:20-21). Leviathan and the Dragon are probably mythological symbols used here of all resistance against God and His people. God will defeat them (27:1). At Ugarit the following lines refer to Lotan: "When thou does smite Lotan the fleeing serpent/(And) shall put an end to the tortuous serpent; Shalyat of the seven heads . . ."[140] Ps. 74:14 speaks of the heads of Leviathan (see Kline above).[141]

---

[140]*ANET*, pp. 137b, 138d.

[141]See Joel Knudsen, "The Archetypes of Evil in Isaiah 13-27" (Th.M. thesis, DTS, 1980). He argues that the serpent, Babylon and sea are symbols of evil known in history and used to personify Satan and the Antichrist. This giant sea creature is

4.   Yahweh promises a time of forgiveness and restoration (27:1-13).

The rejected vineyard of chapter 5 will be restored as a fruitful and productive vine (27:2-6). God next provides an explanation of Israel's suffering. It was caused by their sin and rebellion, but they have suffered sufficiently to atone for it (cf. 40:2, she has received double for all her sins). The result will be a rejection of idolatry. The "fortified city" is surely Jerusalem which sits alone because of former idolatry for which she was punished. The phrases "their Maker" and "their Creator" indicate Israel rather than Babylon as the antecedent.

Finally, the eschatological promise is made to restore the scattered ones of Israel from Assyria and Egypt and to bring them to worship the Lord in the holy mountain of Jerusalem.

Isaiah is of course not stipulating when this situation will come into existence. To him it is in the future, but the time is unknown. We know from the rest of Scripture that there will be a time of redemption of Israel at the end of the church age during the tribulation in which "all Israel will be saved" as opposed to the remnant during this present age.

Thus the instruction to Israel is complete. Trust Yahweh, Ahaz; trust Yahweh, Hezekiah. Do not go to the nations. God will one day visit them and judge them. He will also redeem His people and restore them to the holy city once ruined because of their failure to trust in Him, but restored in that day.

---

probably a remnant of the mythological creature of paganism. In saying that, I am not suggesting that the Israelites believed in the creature as such. I believe such allusions in Isaiah and Job are used much as we would say "Damocles' sword is hanging over my head." I am not giving credence to the Greek myth, but I recognize that the dilemma in which I find myself is comparable to that problem depicted in the myth. It becomes a graphic means of communication without the concomitant acceptance of the reality of the symbol. Here the symbol represents all evil power opposed to God and headed up by Satan. God will destroy it.

E. Yahweh delivers a series of woes to say that true deliverance is to be found in Him, not in Egypt (Chs. 28—33).[142]

In Ahaz's day, the threat was Syro-Ephraim, and he went to Assyria for help. Now, in Hezekiah's day, the threat is Assyria, and the temptation is to go to Egypt (in 38—39, he will make overtures to Babylon). Hezekiah was a good king, but he still played power politics.

1. Woe number one is against the drunkards of Ephraim and the scoffers of Jerusalem (28:1-29).

Isaiah must first indicate that Ephraim and Judah will be judged for not trusting Him.

Verses 1-8 refer to the northern kingdom, ready for judgment because they have chosen to disobey Him and to reject His counsel. The rest of the chapter seems to refer to Judah. These people have convinced themselves that God's judgment will not reach them (they have even made a covenant with Sheol). Consequently, God sends a stumbling block among them—here it probably refers to the prophet speaking the truth, ultimately it refers to Christ—those who believe will be made firm, those who reject will stumble and fall (28:1-29).

2. Woe number two is against the southern kingdom (29:1-24).

The phrase "Ariel" is not clear. As it stands it means "lion of God." Many other suggestions have been made, but the only thing clear is that it is a name for the old city of David, and this judgment is against Judah (29:1-4). Even so, the enemies of Judah, those who besiege the city, will be judged by God (29:5-8). The vision God is trying to give to Judah will be as if they cannot understand it (29:9-12). He condemns them for an external religion that does not reflect true faith

---

[142]Motyer, *The Prophecy of Isaiah,* p. 227, says, "It is the task of chapters 28-37 to demonstrate that the Lord does actually rule world history and that, therefore, his as yet unfulfilled promises and purposes are sure."

(29:13-14). He criticizes them for thinking they can get away with sinning and God will never know (29:15-16).

At the same time there is the promise of conversion and blessing for Judah. Lebanon (representing all nations) will be destroyed and God's blessing will come on His people. They will sanctify His name and obey Him (29:17-24).

3.   Woe number three is against rebellious children (30:1-33). (Cf. 1:2.) Those who go to Egypt for help will be disappointed.

    Judah is condemned for planning her own defenses without consulting Yahweh. These plans will be frustrated, and those who have made them will be disappointed (30:1-5).

    Judah is condemned for taking her wealth to Egypt to buy her support (30:6-7). Egypt is referred to as Rahab in v. 7. This word means basically "pride" or "arrogance." It seems to be used in Psalms 89:10 as a beast or a serpent defeated by God. It should probably be put in the same category as Leviathan as a symbolic use of an ancient mythological creature (see my discussion at 27:1). As such it describes Egypt. The Hebrew of v. 7 is difficult, but the sense is clear: this proud beast will cease to be a threat to anyone.[143]

    This promise is to be written on a tablet as a future witness against these rebellious children (30:8-11). These children refuse to listen to God's spokesmen and hence to God.

---

[143]N. B. *KJV*: "Their strength is to sit still" translates Rahab as strength and follows the MT on יָשֵׁב (*yashab*) *NASB*: "exterminated" repoints MT to מָשְׁבָּת (*mashbath*) from שָׁבַת (*shabath*). The change suggested in BHS is promising and involves only redividing the words: רַהַב הֵם שָׁבֶת (*rahab hem shabeth*) to רְהָבָה מָשְׁבָּת (*rahabah mashbath*): "Her pride is made to cease."

Yahweh promises judgment on Judah for refusing to trust Him and going to Egypt (30:12-17). He tells them (v. 15) that they will be delivered only through repentance, but since they refuse, God will judge them by the very things they are seeking for help.

A beautiful plea is made by Yahweh to Judah to repent (30:18-22), and a promise of messianic blessing if and when they do (30:18-26).

Yahweh promises to judge Assyria and to deliver Judah (30:27-33).

4. Yahweh continues to criticize Judah for going to Egypt for help (31:1-9).

    They are condemned for going to Egypt for help and not trusting in Yahweh (31:1-3). There is a play on words: Judah is "leaning" (*yisha'enu,* יִשָּׁעֵנוּ) on Egyptian horses and not "looking" (*Shau,* שָׁעוּ) to the Holy One of Israel. Egypt is not God, and God will cause Egypt to stumble.

    Yahweh promises deliverance from Assyria (31:4-9). A call to repentance is given in v. 6 with a promise of the fall of Assyria in vv. 8-9.

5. Yahweh speaks of a time when there will be proper leadership and the blessing that ensues (32:1-20).

    Since this chapter flows out of the deliverance in chapter 31, the reference may be to the messianic king first introduced in chapters 9 and 11. The contrast is obvious between this king and the wicked Assyrian king as well as Ahaz the unbelieving king and probably even Hezekiah who, though he was essentially a good king, was not ideal. Verse 8 may be an allusion to the plans to ally with Egypt, and thus forms a backdrop for the next section (32:1-8).

Yahweh challenges the women to leave their luxurious and easy life style and to recognize that in a short time, all that will be stripped away (32:9-14).

He then resumes his discussion of the messianic age when the Spirit will be poured out (יְעָרֶה *ye'areh* "to make bare" as in "baring one's soul") upon the people of Israel, and millennial conditions will exist (32:15-20).

6. The promise of judgment on Assyria (33:1-24).

Destruction is promised to Assyria (33:1-2).

Divine retribution will come even upon the instrument God used to punish his people. As Assyria has meted out judgment, so she shall be judged by others. As she has acted treacherously, so she will be betrayed.

Yahweh promises deliverance of Judah and a time of justice (33:3-12).

Hayes and Irvine may be correct in believing that these verses refer to northern Israelites fleeing to Zion after the destruction of Samaria in 722 B.C.[144] The pain caused by Assyria ("He" in 33:8) created such havoc that many fled to the south.

Yahweh describes the righteous living of the one who trusts in Him (33:13-16).

Yahweh describes the destruction of the enemy by the mighty God (33:17-24).

F. The final message of God's restoration of His people and the land (Chs. 34—35).

---

[144]Hayes and Irving, *Isaiah, loc. cit.*

1. A concluding chapter on the judgment of the nations (34:1-17).

    This is a summarizing chapter to the first part of the book showing judgment on the nations. A special emphasis is placed on Edom who stands out as an example of an implacable enemy of Israel. The language of this chapter is one of the best examples of what I call "destruction genre." As we discussed earlier, this strong language is being used to say that a complete destruction of Edom will take place. The details do not need to be pressed because the language is hyperbolic; however, it is to be understood as a literal, severe destruction.

2. A final promise of blessing (35:1-10).

    The section from chapter 13 to chapter 35 shows the sovereignty of God over the nations. It concludes with this beautiful promise of the messianic age. What a fitting close to the first part of the book that has had so much "doom and gloom" because of Israel and Judah's refusal to listen to God. In spite of that disobedience, they are God's people whom He "will not cast off." This chapter refers to the establishment of the Old Testament Kingdom promises when Israel will be restored to the land in belief, and great blessing will accrue to all.

G. A historical interlude is given to show how the Assyrian threat was carried out and the way Yahweh dealt with it (Chs. 36—39).

    Isaiah has two major historical sections involving Ahaz (Ch. 7) and Hezekiah (Chs. 36—39). The first section responds to the Syro-Ephraimite threat and is followed by the Assyrian threat (Chs. 8—37). The second deals with the Assyrian threat and is followed by the Babylonian threat (Chs. 38—66).

    1. The setting is Sennacherib's invasion of the west to put down rebellion (36:1-3).

        Sennacherib says:

"In my third campaign I marched against Hatti, Luli, king of Sidon, whom the terror-inspiring glamour of my lordship had overwhelmed, fled far overseas and perished. The awe-inspiring splendor of the "Weapon" of Ashur, my lord, overwhelmed his strong cities (such as) Great Sidon, Little Sidon, Bit Zitti, Zaribru, Mahalliba, Ushu (i.e. the mainland settlement of Tyre. See also p. 134), Akzib (and) Akko, (all) his fortress cities, walled (and well) provided with feed and water for his garrisons, and they bowed in submission to my feet. I installed Ethba'al upon the throne to be their king and imposed upon him tribute (due) to me (as his) overlord (to be paid) annually without interruption.

"As to all the kings of Amurru—Menahem from Samsimuruna, Tuba'lu from Sidon, Abdili'ti from Arvad, Urumilki from Byblos, Mitinti from Ashdod, Buduili from Beth-Ammon, Kammusunadbi from Moab (and) Aiarammu from Edom, they brought sumptuous gifts and—fourfold—their heavy ( ) presents to me and kissed my feet. Sidqia, however, king of Ashkelon, who did not bow to my yoke, I deported and sent to Assyria, his family-gods, himself, his wife, his children, his brothers, all the male descendants of his family. I set Sharruludari, son of Rukibtu, their former king, over the inhabitants of Ashkelon and imposed upon him the payment of tribute (and of) ( ) presents (due) to me (as) overlord—and he (now) pulls the straps (of my yoke)!

"In the continuation of my campaign I besieged Beth-Dagon, Joppa, Banai-- Barka, Azuru, cities belonging to Sidqia who did not bow to my feet quickly (enough); I conquered (them) and carried their spoils away. The officials, the patricians and the (common) people of Ekron—who had thrown Padi, their king, into fetters (because he was) loyal to (his) solemn oath (sworn) by the god Ashur, and had handed him over to Hezekiah, the Jew—(and) he (Hezekiah) held him in prison, unlawfully, as if he (Padi) be an enemy—had become afraid and had called (for help) upon the kings of Egypt (and) the bowmen, the chariot(-corps) and the cavalry of the king of Ethiopia, an army beyond counting—and they (actually) had come to their assistance. In the plain of Eltekeh, their battle lines were drawn up against me and they sharpened their weapons. Upon a trust(-inspiring) oracle (given) by Ashur, my lord, I fought with them and inflicted a defeat upon them. In the melee of the battle, I personally captured alive the Egyptian charioteers with the(ir) princes and (also) the charioteers of the king of Ethiopia. I besieged Eltekeh (and) Timnah, conquered (them) and carried their spoils away. I assaulted Ekron and killed the officials and patricians who had committed the crime and hung their bodies on poles surrounding the city. The (common) citizens who were guilty of minor crimes, I considered prisoners of war. The rest of them, those who were not accused of crimes and misbehavior, I released. I made Padi, their king, come from Jerusalem and set him as their lord on the throne, imposing upon him the tribute (due) to me (as) overlord.

"As to Hezekiah, the Jew, he did not submit to my yoke, I laid siege to 46 of his strong cities, walled forts and to the countless small villages in their vicinity, and conquered (them) by means of well-stamped (earth-)ramps, and battering-rams brought (thus) near (to the walls) (combined with) the attack by foot soldiers, (using) mines, breeches as well as sapper work. I drove out (of them) 200,150 people, young and old, male and female, horses, mules, donkeys, camels, big and small cattle beyond counting, and considered (them) booty. Himself I made a prisoner in Jerusalem, his royal residence, like a bird in a cage. I surrounded him with earthwork in order to molest those who were leaving his city's gate. His towns which I had plundered, I took away from his country and gave them (over) to Mitinti, king of Ashdod, Padi, king of Ekron, and Sillibel, king of Gaza. Thus I reduced his country, but I still increased the tribute and the *katru*-presents (due) to me (as his) overlord which I imposed (later) upon him beyond the former tribute, to be delivered annually. Hezekiah himself, whom the terror-inspiring splendor of my lordship had overwhelmed and whose irregular and elite troops which he had brought into Jerusalem, his royal residence, in order to strengthen (it), had deserted him, did send me, later, to Nineveh, my lordly city together with 30 talents of gold, 800 talents of silver, precious stones, antimony, large cuts of red stone, couches (inlaid) with ivory, *nimedu*-chairs (inlaid) with ivory, elephant-hides, ebony-wood, box-wood (and) all kinds of valuable treasures, his (own) daughters, concubines, male and female musicians. In order to deliver the tribute and to do obeisance as a slave he sent his (personal) messenger."[145]

---

[145]*ANET*, pp. 287-288.

Isaiah tells us of this confrontation between the arrogant Rabshakeh, Sennacherib's general, and the representatives of Hezekiah. It is poetic justice that Rabshakeh stands at the identical spot challenging God's people that Isaiah had stood over a decade before challenging Ahaz to trust God and not to trust the Assyrians.

Eliakim is now the steward and Shebna has been deposed to scribe as predicted in 22:15-25. With them is Joah the son of Asaph, the recorder.

2. The challenge was given by the Rab Shakeh (36:4-10).

Rabshakeh tells them the Egyptians will be no help (36:4-6). This is the same thing Isaiah has been telling them.

Rabshakeh tells them Yahweh will be no help since Hezekiah must have offended Him by tearing down His altars and high places (36:7).

Rabshakeh offers the ultimate insult by offering to provide horses if Hezekiah can put men on them (36:8-9).

Finally he even says that Yahweh has commissioned him to carry out this destruction (36:10).

Eliakim, Shebna, and Joah try to get Rabshakeh to speak Aramaic so that the people will not understand. This indicates (1) that Aramaic was the diplomatic language of the day and (2) that only trained people understood it (36:11).

Rabshakeh mockingly tells them that he is talking to the common people not the leaders. He then challenges the common people directly to surrender to him and allow him to take them to a pleasant land. He challenges Hezekiah's trust in Yahweh since none of the other gods have been able to deliver their people from Assyria (36:12-20).

The message is brought to Hezekiah (36:21-22).

3. Hezekiah makes a godly response to the challenge (37:1-38).

The officials bring the report to Hezekiah who responds by tearing his clothes and going into the temple (v. 1). He then sends messengers to Isaiah to ask for God's protection (37:2-5). (N.B. the difference between Hezekiah's response to the threat and Ahaz's.)

Isaiah gives God's word on the matter which is that He will cause Sennacherib to hear a rumor and that he will return to his land and die (37:6-7).

Rabshakeh gets word that Tirhakah the Ethiopian who is now Pharaoh of Egypt has come out.[146] This means that Sennacherib had pulled back from Lachish and Rabshakeh is rushing to join up with him. His Parthian shot is to send a letter to Hezekiah saying that Yahweh cannot deliver from Assyria's hand (37:8-13).

Hezekiah goes to the temple with the letter and prays for Yahweh's deliverance- (37:14-20).

Isaiah sends word to Hezekiah that Yahweh has answered his prayers and that Assyria will be led by a bridle to do whatever Yahweh wants to do with them (37:21-29).

Yahweh gives a sign of his protection in the matter of the food supply. God will see to it that there will be enough to eat from the food as it grows of itself in the first two years after the siege. King Sennacherib will go back home because God is going to defend Jerusalem and deliver it for His sake and David's sake (37:30-35).

Sennacherib returned to Nineveh where he was assassinated by his sons. Esarhaddon becomes king in his place. This act took place

---

[146]Tirhakah is probably called king proleptically since he appears to have taken the throne much later than 701.

twenty years later. The important thing is that it did happen (37:36-38).

The Destruction of Sennacherib

The Assyrian came down like the wolf on the fold,
And his cohorts were gleaming in purple and gold;
And the sheen of their spears was like stars on the sea,
When the blue wave rolls nightly on deep Galilee.

Like the leaves of the forest when Summer is green,
That host with their banners at sunset were seen:
Like the leaves of the forest when Autumn hath blown,
That host on the morrow lay withered and strown.

For the Angel of Death spread his wings on the blast,
And breathed in the face of the foe as he passed;
And the eyes of the sleepers waxed deadly and chill,
And their hearts but once heaved, and forever grew still!

And there lay the steed with his nostril all wide,
But through it there rolled not the breath of his pride;
And the foam of his gasping lay white on the turf,
And cold as the spray of the rock-beating surf.

And there lay the rider distorted and pale,
With the dew on his brow, and the rust on his mail:
And the tents were all silent, the banners alone,
The lances unlifted, the trumpet unblown.

And the widows of Ashur are loud in their wail,
And the idols are broke in the temple of Baal;
And the might of the Gentile, unsmote by the sword,
Hath melted like snow in the glance of the Lord!

— George Gordon, Lord Byron —

5. Hezekiah becomes sick, miraculously recovers, and receives ambassadors from the Chaldeans (38:1—39:8).

Hezekiah is told by God that he will die. Hezekiah pleads with God for life and God grants it along with a sign to assure him that he will live fifteen more years. He also promises him deliverance from Assyria during his lifetime (38:1-8).

Hezekiah composed a lament as part of his prayer to Yahweh for recovery. When he was well, he put it all in writing (38:9-20).

Isaiah had told them to use medicine through which the miracle took place. The sign of the backward movement of the shadow was in response to Hezekiah's request for a sign (38:21-22).

Merodach-Baladan was a member of the Chaldean grouping living at the head of the Persian gulf. He was insinuating himself into the government of the Babylonians and trying to throw off Assyrian control of Babylon. He has sent messengers west to try to stir up opposition to Assyria (39:1).

Hezekiah, because of his anti-Assyrian stance, happily receives the messengers. He will support anyone who opposes Assyria. He shows them everything (39:2).

Isaiah tells Hezekiah that he has made a mistake for these same people will one day plunder Jerusalem and carry off some of the king's descendants to Babylon (39:3-8).

The stage is now set for the history of Israel as affected by Babylon. Chapters 40-66 are set in the Babylonian exile which came about, from a political perspective, because Hezekiah began the policy carried on by his great-grandson, Josiah of supporting Babylonia against Assyria.

Excursus:

Synthesis of Isaiah 1-39

We are working from the construct that Assyria is the dominant political power and that Isaiah's messages are all delivered in connection with the intent of instructing the people to trust in Yahweh instead of going to other nations for help.

I.   Judah is indicted for her sinfulness (1—6).

Chapters 1-6 are an entity. The historical setting is given in chapter 6 as the year that King Uzziah died. Since this chronological reference applies to the reception of the vision, we are assuming that it should be applied backward to the entire unit. The fact that Isaiah was involved in writing some of the memoirs of Uzziah ("Now the rest of the acts of Uzziah, first to last, the prophet Isaiah, the son of Amoz, has written [2 Chron. 26:22]), *could* imply that Isaiah's ministry began *prior* to the death of Uzziah, but not necessarily. (He may have gathered the information from archives and his own pre-call experience.) One would also expect more references to Uzziah's reign within the prophetic framework if Isaiah's ministry were more contemporaneous with Uzziah's life. We are going to argue that chapter 1 is the consequence of the last couple of years of Uzziah's life (c.742-740, see the historical introduction for the invasion of Tiglath Pileser III). However, chapter 6 could still be the inaugural vision, and chapter 1 would be one of Isaiah's early messages making reference to the recently devastated land. Therefore, I am leaning toward chapter 6 being Isaiah's call to the prophetic ministry.

A. A "Riv" case and a call to repentance (1:1-31) followed by a promise of restoration (millennium) (2:1-4).

B. A statement of Judah's sin and promise of judgment (2:5—3:26) followed by restoration (4:1-6).

C. A statement of Judah's sin (vineyard and indictment) and a promise of judgment (5:1-30).

D. Isaiah's call declaring the holiness of God, sinfulness of His people and commission to preach a message of hardening (6:1-12) followed by a promise of a remnant (6:13).

Chapter 6 is the consummation of this unit. It shows that Judah, because of her obduracy, will be judged by God through the preaching of Isaiah. Jesus quotes this passage in connection with the parables, and Paul quotes it in connection with the rejection of the message of the Gospel by the Jews of Rome.

II. Judah will be saved from her enemies and cleansed from her sin, but neither of these will come from human sources (7—12).

This unit grows out of a political crisis and is one of the two major historical centers of the book. God challenges His people to trust him not human deliverers, but they refuse. God therefore promises judgment from those very nations to which Judah looked for help. At the same time, He promises ultimate deliverance by His own supernatural means. This unit is called the "Book of Immanuel" or the "Children's Book" because five boys are mentioned in this section in connection with God's deliverance.

A. Ahaz in response to the Syro-Ephraimite devastation and continuing threat goes to Assyria for help. Isaiah urges him to trust Yahweh, but he refuses. God gives a great sign to all Israel of ultimate deliverance through Immanuel (cf. 8:8). The short space in Immanuel's life is the time left before Israel and Syria will be destroyed (7:1-16).

B. God will bring Assyria (to whom Ahaz is going for help) against not only Syria and Israel, but also against Judah. The time element connected with that invasion (since Immanuel will not be there during Ahaz's time) will be demonstrated by Isaiah's second son, whose name, Maher Shalal Hash Baz, indicates that the invader will come (7:17—8:10).

C. The invasion will bring hard times (8:19-22), but ultimately, God will bring salvation to His people through a divine child who will establish the kingdom (9:1-7), but before that happens, there will be judgment on God's people (9:8—10:4).

D. Assyria, God's "axe," must in turn be judged. Her "trees" will be cut down as she will cut down Judah's trees (10:5-34).

E. The stump of Jesse (house of David) will sprout a twig that will result in the restoration of the people of God to their land in triumph and the branch will rule and reign in the midst of the people. (Since the righteous rule is prominent, it is placed first, although the return of the people from exile must precede it.)

III. By showing that God will judge all the nations with whom she is trying to make an alliance, God is teaching Judah not to trust them but to trust Him (13—23).[147]

A. Babylon is the most important nation in the anti-Assyrian movement. Consequently, that name appears first. However, the unit from 13:2-16 is a general oracle of the Day of Yahweh saying that God is going to judge all the nations, and, therefore, His people should trust Him not them.

B. Babylon herself is dealt with in 13:17-22. This fall of Babylon took place in 689 B.C. when Sennacherib defeated and razed the city of Babylon.

---

[147]Motyer, *The Prophecy of Isaiah*, p. 131-32, says there are ten oracles, consisting of five titles (13:1; 14:28; 15:1; 17:1; 19:1; and four enigmatic titles (21:1, 11, 13; 22:1) and one plain title (23:1).

Within a decade of Hezekiah's response to the overtures of Merodach-Baladan, that city was destroyed.

C. Babylon will someday become an oppressor; therefore, Judah should not go to her for help. Furthermore, Assyria will defeat Babylon in 689 B.C., a second reason for not going to her for help. Thirdly, God will defeat Assyria in His own time apart from the Machiavellian politics of Judah (14:24-27). Finally, 14:29-32 is an example of the folly of revolting against Assyria. Babylon from the beginning (Genesis 10) was considered to epitomize evil. Chapter 14 therefore, probably refers to Babylon as a type of all rebellion against God and persecution of His people. (Since Satan is the ultimate anti-God person, the King of Babylon also represents him.) The opening verses (14:1-3) are described in such a way that the event cannot have been fulfilled in 539 B.C. It has in view the final great regathering of Israel to the land. Does this necessitate the revival of Babylon in the last days? I think not. As Babylon fell in 689 and in 539 as the enemy of God, so will the last oppressors of Israel fall in the Tribulation. The use of "Babylon" in Revelation 17-18 is in this symbolic sense. The literal meaning is still a national aggressor against Israel.

D. The coalition of Syria and Israel against Judah in c. 734 B.C. prompts this oracle against both of them in chapter 17. Some argue that the purpose of the attack against Ahaz was to force him to join a coalition against Assyria. If so, this would indicate the futility of any such movement. However, the nations despoiling the people of God in Israel will be judged (17:12-14).

E. Chapters 18-19 probably all refer to Egypt. 18:2 indicates that messengers have been sent. Chapter 19 indicates that God will judge Egypt through Assyria. The unit 19:16-24 is in prose, indicating possibly that it was preached at a different time than the first part and placed here to complete the picture. A marvelous conversion of Egypt is to take place in the eschatological future.

F. Chapter 20 ties the unit into Sargon II's time (he took the throne in 722 B.C.). He defeated Philistia in spite of the fact that she had joined with Egypt for defense. Egypt will be led away captive. Therefore, do not trust in her.

G. Another oracle against Babylon is found in 21:1-11. The "sea lands" and "Chaldeans" probably stress the fact that Merodach-Baladan and his descendants were not native Babylonians but Arameans. The Elamites and Medians of 21:2 are enemies of Assyria not Babylon. This unit reflects their boast that they will join Babylon against Assyria.[148] However, they will fail to defeat Assyria in this time. (Assyria will fall to them and Babylon in 612 B.C.)

H. The Edomites and Arabians are promised destruction (21:11-17).

I. An interesting judgmental statement is made about the "Valley of Vision" in chapter 22. The title refers to Judah as the language shows. Hezekiah has already been attacked by Assyria (701 B.C.). Note the past tenses in 1-14. The Shebna parenthesis is put here possibly because he was the leader in the anti-Assyrian coalition movement (this conjecture is because the sin of Shebna is not clearly set out).

J. The final nation dealt with is Tyre (chapter 23). Tyrian trade was damaged and controlled by the Assyrian tyranny. From 700-630 B.C. Tyre was under Assyrian control. After that time, Assyria began to decline. Is this the seventy years spoken of?

IV. Chapters 24-27 (often called the little apocalypse) concludes the first 23 chapters with a resumption of the Day of the Lord theme (chapter 24) and the restoration of Israel and Judah (25-27).

A. Chapter 24 is difficult, but the first part (1-13) may refer to judgment on Israel as the people of Yahweh while the latter part refers to the

---

[148]Motyer, *The Prophecy of Isaiah*, p. 174, agrees.

eschatological Day of Yahweh. This great event will culminate in the rule of Yahweh from Mount Zion.

B. Chapter 25 is a marvelous statement of the restoration of Judah. Even the resurrection (end of tribulation) is presented in 25:8. Judah will exult in Yahweh in chapter 26.

C. Chapter 27 presents the restoration of the northern kingdom as well (as in Ezekiel 37). Leviathan and the Dragon are remnants of mythology, but they are not being used here in a mythological sense. Rather, they are terms used of all rebellion against God.

V. Chapters 28—33 pursue the idea that Judah should trust in Yahweh and not go to other nations (cf. 30:1-2). In this unit however, Egypt is dominant, probably because Babylon fell in 689 B.C.

A. Ephraim (the northern kingdom) will be judged (28:1-13).

B. Judah will also be judged (28:14—29:4).

C. Judah's enemies will be judged (29:5-8).

D. Judah's refusal to listen to Yahweh is her problem (29:9-24) (note the tie-in with chapter 6 in 29:9-10).

E. The issue of seeking an alliance with Egypt comes to the fore in chapters 30 and 31. Judah has rejected the word of Yahweh and is trusting in horses (30:12-17). God will judge Assyria (30:31, 31:8) after he has punished Judah. Then there will be a great restoration (chapters 32,33).

VI. Chapters 34—35 are somewhat of a summary of the first part of Isaiah. Chapter 34 shows the results of disobedience (but judgment is on Edom, cf. 63:1-6) and 35 shows the results of God's grace responding to obedience.

VII. Chapters 36—39 are an historical center to link the two parts of the book of Isaiah together.

A. Chapters 36—37 show the results of the folly of Ahaz in going to Assyria. These people have now come to fulfill chapter 8. Rabshakeh stands in the very spot Isaiah stood; the former to blaspheme the God of Judah and the latter to encourage faith in Him.

B. Chapters 38—39 look forward to the Babylonian era (40-66) and show that even godly Hezekiah mistakenly tried to form alliances rather than trust Yahweh. The events of this chapter probably took place in 703 (since Merodach Baladan was deposed at that time) and are placed here for rhetorical reasons.[149] However, 2 Chron. 32:31 speaks of the Babylonian ambassadors coming to enquire about the "sign" which took place in the land. If this refers to the miracle of deliverance, then Chs. 38 and 39 would come *after* Chs. 36-37.

Synopsis of the Events of Isaiah 36-39

1. Sennacherib began his westward campaign to put down rebellion. (Isaiah 36:1; 2 Kings 18:13; 2 Chronicles 32:1)

2. Hezekiah prepared for the battle (2 Chron. 32:2-8; Isaiah 22?).

3. With the fall of Lachish, Hezekiah sent messengers to placate Sennacherib and to offer him tribute (2 Kings 18:14-22).

4. Sennacherib took the tribute, but still sent the Rabshakeh to threaten Jerusalem. Hezekiah prayed and God promised deliverance through a rumor (2 Kings 19:1-9; Isaiah 37:1-9).

---

[149]So Hayes and Irvine (*Isaiah*, pp. 13-14) and J. A. Brinkman ("Merodach-Baladan II," p. 24).

5. Sennacherib withdrew because of the rumor about Egypt, but sent intimidating letters to Hezekiah (2 Kings 19:10-13; Isaiah 37:10-13).

6. Hezekiah prays to the Lord about the letters (2 Kings 19:14ff; Isaiah 37:14ff; 2 Chron. 32:20).

7. God promises deliverance and 185,000 Assyrians died (2 Kings 19:35-37; Isaiah 37:36-38; 2 Chron. 32:21-23).

Part II: Comfort (Chs. 40—66)

Unit I: God's Promise of Restoration: the Work of the Servant (40—55)

The message of Isaiah shifts in the second part of the book to one of comfort. (N.B. that approximately 111 verses of 675 in Chs. 1-35 or 16% deal with comfort and restoration. We must not assume that Chs. 1-39 are only judgment. Conversely, large segments of the second part of Isaiah are judgmental. The larger thrust of the message, however, is "judgment" in 1—39 and "comfort" in 40—66.)

The setting of 40—66 is the exile. This, of course, does not mean that Isaiah was prophesying *during* the exile, but that he was prophesying *about* it.

Some recurring ideas in the book:

"Redeemer": verb, 16 times; noun, 13 times.

"Holy one of Israel": 30 times. (5 times with "Redeemer.")

"Creator" 8 times (40:26; 41:20; 43:7; 45:8,12,18; 54:16,16).

"Babylon" and "Chaldee": Chs. 1—39: 12 times; Chs. 40—66: 9 times.

A. Hermeneutical discussion on the book of Isaiah.

Propositions:

1. Isaiah 40-66 speaks of the return from the exile in 538 B.C. (Cyrus 41:2, 25; 44:28; 45:1-7, 13; 46:11; 48:14; Babylon: 43:14; 47:1; 48:14, 20; Chaldea: 43:14; 47:1, 5; 48:14, 20; building Jerusalem/temple: 44:28) but uses language that must either be interpreted as metaphor, hyperbole or unfulfilled (40:3-5, 9-11; 41:14-20; 42:14-17; 43:1-7, 14-21; 44:1-5; 45:11-17; 49:8-13, 22-23; 51:1-3; 60:4-9, etc.). Furthermore, an extraordinary individual is to lead the deliverance, and the description of his mission is universal in scope (42:1-7; 49:1-13; 50:4-11; 52:13—53:12; 61:1-3). Given the nature of Old Testament prophecy that is, presented in a sort of kaleidoscopic pattern, the *sequential* understanding can only be derived with the passing of time. The promise, in this original form, makes it look like all one discussion (it can only be pulled apart with the progress of revelation).

2. A believing Jew returning under Zerubbabel and Jeshua would have recognized that the very fact of returning to Jerusalem was in some sense a fulfillment of the promise. While he may have been able to interpret the language of return metaphorically or hyperbolically the role of the servant was completely absent. The servant's mission extended to the entire world, involved the restoration of Israel, contained a mysterious element of suffering that was to be vicarious, and involved the whole spectrum of redemption for the people of God.

3. Given the language of the return (returnees from all compass points, victory over Israel's enemies, etc.) and especially the description of the servant's task and even more particularly the suffering of the servant in 52/53, the entire second half of Isaiah takes on eschatological overtones.[150] There are times, of course, when hyperbole is used to

---

[150]Klaus Koch, *The Prophets, the Babylonian and Persian Periods,* vol 2, p. 118,

describe a situation. In that case one must be prepared to accept a limited fulfillment. A case in point in the first part of Isaiah is the destruction language of Isaiah 13.

4. A believing Jew, say in the Maccabean period, would have hoped for the fulfillment of the prophecies of deliverance in their times (cf. 1 Macc 5:53-54).[151]

5. By New Testament times the concept of a forerunner for the deliverer taken on by John the Baptist was not questioned. The role of Elijah was a puzzling one. Jesus himself was identified as Elijah on occasion (Matt 16). He performed miracles like those of Elijah and Elisha (healing lepers, raising a widow's dead son). However, Zechariah was told that John would go in the "spirit and power of Elijah" (Luke 1:17). On the Mount of Transfiguration Jesus made clear that John the Baptist in some sense fulfilled the role of Elijah and thus the forerunner of Isaiah 40. However, Jesus said that Elijah must yet come, and so both Jesus and John the Baptist fulfill this prophecy. The

---

says, "The abrupt change of direction between salvation history and the present time (cf. Jer. 2.7a with 2.7b) will be paralleled by a similar 'bend' in the future as well. History, conceived of metahistorically, therefore emerges as a line broken in two places (cf. Vol I, section 7.6). If we remember this viewpoint when we are considering the prophetic view of history, it is entirely appropriate to use the term 'eschatology' for the prophets' expectation of the upheaval of the times, and the new evolution of the people of God which is to follow."

[151]J. A. Goldstein, *1 Maccabees*, p. 304: "Our author's echoes here of prophesies [*sic*] of Isaiah are so audacious that he must be hinting that he saw their fulfillment in Judas' victories." On p. 3 he says, "The outcome [of the Syrian wars] was entirely unexpected: the desperate resistance of the Jews prevailed, and for a time the 'yoke of foreign empires' was lifted from the Jews as they became independent under the Hasmonaean dynasty. After the centuries of heart-breaking delay, were the glorious predictions of the prophets of a mighty restored Israel being fulfilled? For the Jews, the events cried out for an interpretation in accordance with the teachings of the Torah and the Prophets." Throughout his commentary, Goldstein indicates references to Isaiah which he believes influenced the thinking of the Maccabees.

theme of deliverance represented to some extent in the name Immanuel and more particularly in the names of Isa. 9:6, is taken up in Matthew where the incarnation of Christ is related to Isa. 7:14 and the place of the ministry of Christ is related to Isa. 9:1-2.

6. That Jesus is the fulfillment of the Servant prophecies is indicated when he applies Isa. 61:1 to himself (Luke 4). Matthew applies Isa. 42:3-4 to Jesus (Matt 12:18-21). He also cites Isa 53:4 in relation to the healing ministry of Christ (Matt 8:17) and Peter applies it to the redemptive work (1 Pet 2:24). Philip expounded Isaiah 53 to the Ethiopian by preaching to him Jesus (Acts 8:32ff). These examples could be multiplied.[152]

7. That Isaiah's prophecies are not exhausted in the first coming of Christ is shown by the references to eternal punishment (Isa 66:24 with Mark 9:48) and the new heavens and new earth (Isa 65:17ff; 66:22 with 2 Pet 3:13 and Rev 21:1, 4). Since these features are future even to the time of Christ, it should not be difficult to perceive adumbrations and prophecies of an earthly fulfillment of the many prophecies to the descendants of Abraham.[153]

---

[152]See Nestle-Aland, *Novum Testamentum Graece,* pp. 857-61 for a complete listing of the citations and allusions to Isaiah.

[153]Peter indicates that there will be some sort of physical judgment of the earth followed by new heavens and a new earth in which dwells righteousness (2 Pet 3:8-13), and his language seems to require a literal interpretation. This would fit the scenario of Tribulation followed by Millennium as Isaiah 65 seems to indicate, but what do we make of the reference to new heavens and a new earth in Rev 21:1 which *follows* the Millennium? Before the Edenic-like conditions can be restored, there must be a renovation of the sphere of human existence. Yet, even as Isaiah speaks of the beauties of this restoration, he must speak of death and even of the serpent. When eternity is ushered in, obviously John must speak of a new heavens and a new earth, but this is not the only fulfillment of the promise.

8. The language of Isaiah is thus particular and general. It refers to the return under Zerubbabel in the days of Cyrus the Persian King. It also refers to the coming of John the Baptist and the Servant as the redeemer. Yet, the prophecies referring to the blessed restoration of Israel to their land and city, their triumph over their enemies, Edenic conditions prevailing in the land with the glory of God manifested throughout the earth refer neither to the first coming of Messiah nor to eternity. If the language is to be given its full force, the fulfillment must be upon the earth this side of eternity. The ultimate completion of God's purpose, of course, must be in the eternal state and for this we all long, but we dare not empty these glorious promises to the chosen seed of their Old Testament covenantal meaning.

B. Yahweh states that Judah has suffered enough for her sins and is to be restored (40:1-31).

1. Yahweh calls out rhetorically for Israel to be comforted since her sins are doubly paid for (40:1-2).

2. Yahweh is coming in all his glory to redeem His people (40:3-8).

   Did this happen in 539 when Babylon was defeated and Cyrus' decree was issued allowing the Jews to come home? Young says that there is nothing in this passage about a return from the Babylonian exile. He applies it entirely to the spiritual redemption effected in Jesus Christ and applied to all who believe in Him.

   Yet, to some extent it must refer to the return from the Babylonian exile since this entire section refers to the Chaldeans, Babylonians and Cyrus. At the same time the language of the second part of Isaiah is so universal and comprehensive and is so often applied to New Testament situations that the ultimate fulfillment of these promises must be eschatological.

Was it fulfilled in the first century when Jesus was introduced to Israel by John the Baptist who said he was the "voice of one crying in the wilderness"? In a sense, yes, though Jesus Himself says that "Elijah must yet come" indicating that John the Baptist served in an interim capacity.

The ultimate fulfillment of this prophecy comes when God regathers all His people to restore them in faith to the land.

3. The good news being declared here is that God will restore His people (40:9-11).

    God is depicted here as the shepherd leading his flock. His reward is with him—that is, the redeemed ones. He will gently care for His people as He returns them from the distant lands to place them in the chosen land.

4. Yahweh now gives a statement of His character that when compared to humans, dwarfs them into silence (40:12-17).

    In view of the fact that God's ability to carry out such a magnificent task might be questioned, He begins in this section to show His greatness over all that is known in the human experience.

5. In light of God's greatness, idolatry is utterly foolish (40:18-20).

    Idolatry was being extensively practiced in Isaiah's day and as such comes under scathing denunciation by the Lord throughout these prophecies. Idolatry is so utterly illogical that it hardly deserves denunciation, but because it is the warp and woof of the society of Isaiah's day, it must be shown to be what it is—futile and hopeless.

5. Yahweh gives another statement on His greatness (40:21-26).

This passage constitutes one of the most beautiful statements about the sovereignty and greatness of God in the entire Bible. His control over the universe, nature and humanity is emphasized.

7. He concludes this section by saying that Israel cannot hide from God and that He is able to deliver completely (40:27-31).

On the one hand, God's greatness makes it impossible for people to escape His scrutiny. On the other hand, His greatness makes it possible for Him to help His stumbling, needy people and to deliver them. What a marvelous statement of God's concern for His own.

C. Yahweh speaks of His greatness in redeeming Israel (41:1-29).

1. Yahweh calls upon the world to witness to His greatness in raising up Cyrus (41:1-4).

This is the first reference to Cyrus. The references will grow and become more explicit, culminating at 44:28 and 45:1 when an actual name given. God calls Cyrus in righteousness—not Cyrus' but God's—to His feet, that is, to a place of obedience. Cyrus was unaware that Yahweh was so using him. He was not a worshipper of Yahweh, but the action Cyrus took in returning people to their lands shows the sovereignty of God in the affairs even of pagan kings.

2. Yahweh shows the uniqueness of Israel as His chosen servant (41:5-16).

God points out that the coast lands (usually a reference to the Mediterranean areas) become afraid and consult their deities for help. The idolatry is stressed here as a futile action to prevent Cyrus' takeover of their territory.

Recurring Strands in Isaiah 40-48

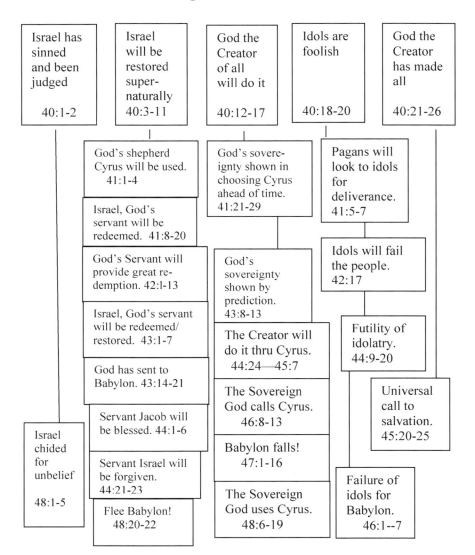

Israel has sinned and been judged
40:1-2

Israel will be restored supernaturally
40:3-11

God the Creator of all will do it
40:12-17

Idols are foolish
40:18-20

God the Creator has made all
40:21-26

God's shepherd Cyrus will be used. 41:1-4

God's sovereignty shown in choosing Cyrus ahead of time. 41:21-29

Pagans will look to idols for deliverance. 41:5-7

Israel, God's servant will be redeemed. 41:8-20

God's Servant will provide great re-demption. 42:l-13

God's sovereignty shown by prediction. 43:8-13

Idols will fail the people. 42:17

Israel, God's servant will be redeemed/restored. 43:1-7

The Creator will do it thru Cyrus. 44:24—45:7

Futility of idolatry. 44:9-20

God has sent to Babylon. 43:14-21

Servant Jacob will be blessed. 44:1-6

The Sovereign God calls Cyrus. 46:8-13

Universal call to salvation. 45:20-25

Israel chided for unbelief
48:1-5

Servant Israel will be forgiven. 44:21-23

Babylon falls! 47:1-16

Failure of idols for Babylon. 46:1--7

Flee Babylon! 48:20-22

The Sovereign God uses Cyrus. 48:6-19

This discussion also allows for an opportunity to contrast the pagan peoples of the world with God's chosen people. Here for the first time, the idea of servant, so prominent in the second half of Isaiah, is presented. Israel as God's servant comes under the protection of God. The time will come when this servant will be able to defeat all his enemies because of God's help.

Excursus:

The servant of the Lord (*'eved Yahweh*, עֶבֶד יהוה)[154] is one of the most important, most discussed, and in some ways the most difficult concepts in the book of Isaiah. It is clear from an exegesis of the individual passages that the phrase is being used in different ways at different times. The following list shows the groupings I have made for the various usages. The occurrence of Israel (Chs. 49) in a group called messianic will be discussed at the appropriate place.

Servant of the Lord:

Plural referring to God's people

54:17	the heritage of the servants of
56:6	the name of the Lord, to be his servants
63:17	Return for thy servants' sake
65:8	so will I do for my servants' sakes
65:9	and my servants shall dwell there
65:13	Behold, my servants shall eat
65:13	behold, my servants shall drink
65:13	behold, my servants shall rejoice
65:14	Behold my servants shall sing

---

[154]See Bernd Janowski and Peter Stuhlmacher, eds., *The Suffering Servant; Isaiah 53 in Jewish and Christian Sources*, for an excellent discussion of all aspects of Isaiah 53.

65:15   and call his servants by another name
66:14   Lord shall be known toward his servants

Singular referring to Israel

41:8   But thou, Israel, (art) my servant
41:9   Thou (art) my servant
42:19   Who (is) blind, but my servant
42:19   and blind as the Lord's servant?
43:10   and my servant whom I have chosen
44:1   Yet now hear, O Jacob, my servant
44:2   Fear not, O Jacob, my servant
44:21   for thou (art) my servant, I have formed thee thou art my servant
44:26   Confirming the word of his servant
        (This probably refers to Isaiah)
45:4   For Jacob my servant's sake
48:20   the Lord hath redeemed his servant Jacob

Singular referring to Messiah

42:1   Behold my servant, whom I uphold
49:3   Thou (art) my servant, O Israel
49:5   that formed me from the womb (to be) his servant
49:6   that thou shouldest be my servant
49:7   to a servant of rulers
50:10   that obeys the voice of his servant
52:13   Behold, my servant shall deal prudently
53:11   shall my righteous servant justify many

"Chosen" (*baḥar,* בָּחַר)

41:8   Jacob whom I have chosen
41:9   I have chosen thee, and not cast away
43:10   my servant whom I have chosen
44:1   Israel, whom I have chosen
44:2   Jesurun, whom I have chosen
48:10   I have chosen thee in the furnace of affliction
56:4   and choose (the things) that please

65:12	did choose (that) wherein I delighted
66:3	they have chosen their own ways
66:4	and chose (that) in which

3. Yahweh declares His greatness in restoring Israel (41:17-20).

The hermeneutical principle established in chapter 40 is that there is an immediate reference to the return from the Babylonian exile, but that the ultimate fulfillment must be eschatological.

4. Yahweh challenges the false religions of that day to prove their reality (41:21-24).

God's greatness is shown in His ability to raise up Cyrus and return Israel to the land. The false religions can do nothing to help their people. Surely we should look upon the work of the government of Cyrus as evidence of the supernatural intervention of Yahweh.

5. Yahweh concludes by referring again to the fact that He has raised up Cyrus- (41:25-29).

God refers again to His greatness in His work among men. He began this dissertation by showing that the raising up of Cyrus demonstrated His sovereignty. Now He concludes it by saying that the idols cannot provide the kind of information or action demonstrated in the calling of Cyrus.

D. Yahweh reveals His servant who is to rule the world (42:1-25).

We now come to the first of the "Servant Songs." The individualistic emphasis in this passage creates problems for those who want to see a collective interpretation.[155]

---

[155]See McKenzie, *Second Isaiah*, for a discussion of the various views. He opts for a vague collectivistic interpretation. He says "The Servant belongs to the future, for he is

1. Yahweh reveals the character and work of the servant (42:1-4).

    The servant's task is to bring forth justice to the nations. He will establish justice in the earth and the coast lands will wait expectantly for His torah. This concept of justice was presented in chapter 11 as the task of the root from the stump of Jesse.

    A major new concept in this servant passage is that the servant will be humble and quiet. He will not cry out or raise his voice. His actions toward the weak are to be ones of compassion. Here the victorious one is seen not using a sword.

    In the midst of Jesus' miracle working, the Pharisees began to look for ways to destroy Him. Jesus quotes this servant passage in connection with His charge to those he had healed to keep quiet about the miracle. At the same time, He is obviously applying the entire passage to Himself since He quotes it *in toto* (Matt. 12:15-21). The people are astute enough to recognize that the work being accomplished by Jesus must be that prophesied in the Old Testament (Matt. 12:23).

2. Yahweh reveals the commission of the servant (42:5-9).

    The stress is on God as creator in v. 5 and then on the servant whose commission includes being a covenant to the people, a light to the Gentiles, opening blind eyes and bringing prisoners from the dungeon.

3. In light of the Servant's work, all people are urged to praise the Lord (42:10-13).

4. Yahweh speaks of His restoration of creation (42:14-17).

---

what Israel must become. But he also belongs to the past, for his character is formed by reflection on Israel's history and on the character of her leaders....Unless Israel accepts the Servant as its incorporation, it cannot keep faith with Yahweh" (LV).

5.   Yahweh speaks of the blindness of Israel and the reason He has punished her (42:18-25).

In this section the servant is not an individual, for he is characterized as being blind. Here it refers to Israel who has not listened to God's word. Because of the blindness of this servant who was to be God's messenger to the world, God brought the judgment of Babylon upon her. Here again is the teaching that Israel was to be the servant, but she has miserably failed. Consequently, the servant, par excellence, is to be raised up to bring the light to the world Israel has failed to bring.

E.   Yahweh calls on Israel to trust Him because He will deliver her (43:1-28).

1.   Yahweh speaks of His redemption and restoration of Israel (43:1-7).

As indicated in the earlier discussion on hermeneutics, there may be some reference to the return in 539 B.C., but the universal language of this passage indicates that the time of fulfillment is subsequent to anything we know about in history for Israel. The exiles are not just in Babylon, but in the North, South, East, West and the ends of the earth.

2.   Yahweh calls upon Israel to bear witness of His faithfulness as evidenced by His redemption of Israel (43:8-13).

3.   Yahweh states His sovereignty in delivering Israel from Babylon (43:14-21).

Again the historic exile is in view, but the language goes beyond it to the ultimate deliverance of Israel.

4.   Yahweh chides Israel for not worshipping Him (43:25-28).

Israel has brought sacrifices, but they have not satisfied God since they do not come with the right attitude. Their sins and iniquities have burdened God. The only one who can redeem them is Yahweh. He is the one who "wipes out their sins."

F. Yahweh again contrasts Himself with the idolatrous practices all around Israel and promises restoration (44:1-28).

1. He promises great blessing on Israel (44:1-5).

    God's promises in this section are far-reaching. He promises to pour out His spirit and His blessing on the descendants of Israel. There will be a great turning to the Lord when that happens.

    Jeshurun is from the Hebrew *yashar* (יָשַׁר) which refers to righteousness. It must mean, "My just ones."

2. He speaks of His uniqueness and calls on Israel to trust Him (44:6-8).

3. He gives a diatribe against idolatry (44:9-17).

4. He shows the judgment of God on them (44:18-20).

    God has judged the nations so that they believe in idols in spite of the utter illogic of their faith.

5. He calls on Israel to recognize Yahweh, His redemption, and to return to Him (44:21-24).

    God has provided the necessary redemptive work for Israel's sins. He calls upon Israel to return to Him and to shout because of God's grace in His redemptive work.

6. He speaks again of His greatness and concludes by showing His sovereignty in raising up Cyrus (44:24-28).

    For the first time Cyrus is mentioned by name. God refers to him as a shepherd who will carry out His desire.[156]

---

[156]These explicit references to Cyrus are one of several issues that cause critical scholars to argue for a sixth century (Babylonian-Persian) period for this section of

G. Yahweh reveals His sovereignty in calling Cyrus to deliver His people and issues a universal call for salvation (45:1-25).[157]

1. He has raised up Cyrus for the sake of His servant Jacob (45:1-7).

   Cyrus says of himself: "All the kings of the entire world from the Upper to the Lower Sea, those who are seated in throne rooms, (those who) live in other [types of buildings as well as] all the kings of the West land living in tents, brought their heavy tributes and kissed my feet in Babylon. (As to the region) from...as far as Ashur and Susa, Agade, Eshnunna, the towns of Zamban, Me-Turnu, Der as well as the region of the Gutians, I returned to (these) sacred cities on the other side of the Tigris, the sanctuaries of which have been ruins for a long time, the images which (used) to live therein and established for them permanent sanctuaries. I (also) gathered all their (former) inhabitants and returned (to them) their habitations. Furthermore, I resettled upon the command of Marduk, the great lord, all the gods of Sumer and Akkad whom Nabonidus has brought into Babylon to the anger of the lord of the gods, unharmed, in their (former) chapels, the places which make them happy."[158]

   Cyrus' policy outlined in this statement is a radical departure from that of his predecessors. Normally, the various idols were brought to the conquering nation. Since Judah had no idols, the utensils of the temple were considered equivalent. It was these utensils that were brought back by Zerubbabel (Ezra 1).[159]

Isaiah. However, those who believe that God can reveal the future to His servants are not troubled by it.

[157]Motyer, *The Prophecy of Isaiah*, p. 352, says, "This new section, along with its parallel 49:1-53:12, constitutes the logical next step in Isaiah's presentation, and the parallels between the two agents involved are very closely worked out: The work of Cyrus (44:24-48:22); the work of the Servant (49:1-53:12)."

[158]*ANET*, p. 316.

[159]References (direct or oblique) to Cyrus

2. He calls on the world to acknowledge His lordship (45:8-10).

God is calling for a day in which righteousness will drop down like water. He is the one who will do it and therefore, He should be accepted as lord. The pericope of 9-10 is characteristic of Isaiah. The fact that God promises an idyllic day cannot be gainsaid by those who complain to God about what He is doing.

2. He speaks of His lordship in terms of the call of Cyrus (45:11-19).

Yahweh's ability to predict the future of Israel (my sons) should convince them of His person. If this were being written *post facto*, it would not provide much proof of Yahweh's existence and power.

41:2   Who has aroused one from the east whom He calls in righteousness to His feet (1-7).

41:25   I have aroused one from the north, and he has come; From the rising of the sun he will call on My name; and he will come upon rulers as upon mortar, Even as the potter treads clay (25-26.)

44:28   It is I who says of Cyrus, He is My shepherd! And he will perform all My desire.

45:1   Thus says the Lord to Cyrus His anointed, Whom I have taken by the right hand (1-7).

45:13   I have aroused him in righteousness And I will make all his ways smooth; He will build My city, and will let My exiles go free (14-16).

46:11   Calling a bird of prey from the east, The man of My purpose from a far country.

48:14   The Lord has loved him . . . I have called him (14-15).

(See Phillip Schafron, "The Importance of Cyrus in the Argument of Isaiah 40-48.")

Verse 13 is a powerful prophecy. God has raised up Cyrus to do His bidding. He will cause two things to happen: Jerusalem will be rebuilt,[160] and the Jewish exiles will be freed.

4. He appeals to the inhabited world to recognize His lordship and to come to Him (45:20-25).

This section is a marvelous appeal to the entire world to turn to Yahweh and experience His salvation. This is one of those universal passages that indicate a message to all the world and not simply to Israel. The fulfillment of this prophecy could not possibly have been in Isaiah's day nor in the return from the exile. It must have far-reaching implications.

H. Yahweh declares the bankruptcy of Babylon's religion and urges Israel to accept His lordship (46:1-13).

1. Bel and Nebo are defeated (46:1-2).

Bel is the Babylonian equivalent to Baal in the rest of the Old Testament. Nebo is the god of science and learning. Both these deities, says Isaiah, will go into captivity. This probably refers to a literal removing of the idols, and indicates that idols are incapable of preventing Yahweh's judgment on the Babylonians.

2. Israel is challenged to receive the person of God (46:3-7).

Bel and Nebo, Babylonian gods, will be *carried* into captivity. However, the God of Israel will *carry* His people to deliverance. There is no limit to the time (gray hairs) that Yahweh will care for His people. The reference to idols provokes Yahweh to launch into his favorite diatribe. This began in 40:18-20 and continues here. How

---

[160]The city was not rebuilt until Artaxerxes' (Nehemiah) time, but Cyrus set in motion the events that made it possible.

foolish to put your hope in idols. How can you possibly compare Yahweh to them?

3. He speaks of His purpose exemplified again in the call of Cyrus (46:8-11).

    The "transgressors" are rebels. This is a conscious refusal to listen to God. Israel was constantly urged to remember the way Yahweh had worked in the past. This should be a basis for them to trust Him for the future. God has a purpose in this world and a goal in which he delights. That purpose will be fulfilled in Cyrus, who is spoken of obliquely as the "man of My purpose from a far country."[161]

4. He chides Israel for stubbornly refusing to recognize His purposes in saving Israel (46:12-13).

5. "Stubborn-minded" is literally "mighty of heart." BHS suggests reading a "d" for the "r" (they look much alike in Hebrew), and read "whose hearts are perishing." However, stubborn-minded goes well with "transgressors" in v. 8. Note the play on Israel being far from righteousness, whereas God will bring righteousness near; and salvation which seems so far off will also brought near to Zion.

I. Yahweh pronounces judgment on Babylon (47:1-15).

1. He declares a debasement of Babylon under the imagery of a woman (47:1-7).

    Before Cyrus can set in motion the actions decreed by Yahweh, Babylon must be dealt with. "Virgin daughter of Babylon" like "virgin daughter of Zion" means "Virgin Babylon" and "Virgin Zion."

---

[161]Gary V. Smith, "The Destruction of Babylon in Isaiah 46-47" JETS 58:3 (2015):527-544, argues that this was fulfilled in 689 BC. when Sennacherib destroyed Babylon.

Chapter 14 describes the fall of the King of Babylon; this passage describes the fall of the city. All her vaunted glory will be reduced to dust and ashes. She will become a peasant woman who wears woolen and grinds grain. Now God discusses the Old Testament theology of retribution on a nation used by God to punish Judah that is in turn punished.

2. He states that Babylon, who thought she could never be punished will undergo disaster (47:8-11).

   The proud, preening Babylon, who is convinced that she can never be harmed; that she can never be a widow nor childless, will be brought low. Known for her wisdom (cf. Daniel 2-3) and her sorceries, she will be utterly unable to "charm" her way out if it (an unusual meaning for this word, but the Arabic supports it). Nor will she be able to atone for her evil.

3. He argues that Babylon's religion will not save her (47:12-15).

   Babylon was noted for her astrology and other related religious practices. These "predictors" of the future will disappear like stubble set on fire. Even though she has spent her lifetime laboring in these practices, she will find herself deserted in the day of calamity about to come upon her. Compare this section with Revelation 17, 18.

J.   Yahweh promises Judah deliverance from Babylon (48:1-22).

   1. He chides Judah for her obstinacy (48:1-11).

      Yahweh declares that He has given prophetic utterances so that Judah cannot claim that her idol has delivered her. The marvelous statements about Cyrus are designed to prove the sovereignty of God.

   2. He appeals to Israel with the reminder that He has chosen her and worked sovereignly in history (48:12-16).

Having reminded Israel of the fact that He has chosen her, God then speaks of the calling of Cyrus. The "him" in v. 14 is probably Cyrus rather than Israel. The word "love" here as elsewhere probably means to choose rather than to have an emotional feeling (Jacob I have loved.) Verse 16 is extraordinary. The subject in the first part of the verse must be Yahweh, but who is speaking in the second part? McKenzie argues that it is "the imagined response of Cyrus to the call of Yahweh."[162] Ridderbos[163] may be correct in believing that the phrase "And now the Lord God has sent me and His spirit" refers to the prophet who is calling upon Israel to listen to the word of the Lord.

3. He tells Judah how good it would have been if they had obeyed (48:17-19).

Yahweh, the redeemer and holy one wants to teach Israel the right way to go. Wisdom is involved here. He longs for Israel to follow the good path. He laments the missed opportunity for Israel to have prospered: if only she had listened to Him.

4. He warns Judah to flee Babylon since He is going to judge her (48:20-22).

This section is a dramatic way of saying that God is going to judge Babylon. Just as he told Lot to leave Sodom, so he tells Israel to get out of Babylon because He is going to judge her.

K. The Servant of the Lord is the redeemer of the world (49:1-26).[164]

---

[162]McKenzie, *Second Isaiah*, AB, 96.

[163]Ridderbos, *Isaiah*, 40-41.

[164]See Norman Podhoretz, *The Prophets*, pp. 283-85, for a discussion and overview from a modern Jewish lay point of view.

1. The Servant is called and protected by God (49:1-4).

    The Servant is called from the womb of his mother; he has been named from his mother's body (to name is another concept for choosing). Under the imagery of weaponry (sword, arrow, quiver) he says that God has made him effective in preaching his message.

    God has called him His servant, Israel, and has promised to show him His glory. If this is an individual, more particularly Christ, why is he called Israel? North argues for an individualistic interpretation in spite of the occurrence of "Israel."[165] Some manuscripts do not have the word Israel, but it appears in 1QIsa[a] and the major LXX MSS. It would be tempting to omit it from the passage, but that might be self-serving since we are assuming that the reference is to Christ.

    Since the reference is clearly to an individual, the appearance of the word "Israel" must indicate that this person is looked upon as the ideal Israel, that is, all that God would like His people Israel to be. However, this does not imply that the individual is not a real person (as is true of those who want to idealize the individual), only that the real person is looked upon as "Mr. Israel."

    The Servant complains of having labored for nothing (v. 4). Did this ever happen in the life of Christ? There is nothing in Scripture that so indicates it, but His prayer in the garden certainly indicates the possibility of a private complaint made by the Son to the Father. The "futility of his work" may be more than an emotional response. It may indicate the refusal of the Jewish nation to receive Him and His kingdom. The rest of the verse shows Him immediately returning to a sense of confidence in God just as in the garden, "Nevertheless thy will be done."

---

[165]See Christopher North, *The Second Isaiah: Introduction, Translation and Commentary to Chapters 40-55,* for an excellent discussion of this passage.

2. The Lord gives the Servant a double commission (49:5-7).

    The first task of the servant is to bring Jacob back to God and to gather Israel to Him (v. 5). The second task reaches beyond Israel to the Gentile world. He is to be a light of the nations, and God's salvation is to reach to the end of the earth. The lowly, despised position of the Servant is presented in v. 7.

    The Servant is spoken of as being a light to the Gentiles in 9:1, 42:6, and 49:6. Simeon says in Luke 2:30-32: "Now Lord, Thou does let Thy bond-servant depart in peace, according to Thy word; For my eyes have seen Thy salvation, which Thou hast prepared in the presence of all peoples, a light of revelation to the Gentiles, and the glory of Thy people Israel." Paul says in Acts 13:47 in connection with his action of leaving the Jews to preach to the Gentiles in Antioch: "For thus the Lord has commanded us, I have placed You as a light for the Gentiles, that You should bring salvation to the end of the earth." Paul is not saying that *he* (Paul) is the light, but that he is bringing the light provided by God in His Son to the Gentiles.

3. The Lord assigns the Servant the task of restoring Israel to the land in great prosperity and peace (49:8-13).

    The addressee is singular "You." This individual will be given as a covenant of the people. This covenant includes the restoration of the land and the freeing of people. They will be brought from distant lands by the gentle hand of the servant.

4. Israel complains that the Lord has forsaken her, but He argues that there is no way He can do so (49:14-21).

    As a mother cannot forget her children, so God cannot forget Israel. They are inscribed on His hands. He will restore them in great prosperity, and she who was barren will have more children than she knows what to do with.

5. God promises to restore Israel as He lifts up His standard to the nations and causes these people who have oppressed Israel to restore them. Then "all flesh will know that I, the LORD, am your Savior, and your Redeemer, the Mighty One of Jacob" (49:22-26).

L. Yahweh gives the reason for Judah's judgment and the Servant speaks again (50:1-11).

1. Judah suffers because of sin (50:1-3).

Yahweh says He is not the cause of Judah's suffering—He did not initiate a divorce, and He was not in debt so as to be forced to sell His wife. Judah suffers because of sin. She is apparently in exile in this portion, and when she reads this she will understand why she is there.

Yahweh says that He is perfectly capable of delivering, but that His deliverance is predicated on a response from His people (50:2-3).

2. The Servant introduces Himself again (50:4-11).

He has the tongue of a disciple (50:4).

Though the word "Servant" is not used until v. 10, the passage by its nature requires it to be speaking of Him. Here the Servant is described as being one who learns of God. God teaches Him to sustain the weak.

He is obedient and suffers (50:5).

The Servant knows how to obey. "To open the ear" is to speak to. God has spoken, and the Servant has chosen to obey. "I do always those things that please the father." This obedience brought Him suffering.

He is vindicated (50:7-9).

The Servant has cast Himself upon the Father ("My God, My God, why hast thou forsaken me"; "In the days of His flesh, He offered up both prayers and supplications with loud crying and tears to the One able to save Him from death, and He was heard because of His piety," Heb. 5:7).

All of this language could apply to some pious man who suffered for his faith, but who would he have been? The context of Isaiah, describing one who will even suffer vicariously, calls for a linking of all these intensely individualistic passages and to see in them statements about the coming Messiah, who we know is Jesus.

He admonishes the remnant to trust in the Lord (50:10-11).

Those believers walking in darkness without light, the Servant admonishes to trust in Yahweh. Those who refuse to trust in Yahweh's light, but have built their own fire, He promises that they will lie down in torment.

M. Yahweh appeals to the faithful remnant to trust Him (51:1-23).

1. "Those who pursue righteousness" are exhorted to look (in trust) to the Lord (51:1-3).

    God encourages the believing remnant to renew their trust in Him (the rock from which they were hewn). He raises images from the past to challenge them: Abraham the faithful one to whom the Lord finally gave children; Sarah who was privileged to produce Isaac in her old age. Eden and the garden of Yahweh are descriptions given to the work God will do for Israel in that day.

2. God's people are told that He will bring justice to the world (51:4-8).

    The theme returns to the time to come when God will bring justice to the world and that justice will be a light of the people. God has the strength (arm) to carry out His promises. God's people are not to fear the reproach of man, for their destiny is well known.

3. God speaks of His great strength and control of the universe (51:9-16).

Rahab and the dragon are mythological creatures we spoke about before. These symbols of myth are being used here without giving credence to the myth itself. Since God can conquer all His enemies, He is able to bring His people from captivity to His own land with great victory.

4. Defeated Judah is addressed (51:17-23).

They have drunk from God's hand the cup of His anger (51:17-20).

Jerusalem is urged to rouse herself from her drunken stupor. She has drunk so much from the wine of God's wrath, that she is incapable of helping herself. Furthermore, there is no help to be had from any of her sons (prophets, kings, priests). All Israel is lying in the gutter of God's judgment. There is none to help.

God will judge the nations and free His people (50:21-23).

God searches for Israel, drunk in the gutter, like a Mother Theresa searching in the slums of Calcutta. Then He will remove the bottle from her hands, and she will never drink again. Conversely, those who have abused her, walked on her, and violently treated her, will now begin to drink from the fatal bottle and suffer what Judah has suffered.

N. Judah is urged to flee from her oppressors (52:1-12).

1. Yahweh will deliver Judah as He once delivered Israel from Egypt (52:1-6).[166]

In 51:17 Yahweh urged Judah to awake from her stupor (*hith'r^eri* הִתְעוֹרְרִי from *'wr* עוּר). Now the same root is being used in 52:1. Judah is to arouse herself, not just from her drunken stupor, but to

---

[166]See H. Wolf, "The Relationship between Isaiah's Final Servant Song (52:13-53:12) and Chapter 1-6," *A Tribute to Gleason Archer.*

clean herself up and put on beautiful clothes. She is to throw off her shackles and leave her captivity.

Verses 3-6 are in prose, probably indicating a unit from another time. It is placed here to indicate some history. Israel was redeemed from Egypt, and now she will be redeemed from Babylon.

2. Yahweh will give good news to His people (52:7-10).

    A beautiful poem follows, indicating Zion's future redemption. There is a modern town near Jerusalem called Mebasereth Zion "Good News for Zion." What good news this is. God is on his throne, and the watchman will declare that Zion is to be restored. Zion, the spiritual name for Jerusalem and the Jewish people, will someday see all this glorious truth fulfilled.

3. The priests are urged to flee the unclean place (52:11-12).

    The command in verse 1 rhymes with the command in 51:17 and 52:1. *Suri, suri* get out of there. Recognize the commands of God relative to ritual purity. Furthermore, as you left Egypt without haste, so you will leave Babylon. Your security is the fact the Yahweh God goes before and behind you.

O. Judah will be redeemed by the vicarious suffering of the Servant (52:13—53:12).[167]

1. The Servant will be successful even though physically abused (52:13-15).

---

[167]For a discussion (with texts) of the Jewish interpretation of this passage, see S. R. Driver and A. Neubauer, *The Fifty-Third Chapter of Isaiah According to the Jewish Interpreters*.

In the sight of God, the Servant's work will be successful. People, however, will see him as a "marred" person. Kings will be amazed at him. He will sprinkle many nations. The word "sprinkle" has sparked endless discussion. This word normally is used in the Old Testament in connection with blood sacrifices. So we should take it here, in spite of the difficulty of the context. The critics cannot accept it because they cannot comprehend such an idea in this context.[168]

2. The Servant was insignificant to the world (53:1-3).

   The human conception of the Servant was that He was utterly insignificant. God chose to have Him born in a manger of lowly Galilean parents—a "root out of parched ground."

3. The Servant suffered vicariously (53:4-6).

   The believing remnant speaks of their failure to comprehend that God was not punishing the Servant when He suffered so, but He was causing Him to bear our sins. "The Lord caused the iniquity of us all to fall on Him."

4. The Servant suffered innocently (53:7-9).

   In spite of His innocence, the Servant suffered silently. Grave and death are used here as parallels. The cross and the tomb are to be identified as grave and death without distinguishing them. Thus with the wicked (thieves) and the rich (Joseph of Arimathea) was his death/grave.

5. The Servant will have reward for His suffering (53:10-12).

   Regardless of what the world thought about the death of the Servant, the Lord having deliberately crushed Him, now rewards Him. He will

---

[168]See E. J. Young, *Studies in Isaiah* for a full discussion.

see the reward of His work (1QIsa[a] has "light" as does the LXX and this is probably to be preferred, since there is no object to the verb. This should be taken to mean that He would live again and refers to His resurrection).

P. God promises a future time of great prosperity (54:1-17).

1. Judah is told to shout for joy because of what Yahweh is going to do (54:1-8).

    Under the imagery of a barren woman who has been allowed to have children (cf. Hannah, Elizabeth), Judah is told she will have so many children she will have to enlarge her dwelling space (54:1-7).

    The imagery continues, only now she is a widow or a forsaken wife. Now Yahweh is her husband and Redeemer. He forsook her for a brief moment, but with great compassion He has restored her (54:4-8). (Compare this with the book of Hosea.)

2. God's covenant with Judah will be like that of the rainbow with Noah (54:9-10).

    Key words in this section are "loving kindness" (*ḥesed,* חֶסֶד) and "my covenant of peace" (*berith shelomi,* בְּרִית שְׁלוֹמִי).

3. God promises a future time of complete protection for Israel when no weapon will be raised against her (54:11-17).

    One must ask when this time of unprecedented blessing will take place. Certainly, it was not fulfilled when Zerubbabel took the little band of Jews back to Palestine where they struggled to exist in the midst of hostility. Nor has any succeeding age fit this description. It must refer to the messianic kingdom in the future called the Millennium.

Q. Yahweh delivers a magnificent call to the people of Israel (55:1-13).[169]

1. An invitation to the grace of God and the covenant of David is issued (55:1-5).

Under the imagery of food, God admonishes them to come for free food and water (His grace). He tells them He will make an everlasting covenant with them based on the faithful mercies shown to David (*ḥasde dawid hane'emanim,* חַסְדֵי דָוִד הַנֶּאֱמָנִים). The faithful mercies shown to David refer to the Davidic covenant in which God promised David that he would have seed to sit upon the throne eternally. It seems that the rest of this section (4,5) refers to that seed, namely, the Messiah who will become a witness to the people of the grace of God. This seed of David will call a nation (collective) not hitherto known and a nation that has not known him. Though this work of the Messiah begins in the church age, this prediction refers ultimately to the outreach to the Gentiles in the time of restored Israel when the Gentiles will seek the Lord through her.

2. God urges Judah to repent and seek Him out (55:6-13).

The wonderful pardon of God is promised to those who turn to Him. God indicates that His thoughts are above those of Judah (8-9). Even so, just as the rain from heaven produces the desired result, so God's promises in connection to the people of Israel will produce His desired end. They will be restored to the land, and they will experience God's wonderful blessing.

---

[169]Motyer, *The Prophecy of Isaiah*, pp. 452ff, has an excellent discussion of this passage.

Unit II—The Sinful Practices that Caused
God's Judgment (56—59)

A. God demands justice and obedience (56:1—57:21).

Up to this point Isaiah's message has grown ever more positive. As a matter of fact, since there is less and less said about idolatry, the context is almost exclusively the end times. But in this unit the old theme is picked up again. Chapter 56 decries the sinfulness of the people of God, and chapter 57 is an indictment of Canaanite religious practices. This is obviously eighth century material in the second part of the book. Just as we have comfort in the first part, so we have judgment and condemnation in the second part.

1. God promises blessing on those who keep His law and seek to do justice (56:1-5).

   The foreigner (*ben hannekar,* בֶּן־הַנֵּכָר) and the eunuch are singled out as ones who are often discriminated against. God says that they will be fruitful and otherwise experience the blessing of God if they will obey Him.

2. God promises to make His house a house of prayer for all peoples when He brings people from other places and joins them to Himself along with His regathered Israel (56:6-8).

3. God gives a pericope denouncing His leaders (56:9-12). They are called blind, dumb dogs, dreamers, shepherds without understanding. One has to wonder whether this chapter was to be applied to the people of Isaiah's day rather than to an eschatological era.

4. God addresses the evil people of Isaiah's day (57:1-10).

   The righteous man (הַצַּדִּיק *hassaddiq*) perishes, and no one pays attention. There is a situation of which Ecclesiastes speaks: the man who tries to obey God dies young and no one cares (57:1-2).

The wicked of that day, however, make fun of the righteous and of their God (57:4-10).

The description given here by Isaiah is that of the cult practices of the Canaanite religion. The high places and the open air chapels (the trees) were used for sexual immorality in the name of religion. Children were sacrificed to the god Moloch (Ahaz is accused of this particular sin, 2 Kings 16:3). On the one hand they practice fertility rites to produce children, and on the other hand they sacrificed them to Moloch. Such is the contradiction of paganism. The Israelites were confronted with this heinous evil from the earliest times. Here the indigenous religion is condemned. We do not yet see the astral religions (Queen of Heaven, Host of Heaven, etc.) that were apparently introduced under Assyrian/Babylonian influence and spoken against by Jeremiah. This should lead us to conclude that this prophecy was against the Jews living in Isaiah's day.

God tells them that, because they ignored Him to follow their idols, they can turn to their idols for help when they are in need (57:11-13).

Despite this awful picture of sin in the early part of the chapter, God promises in His grace to restore His people. Those who are of a contrite heart and a lowly spirit will know the blessing of God in that day (57:14-21).

B. Israel makes a false response to God's overtures (58:1-14).

1. He demands that the people be apprised of their sins (58:1).

2. The people say that they are seeking God (58:2-5).

Here is a people with all the external appearances of being spiritual. They are seeking God for decisions. They act like a nation that has done righteously. They seem to delight in the nearness of God. They are fasting, but they are committing sins as they fast. Because they are fulfilling external form, they think they should be blessed of God and do not understand why they are not being blessed. In actuality they are abusing their workmen. The externals of the fast are totally unacceptable to the Lord. They are not "an acceptable day to the Lord."

3.   God tells them what a proper fast should be (58:6-7).

In consonance with other prophets such as Hosea, Amos, and Malachi, Isaiah says that God is not interested in external ritual, unless it reflects internal devotion. It is to release people under a yoke; to share their plenty; to take care of the poor and homeless.

4.   God tells them of the blessing that will come with obedience (58:8-12).

What a beautiful picture of the way God rewards obedience to His word. Proper obedience will bring God's guidance, strength, rebuilding of ancient ruins and repairing of the streets.

5.   God admonishes them to keep the Sabbath properly (58:13-14).

This emphasis on the Sabbath seems to contradict what has just been said in the previous verses. It is necessary to understand the implication of these verses and to relate them to the verses on the fast. There is nothing wrong with keeping a fast any more than in offering the sacrifices. The problem is that the people were only going through the motions and were failing to have the proper attitude in the process. The same thing applies to the Sabbath. God tells them to keep the Sabbath properly and to delight in Him. This is the same message Jesus brings with regard to the Sabbath. He never condemns the Sabbath, only the abuse of the Sabbath. This understanding will avoid the apparent confusion.

C. God again presents the problem of sin (59:1-21).

1. The problem is not with God's lack of ability to save (59:1-2). (Cf. 50:1-3.)

    God says that He is perfectly capable of delivering Israel, but they are separating themselves from Him by their sinful practices.

2. The problem is Israel's sinful practice (59:4-8).

    This list should be compared with Romans 3. In chapter 57 the condemnation is against religious practices that are part of the Canaanite cult system. Here the sins condemned are more of a horizontal nature. The people are failing to treat their fellow human beings with justice and equity.

3. The result of these sinful practices is a life of futility (59:9-15a).

    Isaiah speaks for the faithful remnant much as does Daniel (Daniel 9), indicating that this sinful practice delineated in 3-8 has resulted in hopelessness, darkness, moaning, and lack of justice.

4. God moves in to bring salvation to Israel and to the entire world (59:15b-21).

    This section contains a marvelous promise of God's rectification of the world system. There is no human source for deliverance. Consequently, God himself must take on the role of a savior (the Hebrew uses a perfect tense because the action is viewed as completed in God's mind—a "prophetic perfect"). He arms Himself with the helmet of salvation, clothes Himself with vengeance, and proceeds to recompense the world for its rebellion against Him.

    When all this takes place, God will place His spirit upon Israel and His words will not depart from them, their children or their grand-children. This is reminiscent of the new covenant promised in Jer. 31:31.

Unit III—Looking to the New Heavens
and the New Earth (60—66)

A. There is going to be a glorious restoration of Israel (60:1-22).

1. Judah is told to rise and shine (60:1-3).

Judah's future glory is depicted under the imperative to "rise and shine for your light has come." When this light shines, nations will come to that light and to the brightness of their rising. This speaks of the kingdom blessing during which time Israel will be the center of things and nations will flow to her.

2. Sons and daughters will be restored from distant lands with great wealth (60:4-9).

In that glorious time (1) there will be a restoration of the dispersed ones of Israel (v. 4), (2) Israel will be restored in great wealth, (3) there will be an altar on which sacrifices will be made (v. 7), (4) the temple will be glorious. In that messianic age, there will be a return of the Jews who will worship at the altar in the temple.

3. The city and temple will be built and glorified (60:10-14).

This section speaks of walls, temple and city. In some sense it must refer to the return in 538 and the rebuilding of the walls by Nehemiah in 445, but the ultimate fulfillment has to go beyond that, for there will be unprecedented glory as all the peoples of the world come to this city and do obeisance to God.

4. The people will be blessed with the wealth of the world and the presence of God (60:15-22).

Isaiah 60	Revelation 21
They will go up with acceptance on My altar,	And I saw no temple in it. For the Lord God/Lamb are

and I shall glorify My glorious house.	the temple.
No sun for light by day. No moon to give light. Yahweh will be everlasting light.	City has no need of the sun or of the moon to shine upon it. For the glory of God has illumined it and its lamp is the Lamb (21:22-23).
No more mourning. All people righteous. Possess the land forever. Branch of My planting. Work of my hands. God will be glorified.	He shall wipe away every tear. There shall no longer be death. (21:4). Nations shall walk by its light. Kings shall bring their glory.

There is much similarity between Isaiah 60 and Revelation 21. There is also much similarity between Revelation 21:1 (new heavens and new earth) and Isaiah 65:17-25 (new heavens and new earth), but we must be careful not to confuse them just because they are similar. There is no temple in Revelation 21 whereas in this section of Isaiah, there is both sacrifice and temple. Revelation 21 is speaking of eternity *after* the Millennium and Isaiah 60-66 is talking about the messianic age or the Millennium itself. It will be blessedly true that a number of the same characteristics of eternity will prevail during the Millennium.

B.   The restoration of Israel must take place through the Servant (61:1-11).

1.   The Servant is given a commission and task (61:1-3).

Once more we have the abrupt appearance of the Servant after a section of great promise. The only way this promise can be carried out is through this unique servant. Jesus applies this section to Himself in Luke 4. It is interesting that Jesus breaks off reading at v. 2a. Christ in His first advent came to save not to judge. The second advent will be to set all things right. The idea of a day of vengeance and a year of restitution appears also in 34:8, 35:4, 63:4.

2. The Servant's work has a result (61:4-9).

   Rebuilding/reconstruction (61:4).
   Foreigners will serve them (61:5).
   Israel will be in a favored position (61:6).
   Israel repaid for her suffering (61:7).
   God's grace is the basis for the action (61:8-9).

3. A testimony of praise is given because of God's work of grace (61:10-11).

   Once again Isaiah, representing the remnant, praises God for His grace in delivering His people because the Lord God will cause righteousness and praise to spring up before all the nations.

C. A statement is given on the beloved status of Zion (62:1-12).

   1. God exults over Israel (62:1-5).

      This chapter is reminiscent of chapter 40. God promises that Jerusalem will be restored to a place of prominence in the world. She has been called "Forsaken" and "Desolate," but she will be called "My delight is in her" *ḥepsi-bah*: (חֶפְצִי־בָהּ) and "married" *beulah*: (בְּעוּלָה). This latter word is from Baal (בעל) which means lord, master, or husband. Here God is the husband and Israel the wife.

   6. God covenants with Israel that she will never be plundered again (62:6-9).

      God has placed watchmen on the walls of Jerusalem to remind Yahweh not to forget what He has promised. That is, that Jerusalem will be reestablished and will never again be oppressed by peoples around her.

7. God promises salvation to Israel (62:10-12).

    This section should be compared with 40:1-11. A highway is to be built there for the return of Israel, and God comes as a shepherd with His reward with Him. If this is taken literally, it tells us that there will be a returning of the people of Israel in faith to the land and in allegiance to the Lord Jesus Christ. If all this is to be applied to the church and to missionary activity in this age, then the language of the passage cannot be taken in its normal literary sense.

D. God speaks of His deliverance in the future and in the past (63:1-19).

    The unit of chapters 1-33 culminates with chapter 34 referencing Edom, Bozrah, Day of Vengeance/Year of Recompense, followed by chapter 35 a Garden for trusting God where the curse is removed. The unit of chapters 40-62 culminates likewise with chapter 63 referencing Edom, Bozrah, Day of Vengeance/Year of Recompense, followed by chapter 63:7-19 where the loving kindness of the Lord is revealed.

    1. God comes from Bozrah (63:1-6).

        Edom was an implacable enemy of the Jews (cf. Obadiah). Bozrah was a capital of Edom. The fact that God is coming from that direction, having trampled the winepress of His wrath, indicates that He is going to punish the enemies of Israel of which Edom is the epitome. This chapter should be related to chapter 34 where Edom is the center.

        Verse 44 speaks of the day of vengeance as does 61:2. It is the year of redemption. This refers to the redemption of Israel and God's judgment on the nations. A time is coming in which the Lord Jesus Christ will judge the nations.

        Verses 5-6 echo 59:16-20, that is, God is alone (here the Messiah) in the task of rectifying all the evil of the world. He was undaunted, however, and determined to carry out the divine injunction alone. This He will do successfully.

2. The remnant recognizes God's deliverance in the past (63:7-14).

Isaiah, speaking again for the remnant, talks about God's loving kindness (*hesed,* חֶסֶד). God has chosen Israel and in the past protected her. However, they rebelled against Him, and God became their enemy. In distress the people remembered God's gracious deliverance from Egypt. This unit should be related to chapter 35 where Israel is promised blessing after God judges Edom.

3. The remnant laments their rejection by God (63:15-18).

As they remember God's gracious acts in the past, they pray to Him in the present through the medium of a lament.

God is not active in Israel's behalf (63:15).
Their ancestors would deny them, but God must not (63:16).
A plea is uttered for God to return them (63:17-18).

At the time of this prayer, the temple is apparently in ruins. The prayer is for the restoration of the people to the land and the rebuilding of the temple. While this happened to a certain extent in 536-516, the ultimate fulfillment of these marvelous promises must yet be in the future.

E. The remnant prays for restoration (64:1-12).

1. They pray for God to manifest Himself (64:1-7).

The allusions are to times when God manifested Himself in a glorious fashion at the Exodus and later at Sinai. The remnant confesses that they are unclean before God and acknowledge the justice of their present situation.

2. They confess their sin and pray for deliverance (64:8-12).

The exile, the destruction of the temple and the waste of the land and the cities are their present lot. They pray for God to forgive and restore.

F.   God appeals to the faithful remnant and condemns the unbelieving elements of Israel (65:1-25).

1.   God has sought Israel, but they have not responded (65:1-7).

God has done everything necessary to reach the people of Israel, but they have rejected Him. They are a rebellious people and continue to follow sinful practices. Consequently God promises judgment on them. (Paul seems to be applying 65:1 to the Gentiles, saying that God allowed Himself to be found by those who did not seek Him. Certainly, the words allow that application, but the primary statement is that He allowed Israel to seek Him, but she refused.)[170]

2.   God promises grace to the remnant (65:8-12).

The doctrine of the remnant in Isaiah began in chapter 1 with the promise of the salvation of a few. Here it is reiterated under the imagery of grapes. Since there is a little good, the cluster will not be destroyed. The servants (note the plural) refer to the remnant who trust in the Lord.

3.   The result of obedience is blessing and of disobedience is cursing (65:13-16).

This section is unique in that an emphasis is placed on the plural concept of servanthood. The people of God are the redeemed remnant who are now in the ideal relationship with God as is His ideal servant (singular) throughout the book.

---

[170]Cf. E. J. Young, *Isaiah*, 3:501, who argues that verse 1 is Gentile and verse 2 is the Jew.

4. The ultimate blessing is the messianic age or the Millennium now delineated (65:17-25).

    There will be a new heavens and a new earth as in Revelation 21. (See footnote #153.) However, here it is in connection with the restoration of Israel to a land with a temple and sacrifice. This must refer to the work of God in connection with preparation for the removal of the curse from the land. Jerusalem will be created for rejoicing. Infant mortality will be gone, and it will not be unusual for people to be considered young at the age of 100. God promises to answer prayer, and there will be a time of unprecedented peace even in the animal kingdom (cf. Isa. 11; Rev. 20)

G. God gives a closing word contrasting His eternal person with man's finiteness and gives a final word on the glory of Zion (66:1-24).

    1. God takes up the theme of His infiniteness (66:1-2).

        No mere temple can hold an omnipresent God. God is interested in people who have a humble and contrite spirit and a willingness to obey His word.

    2. God promises judgment on unbelievers (66:3-6).

        They have sacrificed, but only externally and therefore there is no value in the sacrifice for them. They have persecuted those Jews who did want to believe. Therefore, God is going to judge them.

    3. God promises the restoration of Israel (66:7-17).

        Under the imagery of a woman giving birth, He promises the rebirth of Israel. He promises a time of great peace and prosperity. He promises judgment on His enemies.

4. God declares that He will be glorified among the nations (66:18-24).

All nations will see His glory. He will bring survivors to them who will declare His glory. Who are these survivors? Jewish missionaries who have believed in the Lord? They will bring the Jewish remnant from distant places to Jerusalem. There will be perpetuity for the children of Israel just as there is of the new heavens and the new earth. People will come and bow down before the Lord. There they will see the end of those who rebel against God. They will be suffering eternal torment.[171]

---

[171]Note Jesus' allusion to this verse in speaking of eternal torment in Mark 9:48.

Historical Background of the Seventh/Sixth Centuries

I.   The Assyrian Decline

The great Assyrian juggernaut was grinding to a halt. The rise of Assyrian power had begun in the ninth century under such kings as Ashurnasirpal II (884-859) and Shalmaneser III (859-824). These kings advanced as far as middle Syria without being able to establish lasting control there. Shalmaneser tells of his battle with a Syrian coalition that included Ahab king of Israel. Jehu paid tribute to that same king and has the dubious honor of appearing on the black obelisk of Shalmaneser bowing his face to the ground.

A succession of great Assyrian conquerors began with Tiglath-Pileser III (744-727) (Pul in the Bible). They conquered Syria and Palestine, as well as other lands, and undertook frequent campaigns there. They include Shalmaneser V (727-722) who began the deportation of Samaria, Sargon II (722-705) who completed the deportation, Sennacherib (704-681) who attacked Hezekiah and says "I shut up Hezekiah the Jew like a bird in a cage," and Esarhaddon (681-669) who undertook several campaigns against Egypt and occupied the Delta and the old royal city of Memphis.

The last goal of Assyrian expansion, the overthrow of Egypt, was brought very close. Esarhaddon's son and successor, Ashurbanipal (669-631) could indeed still garrison the upper Egyptian royal city of Thebes, but, under him, the Egyptian adventure soon came to an end, and the decline of the Assyrian might began.

II. The Rise of Babylon (625-609 BC).

Isaiah's great grandfather, Hezekiah, had welcomed ambassadors from the ambitious Chaldean, Merodach Baladan (Isa. 39; 2 Kings 20:12-19). The Chaldeans settled early in southern Mesopotamia at the head of the Persian Gulf (they are first met in the records around the beginning of the first millennium). The tribe from which Merodach Baladan came was situated in Bit Yakin. Because he was Chaldean, as were his better known descendants Nabopolassar and Nebuchadnezzar, the empire and the language were called Chaldean. However, the language of diplomacy used by the Assyrians (2 Kings 18:26) was Aramaic, the speech of a people related to the Chaldeans who were situated east of the Tigris river.

The Chaldeans were apparently not welcomed by the Babylonians, but they were nonetheless able to ensconce themselves as kings after decades of skirmishing with the Assyrians. Finally, as the Assyrian government became weak, Nabopolassar was able to assert his independence and begin to attack the Assyrians.

The Egyptians, once ruled by the Assyrians but now independent, saw the wisdom of defending a weak Assyria against a rising Babylonian menace. The Scythians likewise supported the Assyrians, but for some reason (prospect of plunder perhaps) were persuaded to join the Medes and the Chaldeans in the assault on the capital Nineveh in 612 BC A few of the Assyrians escaped and fled to Haran where Ashur-uballit was appointed the king. He waited for the Babylonian attack on the fort at Haran.

Nabopolassar attacked the Assyrians in 609 BC The Assyrians apparently took the field and the Babylonians captured Haran. The Egyptians under Necho II joined forces with the Assyrians, but were defeated by the Babylonians and their allies. The struggle apparently continued for another five years. Finally the Babylonians defeated the Egyptians at Carchemish and their control of Syria was firm.

King Josiah, following the long standing policy initiated by his grand-father, tried to interdict Necho at Megiddo to prevent him from going to the side of Assyria. (KJV in 2 Kings 23:29 says that Necho went up against the king of Assyria. The Hebrew is *'al*, עַל, which normally means "against" but can also mean "adjacent to." Here it must mean "to the side of" as in *NASB*). As a result, Josiah was killed and his son Jehoahaz was put on the throne. This was in 609 BC. Pharaoh Necho deposed and deported Jehoahaz after just three months reign and placed his brother, Jehoiakim, on the throne. Daniel says that Nebuchadnezzar attacked the city of Jerusalem and deported people in the third year of Jehoiakim.[172] Jeremiah 25:1 indicates that the first year of Nebuchad-nezzar is the fourth year of Jehoiakim. The precise synchronism of these dates is difficult because of the problem of ante- and post-dating systems in vogue at that time.

Jehoiakim submitted to Nebuchadnezzar for three years (2 Kings 24:1) and then rebelled. 2 Chron. 36:6 says that Nebuchadnezzar bound Jehoiakim in fetters to bring him to Babylon. This was his first foray against Jerusalem. Either he did not carry out his threat to deport Jehoiakim or he took him to Babylon and then returned him to Jerusa-lem. The former is more likely since there is no evidence of a viceroy governing until Jehoiakim returned. D. J. Wiseman[173] says, "Jehoiakim may have been personally required to go to Babylon to take part in the victory celebrations as a conquered and vassal king <2 Ch. 36:6> as had Manasseh in the days of Esarhaddon <2 Ch. 33:11>." Yahweh sent local groups against Jehoiakim to punish him. It was no doubt Nebuchad-nezzar who was the human instrument to incite them because he was not yet able to attend the matter himself. By the time Nebuchadnezzar

---

[172]For a discussion of this problem, see R. D. Wilson, *Studies in Daniel*. More recently, Wiseman and Kitchen, *Notes on Some Problems in the Book of Daniel.*

[173]D. J. Wiseman, *Notes on Some Problems in the Book of Daniel*, 18.

arrived, Jehoiakim was dead and his eighteen-year old son Jehoiachin was on the throne to capitulate to Babylon. This event is dated at 597 BC

Zedekiah ruled for eleven years as regent (on the probably valid assumption that Jehoiachin was considered the king even though in exile. He may have been held as a hostage to guarantee loyalty on the part of the Jews in Jerusalem) but was lured into a rebellion against Babylon in 588 (2 Kings 25:1) against the advice of Jeremiah (Jer 27). Nebuchadnezzar besieged the city and took it in 586.

Kings tells us that Evil-Merodach (Ewal Marduk) restored Jehoiachin to favor in the thirty-seventh year of his captivity in twentieth-seventh day of the twelfth month (2 Kings 25:27). This would be the year 560 BC The elevation of Jehoiachin is referred to in two administrative tablets.[174]

The Babylonian Empire lasted less than a century. In 539 Cyrus came into Babylon virtually unresisted by a populace disenchanted with King Nabonidus and his viceroy Belshazzar. The Persian policy of dealing with expatriates was benevolent, and a decree was issued in 538 allowing captive people to return to their homelands with their gods. The Jews were allowed to return with the temple vessels.[175]

---

[174]*ANET*, p. 308.

[175]This historical recapitulation is based on a number of works, including *The Cambridge Ancient History* and *The Babylonian Chronicle.*

SEVENTH/SIXTH CENTURY PROPHETS AND THEIR WORLD

Decade	Prophet	Judah	Assyria	Babylonia	Egypt	Persia
690		Manasseh 696-642				
680			Esarhaddon 681-669	Continued attempts by Chaldean		
670				Tribes to take		
			Ashurbanipal 669-631	Babylon and rebel against		
660	J O Z J H N D E e b e o a a a z r a p e b h n e			Assyria		
650	e d h l a u i k m i a k m e i					
	i a n k l e	Amon 642-640				
640	a h i u l h a k h	Josiah 640-609				
630				Nabopolassar 625-605	*Medes* Cyaxares 625-585	
620	?					
610		Jehoahaz 609	Sinsariskun 631-612	Nineveh defeated 612 Nebuchadnezzar 605-562	Necho fought with Assyria Killed Josiah 609	
600		Jehoiakim 609-597 Jehoiachin 597 Zedekiah	Ashuruballit 612-609 Final defeat in west 605			
590		597-586 Gedaliah			Astyages 585-550	
570				Evil Merodach 562-560		
560		Jehoiachin elevated		Neriglissar 560-556		
550				Nabonidus 556-539 (Belshazzar)	*Persians* Cyrus 558-529 Entered Bab.539	
540					Cyrus' Edict 538	
530		Zerubbabel Temple begun 536			Cambyses 529-522 Darius I 522-486	

520	Haggai/Zechariah	Temple finished 516
		Xerxes 486-465
510	Malachi	Artaxerxes I 465-424

Notes on the Book of Jeremiah

I.   The Historical Era of Josiah (640-609 BC)

Little Josiah became king of Judah at the age of eight. His father, Amon, had been assassinated at the age of 24 after two years of rule. Amon had followed the religious lifestyle of his father, Manasseh, who ruled long (55 years) and lived wickedly. In spite of a repentant attitude in his last years after having been defeated and deported by the Assyrians to Babylon,[176] Manasseh left a legacy of rebellion against the Lord made worse by the length of his reign. In God's sovereignty this wicked work was to be countered by the godly young prince who acted first under tutors and later on his own to restore godly practices in Judah.

In his eighth year (632) he began "to seek the God of his father David" (2 Chron 34:3). In his twelfth year (628) at the age of twenty, he began the reform movement that was to prove so successful. During this purge, Chronicles tells us, he went into the cities of Manasseh, Ephraim, Simeon and Naphtali and tore down their images. This is Assyrian territory. It could be that the Assyrians would tolerate religious activity on the part of a Judean King (as messengers of Hezekiah had gone north to announce the great Passover), but this activity is too blatant for anything that mild. This must indicate some effort on the part of Josiah to extend political control as well. Jeremiah received his call to the prophetic ministry one year later in 627. Ashurbanipal died in 626 or two

---

[176]See *ANET*, p. 291.

years after the beginning of the reform movement complaining of all the misery and misfortune that had befallen him.[177]

Internal troubles resulted in succession squabbles. Ashur-etil-ilani, Ashurbanipal's heir apparent, had to fight for the throne. Babylonia, until now a province of Assyria, broke away under the Chaldean Nabopolassar in 626 when Ashurbanipal died and began fighting Assyria upon Nabopolassar's accession in 625.

An even more extensive reform was carried out in Josiah's eighteenth year (622) during which the law book was found that called for even greater repentance. He again made a foray into the north, tearing down the altar built at Bethel by Jeroboam. He also removed all the houses of the high places that were in the cities of Samaria. A great Passover was held, but except for a passing comment (2 Chron. 35:18), there is no mention of participation by the northern Israelites. The confusion going on in Assyria prevented effective control of the Assyrian territory of Samaria and allowed Josiah to move somewhat at will.

II.   The Man, Jeremiah

Jeremiah is better known than most prophets because of the many biographical sections in the book. We have greater insight into his personality, his struggles, and his commitment to the Lord who called him than in any other Old Testament prophet.

Jeremiah was born in the village of Anathoth north of Jerusalem and was the son of Hilkiah who was a priest. This priestly family was probably descended from Abiathar whom Solomon banished to Anathoth because he supported Adonijah (1 Kings 2:26). Jeremiah was apparently young when he was called (1:6). His ministry spanned forty years from the

---

[177]See Olmstead, *History of Assyria*, p. 414.

thirteenth year of Josiah to sometime after the destruction of Jerusalem in 586 BC[178]

III. The Milieu

This historical background given above describes the situation in which Jeremiah ministered. He began in the thirteenth year of Josiah's reign and so shared in the early period of reform. With Josiah's death, Jeremiah's ministry became increasingly difficult, since there was no support from the throne. In spite of the fact that his early prophecies proved true, he was still treated roughly when he tried to turn the minds of the officials, priests and people to the Lord and to get them to submit to inevitable adversity under Nebuchadnezzar.

5. The Call Theme in Jeremiah

When God calls Jeremiah to the prophetic ministry, he tells him there will be six negative and two positive components in his message: to tear down, destroy, pluck up, and root out and to build and to plant (1:10). These phrases are reiterated in full or in part several times in the book. At least four of the words appear in 1:10; 18:7,9; 24:6; 31:28; 42:10. Between one and three occur in 12:14-17; 31:4,5; 31:40; 32:41; 33:7; 45:4.

6. The Text of Jeremiah

The LXX text of Jeremiah is one eighth shorter than the Hebrew text underlying our English translations. In addition there is somewhat of a different arrangement of material (e.g., the oracles against the nations are situated in a different place than in the Masoretic Text). Qumran frag-ments support a reading unique to the LXX and lead to

---

[178]See LaSor, *et al.* Old Testament *Survey*, 403, 404 and Dillard and Longman, *An Old Testament Introduction* for a discussion.

an inference that there was a Hebrew *Vorlage* (or underlying text) for the Greek translation. But we must stress that it is only an inference since all we have are a few fragments (4QJer[b]).[179] I believe we must deal with these differences as text critical problems (some want to talk about a developing canon, but canon speaks of the book, whereas textual criticism speaks of the changes in the text.)

That the Book of Jeremiah is a compilation of sources written and preached at different times is clear from the text itself. Chapter 25:13 indicates that Jeremiah wrote a "book" of prophecies against the nations. The exiled Jews hear from Jeremiah in a letter written and sent by "diplomatic pouch" that contains a response and a response to the res-ponse (29). The famous "book of comfort" is written at the command of Yahweh (32:2). The large scroll written to present the judgments of God is in chapter 36 where it was written and rewritten. Finally in 51:60 we read that "Jeremiah wrote in a single scroll all the calamity which would come upon Babylon..." All these sub units must have circulated independently. Perhaps Jeremiah with Baruch's help assembled the Book in Egypt where its goal now is to instruct the people of God in exile.

7. The Structure of the Book of Jeremiah.[180]

A. Chapters 1—29

1. It seems that Jeremiah wants us to understand that the Judeans had ample opportunity to repent and thus avoid subjection. This is especially illustrated in the temple sermon (chapter 7) and in chapters 17-18. In the potter imagery, the nation that chooses to

---

[179]See J. Gerald Janzen, *Studies in the Text of Jeremiah*, for a discussion.

[180]For an excellent overall discussion of the problems of the structure of the book of Jeremiah, see D. R. Jones, *Jeremiah,* pp. 18-41.

repent will avoid reshaping in judgment. God will change his mind about the plans for that nation.

2. Moving from the potter in chapter 18 to the pot in chapter 19 is an abrupt change. The smashed pot indicates that judgment is inevitable. Even if they were to repent now, they would only preserve their lives. Submission to Babylon is now unavoidable.[181]

JEREMIAH STRUCTURE
1-29

Repent!	**Potter** **Pot**	**Pashhur #1** **Pashhur #2**	**Bad Leaders**
1-18	19	20-21	21B-23

God's will: Exile

Prophets
Priests
Kings
Branch/Messiah

24 Good/Bad Figs
25 23 Years of Preaching (Rejected)
26 Temple Sermon (Religious)
27-28 Yoke Broken (Rejected)
29 Letter: Exile is God's Will

3. Chapters 20 and 21a are to be viewed together. Chapter 20 represents official rejection of Jeremiah. Pashhur ben Immer persecutes

---

[181]J. G. McConville, "Jeremiah: Prophet and Book," *TynBul* 42:1 (1991) 80-95, shows that texts containing preaching for repentance and inability to repent exist side by side. This is juxtaposed later by Jeremiah. The date for repentance preaching is prior to 597 (I would say 605) and "the necessity of the exile" preaching during Zedekiah's rule.

Jeremiah and denies his message. However, chapter 21 (from after 588 or several years later) shows that Jeremiah's message was fulfilled when another Pashhur (ben Melchiah) entreats Jeremiah to pray for the city, (now under siege by Babylon).

4. Chapters 21b-23 introduce a new element: the leaders of Israel have failed in their responsibility and Judah has suffered. First it is the kings and finally it is the prophets. But in between is the marvelous message of hope of a coming Branch. As in Isaiah, this ideal king will judge with equity and will deliver the people of God.

5. Chapter 24 teaches that the Jews who went into exile in 597 are the good figs, not in the sense that they are more moral, but that God's purpose has been fulfilled.

6. Chapter 25 is a recap of the twenty-three years of preaching, showing that there was ample opportunity to repent, but that the people refused to do so.

7. Chapter 26 is an abbreviation of the temple sermon of chapter 7 with the addition of the persecution and threat of death to Jeremiah. This again shows that there was a clear offer of repentance and avoidance of judgment, but it was rejected.

8. Chapter 27 is the yoke chapter. The Judeans no longer have the option of avoiding subjection; their only option now is to submit to Nebuchadnezzar's yoke. The alliance into which Zedekiah is entering is futile because it is not the will of Yahweh.

9. Chapter 28 is the breaking of the yoke by Hananiah, illustrating the official rejection of Jeremiah's message. His judgment for doing so is death.

10. Chapter 29 is a letter to the exiles urging them to accept Yahweh's will and settle down. The false hope raised by the prophets will only bring pain. They will be there seventy years.

B. Chapters 30—45

    1. Jeremiah 30-33 is one of the clearest units in the book. Here the prophet has collected messages preached over some period of time containing messages of hope and consolation. They are placed here to show that in spite of the judgment of God brought upon his people, that there is still a future for Israel. The New Covenant, especially, gives great hope for the future of Israel. The context clearly calls for the seed of Abraham to be restored in the Eschaton. Chapter 32 is a historical account, but it is in the section on hope, because Jeremiah is instructed by Yahweh to buy a piece of land while the city is under siege! This teaches that the "real estate" will again prove to be valuable. Chapter 33 harks back to the Davidic Covenant and shows that the "Branch" spoken of in chapter 23 will rule and reign in equity and justice.

    2. Chapters 34-38 are a series of "Examples" of why the Judeans had to go into exile. Chapter 34 shows how the covenant of God was broken (on the freeing of slaves) and even the covenant they had made was broken. Chapter 35 is an example of people who kept the covenant of their ancestor, Jonadab, and thus shamed the Judeans. Chapter 36 is an example of the king of Judah flagrantly rejecting the word of God by burning it in the fire. A contrast is being drawn with the response of Josiah to the scroll of the law and that of his son Jehoiakim to the scroll of the prophet. Chapters 37-38 provide two examples of the rejection of God's spokesman, Jeremiah. In 37 he is called a traitor and in 38 he is put into the pit to die.

    3. We come back to a historical unit in chronological order in chapters 39-44. All the prophecies of Jeremiah about the fall of the city are fulfilled. The people continue to reject the word of the prophet even though he has been fully vindicated as a true prophet of Yahweh. They go to Egypt after the violent death of Gedaliah and Jeremiah continues to prophesy in the Delta region. It was presume-ably

sometime after this in Egypt that Jeremiah and Baruch compiled his messages of the previous forty or so years.

Chapter 45 is in a unique position. The time of the prophecy is 605 when Jeremiah wrote the scroll that Jehoiakim burned (chapter 36). Why is it placed last? It forms an appendix, much as do the oracles against the nations (46-51). I am treating it as a negative conclusion: Jeremiah and Baruch are called upon to preach to a God-rejecting people. Their task will not be easy. In the traumatic experience of chapter 36, Baruch became discouraged with the task. God tells him through Jeremiah not to be discouraged. I suspect this chapter stands here to say, "All the prophetic ministry of Jeremiah from 627 to 586 and afterward was rejected, but God's purposes will none-the-less stand. Therefore, Baruch must not be discouraged."

JEREMIAH STRUCTURE
30-45

Book of Comfort	Examples	Prophecy Fulfilled Jerusalem Falls
30-33	34-38	39-45
30 Trouble, but Blessing	34 Covenant Breaking	40 City Destroyed
31 Trouble, but New Covenant	35 Covenant Keeping	41 Gedaliah's Appointment
32 Valuable Property	36 Rejecting the Word of God	42 Gedaliah's Murder
33 David Covenant	37 Rejecting the Prophet	43 To Egypt (Still Rejecting)
	38 Rejecting the Prophet	44 Message in Egypt
		45 Baruch Defeated

C.   Chapters 46—52

1.   Jeremiah gave various oracles against several nations in the course of his ministry. Chapter 26 is a good example of one of those oracles. There Jeremiah is told to make the nations drink the wine of God's wrath. Those nations include: Judah, Egypt, Uz, Philistines, Edom, Moab, Ammon, Tyre, Sidon, Dedan, Tema, Buz, Arabia, Zimri, Elam, Media, Kings of the North, Sheshach (Babylon). As a matter of fact, chapters 46-51 are placed after the middle of 26:13 in the Septuagint. In the Hebrew text, they are treated as an appendix at the end of the book.

STRUCTURE OF JEREMIAH (46-52)

46 EGYPT
  47 PHILISTIA
    48 MOAB**
      49A AMMON**
        49B EDOM**
          49C DAMASCUS
            49D KEDAR AND HAZOR
            49E ELAM
              50-51 BABYLON

**PRESENT AT THE CONSPIRACY

CONCLUDING APPENDICES

SIEGE 52:1-26
TEMPLE 52:17-23
EXECUTION OF LEADERS 52:24-27 (39:5-6)
DEPORTATION 52:28-30
ELEVATION OF JEHIACHIN 52:31-34

2. Egypt is the first nation to receive an oracle and Babylon is the last. As in Isaiah, God wants His people to understand that He is in charge of the universe and determines the events and outcomes of all peoples. Egypt, at first an enemy but later an ally, is shown in 605 BC to be under God's judgment, for Babylon will defeat her at Carchemish. But Babylon, the nemesis of all nations and God's servant for judgment, will one day in turn be judged. Some of the material comes from after 586 and reflects the exile. From that exile, God will deliver his people and judge Babylon. Likewise all the other nations will be defeated sooner or later. Therefore, the puny plans of man are a waste of time.

3. Finally, chapter 52 is an appendix to show the ultimate outcome of all God's work concerning his people Judah. The city and temple were destroyed, the leadership was judged by Babylon for rebelling, people were taken into captivity, and finally, even the king in exile, Jehoiachin was elevated by Evil Merodach (Ewal Marduk) in 560 BC Thus the skein of prophecy is spun out. God's purposes have triumphed over all the plans of man. Ultimately, Judah will be restored both in 539 and in the Eschaton. Then God's plans for Israel will be joyously fulfilled.

VII. Outline Notes

The outline of Jeremiah is difficult because the book is not constructed chronologically. Consequently, events are out of order.[182] The messages of Jeremiah were brought into a continuous whole sometime after the last one had been delivered. The sermons and speeches delivered at different times and under different circumstances over some thirty years have been brought together in this final form with a message: Judah deserves to be punished. Had she repented in the earlier years, the punishment could

---

[182]See, e.g., J. B. Payne, "The Arrangement of Jeremiah's Prophecies," *BETS* (now *JETS*) 7:4 (1964):120-130.

have been averted. However, with the passing of time and the hardening of hearts, the captivity became inevitable. As a completed whole, the book of Jeremiah is an apologetic for God's action against and in behalf of His people. The argument of the book progresses from the call of Jeremiah in chapter 1 to the removal to Egypt after his message had again been rejected in Chapter 43.

A. Undated prophecies and events showing that Judah had ample warning to repent (1:1—17:27).

   1. Jeremiah is called to the prophetic ministry and given a message to preach to Israel (1:1-19).

       The historical note is given on Jeremiah's ancestry and indicates that he prophesied from the thirteenth year of Josiah (627 BC) until the eleventh year of Zedekiah (586 BC). We know that he also prophesied sometime after the fall of the city and was taken to Egypt (1:1-3).

       God sovereignly called Jeremiah to be a prophet before he was even born. In response to Jeremiah's protestations that he is too young, (*na'ar*, נַעַר), God promised to be with him. In spite of that promise, Jeremiah suffered greatly, yet God was with him throughout his ordeal.

       The message of Jeremiah is given in 9-19. He is "to root out, pull down, destroy, throw down, build and plant." There are four negative issues and two positive ones. Watch for these to recur throughout the book (1:9-10).[183]

       Through two symbols God promises to bring judgment on Judah. The first is an almond rod (*shaqed*, שָׁקֵד). By a pun on the word the

_____

[183]All six words occur in 1:10 and 31:28; four or five occur in 18:7, 9; 24:6; 42:10; some of the words occur in 12:14-17; 31:4, 5, 40; 32:41; 33:7; 45:4.

Lord says, "I will hasten (*shoqed*, שֹׁקֵד) my word to do it." The second symbol is a seething pot with its opening toward the north. This indicates that God is going to call the nations of the north against Judah (1:11-16).[184]

Jeremiah is now told to gird himself up and begin prophesying. Kings, princes, priests and people will resist him. Yet God promises that he will prevail over them all (1:17-10).

2. Jeremiah pleads with backslidden Judah to repent (2:1-37).

Looking back to the wilderness experience as a time in the early history of Judah, God reminds them of His devotion to her. Israel was like the first fruits that belong to the Lord. Anyone who interfered with her became guilty (2:1-3).

The Lord asks them what He has done that they are finding fault with Him. He points out that the priests are not asking "Where is Yahweh"; those who handle the law do not know Him; the rulers transgress against Him; and the prophets are prophesying through the pagan god Baal (2:4-8).

The Lord enters a court case with them again (*riv*, רִיב). He calls on all the witnesses of foreign countries to find if anyone has ever left their gods as Judah as left her God. Not only have they forsaken Him, the fountain of living waters, but also they have hewn out cisterns for themselves (2:9-13).

"Israel" here refers to the northern kingdom that went into exile shortly after Jeremiah began prophesying (722 BC). The "you" refers to Judah who has suffered at the hands of Egypt (this must reflect a

---

[184]See the pictures of the siege of Lachish in *ANEP* for an illustration of this activity.

period early in the reign of Jehoiakim rather than Josiah). She goes to Egypt and Assyria (looking for gods), but they have forsaken the Lord (2:14-19).

Judah's apostasy is reflected in the imagery of an ox that refuses to serve under the yoke; as a choice vine that refuses to produce fruit; as a stained person who cannot be cleaned with the strongest detergents; and as a wild donkey in heat who pursues her lovers (2:20-25).

Judah, says God, is ashamed of her idolatrous practice. The word shame (*bosheth,* בֹּשֶׁת) often has the connotation of embarrassed, that is, they let Judah down in a time of need. God demands that Judah call on her idols for deliverance if she believes they can help her. There are as many gods as there are cities in Judah (2:26-28).[185]

The Lord insists that they tell Him why they are contending with Him. He has struck them, but it has not helped. It is not normal for people to forget God, but they have forgotten their God. They were committing the same sins condemned a century before by Amos, Hosea and Isaiah, yet they refused to admit their sin. The historical situation may refer to Assyria prior to 609 when Josiah may have been trying to work out an arrangement with Assyria, but she fell to Babylon. Now they seem to be going to Egypt for help against Babylon (2:29-37).

3.   God appeals to His adulterous wife to repent (3:1—4:4).

The *NASB* has construed the literary structure of chapter 3 as a composition containing poetry (1-5, 11-14, 19-23) and prose (6-10, 15-18, 24-25).[186] The critics will argue that the prose sections are

---

[185]See K. Kenyon, *Digging up Jerusalem,* for a discussion of the idolatry indicated in her excavations.

[186]But see Thompson, *Jeremiah,* who arranges it slightly differently and thus

later "deuteronomistic" additions to Jeremiah's poetic preaching. Thompson argues that like Shakespeare, Jeremiah could have written both prose and poetry.[187] The difference in style may show that Jeremiah preached these passages at different times and later edited them into a continuous whole. The unity of the passage is shown by the concept of divorce (3:1 and 8), "returning" or "turning" (*shub,* שׁוּב: 3:1,1, 7, 7, 10, 12, 14, 14, 19, 22, 22), and calling God "Father" (3:4 and 19).

The Lord appeals to the Deuteronomic law against a husband divorcing his wife and later taking her back again (Deut. 24:1-4). Since that is the law, would it not be improper for Yahweh to take Israel back after she has committed adultery? The phrase "Yet turn to me" is debated (*veshob 'eli,* וְשׁוֹב אֵלִי). Does it mean, as *NASB* implies, "since you have committed adultery, do you think you can return to me?" Or is it be taken as an imperative, "Yet [in spite of this] return to me!" God most assuredly will take Judah back as a demonstration of His grace (cf. Hosea 1-3, Isa. 50:1), but only when there is genuine repentance and not the superficial response recounted in this chapter. If Judah will sincerely repent, He will override His Deuteronomic law in His dealings with Israel (3:1).

Jeremiah charges them with extensive idolatry. He likens them to an Arab sitting along the road. As a result God has withheld the former rains (showers: Oct/Nov) and the latter rains (spring: Mar/Apr). In spite of this Judah is brazen like a harlot and refuses to be ashamed. Under pressure, they have called God "Father" and "friend"; they have prayed that He would not be forever angry. But in spite of this speech, they have done all the evil they were able to do (3:2-5).

---

shows the tenuousness of dissecting this literature.

[187]Ibid.

Yahweh compares Judah to her sister Israel and says that Israel comes off looking better. He cries out to Israel to return to Him because He is gracious. He promises to return them to Zion (3:6-14).

The promise of a return brings Jeremiah to the message on the shepherds whom God will raise up to them (cf. chapter 23); Yahweh speaks of His new covenant which will not need the ark; He speaks of Jerusalem as the "throne of the Lord"; and finally He speaks of the unity that will exist between Israel and Judah (3:15-18).

Jeremiah returns to poetry to appeal further to Israel who has now been judged and sent into exile. God's desire is to set them as sons in his pleasant land, but they have departed from Yahweh like a treacherous wife. The result is "weeping and supplication" because of their captivity. The "hills" (other countries) cannot help them; only Yahweh can be the salvation of Israel. Verses 24-25 are construed as poetry in BHS and Thompson, but as prose in *NASB*. These verses constitute a confession for Israel acknowledging their sin. Some would argue that these verses might address Josiah's attempts to extend the reform into the north (2 Kings 23:15-20). In any event they reflect the deep concern of Jeremiah for the Northern Kingdom and his expectation of their restoration with Judah (3:19-25).

Yahweh appeals to Israel to return with the promise that the blessings of the Abrahamic covenant will be theirs (nations will bless themselves in Israel: *hithbareku,* הִתְבָּרְכוּ). To Judah and Jerusalem He also appeals for repentance. They are urged under the similes of sowing and circumcision to repent so that God's wrath might not break out on them (4:1-4).

4. Yahweh promises destruction of Judah (4:5—6:30).

Yahweh tells Judah to prepare for war by going into the fortified cities because He is going to bring devastation from the north (this of course refers to Babylon) that will lay the land of Judah waste. The mind of the king, princes, priests and prophets will be astounded (4:5-9).

Jeremiah's statement in 4:10 is startling. The direct, stark statement to God sounds blasphemous until we get to understand Jeremiah and realize that he had an intense and close relationship with his Lord. As such he poured out his anguished heart on more than one occasion. Who is telling Judah she will have peace? It can only be the false prophets who continuously speak a lie in the face of Jeremiah's predictions (6:14; 14:13; 23:16-17). "Throat" is the translation of *nepesh* (נֶפֶשׁ) which normally means "soul" or "life." The meaning of "throat" is attested in Ugaritic (4:5-10).[188]

In spite of the word of false prophets, God promises to come against Judah in judgment. This statement is in the first person, but the prophet adds another verse in the third person to say that God will come against Jerusalem in chariots like a whirlwind (4:11-13).

Yahweh appeals again for repentance and promises judgment from the north to punish them for their sin (4:14-18).

Jeremiah is known as the "weeping prophet," and these verses support that identification. Jeremiah laments the destruction of his people. At no point did Jeremiah take delight in the destruction of his people in spite of the way they treated him. To Jeremiah's lament is appended a statement of Yahweh that His people are foolish. Perhaps this is God gently chiding Jeremiah with the truth that the judgment is deserved (4:19-22).

Jeremiah in a series of "I looked" statements (*raithi,* רָאִיתִי of the devastated earth that Yahweh is going to judge (4:23-26).

---

[188]Gordon, *Ugaritic Text Book—Glossary*, p. p. 446.

Yahweh responds by saying that He will indeed bring devastation upon Judah, and yet, He promises that it will not be a complete devastation. Furthermore, Judah will not be able to allay the judgment by primping. She will be despised by her lovers and will cry out in distress (4:27-31).

The reason for the judgment is amplified by the analogy of Sodom and Gomorrah. If Yahweh can find anyone truly faithful in Jerusalem, He will spare Jerusalem from judgment. On the contrary, they have refused to repent (5:1-3).

Jeremiah intercedes for the people by arguing that the poor do not understand the way of the Lord. He expects the great ones (the leaders) to be responsive, but they have broken the yoke of their obedience to Yahweh. As a result judgment must come upon them (5:4-6).

Yahweh argues that there is no basis for forgiveness since they refuse to repent and carry out the fertility practices in real life (5:7-9).

God says that the branches of sin are to be removed from His vineyard. Both houses of Israel have lied by denying that God could ever judge them for their sin. Consequently, the words of Jeremiah are going to be like a fire as he prophesies the coming of a powerful, ferocious nation to destroy them.[189] An addendum is given again that God's judgment will not be final. There is hope, but only after they have served strangers in a land not theirs (5:14-19).

---

[189]The foe from the north even in this earlier period is no doubt Babylon. The old view that it was the Scythian invasion mentioned by Herodotus is not now generally accepted. See Thompson, *The Book of Jeremiah*, pp. 156-16, for a discussion.

Yahweh speaks in terms that we have seen before in His prophets. He is the creator, the one who sets the boundaries of the sea, brings rain, appoints seasons and otherwise shows Himself to be the sovereign God. Yet Israel has turned against Him and refuses to live righteously. Consequently, they must be judged. To compound the egregious nature of their sin, the prophets are false, the priests ignore God in their activity, and the people like it this way (5:20-31).

The motif of the sounding of the trumpet is given again (cf. 4:5ff). The destruction from the north is again promised. Judah will be devastated so that shepherds will graze their flocks there. The reason for this siege is that Jerusalem maintains wickedness and refuses to let go of it (6:1-8).

Under the imagery of grape pickers, God says that the remnant of Israel will be gleaned. The command of 6:9 was probably directed to Jeremiah. God is telling him to preach again to what is left in case he has missed someone. Jeremiah complains that there is no one else left to whom he could speak who would respond to his message. Israel in this context must refer to the people of God in general and not to the northern kingdom. Jeremiah indicates weariness with being rejected when he preaches Yahweh's message, and he calls upon God to carry out His judgment. God's response is melded into Jeremiah's statement. He says He will indeed judge the people because they live wickedly. The prophets will be judged because they are crying "Peace" when judgment is coming (6:9-15).

God cries out for the people to obey Him, but they refuse. He sets a watchman (prophets) but they refuse to listen, He blows the trumpet, but they refuse to hear it. Therefore He will judge them. Jeremiah picks up the theme already heard in Amos, Hosea and Isaiah that empty ritual will have no impact on God. Their sacrifices are not pleasing to Him (16-21).

The foe from the north is again presented. This description of a fierce people could refer to most any nation in those days, since war was conducted without quarter by all those practicing it (6:22-26).

This section on the coming judgment of God is closed with Yahweh's statement to Jeremiah under the simile of an assayer or one who tests metals. Jeremiah's job is to test the character of people to see how they will respond and to separate the dross from the real metal. Unfortunately, they refuse to respond, and so are considered by God to be "rejected silver," in other words all dross. As a result, God has rejected them (6:27-30).

5. Jeremiah delivers his famous temple sermon (7:1-8:3).

Jeremiah attacks the religiosity of the people because they were taking refuge in a superficial response to Yahweh possibly brought about forcibly by Josiah. They were mixing worship of Yahweh with worship of Baal and other deities. "Jeremiah not only had to stand against their wickedness, he had to stand against their righteousness."[190]

Judah has a misplaced confidence (7:1-7).

This sermon is entirely in prose, which leads critics to argue that it is not typical of prophetic preaching style. Why does this need to be true? At best they may be right in assuming it was put in this form (I would say by Jeremiah) after it had been delivered orally. The people are coming into the temple to worship Yahweh. Jeremiah preaches his sermon to them because they are assuming that the presence of the temple (The temple of the Lord, the temple of the Lord, the temple of the Lord) will prevent judgment from coming on them.

---

[190]S. R. Hopper, *Jeremiah*, 5:870.

However, God says that judgment may be averted only by repentance.

Judah practices hypocrisy (7:8-16).

Yahweh says that Judah is breaking commandments 8, 6, 7, 9, and above all number 1 and still has the audacity to come to the temple and claim that Yahweh has delivered her. They should go to Shiloh where the tabernacle was first pitched to see what happened to it. Shiloh was apparently destroyed in the Philistine attacks that captured the ark.[191] If the tabernacle from God's wrath did not protect Shiloh, what makes Jerusalem think she is safe because the temple is there? God will judge them for their sins.

Judah practices idolatry (7:16-20).

This section is not part of the original sermon since God admonishes Jeremiah not even to pray for these people because they refuse to listen and are involved in idolatrous practices. Yahweh tells Jeremiah to take note of what Judah is doing in the streets of Jerusalem. The entire family is involved in the worship of the astral cult Queen of Heaven (*malkath hashamaim*, מַלְכַּת הַשָּׁמַיִם). A full quote from Thompson will help us understand the issue. "In the cities of Judah and in the streets of Jerusalem the cult of the Queen of Heaven was being practiced. The reference is to the Assyro-Babylonian Astarte

---

[191]See R. A. Pearce, "Shiloh and Jer. VII 12, 14, & 15," *VT* 12 (`1973): 105-108 who follows a re-evaluation of the archaeological evidence and argues that Shiloh was not destroyed until Jeremiah's time. He says that Jeremiah links 1 Samuel 4 (the ark/glory departed) and the destruction (recently) of the city. But see, "Did the Philistines Destroy the Israelite Sanctuary at Shiloh?—the Archaeological Evidence," *BAR* 1:2 (1975): 3-5 where the archaeologist Y. Shiloh is quoted in refutation of the revised evaluation. Shiloh (the place) was indeed destroyed about 1050 B.C. and later reoccupied as evidenced by the name "the Shilonite" in 1 Kings 11:29. See also I. Finkelstein, "Excavations at Shiloh 1981-1984, Preliminary Report," *Tel Aviv* 12 (1985) 159-77.

(Ishtar, cf. 44:17). The worship of Astarte along with other Mesopotamian gods was popular in Judah in the days of Manasseh (2 K. 21; 23:4-14). In Mesopotamia this goddess was known precisely as the Queen of Heaven (*sarrat same*) or the Mistress of Heaven (*belit same*). The name was still in use in the fifth century BC in Egypt, as the Aramaic papyri from the Jewish colony at Elephantine testify. Astarte was an astral deity, and her worship was practiced in the open (19:13; 32:29; cf. 2 K. 23:12; Zeph. 1:5). There were local expressions of her cult in Mesopotamia, Canaan, and Egypt. Perhaps, indeed, the cult of Astarte was identified with that of some Canaanite goddesses."[192]

God speaks of His true revelation (7:21-28).

When God first spoke to the people of Israel, He gave the Decalogue and the people agreed to accept it and follow it. At that time God did not speak of ritual—that would come later. Therefore, Judah should recognize that the ritual is secondary to what Yahweh really wants: obedience. On the contrary there has been disobedience from the very beginning. God now says that He will not answer them when they pray.

God gives a final promise of judgment (7:29-8:3).

The people are told to enter into the mode of mourning because God is going to judge His people. Topheth is in the valley of Hinnom where Judah practiced child sacrifice.[193] God will turn that place into the "valley of slaughter" when He brings judgment on Judah. It is considered disgraceful for a body to be disinterred and the bones

---

[192]Thompson, *Jeremiah*, 284.

[193]See Heater, *Bible History and Archaeology—an Outline*, p. 61 for a discussion.

scattered.[194] When God brings judgment on Judah, the bones of all the leaders will be scattered, and death will be chosen over life at that time.

6. Through a series of first person statements, Yahweh charges Judah with her sin (8:4—9:26).

    Judah in her conduct goes against all natural laws. When one falls, he gets up. The stork knows her seasons, etc., but Israel does not have enough sense to know the ordinance of Yahweh (8:5-7).

    Judah considered herself to be wise, but Yahweh says that the wise men are a disappointment because they have rejected the word of Yahweh. Because of this, Yahweh will judge them. Everyone is greedy; even the prophet and the priest are involved. The only message they bring is "Shalom" (peace) when in reality there is no Shalom. Therefore, they will be punished (8:8-13).

    A confession is written for Judah to say: "We must prepare for judgment for we have sinned against Yahweh" (8:14-17).

    Jeremiah speaks for himself and almost for Yahweh in his lament for the people of Judah because of the suffering that is going to come upon them. There is no healing for His people (8:18-22).

    Jeremiah's lament goes on in chapter 9. Again he speaks for himself and for Yahweh. He wishes he could get away from the people because of their sinfulness. Yahweh laments that they do not know Him (9:1-6).

    Because of their sin Yahweh is going to refine them and assay them as metal (cf. 6:27-30). What He finds is a deadly poison. He must punish them for their sin (9:7-9).

---

[194]Note the present Jewish/Arab struggle as it impinges on the cemeteries outside Jerusalem.

Yahweh will bring terrible destruction upon Jerusalem. The city and its environs will be desolate. When the question is asked: Why has this been done, the answer will be that Yahweh has punished His people (9:10-16).

A dramatic presentation is given of professional women being called to mourn Jerusalem's destruction (9:17-22).

A final challenge is made to the "wise men." True wisdom is to understand and to know Yahweh who exercises *ḥesed*, justice, and righteousness. These are the things in which He delights. Furthermore, in the future God is going to judge both Israel (circumcised) and the Gentiles (uncircumcised). Indeed Israel is uncircumcised of heart (9:23-26).

7. Yahweh speaks of the futility of idolatry (10:1-16).

Israel is warned not to learn the way of the nations. They should not fear the astrological religion of the pagans. The idols are only wood and stone. It is utter foolishness to fear them (10:1-5).

Jeremiah extols Yahweh as the one who is great and to whom reverence is due. The wisest of men are stupid when compared to God. Their foolishness is magnified in their following after lifeless idols. Yahweh is the true God and sovereignly in charge of the nations (10:6-10)

Verse 11 is very strange for it is in Aramaic. Most critical scholars assume it to be a gloss. Thompson says: "It is not impossible that it was a well-known saying. That it is in Aramaic is no necessary argument for a late date, since Aramaic was widely known in Western Asia and among people on Israel's borders. Even so, it may represent a marginal note added later by an Aramaic speaker. The thought is in any case not inconsistent with Jeremiah's outlook."[195] The verse is in LXX and Qumran fragments. The Qumran Hebrew seems to follow the LXX.

Jeremiah returns to the greatness of God. Notice the alternating patterns between God the Unique One and idols (idols: 1-5; God: 6-7; idols: 8-9; God: 10; Aramaic on false gods: 11; God: 12-13; idols: 14-15; God: 16). Note that verse 11 as a promise of the demise of idols fits into the last two "God" sections.[196]

8.   Jeremiah gives a graphic message of captivity (10:17-25).

It is difficult to know how to relate this section to the rest of the chapter. Unless Jeremiah is speaking prophetically, or giving a dramatic presentation of what will happen in the future, there is captivity going on at this time. Perhaps it should be related to 597 BC when Jehoiachin was carried away captive.

---

[195]Thompson, *Jeremiah*, p. 330.

[196]See my notes on Jeremiah 10:11 and the LXX:

1.   The MT has a beautiful symmetry in four parts, each contrasting idols with Yahweh the God of Israel.

2.   The LXX has marred this symmetry by omitting two of the four units extolling the power of God and the life in God (vv 6, 7, and 10).

3.   Verse 9 is elided with verses 2-5 to complete the diatribe as a unit. Assuming the there is a Hebrew *Vorlage*, the same thing was done by Jews working in the Hebrew text. It is the kind of harmonization one sees in 1QIsa[a] where similar passages are brought together. This may be the explanation for the textual dislocation and would argue for a later version of the text of the LXX.

Jerusalem is under siege, and Jeremiah tells them to pack their bags for they are leaving. However, it is no accident that they are going, for it is God Himself who is "slinging" them out (10:17-18).

Jeremiah then identifies with the people and weeps over their calamity. Jeremiah never rejoiced in the judgment on his people. He blames the problem on the shepherds (leaders) who are stupid and have not sought the Lord. Judgment is therefore coming (10:19-22).

Jeremiah gives a subdued testimony in the last unit of the chapter. He acknowledges man's sinfulness; he recognizes the necessity of God's chastening hand; but he asks for God to use moderation and to judge those nations that have devoured Judah (10:23-25).

9.   Jeremiah delivers the covenant sermon (11:1-17).

This sermon stresses the covenant Yahweh made with the Israelites at Horeb when He brought them out of Egypt. He swore to them at that time to give them a land flowing with milk and honey. A number of covenants were given to Israel (Abrahamic, Mosaic, Palestinian, and Davidic), but the one stressed here is the one given in Exodus 20 and following. Jeremiah responds by saying Amen, Yahweh! (11:1-5).

Jeremiah is admonished to preach the covenant sermon all around Judah. The people are to learn that Yahweh judged the people of Israel for disobeying His covenant. The same fate awaits those who disobey Him now (11:6-8).

Judah is viewed as having entered a conspiracy against Yahweh. They have violated the covenant He gave to their ancestors, and they have sinned in idolatry as their ancestors did. When they are in trouble, God tells them to cry out to their idols for help, but that they will not help them. They have as many idols as they have cities. Because of their violation of the covenant, they are going to be judged. There is no point in Jeremiah praying for the judgment to be lifted (11:9-14).

The next two verses are difficult. They are in poetic form and therefore were probably delivered at a different time from the rest of the sermon. The mention of idols in v. 13 leads to a condemnation of the Jews who are going to the temple for worship while they follow idols. Yahweh called them a green olive tree, but he is going to set their worthless branches on fire (11:15-16).

10. Jeremiah's life is threatened and he complains to Yahweh (11:17—12:6).

Yahweh revealed to Jeremiah that some people were seeking his life. Jeremiah laments his vulnerability and naiveté toward those who planned to kill him. He appeals to the righteous God to judge his case and avenge him of his enemies (11:17-20).

Yahweh reveals to Jeremiah that it is the men of his own village Anathoth who are plotting against him. He promises to punish them because of their opposition to Jeremiah (11:21-23).

The poem at the beginning of chapter twelve is placed here because it is the personal complaint of Jeremiah as to why the wicked prosper. He says that God has planted the wicked and caused them to prosper. This is true in spite of their hypocrisy. Jeremiah points out that Yahweh knows him and his attitude toward God. Therefore, Yahweh should judge his enemies since because of their sin, the land is in trouble (12:1-4).

Yahweh's response is to chide Jeremiah for his impatience. If you have run with the footmen (false prophets?) and become weary, how can you run with the horses (Babylonian war?). "The land of peace is contrasted with the "swelling of Jordan." The swelling of Jordan (*gᵉ'on hayarden,* גְּאוֹן הַיַּרְדֵּן) is the area on each side of the river where the water floods and leaves rich soil. This caused the under-brush to grow thickly and became a good place for lions to hide; hence a dreadful place. He goes on to tell Jeremiah that members of his own family are plotting against him and that he is to ignore them if they entice him. Since his own family and villagers are mentioned (11:21; 12:6), these pericopes may come from the same period of time in Jeremiah's life (12:5-6).

11. Yahweh laments the damage He has had to inflict on His people (12:7-17).

Without transition, our attention is turned to Yahweh's lament for His people. He has forsaken Israel, and she has suffered greatly at the hands of her enemies. Shepherds (v. 10) refers to foreign rulers who have attacked Israel and desolated the land. When this took place is not stated, but it could have been the situation spoken of in 2 Kings 24:1-2, when bands of marauders were sent by Yahweh against Jehoiakim prior to Nebuchadnezzar coming against the city in 597 BC (12:7-13).

A prose section is added here to say that those "shepherds" who despoiled God's people will in turn be despoiled. In universal terms God speaks of restoring Judah from the lands where she will be taken captive and of His restoration of the Gentiles who have captured her. This can only speak of the messianic era which the Gentile peoples will be turned to Yahweh (12:14-17).

12. Yahweh illustrates by a waistband and a proverb His promised judgment on Judah (13:1-27).

The first illustration is that of the waistband. Jeremiah was to hide it in Perath (פְּרָתָה). This word is usually identified as the Euphrates River, which would be some six or seven hundred miles away. Jeremiah may have made that trip or he may have gone to a nearby stream called Wadi Farah, or he may have had a vision. I would incline to the second view. The rotting of the waistcloth is interpreted to be God's destruction of His people. The identification with the River Euphrates or a stream sounding like that river should indicate that God will "rot" them by sending them to Babylon in exile (13:1-11).

The second illustration is the quotation of a proverb: "Every jug (wineskin, *nebel,* נֵבֶל) will be filled with wine," that is, the purpose of jugs is to be filled with wine. When the people answer with derision: "Of course we know this proverb," Jeremiah is to say: "You will drink the wine and become drunk." Drunkenness represents Yahweh's judgment upon the people. Jeremiah thrusts at the ruling family in v. 13 (13:12-14).

The following section speaks of captivity, and since it even speaks of the captivity of the king and queen mother, it may refer to the deportation of Jehoiachin in 597 BC, although the tenses could be prophetic perfects. The compassion of God is evident in His deep groaning for the people who are made to suffer so. Yet they deserve what has happened because they seem to be utterly unable to stop sinning (Ethiopian/leopard) (13:15-27).

13. Jeremiah identifies with the people in time of drought and judgment (14:1-22).

This section (1-9) should not be linked chronologically with the one following for the simple reason that the false prophets are saying there will be no famine, but rather peace (v. 13). A drought has taken place that brought with it famine and devastation. Jeremiah, speaking for the people, confesses his sin and cries out for forgiveness and care on the part of God. Even though He acts helpless, He is indeed in their midst and able to deliver (14:1-9).

Yahweh tells Jeremiah not to pray for Israel because their sin is so great, He is going to call them to account for it. Jeremiah pleads on their behalf that the false prophets are to be blamed for telling them that there will be only peace and prosperity. Yahweh's reply is that the prophets will be judged by the very things they say are not coming. However, the people are still responsible for their actions and will be likewise judged for their sin (14:10-16).

The following section like 13:15ff refers to some kind of military campaign. People are crushed, slain, subject to famine and disease and prophets and priests have been deported. Yahweh gives an interesting command to Jeremiah: he is to speak words to them that they themselves would be saying. They cry out to God asking Him if He has completely rejected Judah. They confess their sin and ask Him to remember His covenant. They conclude with a word of confident hope (*neqaweh,* נִקְוֶה) in Him (14:17-22).

14. Jeremiah speaks words of judgment and personal complaint (15:1-21).

Yahweh tells Jeremiah that even though Moses and Samuel, the two great intercessors, were to pray for the people, He would still send them away. Their judgment will consist of four things: death, sword, famine, and captivity. There will be four dooms: sword, dogs, birds, and beasts. All this is because of the sin of Manasseh the son of Hezekiah who led Judah into such sin (15:1-4).

Yahweh speaks in poignant terms of Judah's judgment that will lead them to the point where no one will have pity. The anguish will be unbelievable (15:5-9).

Jeremiah laments his birth because he has become a man of contention and strife (*madon, riv,* רִיב מָדוֹן). These are court terms again and may mean that Jeremiah is always indicting the people. Yahweh's answer is not very clear. He seems to be promising Jeremiah protection from the enemy when he comes. This is precisely what happened (Jer. 39:11-14) (15:10-11).

The futility of Judah's resistance against the coming attack is represented in the question: "Can anyone smash iron from the north?" God's judgment will be irresistible (15:12-14).

Jeremiah laments again to Yahweh and asks that vengeance be wrought on his enemies. His statement about eating the word of God shows the joy of his ministry in spite of suffering. Furthermore, he does not take any pleasure in the suffering of his people even though they have badly treated him (15:15-18).

Yahweh gives a very encouraging word to Jeremiah. He must be willing to return (does this imply that Jeremiah had stepped aside for a while?). God promises to make him His spokesman who will deliver messages. Yahweh will protect him. He will receive stiff opposition, but they will not prevail over him (15:19-21).

15. Jeremiah, by his life, will communicate a message of judgment to the people (16:1-21).

Jeremiah is not to get married. The reason he is to give when asked is that those with children and family will suffer dreadfully when the judgment comes (16:1-4).

Jeremiah is not to enter a house of mourning. The reason is that God is going to bring the judgment of death upon many people and there will be no one to mourn them (16:5-7).

Jeremiah is not to go to a festive party. The reason is that God is going to eliminate festivity from the people of Judah (16:8-9).

The people will protest innocently: What have we done? Jeremiah is to answer that their ancestors have sinned and so have they. Therefore, He is going to hurl them out of the land (16:10-13).

In spite of this negative promise, Yahweh declares that He will return the people of God to their land. As if to smash premature hope, He says He will send for fishermen and hunters to catch them all in their sin for judgment. Finally there is another universalistic statement about the fact that God is going to receive the nations who will forsake their idolatry when they see the greatness of God (16:14-21).

16. This chapter is a series of miscellaneous messages delivered probably over a period of time (17:1-27).

    Judah's sin is so indelibly impressed upon their hearts that it is as though it were written with an iron stylus. Consequently, God will judge her (17:1-4).

    A wisdom poem is given on the analogy of Psalm one contrasting the man who trusts in humanity to the man whose trust is in Yahweh (17:5-8).

    A beautiful Psalm is presented showing Jeremiah's trust in Yahweh and praying for God to protect him from the enemies around about (17:9-18).

    The chapter is concluded in an uncharacteristic way, for Jeremiah admonishes them to observe the Sabbath properly. Heretofore, he has denounced them in scathing terms for their ritualism without reality. However, he is probably using the Sabbath here as part for the whole: because they are abusing the Sabbath and not honoring God on it, they are not honoring God at all.[197]

B. Potter and Pot—from opportunity to repent to inevitable judgment in captivity (18:1—23:40).

    Chapters 18-20 form a triad around the issue of the "pots." Chapter 18 shows God's sovereignty in dealing with His people—but they can still repent; Chapter 19 shows through the breaking of the pot the inevitability

---

[197]See Thompson's discussion and defense of the unit (*Jeremiah*) 17:19-27.

of judgment; Chapter 20 describes the persecution of Jeremiah because of his prophecies of judgment. Chapters 21-23 argue that the responsibility for judgment rests primarily on the leadership.

1. Yahweh uses the potter to illustrate His own dealings with the Jewish people and to show that they had an opportunity to repent (18:1-23).

    Yahweh tells Jeremiah to go to the potter's house. He probably has a crowd following him to whom he makes his point. The potter is making a vessel of some kind on his wheels. When a defect shows up in the work he crushes it and begins again (18:1-4).

    Yahweh says that the potter illustrates His sovereignty. If He has promised calamity against a nation or good for a nation, He is able to change His mind on the basis of their changed attitude. The application is that Israel should recognize that Yahweh is "fashioning" calamity against them. They therefore should repent. "To fashion" is *yatsar* (יָצַר). "Potter" is *yotser* (יוֹצֵר). The same word is used in Genesis 2:7 to describe the creative process. All of this play on words as well as the illustration itself is to warn Judah to repent. However, they say: It is no use! (18:5-12).

    Yahweh then indicts Judah for the foolishness of turning away from Him. He says that one could search far and wide to see if anyone has ever done anything like this and the search would be futile. They have moved from the ancient paths where truth is known. Therefore, God will judge them (18:13-17).

    The response of the people to Jeremiah's message is plainly seen in v. 18. The general consensus is that "the law will not be lost to the priest, counsel to the sage, nor the word to the prophet." Jeremiah is just a troublemaker. Consequently, they want to bring him down (18:18).

Because of this terrible response, we hear of one of Jeremiah's most vitriolic statements against his opponents. He calls upon God to wreak vengeance upon his enemies. This is not what we normally hear from Jeremiah as he identifies with his people. He is probably responding very emotionally to the constant refusal of the people to respond to his message and their insistence that all is well and God cannot judge them because they are fulfilling the ritual (18:19-23).

2. The message of judgment on Judah (the broken pot—the opportunity is past) (19:1-15).

God tells Jeremiah to give an illustrated message of promised judgment to the people of Judah. In chapter 18 (probably early in Jehoiakim's rule) there was still the possibility of repentance. In chapter 19, the opportunity has passed—judgment remains. The components of the illustration are a potter's earthenware jar (*baqbuq yotser ḥarash,* בַּקְבֻּק יוֹצֵר חֶרֶשׂ), some of the elders and some of the senior priests, valley of ben-Hinnom, and the potsherd gate.[198] There are three valleys around Jerusalem: east is the Kidron valley; central is the Tyropoean (cheese makers) valley; west is the Hinnom valley. All three converge south of the city of David. The Hebrew word for valley is *gai*. And so the name of the west valley is sometimes called *Gai Hinnom* (the valley of Hinnom) or *Gai bene Hinnom* (the valley of the sons of Hinnom). From that comes the corrupted name in Greek of *Gehenna*. The valley of Hinnom was infamous as a place where people (including King Ahaz) forced their children into a fire to offer them to the god Moloch (2 Kings 16:3, 23:10; Jer. 19:4-5). It thus becomes a symbol of evil and of burning. By New Testament times it had become a symbol of eternal punishment and so Jesus used it (Matt. 5:22).

---

[198]Remember the type of jar; Hebrew: *baqbuq*; we will come back to it later.

3. The warning of impending doom is given. The calamity will be so great it will make people's ears tingle (19:3).

The reason given for the coming judgment is their idolatrous practices. They have forsaken Yahweh, made the temple "an alien place," worshipped other gods, filled this place with the blood of the innocent, built high places to Baal and burned their children in the fire to Baal (19:4-5).

The judgment is pronounced through a series of word plays. The name of the valley will be changed from Topheth or ben-Hinnom to the valley of Slaughter. Topheth is difficult. It may mean place of burning. Next Yahweh says he will make void the counsel of Judah and Jerusalem; that is, He will frustrate their plans. The word for the jar Jeremiah carries is *baqbuq*. It is an onomatopoeic word: the name is like the sound. In this case it is the sound of emptying out a bottle. As Jeremiah holds the jar (*baqbuq*) he says, "I will void (*baqothi*, בַּקֹּתִי) the counsel of Judah and Jerusalem." There will be a horrible slaughter, and in the siege parents will eat their children[199] (19:6-9).

Jeremiah then carries out the object lesson by breaking the earthenware jar. The breaking symbolizes the fact that God is going to break Judah. The houses will be defiled like Topheth. Josiah had defiled Topheth to prevent any more child sacrifice there. Precisely what this means is not clear. Did he make it a city dump, so that there was always trash burning there and no one would want to use it for sacrifice? In any event, the city of Jerusalem will be like Topheth when God finishes with it (19:10-13).

Jeremiah then returns to the city, stands in the court of the temple and extends the same message to the people in general (19:14-15).

---

[199]See 2 Kings 6 for an example of this.

3. Jeremiah is persecuted because of his message (20:1-18).

At the end of Jeremiah's message, he is arrested by Pashhur ben Immer who was chief officer (*paqid nagid,* פָּקִיד נָגִיד) of the temple. 52:24 may indicate that he was next to the high priest. He has Jeremiah beaten (40 stripes, Deut. 25:3?) and put in stocks. The word for stocks is *mahpeketh* (מַהְפֶּכֶת) which refers to turning. It probably means that Jeremiah was tortured (20:1-2).

Jeremiah confronts him the next day when he is released and says that Pashhur's name is being changed to Magor-missabib (מָגוֹר מִסָּבִיב). This word means "fear on all sides" and seems to be a relatively common expression in Jeremiah (6:25; 19:3,4,10; 46:5; 49:29; Lam. 2:22). Pashhur will suffer the fate of the city. He will go into captivity and die. We now have serious confrontation over the issue of true versus false prophecy (20:3-6).

The rest of the chapter gives us a glimpse of the private response of Jeremiah to his persecution. The public response was bold and unequivocal; the private response is bitter. He begins by saying that God has deceived him in leading him into the ministry of prophecy. His bitterness because of the daily derision led him to the point of refusing to speak in the name of the Lord any more. However, the word was so strong in him that he was unable to refrain (20:7-9).[200]

Jeremiah has heard of the efforts to defeat him. He seems to imply that his own name is Magor-missabib. Yet he concludes that Yahweh is with him like a mighty champion (*'arits gibbor,* עָרִיץ גִּבּוֹר the first word usually refers to a tyrant and the second to a soldier. These are powerful words to use of God's ability to deliver). He concludes by singing to the Lord of His deliverance (20:10-13).

---

[200]May God give us that same sense of urgency.

A bitter lament follows on the order of Job's poem (Job 3) decrying the day of his birth. Keil argues that it is psychologically possible for a person to go from verse 13 to verse 14,[201] but it is more probable that Jeremiah composed this section at another time and appended it here as an illustration of his struggle with God when he was persecuted (20:14-18).

4.   Zedekiah sends Pashhur to ask for Yahweh's help in the Babylonian siege (21:1-10).

With this unit we turn to the last king of the Judean monarchy. Zedekiah was placed on the throne in 597 BC after his nephew, Jehoiachin, had been taken to Babylon. Zedekiah was twenty-one years old and ruled until 586 BC. In 588 BC he rebelled against Babylon, and Nebuchadnezzar put the city under siege (2 Kings 24:18—25:3). It is in this latter period that chapter 21 takes place.

The king sent messengers to Jeremiah to seek a word from Yahweh. The Pashhur mentioned here is not the same as the one in chapter 20 (this man shows up again in chapter 38), but the common name is used in the argument. The first Pashhur rejected God's word of judgment, the second Pashhur comes for help in the midst of the fulfillment of that very word. They ask Jeremiah to inquire of Yahweh (*darash*, דְּרַשׁ "to seek God's mind") in behalf of Jerusalem. Their hope is that God will act miraculously (*niphlaoth*, נִפְלָאֹת as in Judges 6:13 when Gideon asks the Angel of Yahweh where the miracles are of which his fathers spoke) in behalf of the city to deliver her from Babylon. The time for repentance was some ten years prior, but that Pashhur rejected the opportunity. Now only judgment remains (21:1-2).

Jeremiah reports God's just response to the request of the king. He will help Judah's enemies. He will fight against Jerusalem. The

---

[201]Keil and Delitzsch, *loc. cit.*

"outstretched hand and mighty arm" are a victory motif used by God usually in His defense of His people. He finally promises to deliver the king and the people into the hand of Nebuchadnezzar (21:3-7).

Yahweh then gives the people a choice. They can choose to surrender to Babylon and live, or they can fight and die. God has set His face against the city for harm (21:8-10).

5. Yahweh indicts the leaders of Judah to show one of the major reasons for the catastrophe (21:11—23:40).

We now move into a section of the book where the events and messages are not at all chronological. They jump back and forth between Jehoiakim and Zedekiah, and include references to Jehoahaz and Jehoiachin as well. These messages lead to the conclusion that the captivity is unavoidable, and that bad leadership has brought them to this point. Judah has reached the point where she must receive the punishment for her sin.

This series of messages is a compilation of several sermons delivered by Jeremiah against the leadership of Judah with a promise of future leadership that will do God's bidding. The diversity of these messages is indicated by the prose/poetry constructions as well as the chronological indicators that show them to have been delivered over a period of time.

Jeremiah gives Yahweh's word against the royal house. This section is in poetry and so was probably given at another time, but it is in this unit because it concerns the same topic. The royal house is admonished to be just in its dealings with the people so as to avoid God's wrath. The valley dweller/rocky plains refers to Jerusalem (21:11-14).

These chapters (21-23) contain a scathing denunciation of all the kings after Josiah (except Zedekiah). Jehoiakim comes in for the most scathing denunciation of any Jeremiah makes. After dealing with the sinfulness of these kings, a promise is made of God's coming Messiah who will rule properly. Finally the section closes with a diatribe against false prophets who are also leaders of the people. These messages were no doubt delivered while each pertinent king was alive. They consist of both prose and poetry and have been brought together here because of the similarity of subject matter.

The genealogy according to 1 Chron. 3:14-15 looks like this:

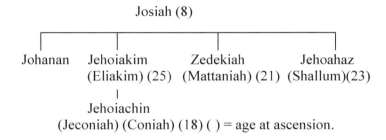

Josiah (8)

| Johanan | Jehoiakim | Zedekiah | Jehoahaz |
| | (Eliakim) (25) | (Mattaniah) (21) | (Shallum)(23) |

Jehoiachin
(Jeconiah) (Coniah) (18) ( ) = age at ascension.

Johanan is not known outside Chronicles. He must have died young or have been insignificant. Jehoahaz (Shallum) was younger than Jehoiakim, but for some reason was chosen over his older brother to be king. He is listed as the fourth son in Chronicles because he has the same mother as Zedekiah. He had to be older than Zedekiah to have been able to reign in 609 BC

The first unit is not addressed to any particular king. It may have been early in Jehoiakim's reign before his actions demonstrated an ungodly attitude. In any event the philosophy of kingship is to show justice to all people and particularly to vulnerable ones. God promises that there will be kings on the throne if they obey, but that the temple will be destroyed if they do not. Chapters 24-29 show the results of the failure of the Judean kings to obey—captivity came (22:1-5).

The second unit is likewise not directed to a king by name, but the tone is hostile. In spite of the position held by David's descendant in God's plan, He will bring them down and judge them for forsaking the covenant and worshipping idols (22:6-9).

The third unit gets specific. It was probably written in 609 BC just after Jehoahaz had been removed from the throne and taken to Egypt. The "dead" in this context is Josiah, the one who "goes away" is Jehoahaz. Then a doleful prediction is made that Shallum will never return to his home. Shallum (שַׁלֻּם) has to do with repayment. A name like Shelemiah would mean "Yahweh repays" (in a good sense). Shallum is the natural name for Jehoahaz as we know from Chronicles, and that may be the only reason it is given here. On the other hand, Jeremiah may be referring to the irony of the name "He got what he deserved" (22:10-12).

The longest unit is a poetic statement written in vitriolic tones against Jehoiakim. He had apparently set out to build a new palace with cedar walls in spite of the poverty of the people created by raising taxes to pay the tribute demanded by Egypt. His father is held up to him as an example he should follow (v. 15), and he is told that he will die an ignominious death (22:13-23).

The final unit is delivered against Jehoiachin the young son of Jehoiakim who ruled only three months—long enough to surrender the city to Nebuchadnezzar. The first section is prose and is written prior to his deportation. Here God likens him to a seal ring (a very important item) that He will cast off in spite of its importance. He and the queen mother will be hurled to another country where they will die. The second section is in poetry and takes place after the deportation. Jehoiachin (Coniah) is a despised, shattered jar. God writes him childless, not that he would have no children (we know he had children), but that none of his immediate descendants would sit on the throne (22:28-30).

The shepherds of Israel are denounced in the beginning of chapter 23. The imagery of sheep and shepherds is common enough in the Old Testament and is, of course, followed in the New Testament as well, with Christ being the Good Shepherd. The shepherds are castigated for not doing their job well and are promised judgment. At the same time there is a promise that God will gather His flock and bring them back to pasture (their land) and will raise up over them good shepherds (23:1-4).

This promise of a future return from captivity and a leadership of good shepherds is the occasion for the next poetic unit to be placed here. The promise is given of a coming "Branch" (*tsemaḥ,* צֶמַח). The idea of a "shoot" coming out of the stump of Jesse begins with Isaiah (11); the root out of dry ground is presented in Isaiah 53. In the post-exilic period this "Branch" is developed in Zechariah (Chs. 3,6) where the Targum even translates it as Messiah (*mshiḥa'* מְשִׁיחָא). All the ideal actions of a king set forth in this major unit will be carried out by the Branch. As such he will be called "Yahweh, our righteousness" (*Yahweh tsidkenu,* יהוה צִדְקֵנוּ) which is surely a play on the name of Zedekiah (Yahweh is righteous). A parallel passage is in 33:16 (23:5-6).

Because of that future glorious work of restoration, the Exodus will pale into insignificance. They will no longer make the creedal statement: "Yahweh who brought us from Egypt," but they will say "Yahweh who brought us from the land of the north" (23:7-8).

Jeremiah, mingling his own feelings with those of Yahweh, speaks of the desolation that has come over the land because of the pollution of both prophets and priests. As a result they are promised judgment (23:9-12).

Yahweh compares the prophets of Judah to those of Samaria. The implication is obvious: the false prophets of Baal misled the northern kingdom and they went into captivity. The same thing will happen to Judah. Their wickedness has become so awful that God must judge them (23:13-15).

The message of the false prophets can be discerned from the condemnation of their words of peace and prosperity. These prophets do not know the counsel of God. God has sent out His whirlwind and it will not turn back. Furthermore God is near, not far off. No one can hide from Him (23:16-24).

Yahweh denounces the prophets for their dreams, which He likens to straw (as opposed to grain). God therefore sets Himself against the prophets (23:25-32).

He tells Jeremiah (singular pronoun) that the only response he is to give when he is asked "what is the oracle of the Lord" is "There is no oracle (What oracle)," Instead the word from God is "I shall abandon you." The prophets along with the people will be cast out (23:33-40).

This unit began with the house of David, went on to denounce Jehoahaz, Jehoiakim, and Jehoiachin, and finally attacked the religious leaders, particularly the prophets. In the midst of this negative statement is the beautiful prophecy of the Messiah.

C. A series of messages to show the necessity of submitting to Babylonian over lordship (24:1—29:32).

1. Jeremiah delivers a message under the imagery of good and bad figs shortly after the deportation of Jeconiah in 597 BC (24:1-10).

   The vision Jeremiah sees is two baskets of figs sitting before the temple. One basket contains very good figs and the other rotten figs (24:1-3).

   The basket of good figs represents the captives. Those who have gone to Babylon, says Jeremiah, are better off than those who remain, because God is going to bring them back to the land and establish a wonderful spiritual relationship with them (notice the rubric "they will be My people and I will be their God") (24:4-7).

The basket of bad figs represents those who will remain in the city as well as those who have fled to Egypt (to escape the Babylonian captivity). They will be given up to the sword, famine, and pestilence. The purpose of the "fig" messages is to say that captivity is God's sovereign purpose for His people. The fact that that purpose is being carried out is good, even though the effects in the short run are painful. This chapter should be tied in with 23:39-40 (24:8-10).

Small wonder Jeremiah's message was despised. The captivity in Babylon was looked upon as a horrible thing and prophets even predicted a return within two years. Jeremiah, on the other hand, tells them it is better to be in Babylon than Jerusalem and predicts the desolation of Jerusalem.

2. Jeremiah predicts seventy years of captivity. The time is the fourth year of Jehoiakim and the first year of Nebuchadnezzar (25:1-38).

    The chronology of this chapter is very important. Pharaoh Necho had put Jehoiakim on the throne in 609 BC Now Nebuchadnezzar has forced Jehoiakim to capitulate to his rule. This takes place in the first year of Nebuchadnezzar (605 BC) and in the fourth year of Jehoiakim. Daniel lists this as the third year of Jehoiakim (25:1-2).[202]

    The message of Jeremiah is that he has spent twenty three years prophesying to them; that God has sent prophets continually to prophesy to them, but they have not listened to anything God told them to do. Chapter 25 seems to have been placed here to reinforce the message of Chapter 24, namely, the disaster that came upon

---

[202]See Thiele, MNHK, for a discussion of the systems that led to this apparent but non-real contradiction.

Judah was engineered by God in response to a rebellious people (25:3-7).

The result of this disobedience through idolatry is that God will bring Nebuchadnezzar (note the phrase "My servant" in v. 9) to attack the city and carry the people away for seventy years (25:8-11).

Yahweh then promises deliverance after the seventy years are expired. The Babylonians will be appropriately punished[203] for their abuse of God's people (25:12-14).[204]

---

[203]Note the "destruction language": "Babylon will be destroyed *forever*" after the seventy years. This *must* refer to 539 BC.

[204]Excursus on seventy years:

This prophecy (repeated in Jeremiah 29) is very important to Old Testament studies. While there are some problems in the following assumptions, they will form the basis for the discussion of the prophecy. Between the Battle of Carchemish and Nebuchadnezzar's return to Babylon to receive the crown, Jerusalem would have been forced to capitulate to Nebuchadnezzar (referred to proleptically as king), and captives would have been taken including Daniel. It is difficult to determine the termini of the seventy-year period. 605 (first attack and captivity) to 539 (Babylon's defeat) provide only sixty-six solar years. Since the terminus of the seventy years is to involve the return to the land (29:10), the terminus might be 536 when Zerubbabel returned and the foundation of the new temple was laid. It may be that we should consider the years to be 360 days each as seems to be the case in the book of Daniel. Whatever may be the variables, the seventy years should probably begin with the first deportation in 605 and end with the return to the land in 538 and/or the founding of the second temple in 536.

Zechariah 7 indicates that the Jews have been fasting for the fallen temple for seventy years. Now that it is nearing completion (516 BC) they are asking whether they should stop fasting. To the Jews of Zechariah's day God's indignation against *the temple* has lasted seventy years and seems to be still going on. This reference may have nothing to do with Jeremiah's prophecy: it may only indicate that they have been fasting for the temple since 586, i.e., seventy years.

Through the commonly used imagery of drinking a wine cup of wrath, Jeremiah tells the surrounding nations that God is going to judge them as well as Judah: Egypt, foreign people, Uz, Philistines, Edom, Moab, Ammon, Tyre, Sidon, coast lands, Dedan, Tema, Buz, Arabia, foreign people (desert), Zimri, Elam, Media, north, earth. Last of all Sheshach will drink the cup. This latter name is called an *athbash* or a reversal of the alphabet (a=t [a=z], b=sh [b=y]. Hence,

Sh=b, sh=b, k=l or Babel (בָּבֶל=שֵׁשַׁךְ). One wonders whether ambassadors from other nations might have been at Jerusalem to whom Jeremiah offered the drink. If they refuse, he is to tell them that they will drink regardless of whether they accept the cup (25:15-29).

The wrath of God against the nations is depicted as God roaring from on high and carrying out a court case against the nations. There will be great judgment against the nations. Finally, Yahweh, under the imagery of a lion, attacks the shepherds of the flocks (kings and rulers) and brings devastation to them (25:30-38).

Small wonder that Daniel (9:1ff), reading from Jeremiah and noting that almost seventy years had transpired since his deportation in 605, prays and confesses in behalf of Israel. As a result he is given a vision of the future of Israel the chronology of which is in terms of sevens or heptads. As the seventy-year captivity represented in a fashion the 490 years of disobedience, so it also represents 490 years in the future during which God will fulfill His purposes for Israel.

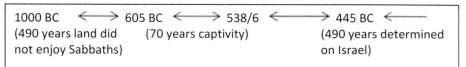

1000 BC ⟷ 605 BC ⟷ 538/6 ⟷ 445 BC ⟵

(490 years land did   (70 years captivity)   (490 years determined
not enjoy Sabbaths)   on Israel)

See Wm. A. Troth, *A Study of the Termini of the Seventy-Year Captivity* (Th.M. Thesis, DTS, for a discussion).

3. Jeremiah delivers another "temple" sermon and almost loses his life (26:1-24).

This message takes place in the beginning of Jehoiakim's reign. That is prior to his submission to Babylon. Bright says that this is a technical expression for the time before his first regnal year, i.e., between Sept. 609 and April 608.[205]

The reason for the positioning of this unit is not obvious.[206] It may be that, like Chapter 25, the point of the placement is to show that from 609 on there was a bitter rejection of Jeremiah's message. Therefore, the calamity of 586 was inevitable, given the hardened attitude of the king and people to a message requiring repentance. The sermon is an abbreviated version of the one given in chapter 7. Failure to obey God will result in the temple becoming like Shiloh and the city becoming a curse (that is "may you become like Jerusalem" or some such) (26:2-9).

The priests, prophets and people demanded Jeremiah's death because of his prophecy against the city, but the princes intervened by sitting in judgment on the case. Jeremiah defended his ministry to the princes, called for repentance, and placed himself in the hands of the princes with the warning that they must give an account to God (26:10-15).

For unknown reasons, the officials sided with Jeremiah against the priests and the prophets. They cited Hezekiah's willingness to listen to Micah when he prophesied against Jerusalem (26:16-19).

---

[205]See also Thompson, *Jeremiah*, p. 1.

[206]G. von Rad, *The Message of the Prophets*, p. 17, no. 3, says, "In connection with the so-called temple address in the year 609, the tradition contains the prophet's words (Jer. 7:1-165) and independently a story which describes the incident (Jer. 26)."

The next unit is treated by some as a continuation of the official's argument, but it is more likely another example of Jehoiakim's arrogance against the prophets of God and has been included here to reinforce the picture. Uriah prophesied in the same manner as Jeremiah and was killed, while Jeremiah was protected and survived. Such are the ways of God! (26:20-24).

4. Jeremiah preaches submission to Babylon under the symbolism of a yoke (27:1—28:17).

It would appear that early in the reign of Zedekiah international intrigue was carried out against Babylon. Various ambassadors were in Jerusalem consulting with Zedekiah when this message was delivered. The symbolism consisted of yokes and ropes around Jeremiah's neck (27:1-2).

The message to be delivered to the nations (Edom, Moab, Ammon, Tyre, and Sidon) gives us a pretty good awareness of Jeremiah's theology that God is working through Babylon. They were to recognize first God's sovereignty (v. 5), and secondly, His right to give control of the world to whom He chooses (v. 6). Nebuchadnezzar was Yahweh's servant. Those nations who refused to submit to the yoke of Babylon would be judged by the Lord. They were not to listen to their religious leaders because they would cause them to go into captivity (27:3-11).

Jeremiah made a personal plea to young king Zedekiah, to the priests and to all the people. He tells them that the vessels left by Nebuchadnezzar in his first foray would eventually go to Babylon. They would stay there until Yahweh in His grace brought them back to Jerusalem (27:12-22).

We now come to a major confrontation between a true prophet and a false one. Hananiah called himself a prophet and came from the town of Gibeon. He addressed a crowd of people in the temple and told them that within two years the temple vessels, Jeconiah, and all the exiles would come back to Jerusalem. God would have broken the yoke (symbolically worn by Jeremiah) of the King of Babylon (28:1-4).

Jeremiah seemed to be somewhat puzzled in his response. He said "amen" to Hananiah's prophecy but reminded him that the test of prophecy is fulfillment. Hananiah then broke the wooden yoke Jeremiah was wearing and reiterated his prophecy of the defeat of Nebuchadnezzar within two full years (28:5-11).

Yahweh sent Jeremiah back with the message that the yoke of wood would become a yoke of iron since He had assuredly given Nebuchadnezzar charge of the human arena. Then in a dramatic statement Jeremiah told Hananiah that he was a false prophet. To demonstrate the veracity of the true prophet, Jeremiah predicted Hananiah's death two months later (cf. 28:1). Hananiah died on the seventh month of that year (28:12-17).

5. Jeremiah reinforces his message of judgment from God through Babylon by telling the captives to settle down for a long stay (29:1-32).

Jeremiah sends a letter in a diplomatic pouch to the exiled leaders (elders, priests, prophets, and people) who were in Babylon. Zedekiah had sent official letters to Babylon by Elasah ben Shaphan (29:1-3).[207]

The contents of the letter in fine are that they are to settle down, build houses, enter into marriage contracts, and pray for the peace of

---

[207]See our excursus on Jeremiah's writing at the discussion on chapter 36.

the city. They are not to let the prophets in exile deceive them when they tell them not to unpack (29:4-8).[208]

The letter goes on to give good news. The exile will be long, but only seventy years. After that God's good plans for them is to bring them back and to restore a relationship between Him and His people (29:9-14).

This chapter is a collage of material derived from more than one letter and from responses to the letters. There may have been several pieces of correspondence between Jeremiah and the exiles. Verses 1-23 are the first letter to which Shemaiah responds in 24-32. A second letter *quoting* Shemaiah and telling how his letter was handled follows (29:15-32).[209]

Prophets in Babylon. These prophets are again apparently prophesying an early return of the captives, because Jeremiah says that those remaining behind will suffer more than those who went into captivity (29:15-20).

Ahab ben Kolaiah and Zedekiah ben Maaseiah. These two men are prophets who are prophesying falsely. They will be delivered to the king of Babylon and be roasted in fire (Kolaiah, קוֹלָיָה sounds like roasted grain, *qali,* קְלִי, and roasted [in fire], *qala,* קָלָה and curse (*qelalah,* קְלָלָה). Their sin is two-fold: they have prophesied falsely and committed adultery. D. J. Wiseman discusses a rebellion against Nebuchadnezzar about 595 BC and says "It has also been suggested that the rebellion involved some of the Judean deportees in Babylonia since Nebuchadrezzar also put to death by burning Ahab

[208]See W. L. Holladay, "God Writes a Rude Letter (Jeremiah 29:1-23)," *BA* 46 (1983): 145-146.

[209]See Meindert Dijkstra, "Prophecy by Letter Jeremiah XXIX 24-32" *VT* 33 (1983): 319-322.

ben Kolaiyah and a Zedekiah ben-Maaseyah who had prophesied that the Jewish exile would last only two years in contrast to the seventy predicted by Jeremiah" (29:21- 23).[210]

Shemaiah the Nehelamite. Nehelamite means "the dreamer" and may have reference to claims to revelation through dreams (cf. 23:25). Shemaiah's letter to Zephaniah is in response to the letter of the first part of this chapter. He urges Zephaniah to lock Jeremiah up since his words are discouraging. Zephaniah read the letter to Jeremiah (did they have a laugh together?), and Jeremiah sent a word to all the exiles denying Shemaiah's prophecies and predicting that he will have no descendants (29:24-32).

D. Jeremiah gives several messages of hope for the future of Israel (The Book of Comfort) (30:1—33:26).

Verses 1-3 seem to be a heading to the unit of hope. Jeremiah's messages have contained dismal predictions, at best (including the seventy years of captivity in chapter 29). Now Judah's attention is turned to the future. She indeed must suffer because of her sin, but the covenant keeping Yahweh will not forget His own. The messianic allusions earlier in the book are augmented by some of the most beautiful prophecy in the Old Testament (30:1-3).

Before Israel can enjoy God's ultimate blessing, she must endure suffering. This "time of Jacob's trouble" is to be equated with the tribulation period from which God promises to save Israel. When that salvation takes place, the yoke will be broken off and they shall serve the Lord their God and David their king. This refers to the Millennium. Will David rule as king during the Millennium (cf. Ezek. 37:25)? I believe the reference to David here is to the Messiah of whom David is the type (30:4-9).

---

[210]D. J. Wiseman, *Nebuchadrezzar and Babylon*, 34-35.

A message reminiscent of Isaiah's servant songs is next appended (it is poetry). This is a promise of restoration after chastening. The chastening is necessary because "her wound is incurable" (30:9-17).

A beautiful poem on the restoration of Israel follows describing the rebuilding of the city. In addition their leader will be "one of them" who will be able to approach God. They will "be my people and I will be their God" (30:18-24).

The message of hope continues with a depiction of God's everlasting love. He uses the words of Jeremiah's call in describing the rebuilding and replanting of Israel. "Arise, and let us go up to Zion, to the Lord our God" (31:1-6).

The references to Israel probably indicate messages directed to the North early in Jeremiah's ministry when Josiah was extending his rule to the North.[211] Specific statements are made about the return of Israel form the north. What a marvelous and miraculous event this will be. This is no modern "Zionist" movement where a limited number of Jews return to Israel. This is a worldwide restoration of Jewish people in preparation for the Millennium (31:7-9).

Yahweh summons the nations and coast lands to witness His miraculous work in restoring Israel to happiness and satisfaction (31:10-14).

This idyllic scene is interrupted with a reminder of the suffering through which Israel must go before she can be restored. Rachel weeps for her children who languish in the exile (Matthew uses this picture to describe Israel's anguish over the slaughter of the infants by Herod). God agonizes over the pain of His people (31:15-20).

A series of messages are joined together promising the return of Israel. "A woman will encompass a man" is most difficult. It seems to be a

---

[211]See Bright, *Jeremiah,* pp. 284-85.

proverb of sorts and is to represent something most unusual ("a new thing the Lord has created in the earth"). It may mean that Israel (a woman) is to turn and embrace the Lord (the man), that is, she will repent.[212] Another brief statement is given about the restoration of Judah (31:21-26).

The only place a new covenant is mentioned in the Old Testament is in this context (but the *conditions* are promised in Ezek. 36:22-32). God promises restoration again, but he speaks of the fact that He will make a new covenant with Israel that will involve internal conversion. This covenant will be different from the Mosaic covenant. They will know Yahweh so well, that they will not even have to teach one another. Their sins will be forgiven. This passage underlies Hebrews 8 where it is cited fully. The work of Christ at Calvary is the basis for the new covenant including the church and the new covenant that will restore Israel's fortunes (31:27-34).

The assurance of God's faithfulness to Israel is His comparison with the astral heavens. If this fixed order should depart, then He could cast off Israel, but since it cannot, than He can never cast off His people (31:25-38).

By citing specific physical characteristics of the city of Jerusalem, Yahweh promises the restoration and protection of Israel.[213]

The siege is coming to a conclusion. Things look hopeless; and from a human point of view they are. Jeremiah, because of his "seditious views" is locked up. He has predicted that Jerusalem will be taken, Zedekiah carried off to Babylon, and the futility of resisting Babylon (32:1-5)

---

[212]But see Holladay, "Jer. 31:22b Reconsidered: 'The Woman Encompasses the Man,'" *VT* 16 (1966): 236-239.

[213]See G. Barkay and A. Kloner, "Jerusalem Tombs from the Days of the First Temple," *BAR* 12 (April 1986):23-39 for a discussion of this area. They argue that it may refer to the section north of the broad wall discovered by Avigad.

The Lord tells Jeremiah to prepare for an unusual request from his uncle with reference to a field. The purpose of this divinely planned incident, is to give hope to the people. This situation is the matter of *goel* (גּאֵל) re-demption of land sold due to poverty as set out in Lev. 25:25. Hanamel asks him to buy his property in the hometown village of Anathoth. This is a notoriously poor investment. The land is surrounded by Babylonians; everyone is about to lose their property; nothing is worth anything, and yet Hanamel wants Jeremiah to buy his land. Since Jeremiah knows now that it is from the Lord, he proceeds to carry out the transaction. He takes witnesses, writes a deed, pays seventeen shekels of silver and tells Baruch to put the deed where it will endure for a long time. The key words are "houses and fields and vineyards shall again be bought in this land" (32:6-15).

Jeremiah offers a marvelous intercessory prayer following the general pattern of Hebrew prayers: extolling God for His greatness, mercy, justice and redemption of Israel and finally confessing the sin of the people. "Nothing is too difficult for you" (*lo yipale' mimeka kal davar* לֹא יִפָּלֵא מִמְּךָ כָּל־דָּבָר) echoes Gen. 18:14. Jeremiah believes God is able to deliver His people. Furthermore, he appeals to the "loving kindness" (*ḥesed,* חֶסֶד) of God in the past and reminds Him of His justice and redemption. At the same time he acknowledges that Israel has not obeyed God. At the conclusion of his prayer he points out to God the obvious: the siege mounds are against the city, and all that God has pro-mised has come to pass. What puzzles Jeremiah is why God would ask him to buy land in this hopeless situation (32:16-23).

God's answer comes in the form of a question (echoing Jeremiah's reference to Gen. 18:14) and restatement of the litany of Israel's sins against Him. However, in spite of the fact that Israel must be judged because of her sin against Yahweh, He purposes a hopeful future for her. God will gather them from all the lands and "they shall be His people and He will be their God." There will be an everlasting covenant in which God's fear will be in their hearts (cf. 31:32). As a result *fields shall be bought in this land* when God restores their fortunes (32:24-44).

Yahweh brings a word of encouragement to Jeremiah while he is still locked up during the siege. He reminds Jeremiah of His sovereignty again. He is the one who made the earth and formed (*yotser,* יוֹצֵר) it to establish it. This statement indicates that no matter how bad the circumstances, people can trust the creator God to effect His will. He then tells Jeremiah to pray to Him so that He can show him great and mighty things. The word "mighty" usually refers to fortified cities (*betsuroth,* בְּצֻרוֹת as in Josh. 14:12). In this context it means inaccessible ideas. God will admit Jeremiah into His confidence (33:1-3).

In the present context things look hopeless. The Chaldeans are attacking in fulfillment of God's judgment and people are going to die. Yet, in spite of all the apparent hopelessness, God promises the restoration of Judah and the fortunes of Israel. The word "rebuild" shows up again. In familiar language, God promises to cleanse and forgive them. All the nations will testify of the grace of God (33:4-9).

A series of promises follows concerning the restoration of the city of Jerusalem and Judah. Israel is included in the other passages and so should be here. The reason for the emphasis on Jerusalem is because of her imminent fall. The promise is specifically applied to the city including even the name "*Yahweh Tsidkenu*" which in 23:6 is applied to the Messiah. The city has received the name in this parallel passage because she is the recipient of the righteousness brought by the "righteous branch." The Davidic covenant is prominent in this chapter (33:10-18).

A promise similar to that in chapter 31 is given. Since the covenant with nature made by God cannot be abrogated, neither can the seed of David be cut off. Even though there were gaps during which no king was on the throne, God's promise is that there will be a continuity of seed (33:19-22).

A closing word is appended similar to the preceding: the two houses (Israel/Judah) have been apparently destroyed. However, Yahweh insists that He will not reject the descendants of David or the descendants of Jacob (33:23-26).

E. Messages and events giving examples of the reason for the catastrophe (34:1—38:28).

1. Two events during the siege of Jerusalem: a word to Zedekiah and the abuse of slaves (an act of covenant breaking disobedience) (34:1-22).

Jeremiah delivered a message to King Zedekiah while Nebuchadnezzar was besieging the city and its outpost defenses of Azekah and Lachish. Yahweh promises Zedekiah his life even though he will go into captivity (34:1-7).

The second message was given in conjunction with the hypocritical action of releasing slaves in fulfillment of law (Exod. 21:2). This action was designed to secure Yahweh's favor, which they seem to have attained when the threat of Egyptian intervention caused the Babylonians to pull back (cf. 37:11). As soon as that happened, however, the leaders thought they were home free and took the slaves back again. Jeremiah denounced this self-serving action and promised to give them the "release" they refused to give to their people. This "release" would be to the sword, pestilence and the famine. Furthermore, the Babylonians who have withdrawn will return to take up the siege and leave Judah desolated (34:8-22).

2. Jeremiah uses the Rechabites to show Judah how she should have obeyed (35:1-19).

The events of this chapter take place toward the end of Jehoiakim's reign. 2 Kings 24:1-2 tells us that Jehoiakim rebelled against Babylon in 602/1 BC Nebuchadnezzar, unable to deal with the situation directly, sent bands of Arameans and others to harass Judah. This would be the kind of situation that would have driven the Rechabites into Jerusalem. Jeremiah put this chapter here to contrast the Jews of Zedekiah's day with the Rechabites of Jehoiakim's day. (35:1).

Jeremiah brought representatives of the Rechabite clan into a special room off the temple. There were probably plenty of witnesses. He then set wine before them and asked them to drink. They refused and gave him the reason: It seems their ancestor, Jonadab, commanded them never to drink wine, practice agriculture, nor live in permanent buildings. The only thing that had disrupted their obedience of that command was the attacks being carried out against them by the marauding bands mentioned above (35:2-11).

The Rechabites are identified with the Kenites in 1 Chron. 2:55. The Kenites have a long relation with Israel and seem to be virtual proselytes. Judges 1:16 identifies them with Moses' father-in-law. Jael, who killed Sisera the enemy of Israel, was in the Kenite clan. They were treated favorably by Saul (1 Sam. 15:6). Finally, the ancestor mentioned in Jeremiah joined with Jehu in the war against Baalism (2 Kings 10:15-16). Jonadab made his vow and enjoined it upon his descendants some three hundred years prior to the events of Jeremiah 35.

Yahweh then tells Jeremiah the import of the example. Israel has refused to listen to the warnings of Yahweh in spite of His tenacity in sending messengers, whereas the Rechabites have kept the word of their ancestor for some three hundred years. Consequently, God says that He is going to bring judgment on the city of Jerusalem. This would have been a devastating word as the city was under attack from various groups (35:12-17).

Because of this faithful attitude on the part of the Rechabites, God promised them that Jonadab would not lack a man to stand before Him (serve Him) forever. Keil reports that a fifteenth century Jewish missionary recounted that some people claiming to be Rechabites lived in Mesopotamia (35:18-19).[214]

3. Yahweh presents His word in written form and Jehoiakim disdains it (another example of radical disobedience) (36:1-32) (see also 45:1-5).

The events of this chapter are prior to those of chapter 35. They take place during that frightening fourth year when Nebuchadnezzar forced Jehoiakim to accept his suzerainty. It was a time of consternation and fear (35:1). The chapter is probably in this unit to show how the leadership despised the Word of God and therefore deserved judgment.

We have in this chapter a glimpse into the production of Scripture. Yahweh tells Jeremiah to take a scroll and write on it the messages he has been speaking about Israel and Judah from the year 627 BC to the present (605 BC). The purpose of this scroll is to entice Judah to repent so that God may be able to forgive their sin (36:2-3).

Jeremiah calls his secretary, Baruch, and dictates to him the words of Yahweh that He had spoken to him. He then tells Baruch to read it on a fast day since Jeremiah is restrained (prevented) from speaking in the temple (36:4-8).

---

[214]Keil, *Jeremiah,* 2:92.

The first occasion to read the scroll on a fast day comes in the fifth year of Jehoiakim when people had been summoned to fast (for Yahweh's deliverance). Baruch read the scroll before everyone (36:9-10).

A comparison is being drawn between this scroll and the one found by Josiah (2 Kings 22). The Scribe's name in Josiah's day was Shaphan. Jeremiah's scroll was read by Baruch in the room of Gemariah, Shaphan's son. It is Shaphan's grandson, Michaiah, who reports on the words of Baruch. A certain Elnathan (v. 12) is among the officials. This Elnathan is the son of Achbor who is probably the Achbor of 2 Kings 22:12. As God's word was preserved in the temple and resulted in a great reformation, so God's word is being preserved and read to the people to produce repentance.

The officials have Baruch read the scroll and question him about the way it was written. They decide to report the situation to the king, but warn Baruch to hide himself and Jeremiah (36:11-19).

At the king's command, the scroll is read, and, in spite of remonstrations by the godly officials, Jehoiakim cuts the scroll up column by column and throws it into the fire. He then sends out word to arrest Jeremiah and Baruch, but God hides them (36:20-26).

Yahweh's word cannot be destroyed by lesser or greater men. He orders Jeremiah to make another copy of the previous messages to expand on them. He also has a special message to Jehoiakim: none of his descendants will sit on the throne (Jehoiachin does not count, since he was only there to surrender the city), and he would die an ignominious death (36:27-32).

Chapter 45 should be read in this connection as God's personal word to Baruch when he apparently became discouraged over the way the king handled the word of God.[215]

4. Jeremiah suffers under the hands of the wicked officials when the city comes under siege (further examples of rejection of God's word and messenger) (37:1—38:28).

The heading in 37:1-2 is necessary because chapters 35-36 from the period of Jehoiakim have intervened. The arrangement may be in this order to show the crescendo of disobedience, culminating in Jehoiakim's destruction of the scroll but finalized in the defeat of Zedekiah.

In spite of the king's disobedience, he still respected Jeremiah and knew that he spoke from Yahweh. Consequently, when the sally of the Egyptians forced the Babylonians to retire from the siege, Zedekiah sent to Jeremiah to ask him to pray, with the understanding that he would give advice to the king. Jeremiah's response to the king was that the Babylonians would return and lay siege to the city again and the city would be burned with fire (37:3-10).

---

[215]Much ink has been spilled trying to identify the scroll of Jeremiah written in 605 BC., with sections of the book of Jeremiah. Most people (see, e.g., Bright) will assume that it is contained within the first 25 chapters of the book of Jeremiah. It would have been expanded and updated for the final form as we have it in the present text (by Jeremiah and Baruch). By way of speculation, is it possible that scroll floated around and was read by people as the authoritative word of God (much as Paul's non-canonical letters would have been)? We know that in addition to chapter 36, Jeremiah wrote letters to the exile (chapter 29). Likewise in chapter 30, Jeremiah is told to write "all the words which I have spoken to you in a book." Could there be some relation between these several written documents of Jeremiah and the text we now have in the LXX? Technically, we would refer to the book of Jeremiah in our Hebrew Bibles as the canonical Jeremiah (and as the autograph) while the shorter work would have to be referred to as pre-canonical. It was just as surely the word of God as were Jeremiah's oral messages, but *in that form*, it was not canonical.

During the respite that came from the Babylonian withdrawal, Jeremiah decided to go check out some property in Anathoth. (The word in *NASB* "take possession of property" and KJV "to separate himself" is from the Hebrew *laḥeliq,*(לַחֲלִק) a shortened form of לְהַחֲלִיק (*lᵉheḥeliq*) which means "to divide up as property." This is supported by the LXX rendering.) Since Jeremiah was in prison when he purchased the property from his uncle (Ch. 32), this situation must have taken place prior to that purchase. Consequently, we can only assume that he was considering this property ahead of time. Looking for a pretext to punish Jeremiah, Irijah arrested Jeremiah, accusing him of deserting to the Chaldeans. He was beaten and thrown into a temporary jail for many days (37:11-16).

Zedekiah, demonstrating his weak character, summoned Jeremiah secretly to inquire of the Lord. Jeremiah stands behind his original statement that Zedekiah would be delivered over to the king of Babylon. He then protests his treatment asking what he has done to deserve such treatment. He even throws the false prophets into Zedekiah's face by asking where they are now that their prophecies have proven false. Finally Jeremiah petitions Zedekiah not to leave him in the temporary prison. Apparently the conditions were so bad Jeremiah feared for his life. Zedekiah had him moved to more favorable quarters (37:17-21).

The officials of the city decided Jeremiah had to be silenced. His messages to a city under siege would either have to be obeyed or he would have to be eliminated. The hands of the people who were being urged to defend the city were being weakened. The officials chose to kill the bearer of bad news. The weak-kneed king capitulated to their demands and Jeremiah was put into an empty cistern that had only mud at the bottom (38:1-6).

An Ethiopian eunuch (remember the one in Acts 8) whose name was even generic (king's servant) had compassion on Jeremiah. How pathetic that only a foreigner believed in Jeremiah sufficiently to risk his life for him. He went to the king and begged for Jeremiah's life. The king consented and Ebed-melech pulled Jeremiah from the cistern (3 men rather than 30 accompanied him: shalosh vs sh⁽ᵉ⁾loshim), and he was allowed to stay in the guardhouse. Ebed-melech's reward is stated in 39:15ff (38:7-13).

Zedekiah once again secretly meets with Jeremiah to find out Yahweh's plans. Jeremiah tells him they have not changed. Zedekiah will be delivered over to the Babylonians. His only hope is to surrender to Nebuchadnezzar. Zedekiah's weakness is demonstrated in his excuse that he fears the deserters. Jeremiah promises him that nothing will happen, but he still refuses to follow Jeremiah's direction. To protect Jeremiah, Zedekiah tells him to inform the officials who will probe him, that he was petitioning Zedekiah not to send him back to Jonathan's prison house. This was not a lie since we know that Jeremiah had petitioned the king to remove him from that house (37:20), and no doubt was now asking the king not to return him there (38:14-28).

F.   The city falls to Nebuchadnezzar (39:1-18).

The denouement has arrived. The promised catastrophe designed to fit a disobedient king and people has come as Jeremiah, God's messenger predicted it. After a siege lasting eighteen months, the army of Nebuchadnezzar was able to break through the outer defenses and the representatives set up thrones to begin judgment on the city. Zedekiah and his advisors tried to flee in the night toward the south. The statement 39:4 should not be understood to mean that Zedekiah did not flee until after the walls were breached. They were caught as they approached Jericho and brought to Riblah in Hamath (in the north) where King Nebuchadnezzar pronounced judgment on him as a rebel vassal. Nebuchadnezzar killed Zedekiah's sons before his eyes along with the nobles of Judah, put out Zedekiah's eyes, and carried him to Babylon (39:1-10).

A recapitulation of these events with additional details is given in chapter 52. There we learn of the burning of the king's house, the tearing down of the walls of the city, and the deportation of the people. The numbers differ from 2 Kings possibly, as Thompson says, because only the males are numbered in Jeremiah.[216] The third deportation is otherwise unknown. It may have been a punitive raid after the assassination of Gedaliah.

The deportation of the temple furniture is mentioned in this chapter as well. Priestly and civil leaders caught in Jerusalem were taken to Riblah where they were killed at Nebuchadnezzar's command.

Nebuchadnezzar had heard of Jeremiah's messages, which, of course, he regarded favorably. As a result he commanded his officers to treat Jeremiah kindly. They took him from the guardhouse and turned him over to Gedaliah whom they would appoint as governor of the land (39:11-14).[217]

A postscript in chapter 39 gives the message revealed to Jeremiah in behalf of Ebed-melech: in the imminent destruction of the city, Ebed-melech will be delivered. He would have his life for booty because he trusted in Yahweh (39:15-18).[218]

---

[216]Thompson, *Jeremiah, loc. cit.*

[217]See the discussion in chapter 40 for the different accounts.

[218]Chronology of the Siege of Jerusalem:

Ninth year
Mo. 10   Siege began on 10th day (588)
 11
 12
Tenth year (587)
 1 [Precise dates for following events unknown]
 2 Jeremiah free to move (37:4)
 3 Slaves released (34:8)

G. Prophecies and events after the fall of Jerusalem (40:1—44:30).

1. Gedaliah is appointed governor (40:1-16).

The heading "The word which came to Jeremiah" cannot refer to this chapter for there is no word. It must be a heading for this entire section and includes the prophecies in Egypt (40:1).

More details are added about the release of Jeremiah to those in chapter 39. There he was taken from the guardhouse; here he is taken at Ramah where he had been confined with other non-combatant personnel. The events of chapter 40 are expanded and provide the full sequence of events. Chapter 39 is abbreviated and omits entirely the trip to Ramah. From the perspective of that chapter, Jeremiah was taken from the court by the Babylonian officer because the intermediate step is ignored. Jeremiah is given the option of going to Babylon or remaining in the land with Gedaliah. When he makes no decision, the officer makes it for him and sends him to Gedaliah (40:2-6).

---

4 Egyptian threat; siege lifted (37:5; 34:21)
5 Jeremiah went out to check property (37:12)
6   (was this in anticipation of the offer in 32?)
7 Jeremiah was arrested (37:15,16)
8 Zedekiah appealed to him and released him to an
9   easier confinement (37:17-21)
10 Jeremiah, in prison, bought property (32:6-15)
11 Jeremiah preaches from jail and is put in pit (38:6)
12 Jeremiah is removed from pit and sent to the court (38:28)
Eleventh year (586)
1
2
3
4 City broken into 9th day (586)
5 City burned, temple destroyed 7th day (586)
7 Gedaliah assassinated

Gedaliah's father had already been instrumental in protecting Jeremiah (26:24). When the Judean officers who had been able to escape heard about Gedaliah, they returned to him. Their group included one Ishmael ben Nethaniah. Gedaliah urged them to accept the Babylonian victory and get on with the business of making a living. Other Jews who had fled to Moab, Ammon and Edom came back and submitted themselves to Gedaliah's rule (40:7-12).

The Jewish officers became aware of a plot on Gedaliah's life by Ishmael ben Nethaniah. Ishmael was a member of the royal family and perhaps part of that bitter anti-Babylonian faction that could not tolerate defeat. He was being used by Baalis the Ammonite, perhaps because the latter wanted to meddle in the Judean affairs. Gedaliah refused to believe the report and turned down Johanan's offer to assassinate Ishmael (40:13-16).

2.   Gedaliah is assassinated (41:1-18).

Ishmael joined Gedaliah at Mizpah for a meal and treacherously killed him. He also killed the Jews who were with Gedaliah and the Babylonian garrison left there to keep the peace (41:1-3).

Ishmael showed his true character when he slaughtered seventy of the eighty pilgrims who were on their way to Jerusalem to offer sacrifice on the ruined altar. Ten were able to escape because they told him they had treasures buried in the ground. Ishmael then took the people who were at Mizpah and headed toward Ammon (41:4-10).

Johanan and the other officers pursued Ishmael and overtook him at the large cistern.[219] The prisoners broke away from him and went with Johanan, but Ishmael and eight men got away and fled to Ammon. Johanan then took the people to a place near Bethlehem to

---

[219]See *ANEP* #'s 877-79 for pictures of the cistern.

prepare to flee to Egypt. They assumed that there would be retaliation from the Babylonians for the assassination of Gedaliah (41:11-18).

3. Direction from the Lord is sought from Jeremiah and then rejected (42:1-43:7).

    Johanan and the officers and all the people approached Jeremiah and asked him to seek Yahweh's mind about going to Egypt. They gave their solemn word that whatever the response was—pleasant or unpleasant—they would listen to it (42:1-6).

    Jeremiah returned within ten days with a message from the Lord. That message was that if they would stay in the land that Yahweh would *plant* and not *uproot* them. They did not need to fear the Babylonians, for God was with them. On the other, hand should they insist on going to Egypt, they need not expect God's protection. On the contrary, He would judge them if they went to Egypt. God's only plan of protection for His people was to surrender to the Babylonians. He offered no other (42:7-22).

    It is the ultimate irony that Jeremiah, after seeing all his prophecies come true, was called a liar by these blasphemous and rebellious people. An evidence of Baruch's stature may be that they accused Jeremiah of following Baruch's directions. It could also be that blaming Baruch removed some of the onus of rejecting Jeremiah's word. Johanan and the officers then took all the people along with Jeremiah and Baruch and went to Egypt (43:1-7).

4. Jeremiah's prophecies in Egypt (43:8—44:30).

    Jeremiah stood resolute even though alone in Egypt and insisted that God's judgment would be carried out on this rebellious people through Nebuchadnezzar. Jeremiah placed stones to represent symbolically that Nebuchadnezzar would place his throne in Egypt to conquer it. We know that Nebuchadnezzar invaded Egypt in 567 BC ". . . [in] the 37th year, Nebuchadnezzar, king of Bab[ylon] mar[ched against] Egypt (Mi-sir) to deliver a battle."[220] Jeremiah predicted that Nebuchadnezzar would invade Heliopolis (north of Cairo) and shatter the obelisks (*matseboth,* מַצֵּבוֹת), and burn temples.[221]

Jeremiah confronted the Jewish remnant once again and recited the abysmal history of the Jewish people to them. They disobeyed Yahweh continuously, and the result was this exile in Egypt. He told them that God was going to punish the remnant in Egypt (44:1-15).

The people responded angrily to Jeremiah that they were not going to listen to his message from Yahweh. They were going to do what they chose to do for they had had nothing but trouble since they stopped worshipping the Queen of Heaven. Furthermore, the women were not alone in the worship—their husbands were with them in it (44:16-19).[222]

Jeremiah's last recorded word is one of denunciation of these stubborn people. He told them to go ahead with their syncretistic religion. God was going to punish them so that only a few would be able to creep back to the land of Abraham. This remnant would no longer say "As the Lord lives" for the simple reason that He will be judging them, and they will not be worshipping Him. The sign to prove the veracity of Jeremiah's prophecy was that Pharaoh Hophra

[220]*ANET*, p. 308.

[221]Cf. The Elephantine papyri where the Jews seem to say that Cambyses (525 B.C.) tore down Egyptian temples, but did not tear down the Jewish temple, but see my excursus on Babylon/Persia and Egypt at Ezekiel 29.

[222]This seems to indicate that the Queen of Heaven cult was especially attractive to women as a fertility cult.

would be defeated by Nebuchadnezzar just as Zedekiah was (44:20-30).[223]

H. God gives a special personal message to Jeremiah's Scribe, Baruch (Appendix I) (45:1-6).

The background for this chapter is found in chapter 36 when Jehoiakim burned the scroll containing the promise of judgment unless repentance was forthcoming. It is probably placed here to show that the predictions found in the scroll indeed came to pass. Baruch, the faithful but discouraged scribe, was kept alive by the promises of God to go to Egypt. So ends the sad story of the fall: all that God promised in the written word has come to pass.

I. Jeremiah delivers a series of oracles against the nations (Appendix II) (46—51).

As noted above this section on the nations occurs in the LXX after 25:13 and is arranged somewhat differently internally as well. This was no doubt a unit and was assembled in a different way in the Vorlage (underlying text) of the LXX than was done in the Masoretic Text (by Baruch?). As it stands in the Masoretic Text, it is an appendix expanding on the small list of oracles in chapter 25. There, as here, the surrounding nations are dealt with first and the last word is reserved for Babylon (Sheshach).

---

[223]Apries (Pharaoh Hophra of the Bible, 588-566 B.C.) was essentially in the hands of his Greek mercenaries (much to the resentment of the population). He supported King Zedekiah in his revolt against Babylon and attacked Phoenicia from the sea. The army revolted and put an officer, Amasis (d. 526), in as co-regent. Apries tried to reestablish himself, but was defeated and slain by his own men. See Kitchen, *Third Intermediate Period.*

1. Egypt

    The first oracle against Egypt was given after Nebuchadnezzar had defeated Egypt at Carchemish. A vivid, poetic description is given of Egypt's fall (46:1-12).

    The second oracle is delivered when Nebuchadnezzar, after returning home to be crowned king, presses on into Egypt. Egypt is told to prepare for the exile as Judah had already done (46:13-26). In contrast to Egypt, Judah/Israel are promised deliverance. This unit comes from 30:10-11 where it fits the context. It has been placed here to draw a contrast between the judgment on Egypt and the hope for Judah (46:27-28).

2. Philistia

    It is not clear at what point in Nebuchadnezzar's defeat of the west that this oracle fits. It predicts the fall and defeat of the cities of Philistia and her allies (47:1-7).

3. Moab

    A series of oracles against Moab are brought together in which the many small cities of Moab are mentioned and the promise is made of the destruction of the nation. At the same time a promise is made of the restoration of Moab in the latter days (48:1-47).

4. Ammon

    Ammon is chastened for taking possession of territory belonging to Gad. Her god is Milcom, and Yahweh is going to take them into judgment. Again the promise is given of restoration of Ammon (49:1-6).

5. Edom

   This message against Edom consists of a mélange of prophecies, some of which may have existed before Jeremiah's time. They have been brought together to show God's judgment against this little country that was always at odds with Israel. Sections of this oracle are virtually identical with sections of Obadiah, which I assume was written (compiled) after Jeremiah (see notes on Obadiah) (49:7-22).

6. Damascus

   The capital of Aram will also fall prey to Nebuchadnezzar's attacks (49:23-27).

7. Kedar/Hazor

   These names refer to Arab tribes living east of Palestine. Hazor is not the well-known town north of the Sea of Galilee. It may refer to unwalled villages (49:28-33).

8. Elam

   Elam was an Indo-European country east of Babylon. Her defeat is here predicted, but she is also promised restoration in the last days (49:34-39).

9. Babylon

   In Jeremiah's earlier ministry, Babylon was considered to be God's servant. Nebuchadnezzar's God-ordained task was to punish Israel for her sins. Now at the end of his book, Israel having been taken into exile, God's wrath turns on the one who pridefully rejoiced in the destruction of Israel. One hundred verses are devoted to prophecies about Babylon. Merathiam and Pekod are known places within Babylonia (v. 21). However, they have other meanings in Hebrew: Merathiam means double rebellion and Pekod means judgment.[224] We read at the end of chapter 51 that Jeremiah wrote a series of oracles against Babylon and sent them to the captives in Babylon to reassure them about God's future deliverance. These oracles were composed over a period of time and under different circumstances. Jeremiah now brings them together and sends them to Babylon after the fall of the city in 586 BC The closing statement ("Thus far are the words of Jeremiah") indicates that the prophecies of Jeremiah end at this point (50:1—51:64).[225]

J. An epilogue is provided to show the subsequent history of Judah (52:1-34).

   1. The fall is recapitulated and the reasons for it are provided (52:1-30).

   The purpose of this chapter is to provide at the end of this long prophecy the final statement on the fate of the nation to whom Jeremiah had prophesied over many years, a nation which had consistently rejected that message to their own detriment. Chapter 52 says that God fulfilled his predictions of judgment against His own people.

   2. A post-script is given on the elevation of Jehoiachin in captivity (52:31-34).

   This unit appears also in 2 Kings 25. Ewal-marduk decided to honor Jehoiachin by taking him out of prison and giving him a daily ration. Since this happened in the thirty-seventh year of the captivity the date would be 560 BC "...t[o] *Ia-u-kin*, king...10 (sila of oil) to...[*Ia*] -*kin*, king of Ia[...]."[226]

---

[224]Thompson, *Jeremiah*, p. 741.

[225]See my discussion below on the composition of the epilogue.

[226]*ANET*, p. 308.

We know from the Elephantine Papyri that there was communication between the Jews of upper Egypt and Palestine in the fifth century. It is not inconceivable that Jeremiah could have written this addendum when he, with the assistance of Baruch, compiled the book. If he were eighteen, say, when he was called as a youth, he would have been eighty-five when Jehoiachin was elevated. It is also possible that Baruch as his amanuensis added this post-script that signified the conclusion of an era—the last act of the last official king of Judah. ("...till the day of his death" may take the postscript beyond both Jeremiah and Baruch. If so we would have someone like the Chronicler adding this last item.) In a sense also it closes the book on the divine judgment brought upon the spiritually bankrupt leadership of Israel, those descendants of David who failed to follow their Master.

A Synopsis of Events in the Seventh Century: Josiah and Sons

640 Josiah became king at age eight (640-609).

632 At age sixteen, he began to seek the Lord.

628 At age 20, he began to purge Judah and Jerusalem of idolatry.

627 Jeremiah was called to the prophetic ministry at a young age.

625 Nabopolassar was able to declare complete independence from the Assyrians and to begin the Neo-Babylonian Empire.

622 The Book of the Law was found in the temple, bringing further reform.

The waning power of the Assyrians allowed Josiah to take the reform movement into the northern area that was formerly Israel. These people were still Jewish, however mixed with foreign blood. They were basically apostate, and Josiah tried to influence them spiritually.

612 Nabopolassar, joined by the Medes and Scythians, attacked and defeated the Assyrians in Nineveh.

609 The Assyrians fled to Haran where they prepared to take a stand against General Nebuchadnezzar. The Egyptians, preferring a weak Assyria to a strong Babylon, went to Assyria's side at Haran. Josiah, following his great-great grandfather Hezekiah's foreign policy, wanted to see the Assyrians defeated and so tried to stop Pharaoh Necho at Megiddo. He was killed at age 39.[227]

The people placed Josiah's son, Jehoahaz (Shallum) on the throne, but Pharaoh Necho, asserting his desire to control Syria and Palestine, removed him, took him to Egypt, and placed his brother, Jehoiakim, on the throne (609-597).

605 Final defeat of Assyria (and Egypt) at Carchemish. Nebuchadnezzar hurried back to Babylon to assume the crown on the death of his father. Sometime that year, he had forced Jehoiakim to change allegiance from Egypt to Babylon. He may even have taken Jehoiakim to Babylon as part of the victory parade and then returned him (2 Chron 36:6).

601 In December Nebuchadnezzar marched against Egypt. Judah was probably still a vassal of Babylon (he would not likely have left his rear exposed to a hostile army). The battle was fierce and Babylon suffered heavy losses. Nebuchadnezzar returned to Babylon to regroup his army (*ANET* sup. p. 564). It was probably at this time that Jehoiakim rebelled (2 Kings 24:2).

597 Jehoiakim had plotted revolt against Babylon and Nebuchadnezzar, having gotten affairs in order in the east, marched against Jerusalem to reckon with Jehoiakim's rebellion. Jehoiakim was killed, possibly in a palace coup in an effort to placate Nebuchadnezzar. The strategy apparently worked, for Nebuchadnezzar spared the city. However, he took Jehoiakim's son, Jehoiachin, who had reigned three months into captivity as a hostage. He placed another son of Josiah, Zedekiah, on the throne (597-586).

586 In spite of Jeremiah's constant urging to submit to the yoke of Nebuchadnezzar as God's servant, Zedekiah entered into alliances to

---

[227]See a summary of events by D. Wiseman, *Chronicles of Chaldaean Kings,* pp. 43-49.

revolt against Babylonia. Nebuchadnezzar came west and besieged the city of Jerusalem in 588. After one and a half years, the walls were breached. Zedekiah tried to escape, but was captured and sent to Babylon. The city was destroyed, the temple was torn down and many people were taken into captivity. The date was 586 BC

Gedaliah, a member of the royal family, was appointed governor by the Babylonians. Just three months after the fall of the city, he was assassinated, and the remnant fled to Egypt. Jeremiah and Baruch were also taken to Egypt, where Jeremiah continued to prophesy to an unrepentant people.

582 Jeremiah 52:30 speaks of a deportation of 745 people in this year. Was this a punitive raid to deal with the assassination of Gedaliah?

560 Jehoiachin is taken from prison in Babylon and given a stipend and provisions "until the day of his death." He was fifty-five years old when elevated.

Notes on the Book of Lamentations

I.   The Position of Lamentations in the Canon.

Lamentations is being studied in this course on the prophets because it has been traditionally linked with the prophet Jeremiah and in our English Bibles follows Jeremiah. There is nothing in the Masoretic Text that attributes it to Jeremiah. The Greek Text does attribute it to him as do other versions of the Old Testament. Arguments are posited for and against Jeremianic authorship, but the contents of the book do not prove conclusively whether or not they come from Jeremiah's hand. Certainly, the thought and style are similar to Jeremiah's, and since there is no other known person to whom the work might be attributed, we will follow the traditional position.

II. The Name of the Book.

The Hebrew name of the book is *'Ekah* (אֵיכָה), the Hebrew word for "How" or "Oh" that appears at 1:1, 2:1, and 4:1. The Greek title is *Threnos* meaning lament, and that title came through the Latin into English.

III. The Date of the Book.

There is virtual agreement among scholars that the book of Lamentations is contemporaneous with the events of the fall of the city and temple in 586 B.C. There is no internal evidence that it is written from the exile, and the events seem to be presented by an eyewitness to the tragic events of Judah's last days.

V. The Poetic Style of the Book.

The poetic structure of Lamentations is what is called an acrostic, that is the poem is built around the alphabet. Remember that the Hebrew alphabet has twenty-two letters beginning with "A" and ending with "T." Chapters one and two consist of twenty-two stanzas, the first word of each beginning with the appropriate letter of the alphabet. Chapter three also has twenty-two stanzas but each of the three lines in each stanza begins with the appropriate letter. Chapter four goes back to the pattern found in chapters one and two with the exception that it has two-line stanzas rather than three. The fifth chapter has twenty-two stanzas (or lines in this case), but the lines do not begin with successive letters of the alphabet.

One possible reason for acrostic poetry may be to aid the memory, but if that were its only purpose, one might expect more Scripture to have been written in that style. It is primarily an alternate style of writing poetry and is thus a piece of artistry.[228]

V. Structure of Lamentations[229]

Chapter 1

א (all verse 1)

ב (all verse 2)

Twenty-two verses—sixty-six lines.

---

[228]See also D. R. Hillers, *Lamentations,* and R. K. Harrison, *Jeremiah and Lamentations,* for a good discussion.

[229]See H. Heater, "Structure and Meaning in Lamentations," *BibSac* 149 (1992) 304-15 (Reprinted in *Vital Old Testament Issues*).

Chapter 2

Same as chapter 1.

Chapter 3

א (verse 1)
א (verse 2)
א (verse 3)
ב (verse 4)
ב (verse 5)
ב (verse 6)

Sixty-six lines (one per verse).
Each line begins with the appropriate letter.

Chapter 4

Same as chapters 1-2 except that there are two lines per stanza rather than three.

Chapter 5

The alphabet is not used, but there are twenty-two lines. Verses 19-20, the greatest confession of the book, may be a mini-acrostic. Aleph to Kaph (first half of alphabet) and Lamedh to Tau (second half of the alphabet).

אַתָּה יהוה לְעוֹלָם תֵּשֵׁב   כִּסְאֲךָ לְדֹר וָדוֹר
לָמָה לָנֶצַח תִּשְׁכָּחֵנוּ   תַּעַזְבֵנוּ לְאֹרֶךְ יָמִים

The chapters are not uniform in their use of the alphabet. Chapters one and two are the same: there are sixty-six lines (three lines per verse) and each *verse* begins with a letter of the alphabet. Chapter one also breaks the sense in the middle of the alphabet. Thus A to K is the author speaking of the awful fall of Jerusalem. L-Z (L-T in Hebrew) personifies Zion who speaks of her desolation.

Chapter 3 (the middle chapter) intensifies the use of the alphabet. There are still sixty-six lines, but *each* line begins with a letter of the alphabet. The subject matter of chapter 3 is also somewhat general. The writer expresses his dismay, his contrition, and his hope of restoration. This then is the "peak" chapter in the book.

But just as crescendo can express emphasis, so can diminuendo, and this is what takes place in the remainder of the book. Chapter 4 reverts to the pattern of chapters 1-2, with the difference that there are only two lines per stanza instead of three. In this chapter the writer relives the agony of the destruction.

The volume of the composition drops to a whisper in chapter 5. Here there are no letters used at all, although the 22 lines represent the 22 letter alphabet. Moreover, verses 19-20 are themselves a mini-acrostic used to express the highest praise for Yahweh in the book followed by a tentative, but hopeful cry for help.

Yahweh is sovereign!

A—You, O Lord, do rule for ever;
K—Your throne is from generation to generation.

But O Lord do not abandon us!!

L—Why do You forget us forever;
Z—Why do You forsake us so long?

VI. The Theology of the Book

From the Jewish point of view an unmitigated tragedy took place in 586 B.C. The city and temple, visible evidences of God's presence and therefore constant reassurances that God had elected the city and the people, were gone. Popular sentiment apparently held that as long as the temple was in the city, the city was impregnable (cf. the temple sermon in Jeremiah 7). God's people were in disgrace in exile and thus defeated by the nations. The author of Lamentations does not question the rightness of what God did, but he is confessing his grief that it happened. The people had to wrestle with the question of God's purpose. LaSor, *et al.*, say: "In Lamentations the three great strands of Israel's literature and faith are woven together: the prophets' insights into the judgment and grace of the covenant Lord; the priests' liturgical expression of contrition and hope; the wise men's wrestlings with the mysteries of suffering. The poet of Lamentations is heir to them all, but not as mere scribe or recorder. The texture and pattern of the weaving are his own, adding a subtlety and beauty that make the book a treasured tapestry of biblical revelation."[230]

VII. Outline of the Book.

A. A vivid, dramatic description of the tragic fall of Jerusalem is given (1:1-22).

   1. The Prophet speaks of the desolate city (1:1-11).

      This unit is in the third person and speaks of the fall from greatness to that of a forced laborer. Her friends (other nations) have betrayed her. She weeps at night in exile and harsh servitude. She dwells among nations without rest. Her adversaries have become her masters (1:1-5).

      Her precious things are remembered. She has become unclean. She has no comforter (cf. 1:2, 16, 21). Her precious things are mentioned again (v. 10) and they are given for food (v 11). Zion personified breaks out in the first person in 9 and 11 to prepare the way for the last section (1:6-11).

---

[230]LaSor, *et al.*, *Old Testament Survey*, p. 622.

LAMENTATIONS: A MUSICAL COMPOSITION

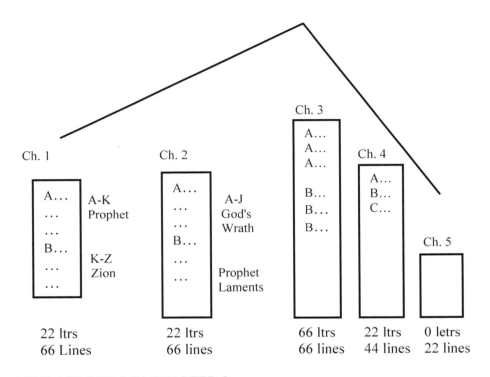

MINI-ACROSTIC IN CHAPTER 5

V. 18 A-K You are sovereign   V. 19 L-Z Why do you forget

2. Zion speaks of the desolate city (1:12-22).

    The poem is divided in half. The second part of the alphabet uses the
    poetic device of personification. Zion speaks and laments her troubles.

    Zion confesses the justness of what has happened to her, but she cries
    out bitterly that no one takes note of her distress. She acknowledges
    that what God has done to her was deserved, but she gives in detail
    what He has done: fire into my bones, spread a net for my feet, turned
    me back, etc. (1:12-15).

Zion confesses her sin. "The Lord is righteous, for I have rebelled against His command." She sought help from her lovers (Egypt, Philistia, etc.), but they deceived her. She calls out to God to judge her enemies as He has promised to do. She longs for the Day of the Lord that her enemies might experience what she has endured (1:16-22).

B. A detailed description of the city from the point of view of Yahweh and the prophet is given (2:1-22).

1. The havoc wreaked upon the city came from Yahweh (2:1-10).

Yahweh is referred to by name or pronoun some forty-five times. The prophet is clearly referring to this tragedy as an act authored by Yahweh. It did not happen accidentally. Six references are made to God's anger and more are obliquely given. Yahweh has become an enemy to Judah, and He has destroyed the temple (under the picture of a booth [שֻׂכּוֹ sukko]). He has rejected His altar and abandoned His sanctuary. The walls, gates, and bars of the city have been torn down by Yahweh as well. The king is gone, the law is no more, the prophets find no vision, the elders are silent, the virgins have bowed their heads—Yahweh has done it all.

2. The prophet speaks a lament over the "daughter of Zion" (2:11-22).

The sense break in this chapter does not come in the middle as it did in chapter 1. At verse 11 the prophet speaks of his grief over the city. In gentle, compassionate tones he speaks of the suffering of the little children (11), of the deceit of the false prophets that led them astray (14), and of the people who pass by mocking the city (15-16). But all of this is in God's eternal plan. It is not something that caught Him by surprise (17). The prophet urges Yahweh to look at the devastation wrought; to see the mothers eating their children. He uses a phrase we have encountered in Jeremiah: *Terrors on every side* (*m^{e}gure misabib*, מָגוּרֵי מִסָּבִיב).

C. The third chapter (the middle chapter of the book) is different from the others: it is a general rather than specific lament and it begins each line with the appropriate letter of the alphabet (3:1-66).

   1. The prophet laments God's judgment on him (3:1-19).

      This first person section should be viewed as the prophet speaking for the people. With repeated references to Yahweh as the author of his problems, the prophet struggles with all the suffering he is undergoing. These words are reminiscent of Job in a number of details. He concludes the unit by calling upon Yahweh to remember his afflictions (19).

   2. The prophet expresses hope in God (3:20-39).

      He reminds Yahweh of His *hesed* (mercy, grace) (22), and says that the one who waits patiently for the Lord is rewarded (26). This quiet confidence is the underpinning for Judah's hope in the dark days of the exile. God does not afflict willingly (33), He does not deprive people of justice (35), both good and will come from God (38), therefore, the Jews can trust Him in this calamity, and complaint is out of order (39).

   3. The prophet acknowledges that confession and repentance are proper (3:40-42).

      This little section is an asseveration of the prophet's confidence in God's forgiveness for those who will acknowledge their sinfulness and humbly return to Yahweh. He will receive and pardon them.

   4. The prophet returns to the dismal state of the people and prays for vengeance on the enemy (3:43-66).

      He laments God's judgment, though he confesses Judah's transgression, which, he says, God has not pardoned (42-44). The recurring phrase "My eyes run down with streams of water" brings him to speak again of his vulnerability and helplessness before the enemy (45-55).

He states that Yahweh has heard (56), drawn near, encouraged, and pleaded his case (58).

He concludes the unit by calling upon Yahweh to avenge Judah of her enemies: those who have mocked her and had schemes against her (59-66).

D. The prophet returns to a poem with two line stanzas, with the first word having the appropriate letter, to relive the terrible days of destruction (4:1-22).

   1. The people of Judah are compared to marred metal (4:1-6).

The precious sons of Zion are considered to be worthless, like earthen jars. His people have become cruel, refusing to feed their young. Delicate people have become desolate. The reason for the judgment is that Judah's sin is like that of Sodom and Gomorrah which were overthrown without human hand.

   2. The dramatic change wrought in the people because of the Babylonian attack is detailed (4:7-13).

He refers to her consecrated ones (7). This is the word Nazirite, but he seems to be using it here to describe all the Judeans as God's special ones. They once were beautiful, but they are now ugly. The horrors of dying of starvation are depicted here. People boiled their own children (10). This has come about because of the wrath of Yahweh (11). No one believed it would ever happen to Jerusalem—but it happened because of the sins of her prophets and priests (12-13).

   3. The prophet speaks of the creeping conclusion of their lives (4:14-22).

One can see the people with their leaders desperately casting about for help from any source (17). Their plea to Egypt yielded little fruit and only raised false hopes. The enemy hunted their steps and brought them down. The king (Lord's anointed) was captured (20). A brief allusion is made to Edom (see Jeremiah 49 and Obadiah) who rejoiced at the destruction of Judah. Your turn will come, says the prophet. Judah has suffered and gone into exile, but Edom will one day be punished as well (21-22). How they must have chafed to see their arch enemy rejoicing from the side lines, while they as God's elect went into captivity.

E. A final plea is made to Yahweh to remember them (5:1-22).

1. A final statement is made of the desolation of Zion (5:1-18).

The tone of this chapter is a bit more remote than the preceding. The extent of the calamity has begun to be apparent. The Judeans recognize that they have had to submit to others for daily subsistence. This reference to Egypt and Assyria alludes to the past alliances with these nations. Could it refer to the "lovers of Judah" who provided them with "bread."[231] The terrible treatment of the women (11), the rulers and elders (12), and the boys (13) is set out. Judah's glory has turned to shame (15-18).

2. The book closes with a tribute and a plea to Yahweh (5:19-22).

Yahweh is great and glorious, but He is urged not to forget His people but to restore them so that they might return.

Yahweh is sovereign!
(Mini-Acrostic)

A—You, O Lord, do rule for ever;
K—Your throne is from generation to generation.

But O Lord do not abandon us!!

L—Why do You forget us forever;
Z—Why do You forsake us so long?

---

[231]So Hillers, *Lamentations*, 4-6.

A final tentative note is sounded: "Unless You have utterly rejected us," a position the prophet cannot and will not hold because of his confidence in God's grace.

PROPHETS DIRECTED AGAINST CERTAIN NATIONS

Four prophets directed their messages exclusively to one nation. These men lived centuries apart (Jonah in the eighth century; Nahum prior to 612 B.C.; Habakkuk sometime in the vicinity of the Neo-Chaldean empire [625-539]; Obadiah probably after the fall of Jerusalem).

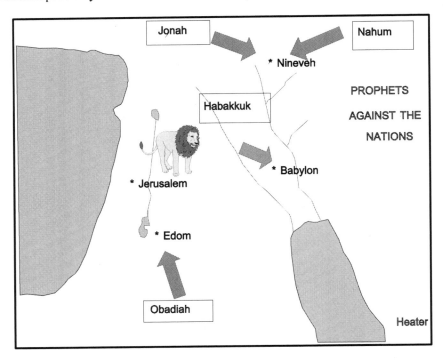

Notes on the Book of Obadiah

I.   Historical Background.

The Edomites were descendants of Esau, Jacob's brother. There was implacable hostility between the two groups from the time the Israelites were denied passage through Edomite territory. Much of the period of the monarchy showed Israel dominant over the Edomites. The area was important for two things: trade and copper.

The present day site of Petra was the original home of the Edomites. There they lived in the rocks and laid a foundation of culture that was later built upon by others. Probably around 580 B.C. the Edomites began to creep into the southern area of Judah now vacated by Nebuchadnezzar's removal of so many of the people. On their heels and taking over Petra was a new peoples group called Nabatean. These Nabateans were Arabs, but they were speaking Aramaic. They left most of the rock carved structures seen in Petra today. They also left many inscriptions.

The Edomites were subjugated in the Maccabean era by John Hyrcanus (134-104 B.C.). He forced them to be circumcised and to accept the Jewish faith. The Greek name for this section was Idumea. Alexander Jannaeus appointed Antipater I as governor of Idumea. He was the grandfather of Herod the Great.[232]

---

[232]See I. Browning, *Petra.*

II. The Setting of the Prophecy.

The prophet Obadiah is otherwise unknown, and nothing of his family or background is given in his prophecy. The name means "Servant of Yahweh" and so would be a popular one. Ahab's steward who met Elijah (1 Kings 18) was so named. There is insufficient historical data in the book to identify its historical setting. A major catastrophe has taken place in Judah that has led to exultation on the part of Edom. The most likely time for that catastrophe was the destruction of the city and temple by Nebuchadnezzar. It most certainly could have been earlier, but I believe it belongs to this horrible period of Judah's greatest devastation.

II. Links with Other Prophecies.

Some of the contents of Obadiah are found elsewhere. Below are two sections compared with the 49th chapter of Jeremiah. Some links with Joel are apparent as well.[233] The question is which material came first. Soggin, is probably right that there was older material incorporated by both Jeremiah and Obadiah.[234]

Comparison of Obadiah 1:1-4 and Jeremiah 49:14-16 and Obadiah 1:5-9 and Jeremiah 49:7-11(NASB)

We have heard a report from the Lord, And an envoy has been sent among the nations saying, Arise and let us go against her for battle—Behold, I will make you small among the nations; You are greatly despised.	I have heard a message from Lord, And an envoy is sent among the nations, *saying* Gather yourselves together and come against her, And rise up for battle! For behold I have made you small among the nations, Despised among men. As for the terror of you, The
The arrogance of your heart has deceived you, You who live in the clefts of the rock, In the loftiness of your dwelling place,	arrogance of your heart has deceived you, O you who live in the clefts of the rock, Who occupy the height of the hill,

---

[233] See LaSor, *et al., O. T. Survey,* 457.

[234] J. A. Soggin, *Introduction to the Old Testament,* p. 341.

Who say in your heart, Who will
bring me down to the earth?
Though you build high like the
eagle, Though you set your nest
among the stars, From there I
will bring you down, declares
the Lord.

Though you make your nest as
high as an eagle's, I will
bring you down from there, declares the Lord.

Is there no longer any wisdom in
Teman? Has good counsel been lost to
the prudent? Has their wisdom
decayed? Flee away, turn back, dwell in
the depths, O inhabitants of Dedan, For
I will bring the disaster of Esau upon
him At the time I punish him.

If thieves came to you, If robbers by night—O how you will be
ruined—Would they not steal *only*
until they had enough? If
grape gatherers came to you,
Would they not leave *some* gleanings? O how Esau will be ran-
sacked, And his hidden treasures
searched out! All the men allied
with you Will send you forth to
the border, And the men at peace
with you Will deceive you and
overpower *you. They who eat* your
bread Will set an ambush for you.
(There is no understanding in
him.) Will I not on that day,
declares the Lord, Destroy wise
men from Edom and understanding
from the mountain of Esau? Then
your mighty men will be dismayed,
O Teman, In order that everyone
may be cut off from the mountain
of Esau by slaughter.

If grape gatherers came to you,
would they not leave gleanings? If thieves *came* by
night, They would destroy *only*
until they had enough. But I
have stripped Esau bare, I
have uncovered his hiding
places So that he will not be
able to conceal himself; His
offspring has been destroyed
along with his relatives And
his neighbors, and he is no
more, Leave your orphans behind,
I will keep *them* alive; And
let your widows trust in Me.

IV. The Theology of the Book

Obadiah says basically that Edom, an implacable foe of Israel, who laughed and mocked when Judah was in the straits of Nebuchadnezzar's siege, will one day receive divine retribution for her sins. Known for her wisdom (cf. Job 2:11), the wise men will perish from Edom, that is, she will not have proper counsel for the operation of her nation. No matter how high she makes her nest, she will be brought down and judged.

V. Outline of the Book.

A. The vision concerning Edom (1-14).

Edom's fall is announced as an envoy is sent among the nations. Even though the arrogance of her heart has deceived her into thinking she is inaccessible because she lives in the heights of the rocks, God will bring her down to the earth and judge her (1-5).

The completeness of her destruction is shown through the imagery of the grape gleaners and robbers. These would only take what was needed, but nothing will be left of Esau. His hidden treasures will be searched out. The wise men (for which they were famous) will be destroyed. Teman will also contain mighty men who will be dismayed (6-9).

The reason for the judgment is their attitude and action toward Judah. The Edomites joined with Judah's enemies to gloat over her misfortune. Edom is admonished not to loot the wealth of Judah (an indication that they did). They are admonished not to stand at the fork of the road to cut down the fugitives and to enslave survivors (10-14).

B. The Day of the Lord is promised (15-21).

The promised day of the Lord is set forth here in Obadiah also. It will be a time in which all things will be set right. Nations will be judged (along with Edom). Drinking the wine cup of Yahweh is a common enough imagery. They will drink and thus be judged.

Mt Zion however will be a holy place containing escapees from exile. The house of Jacob will be a fire and Edom will be the stubble. The roles will be reversed.

In the day of the Lord the Jews will re-inherit the land. They will inherit Esau's territory, Philistia's territory, Ephraim and Samaria will be repossessed as will Gilead. Jews in exile in Sepharad will possess the cities of the Negev. (This place is really unknown, but the latest opinion is Sardis in which a bilingual inscription in Lydian and Aramaic was found naming the place *sprd*. This infers that a Jewish colony was located in that area. Wherever it is, the point of the prophecy is that exiled Jews will return to reclaim the land and "the kingdom will be the Lord's.")[235]

---

[235] Allen, *The Books of Joel Obadiah, Jonah, and Micah*, p. 171.

Notes on Habakkuk

"The book of Habakkuk stands in the eighth position among 'The Twelve' in the Masoretic and Greek texts. It follows Nahum and precedes Zephaniah. It is generally acknowledged that these three prophets were contemporaries and shared a common conviction that Yahweh was sovereign in the affairs of men and would judge the wicked and deliver the righteous."[236]

I. The Prophet. We know nothing about the prophet beyond his name which appears no other place in the Scriptures. The name comes from the Hebrew word "to embrace" and is probably a shortened form of Habakkukiah, "whom Yahweh embraces."[237]

II. The Time. No dates are provided in the book. Most statements are of a general nature and could fit into many eras, but the mention of the Chaldeans (1:6) places the book in the late seventh century B.C. The Chaldeans made their move against Assyria with the defeat of Asshur in 614 and Nineveh in 612 and then chased them west to Haran. By 605 the Assyrians were completely defeated and to be heard from no more. Consequently, the date of the book should be between 625 and 605 B.C.

III. Habakkuk was of great interest to the Qumran sectaries. In 1950 Millar Burroughs published the Habakkuk Commentary. The commentary deals only with the first two chapters. From a history of religions point of

---

[236]Ralph L. Smith, *Micah-Malachi*, p. 93.

[237]But see Smith, ibid., who argues that it is a foreign word.

view, the commentary is very interesting. But it is of little value in interpreting the prophecy.[238]

IV. Structure of the Book. The prophet asks two questions (1:2-4 and 1:12-2:1). A parenthesis follows the second question (2:1). God answers the two questions (1:5-11 and 2:2-20). The first part of His second reply is an admonition to Habakkuk and to believers to trust Him (2:2-4). The second half is a series of five woes in which He condemns the wicked. Finally, unique to Habakkuk, He gives a psalm patterned after the Psalter with a heading, "A Prayer of Habakkuk the prophet on Shigionoth" and a conclusion, "To the Chief Musician with My Stringed Instruments."[239]

V. Notes on the Text.

A. The first question: Why does God not punish the wicked (1:1-4).

This prophecy is called a burden (מַשָּׂא *Massah*), a word used to describe a weighty message usually with negative consequences and usually against other nations (1:1).

Habakkuk laments in the fashion of Jeremiah (12:1-4) and of the Psalmist (Ps. 73) that God is not just. The wicked prosper, and the righteous suffer. He has prayed for God to intervene, but nothing has happened. He blames God for allowing him to see the perversion of justice without the intervention of justice. Habakkuk piles up words: violence, iniquity, trouble, plundering, strife, and contention.

---

[238]Millar Burrows, ed., *The Dead Sea Scrolls of St. Mark's Monastery*, vol. 1, plates LV-LXI. For example, when Habakkuk mentions the Chaldeans, the sectaries say that its interpretation is the Kitim. We know from elsewhere that the Kitim refer to the Romans.

[239]Smith, op.cit., p 95 says, "The last chapter of Habakkuk is a prayer in the form of a psalm. The reference to Habakkuk as a prophet in the superscription, along with the reference to the *Shigionoth*, may indicate that Habakkuk was a cultic or a temple prophet."

The result is a powerless law. Habakkuk views the Torah (law) as God's correction of human life—but now the law is powerless to change things. Justice never manifests itself and the wicked surrounds the righteous (hems them in). Instead of justice, a perversion of justice comes forth.

B. God's answer (1:5-11).

God tells Habakkuk that He is about to do an astounding thing: He will raise up the Chaldeans, the Aramaic peoples who took over Babylon after centuries of infiltration. This is God's answer: a devastating military invasion of Judah to punish her for her sins.

A long description of the Chaldeans follows.[240] God uses similes to get across His point: leopard, wolves, and eagles. They are utterly unintimidated. Verse 11 states, "Then his mind changes and he transgresses." Smith's translation is better, "Then he passes by like wind and passes on."[241]

C. Habakkuk's second question (1:12-2:1).[242]

It is difficult to identify the subject of Habakkuk's second question. He is not satisfied with God's answer to his first question, but is he referring to Israel or to Babylon? The occurrence of the word "nations" in 1:17 suggests the latter. In which case, Habakkuk is now defending his people against the cruel judgment brought by the Babylonians.[243] He confesses

---

[240]Smith, *Micah to Malachi*, p. 94, says, "The majority of Old Testament scholars would probably date a large portion of the book of Habakkuk in the period between 612 and 587 B.C., although some editing was probably done later."

[241]Ibid., p. 100. NIV "Then he passes by like the wind and passes on."

[242]Ibid., p. 95, argues that this may be later—in 597 when Nebuchadnezzar was pressuring Jerusalem.

[243]See Chisholm, *Interpreting the Minor Prophets,* pp. 187-188.

to God's sovereignty and justice. Indeed God has marked out those who will be judged, but He is going to bring the cruel Chaldeans against the Jews. Habakkuk laments that God looks on iniquity (tolerates it).

Habakkuk then presents and develops an amazing simile. God has created mankind to be like leaderless fish in the sea. "They" (the Chaldeans) cast their nets and haul in a great catch of people. Then they worship their net. Habakkuk asks God how long He plans to allow this to happen (1:17).

Finally, he rather petulantly says he is going to stand his watch until God gives him his answer (2:1).

D. God's second reply (2:2-20)

God's reply is a bit of a rebuke. "I've told you that I will judge Judah through the Chaldeans, but you are not happy with that. Now I'm telling you again that you must accept the fact that things will happen in My time, not yours. But it will happen! Furthermore, you must trust Me and recognize that just people in Israel even if they are being treated unjustly by the Chaldeans, must live by their faithfulness" (2:2-4).[244]

This latter phrase became a foundational soteriological statement by the Apostle Paul in Romans 1:17. The context is different, but the premise is the same. Just people must walk by faith, Habakkuk says, because they cannot see the outworking of God's plans. Likewise, people must act in faith on God's promise to provide redemption apart from what they can see or touch—their own works.

Through a series of "woe" statements, God indicates that He will judge the Chaldeans (cf. Isaiah 10:15-19 where Assyria is rebuked for her arrogance when God uses her to punish Judah).

---

[244]Chisholm, *Interpreting the Minor Prophets,* p. 191

Woe #1 to the drunkard and plunderer (2:5-8).

Assuming that these woes are directed against Babylon, the charge here is that the Chaldeans are proud, covetous, and swallow up nations and peoples. Like a drunkard pursuing drink and death looking for corpses, so the Chaldeans are pursing nations. Since 1:5 is written from a point where the Chaldeans are just beginning to rise up, and 2:5-19 indicates a people already on the march and conquering many people, the date should probably be after 605 when Nebuchadnezzar completely routed the Assyrians and took over their hegemony.

Taking many pledges is a metaphor for conquering many peoples. The conquered ones will say, "You owe us" and start collecting later on.

Woe #2 to the one who covets evil gains (2:9-11)

The Chaldeans hoped to create enough wealth to be secure (nest on high and power of disaster). He advises the people of his house to do things contrary to the Law (shameful counsel) that takes advantage of people. However, God will cause the very house he is building through fraudulent activities to cry out against him.

Woe #3 to the one who builds a town with bloodshed (2:12-14).

The Chaldeans build a city with bloodshed, but God builds eternally— like Isaiah (Chapter 11) Habakkuk foresees a time when people all over the earth will know the Lord. His glory will not only fill the temple, it will cover the earth.

Woe #4 to the one who gives drink to his neighbor (2:15-17).

The Old Testament often uses the imagery of handing a cup of wine (often a picture of wrath) to the nations to make them drink (cf. Jer. 25:15-19). As the Chaldeans have made nations drunk, so God will make them drunk. Thus exposing their nakedness (no standing with God), and instead of glory they will have shame. The violence of the Chaldeans will be returned on their head.

Woe #5 the vanity of idolatry (2:18-20).

It is difficult for us today to understand the pervasive influence of idolatry in the ancient world. A visit to Hindu India is instructive in this respect. The Babylonians, as the entire ancient near easterners worshipped idols (note 1:16 where they worship the net used to catch fish).

The Old Testament prophets constantly inveighed against idolatry as being the ultimate of futility. All their religious efforts are directed toward a speechless, handmade idol. In contrast the living Yahweh is in His holy temple—all the earth is commanded to submit to Him in silence. With this last profound statement, God through Habakkuk sums up His argument—I am sovereign, and I will carry out my divine plans.

E. A prayer of Habakkuk for God's manifestation (3:1-19).

This prayer is stylized like many of the Psalms. The overall context calls for God to fulfill His promises in behalf of His people.

1. A theophany (3:3-7).[245]

This passage contains old ideas and words used to describe God's coming forth in behalf of His people and against His enemies (cf. Isa 63:1-6; Exodus 15). God's manifestation at Mount Sinai is alluded to here.

2. The battle (3:8-15).

Using graphic and symbolic language, Habakkuk reminds the Lord of His cosmic battle against His enemies. The rivers, mountains, the deep, and the heavenly bodies are all personified as doing battle with Yahweh but losing.

---

[245]See Smith, *Micah-Malachi*, p. 115, for a discussion of Sinai theophany.

3. Habakkuk's response of faith (3:16-19).

Habakkuk is expecting the Chaldean attack on his people. He recognizes this as a necessary judgment of God. No matter the disaster, he will rest in the Lord. God's strength will give him the ability to triumph.

Sing it!

Notes on the Book of Zephaniah

I.   The Prophet Zephaniah.

The name Zephaniah means "Yahweh hides" or "protects" (צְפַנְיָה). He is unknown apart from the book that bears his name. His genealogy traces him back to Hezekiah (although a few Hebrew MSS and the Syriac read Hilkiah). It is unusual to trace a prophet's genealogy this far back—an argument for the importance of the name Hezekiah, and, therefore, it may be that Zephaniah is a member of the royal family descended from another son of Hezekiah. He and Josiah, under whose rule he prophesied, would have been related.

II. The Time of the Prophecy.

The time of his prophecy is during the reign of Josiah who ruled from 640 B.C. to 609 B.C. Since Nineveh has not yet fallen (2:13), his prophecy must have taken place prior to 612 B.C. and was probably fairly early in Josiah's reign. Since Jeremiah began to prophesy in 627 B.C., there may have been some overlap in their ministries.

III. The Message of the Book.

Like Jeremiah, Zephaniah condemns the idolatrous religious practice of the Jews. He speaks against Baal (1:4), idolatrous priests, those who worship the host of heaven and swear to Milcom (1:5), and have turned back from following Yahweh (1:6).

Zephaniah speaks of the day of Yahweh as a time when He will punish the princes of Judah and those who leap on the threshold and fill the house of their lord with violence and deceit (1:9). The day of Yahweh is described in similar terms to that of Joel (1:14-16 with Joel 2:1-2). He speaks of the day of Yahweh also in terms of judgment on the nations (2:1-7). The last part of the book (chapter 3) speaks of God's judgment on His people, but also of their restoration to a place of prosperity and obedience to the Lord.

IV. The Outline of the Book.

A. Zephaniah predicts a time of judgment on the earth (1:1-18).

1. There will be a time of general judgment (1:2-3).

   Yahweh predicts that he will remove all things from the face of the earth. (The phrase "completely remove" is a translation of the Hebrew אָסֹף אָסֵף, (*asoph aseph*) meaning to "gather in" in the sense of taking away life.) Is this statement teaching that God will someday destroy all life? More likely it speaks of judgment in general—that all will be judged by God (though a remnant will be left). "The ruins along with the wicked" (1:3) is difficult. "Ruins" is a word meaning "to cause to stumble" (הַמַּכְשֵׁלוֹת *hammaksheloth*). The NASB has treated it as ruins that cause stumbling, but it is better understood as people that cause stumbling. The only problem with this is that the word is feminine where one would expect masculine, but this may be because it refers to religious systems run by people.)

2. There will be a time of Judgment on Judah (1:4-6).

   The idolatry of Judah will bring God's judgment (this is the same message Jeremiah preached). People are worshipping Baal, there are idolatrous priests (a special Hebrew word) and regular priests who will be cut off, there are people worshipping the host of heaven (cf. Jeremiah's condemnation of the same system [8:2; 19:3]. It probably refers to astral deities from Assyria). They are also worshipping Milcom (lit. Malcam, but probably a variant of the Ammonite god

Milcom, and so the NASB spelled it). The crowning description is that
they have turned back from following the Lord (1:6).

3. Zephaniah predicts the coming of the day of Yahweh in which He will
    judge His people (1:7-13).[246]

The coming day is depicted in terms of a sacrificial feast (cf. 1 Samuel
16). God will (metaphorically) call His people to the feast (His
sanctified ones) and will then punish the king's sons who wear foreign
garments. (This latter expression probably is metonymy for adopting
foreign customs—especially religious ones.)[247] Other people who will
be punished will be those who have false religious practices and fill
the temple with violence and deceit (1:9, cf. Jeremiah 7, the temple
sermon). (Another possible meaning is that they leap over people's
thresholds to steal and thus, fill the king's house with plunder) (1:7-9).

The judgment of God will bring a cry from every quarter of the city.
"The Mortar" refers to a declivity in the city probably in the Tyropean

---

[246]Excursus on the Day of the Lord:

Isa. (2:12); 13:6, (22:1ff); (34:1ff) (Jer. 46:1ff), Eze.(7:1ff) 13:5; 30:2-4; Joel 1:15;
2:1,11; 3:14; Amos 5:18,20; Obad. 15; Zeph. 1:7,14; 2:2; Zech. 14:1,7; Mal. 4:5. [()
means that the phrase does not occur (at least the precise phrase), but the idea does.]
M. Weiss, "The Origin of the 'Day of the Lord'—Reconsidered," HUCA 37 (1966):
29-71 refutes von Rad's theory that the Day of the Lord concept originated in the idea
of the Holy War and is therefore pre-prophetic. He argues (1) that while the idea of
theophany is pre-prophetic, it is Amos who coins the phrase which would have been
identified by the people with the old concept of theophany, (2) the use of the "Day of
the Lord" by Isaiah, Joel, etc., was influenced by Amos. He also argues that Day of the
Lord can refer to past events (Isa. 22:5; Ezek. 13:5) as well as future. Therefore, it is
used at times of the application of a prediction of God's judgment on the nations. Yet,
(I would say) the prophets have in mind a future Day of the Lord, unspecified in time,
in which all things will be set right including the judgment of God's people who have
disobeyed Him.

[247]Cf Jesus' remarks on those without proper garments (Matt 22:11-14).

valley.[248] The "people of Canaan" refers to merchants, i.e., these are those who are using the temple for commercial purposes, a situation still existing when Jesus came. Yahweh, in His day, will carefully search out Jerusalem and will punish those who are "stagnant in spirit." This is literally "to thicken on their lees," i.e., undisturbed wine. These men are "neutral" in that they say that "The Lord does neither good nor evil" (1:10-12).

4. Zephaniah speaks of the Day of Yahweh in terrible terms (1:14-18).

    The great day of the Lord is near and coming very quickly. This is similar to the idea of imminence in the NT. It is the next great event on the horizon. The description of the Day of Yahweh is similar to the Lord's statements in Matthew 24. How are we to understand such phrases as "all the earth will be devoured" and "he will make a complete end…of all the inhabitants of the earth"? It refers to a terrible judgment such as found in Revelation 6-19. The phraseology must be hyperbolic and that there will not be complete annihilation.

B. Zephaniah calls upon Judah to repent (2:1-15).

    1. The shameless nation is urged to seek Yahweh (2:1-3).

        Judah does not blush for shame (נִכְסָף לֹא *lo niksaph*), but she is urged to prepare herself so as to avoid the day of wrath that is coming.

    2. Surrounding nations will be judged (2:4-7).

        The Philistine cities (Gath is not mentioned here nor in Amos 1 probably because she was in Judean territory) will be judged. Yet Judah will inherit the land of the Philistines and God will care for them.

---

[248]See N. Avigad, *Discovering Jerusalem*, p. 54.

3. Moab and Ammon will be judged (2:8-11).

    This section is reminiscent of Obadiah's prophecy against Edom. These nations have been involved in making fun of Judah in her sufferings (just when this happened is not stated). As a result they will be terribly judged by the Lord.

4. The Ethiopians and the Assyrians will be judged (2:12-15).

    The purpose of mentioning Ethiopians may be to show a north-south axis that God will judge. On the other hand, the regime in Egypt at this time was Ethiopian. In any event, the people south will come under God's judgment as will the mighty Assyria. Nineveh will become a desolation. This indicates that Zephaniah is prophesying prior to 612 B.C. when Nineveh was destroyed by the Babylonians and the Medes.[249]

C. Zephaniah speaks of Judah's sin and restoration (3:1-20).

    1. Judah's sin is set forth (3:1-7).

        Judah is depicted as a stubborn person who refuses any instruction. The princes, judges, prophets and priests are described as wild animals that destroy people and sanctuary. Yet, in spite of this terrible state of affairs, the righteous Yahweh is in her midst. He is the epitome of justice. He has shown His power in cutting off nations, expecting Judah to acknowledge His Lordship, but they have refused and proceeded to corrupt all their deeds.

    2. Yahweh speaks of a day of world conversion (3:8-13).

        The first phase of God's work will be judgment on the nations. After that judgment, He will give purified lips to the peoples. This seems to be a wider group than Judah. He will have worshippers from beyond

---

[249]Note the similar language to Isaiah 13 and Babylon.

Ethiopia who will serve him. The Jews will then be dealt with by God, and the proud ones will be removed, and the remnant will do no wrong.

3.   Yahweh encourages Judah to rejoice (3:14-20).

A marvelous time is coming when the King of Israel, Yahweh, will be in their midst. They will fear disaster no more. They will be regathered and their fortunes will be restored.

The question is "when will all these amazing events take place?" The judgment of the nations (referred to in Matthew 25) will take place during the tribulation. Likewise the national conversion of Israel will occur as they are undergoing intense persecution after the Antichrist has broken his covenant with them (2 Thes. 2; Revelation 11). All this will be preparatory to entrance into the kingdom or Millennium as it is known in Revelation 20.

Notes on the Book of Joel

I. The Prophet.

The prophet, Joel, is unknown outside this book. The name means Yahweh is God (the reverse form of Elijah). He is the son of Pethuel.

II. The Historical Setting.

The internal references are sufficiently vague as to make it impossible to identify the time and setting of the prophecy with certainty. Wolff says the book was placed between Hosea and Amos because of similarity of ideas rather than for any chronological reasons.[250] Some kind of a devastating invasion of insects has taken place. In the midst of this devastation, the temple has been plundered (3:5). Tyre, Sidon and Philistia have sold Judeans into slavery (cf. Amos 1:6). Some would place the prophecy during the time of Joash (2 Kings 12), because the Arameans threatened Jerusalem and Joash bought them off. However, the Arameans are not mentioned in Joel. Ammon and Moab are mocking Judah in Zephaniah (2:8-11) and Edom in Obadiah. There were probably a number of incursions against Judah that would fit this situation, but the terrible locust plague (a fairly common event in the Middle East) is not mentioned elsewhere and so we are unable to date the book. However, the idea of the "Day of the Lord," incipient in eighth century Amos (5:18-20) is well known in Joel.[251] This may imply that Joel is later than Amos. It could

---

[250]Hans W. Wolff, *Joel and Amos*, p. 3.

[251]See Richard H. Hiers, *Day of Yahweh* in *ABD*, 2:82-83 for an excellent discussion. He says, "There is wide agreement, however, that for most of the prophets, the Day of Yahweh meant that time in the relatively near future when

even have taken place at the destruction of Jerusalem in the last days of the Judean monarchy (605-586 B.C.), since the word "fortunes" (3:1) is the Hebrew word often translated captivity (שְׁבוּת *shebuth*). The temple is still standing in chapter 1.[252] In light of these considerations, I believe Joel was somewhat contemporary with Zephaniah.

III. The Message of the Book.

The most difficult issue in the book is the significance and relationship of the locusts in chapters one and two. This is tied into the issue of the meaning of the day of Yahweh. The problem is exacerbated by the tendency of the prophets to merge the past or present with the future. The concept of the day of Yahweh is discussed briefly in the Zephaniah notes. The ultimate concept is that God will set all things right in the eschatological future, and that this will include judging Israel and the other nations and the restoration and conversion of Israel as God's people on their land. At the same time, God's judgment at any period can be referred to as the day of Yahweh. My approach to the book of Joel is to see both chapters one and two as the same event (one that happened sometime in the history of Judah) that is being treated as a type of what is yet to come when God judges the world. As such Joel can slide into the great eschatological outpouring of the Spirit (2:28-32) and the complete restoration of Israel (3:1-21).[253]

Yahweh would punish not only his people's enemies, but also his people (Israel, Judah, or the Jewish people) for breaking the covenant. Then, either through a new Davidic king or messiah or by acting directly, Yahweh would establish his own rule or kingdom over all the earth."

[252]Wolff, *Joel and Amos,* p. 4, argues that the temple referred to in Chapter 1 has been rebuilt and the memory of the Babylonian siege is faded. Hence, he places the book after 445 B.C. when the walls of the city have been rebuilt.

[253]See also D. A. Garrett, "The Structure of Joel," *JETS* 28 (1985): 289-297.

IV. The Outline of the Book.

A. The locust invasion (1:1-20).

1. Joel calls the people to witness the devastation that has come about and to ask them if any such thing has ever happened before (1:1-3).

2. Joel describes the invasion (1:4-7).

   He speaks of four kinds of locusts. Each succeeding group finishes off what was left by its predecessor. This is a destruction of crops that is indescribable. He refers to the locusts as a nation because of their apparent organization. They have teeth and fangs like lions with which they strip the vegetation.

3. Judah is called upon to weep and beseech Yahweh for deliverance (1:8-20).

   The people are told to wail because the loss of crops has affected the temple worship (thus the priests mourn). The land mourns, the farmers are disappointed. Even rejoicing is "dried" up, the rejoicing that is characteristic of the harvest (1:8-12).

   The priests are admonished to wail and lament over the terrible devastation. They are to cry out "Alas for the day! For the day of the Lord is near." This seems to indicate that the locust plague was identified with the day of the Lord and would support Weiss's arguments (set out in the Zephaniah notes) that the day of the Lord was sometimes applied in a general way to judgment and was not always *the* day of the Lord yet to come. At the same time, the plague as a local "day of the Lord" should warn Israel of the eschatological day of Yahweh (1:13-20).

B. The day of the Lord and God's deliverance (2:1-32).

There is an integral relationship between chapters 1 and 2. Chapter 1 speaks of all that the various locusts have eaten and chapter 2 speaks of restoring what those same locusts have eaten (2:25). Consequently, if we relate the day of Yahweh in 1:14-15 to the terrible locust invasion, we must see a similar connection in chapter 2.

1. The alarm is to be sounded because of the dreadful invasion of locusts (2:1-17).

The day of the Lord is a time of darkness and gloom. This may be a metaphor of the attitude of the people or it may be literal due to the thick clouds of locusts. The situation is so bad, the prophet can say that nothing like it has happened or will happen (2:1-2).

The description of the locust invasion is awe inspiring. They are like fire going through stubble. Land like the garden of Eden before them becomes like a waste desert behind them. People are pale with fear. These locusts move inexorably toward the destruction of all the crops. The sun, moon and stars grow dark (2:3-10). [254]

However, this is not happening by chance: this is Yahweh's army, and He marches at its head. He is using this plague to call His people to Himself. He urges them to rend their hearts and repent. He had called on them to blow the trumpet of alarm in 2:1, now He urges them to blow the trumpet of assembly to beseech the Lord for mercy (2:11-17).

---

[254]Some, e.g., H. Wolff, *Joel and Amos,* argue that chapter 2 speaks of an actual army.

2.   Yahweh was zealous[255] for His land and had pity on His people (2:18-27).

He will send crops to replace those that have been removed. He will destroy the "northern army" that has invaded. His people will never again (better translated "no longer") be a reproach among the nations. This section had its fulfillment in historical days, but as God expands on His wonderful promises of restoration, He begins to telescope the distant future into the historical past. This begins at 2:26b: "Then My people will never be put to shame" (וְלֹא יֵבֹשׁוּ עַמִּי לְעוֹלָם *welo yeboshu 'ammi le'olam*). In the same way the Lord Jesus jumps into the Eschaton from a historical situation in Matthew 10, so God moves from the beautiful statements of restoration in the historical past to the beautiful spiritual restoration of Israel in the future (2:18-20).

He promises them restoration of the land, the early rain and the latter rain (Fall and Spring),[256] full threshing floors, and a repayment for all the destruction wrought by the locusts. This will lead them to acknowledge His presence and again "My people will never be put to shame" (2:21-27).

3.   Yahweh promises a blessed time in the future when there will be a great spiritual movement among His people (2:28-32).

This unit is related to what precedes in that it speaks of great blessing by Yahweh upon His people. However, the *complete* restoration of the land will be accompanied with a pouring out of the Spirit. The Hebrew text makes a separate chapter out of this section (3:1-5).

The introductory phrase, "And it will come about after this" (וְהָיָה אַחֲרֵי כֵן *wehyah 'ahare ken*), is a loose connective phrase that should

---

[255]Note my translation "was zealous." This tense would normally be translated past.

[256]F. S. Frick, "Rain," in *ABD*, 5:612.

not be pressed too hard. "In the future, God will bless His people by restoring to them what the locusts destroyed, and He will also pour out His Spirit upon them" seems to be its primary import.

Yahweh promises to pour out His Spirit upon all mankind (lit.: flesh). There will be prophecy, dreams and visions. Even common people will have the Spirit poured on them (2:28-29).

Miracles will be wrought in the sky and on earth. All of this will be tied in with the "great and awesome day of the Lord." Sections of Revelation 6-19 seem to refer to this passage in describing events of the tribulation. During that time those who call upon the Lord will be delivered (cf. Paul's use of this verse in Romans 10:13) (2:30-32).

How are we to understand Peter's use of this passage? Peter, in explaining the phenomenon of Pentecost, says "this is that which was spoken by the prophet Joel." He then quotes this extensive passage. It is clear that not all of the prophecy was fulfilled in Acts 2. The wonders in heaven and signs on earth, blood, fire, etc., were not fulfilled. Furthermore, the simplest reading of the Old Testament concept of the day of Yahweh would argue against the church age being its fulfillment. What then is the relationship between Joel 2 and Acts 2? Peter believed, rightly, that the messianic era could only begin with the Messiah. He was also aware that the messianic era as it affected Israel required repentance. The "times of refreshing" could not come until there was national repentance (Acts 3:19-23). Pentecost represents the beginning of that great work of God, but the ultimate fulfillment can only come when the Messiah returns for the church and resumes His work with Israel. Peter could not perceive that there would be two thousand years between his preaching and the fulfillment of all of Joel; he could only know that God was beginning

His great redemptive work after the risen Savior had returned to glory.[257]

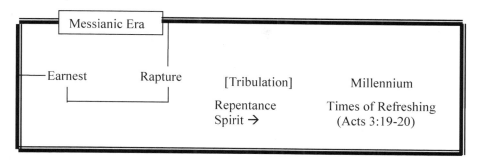

C. Yahweh promises to restore Judah and to judge the nations (3:1-21).

1. Yahweh will judge the nations at Jehoshaphat (3:1-8).

   Judah will be restored and when that happens, Yahweh will gather the nations to the Valley of Jehoshaphat. Jehoshaphat means "Yahweh will judge" and may be an *ad hoc* name for this task. It is usually related to the Kidron Valley. It is to be related to Matthew 25 where the nations will be judged in accordance with their treatment of Israel during the tribulation. Here Yahweh promises to restore the Jews who have been scattered and to judge those who scattered them.

2. Yahweh declares holy war against the nations (3:9-21).

   Here the day of Yahweh refers to His judgment of the Gentile nations (whereas earlier it referred to His judgment of His own people). The people are to be stirred up for war against the Divine Warrior and be brought to the valley of Jehoshaphat for judgment (3:9-12).

---

[257]See further, R. Patterson, *Joel*, in EBC.

Under the imagery of the harvest, He promises to thrust in the sickle, to tread the wine press, and to bring them to the valley of decision (= Jehoshaphat) (3:13-14).

There will be changes in the heavens (here in the stellar heavens them-selves; in chapter 1 it was the way the people viewed them as the locusts blotted them out) (3:15).

Yahweh roars out against the nations, but He is a refuge to His people (3:16). Then His people will know who He is and Jerusalem will be holy (3:17).

Finally, the tables will be turned in favor of God's people. Judah will prosper. The land will be productive, but Judah's enemies will be judged (3:18-21).

V.   The Structure of Joel as it Bears on the Argument of the Book.

The little book of Joel contains a number of issues that bear on both Old and New Testament studies. Some of the more significant ones are (1) the relation of chapter 2 to 1: do they refer to the same situation, or is one a prefigurement of the other; (2) the significance of the Day of Yahweh and whether the Day of Yahweh in 1:15 is the same as the one in 2:1ff; (3) the use of 2:28-32b by Peter in Acts 2. A critical issue in the solution of #'s 1 and 2 is the translation of the tenses in 2:18,19. The Hebrew divisions are 1:1-20; 2:1-27; 3:1-5; 4:1-21.

The Hebrew tenses in 2:18-19. In the MT, these verbs are what used to be called waw consecutive imperfects but are now usually referred to as preterites. They are the typical syntactical form for narration in past time. They may be used for future time, but in such cases they are usually anchored to a perfect tense cast in the future with the waw consecutive.[258] Joüon says, "The wayyiqtol (like a qatal #112 g-h) is rarely used in the

---

[258]Gesenius, Kautzsch, Cowley, *Gesenius' Hebrew Grammar*, #111w.

future. After a prophetic perfect (#112h): Isaiah 9:5; Joel 2:23."[259] Some have tried to repoint the forms as jussives, but Wolff cogently argues against the effort. The normally expected translation of these four verbs would thus be, "Then the Lord *was* zealous for His land, and He *had* pity on His people. And the Lord *answered* and *said* to His people, 'Behold, I am going to send you grain…'" In spite of this, *KJV, NASB*, and *NIV* have translated it future, because they see all of chapter 2 as eschatological.

Hans Wolff,[260] in his insightful analysis of the book, argues that chapter 1 is a historical plague of locusts, but that chapter 2 takes that historical situation and draws from it a warning about the eschatological Day of Yahweh. He argues, quite rightly I believe, that the tenses of 2:18,19 are narrative tenses picking up the point made in 1:2-3. In other words, the task of telling later generations about the plague is continued as the prophet tells of God's forgiveness of His people, and so the content of 2:18-19 is historical, not prophetic. However, he believes that 2:1-11 refers to the eschatological Day of Yahweh as does 2:19ff. Consequently, his structure is a = locusts (1:1-20); a[1] = eschatological Day of Yahweh (2:1-11); c = plea for repentance (historical) (2:12-17) to which the people responded and God was merciful; a[2] = eschatological blessing (2:19b-32) and judgment on nations (3:1-21). Keil holds to a similar position. Chisholm[261] generally follows Wolff.

I find it awkward to have a historical situation (2:18-19) thrust into an eschatological section. It seems to me better to see a unitary structure in the first two chapters.[262] There are four main imperatival units in these

---

[259]Joüon, *Grammaire de l'Hébreu Biblique,* #118s. "Dans la sphere du futur, wayyiqtol (comme qatal #112 g-h) est rare. Apres un parfait prophetique (#112h): Is 9,5; Joel 2,23."

[260]Hans Wolff, *Joel and Amos, loc cit.*

[261]Chisholm, *Joel.*

[262]So Allen, *Joel.*

chapters: 1:2 "Hear this, O elders, and listen, all inhabitants of the land"; 1:14 "Consecrate a fast, proclaim a solemn assembly, gather the elders and all the inhabitants of the land"; 2:1 "Blow a trumpet in Zion, and sound an alarm on my holy mountain!"; 2:15 "Blow a trumpet in Zion, consecrate a fast proclaim a solemn assembly." In light of the calamity in chapter 1, they are to consecrate a fast (obviously for the purpose of intercession). This idea is pursued in 2:1 where the alarm is to be sounded because of the invasion of the "army." *Both* ideas are included in 2:15 where the injunction to fast and to sound a warning are given.

I would conclude then, that the historical scene of a terrible locust plague is in view in both chapters. The parallel similes and descriptions link them. Even the description of the earth and heavens should be understood as coming from the impact of the awful locust invasion. The locusts are called God's army in 2:11 and a nation in 1:6. The Day of Yahweh in chapters 1 and 2 should be understood as a "local" day of Yahweh when he brings judgment on His people. God's earnest plea for repentance does not come until 2:12-17 where He proclaims His compassion toward His people. To this plea the people responded, and God graciously forgave them. In light of that forgiveness, He promised to restore all that the locusts had eaten (2:25) and to bring abundance of rain.

An objection might be raised about the statement in 2:19 translated in *NASB* "And I will never again make you a reproach among the nations." This phrase is clearly an answer to the "paradigm prayer" God gave them in 2:17: "Spare Thy people, O Lord, and do not make Thine inheritance a reproach, a byword among the nations." The phrase "never again" is עוֹד... לֹא (*lo'... 'od*). This syntactical combination occurs over 100 times. It is often translated "never again" as here, because it occurs often in prophetic passages containing promises. However, it often simply means "no longer" with no reference to whether the situation could be repeated (e.g., Judg. 2:14; Ezek. 33:22). The context refers to the historical reproach brought on Israel because of the locust plague. That reproach was removed when God destroyed the locusts and restored the vegetation to the people.

However, as God expands on His wonderful promises of restoration, He begins to telescope the distant future into the historical past. I believe this begins at 2:26b: "Then My people will never be put to shame" ולא יֵבשׁוּ עַמִּי לְעוֹלָם *v*^elo' yeboshu 'ami l^e'olam). In the same way the Lord Jesus jumps into the Eschaton from a historical situation in Matthew 10, so God moves from the beautiful statements of restoration of Israel in the future.

Joel is teaching the people of Israel (1) the Day of Yahweh will bring discipline to His people to bring them to Himself; (2) God's forgiveness is conditioned on repentance, but when that repentance is present, He forgives and restores (2:18-27); (3) The lessons taught in chapters 1-2 (God leads his army [locusts] against His people to force them to Himself, but upon genuine repentance, forgives and restores) are to be applied to the Eschaton, and therefore, the day of the Lord will include a spiritual renewal of Israel (וְהָיָה אַחֲרֵי כֵן *v*^ehayah 'ah^are ken; these time references are general, not specific) (2:28-32). The day of the Lord will also be a time of judgment on the nations who have mistreated Israel (כִּי הִנֵּה בַּיָּמִים הָהֵמָּה וּבָעֵת הַהִיא *ki hineh baymim hahemah uba'eth hahi'*). At that time Israel will be restored (3:1-21).

Structural Diagram of Chapters 1 and 2

a¹ Call for Elders and Inhabitants of land to hear (1:2-3)
שִׁמְעוּ זֹאת וְהַאֲזִינוּ *shim*^e'u zo'th v^eha^azinu

b¹ Reason: an event has transpired (1:4-7)

Perfects: אָכַל (3 x's); נִכְרַת עָלָה שָׁם חָשַׂף הִשְׁלִיךְ הִלְבִּינוּ
'akal, nikrath, 'alah, sam, hasaph, hishlik, hilbinu

c¹ Wail drunkards and wine bibbers (1:5)
Three imperatives: וְהֵילִילוּ וּבְכוּ הָקִיצוּ *haqitsu, ubeku, v*^e*helilu*

b² Reason: a NATION has come up (6-7)

    c² Wail everyone—8
    One imperative: אֵלִי   *'eli*

b³ Reason: devastation of agriculture (9-12)
Effects on priests: אָבְלוּ   *'abᵉlu*

    Facts: יָבֵשׁ hiphil (4 x's); שֻׁדַּד אָבְלָה אֻמְלַל אָבַד   *Yabesh, shudad, abelah, 'umelal, 'abad*

        d¹ "The grain and drink offering have been cut off from the house of Yahweh"

    c³ Wail priests (13a)
    Five imperatives: לִינוּ בֹּאוּ הֵילִילוּ וְסִפְדוּ חִגְרוּ   *higeru, vᵉsiphedu, helilu, bo'u, linu*

        d² "The grain and drink offering have been withheld from the house of God"

a² Call for Elders and Inhabitants to Repent (14)

    Four imperatives: זַעֲקוּ אִסְפוּ קִרְאוּ קַדְּשׁוּ   *qadeshu, qire'u, 'sephu, zaᵃqu*

    b⁵ Reason: Day of Yahweh is near (קָרוֹב *qarob*), it is coming (יָבוֹא *yabo'*)

a³ Call for an Assembly (2:1a)
Blow, Shout, Tremble—all inhabitants of the earth

    b⁶ Reason: Day of Yahweh (2:1b)

        c⁴ Description (2:2-11)
        Earth (2:3-9)
        Heaven (2:10-11)

a⁴ Plea for Repentance (2:12)

Fasting, weeping, mourning

    b[7] Reason: (2:13-14)
        Gracious, merciful, patient, great kindness, repents of calamity, who knows whether…

        d[3] "And leave a blessing behind Him, *Even* a grain offering and a libation."

a[5] Call for Repentance and an assembly (2:15-17)

2:1	2:15
Blow trumpet	Blow trumpet
1:14	
Consecrate fast	Consecrate fast
Call assembly	Call assembly
Gather elders	Gather people

    Cry out
    Consecrate assembly
    Gather elders
    Gather children
Let…go out
Let…weep
Let…say

GOD'S RESPONSE (2:18-27)

"And Yahweh *was* zealous (וַיְקַנֵּא *way^{e}qane'*) for His land, and He *had* compassion (וַיַּחְמֹל *wayaḥmol*) on His people. And he *answered* (וַיַּעַן *waya'an*) and *said* (וַיֹּאמֶר *wayomer*) to His people, behold I am about to send to you the grain, new wine, and oil. And you will be satisfied with them and I will not permit you any longer to be a reproach among the nations" (2:18-19).

Joel —Page 312

Notes on the Book of Nahum

I.   The Prophet.

Nothing is known about Nahum beyond what is in 1:1. The name is probably a passive form (comforted) with the name Yahweh omitted. The short prophecy against Nineveh is considered to be some of the highest quality of Hebrew poetry.[263] The town of Elkosh is likewise unknown.[264]

II. The Historical Setting.

The fall of Nineveh seems to be imminent throughout, but it has not yet taken place. On the other hand the city of No-Amon (Thebes) has already fallen to Esarhaddon (either 671, 667 or 663). In light of this, the date ought to be some time close to 612 B.C. We will place it about 615 B.C., and so Nahum will be somewhat contemporary with Zephaniah and Jeremiah and perhaps Joel. Sennacherib attacked Jerusalem in 701 B.C. and for a century Assyria had dominated the politics of Syro-Palestine. Their cruelty was notorious (though perhaps no more so than any other world power). The city of Nineveh was large, well-fortified, and well-adorned. Archaeology has revealed a city of splendor. Under Ashurbanipal, a large literary collection was made of ancient materials. Some 20,000 tablets were recovered including the flood and the creation accounts. The city fell to the combined attack of the Medes, Babylonians and Scythians in 612 B.C.

---

[263]See LaSor, *et al.*, *Old Testament Survey*.

[264]See Y. Kobayashi, "Elkosh" in *ABD*, 2:476.

III. The Message of the Book.

Nahum, like Obadiah, has only a negative message of judgment against Nineveh. There is no counterbalancing condemnation of Judah for her sin, but that is well taken care of elsewhere. Nineveh, notorious for her arrogance against Yahweh (cf. Isa. 36- 37), must be dealt with for her inhumanity to all people and particularly to God's people. Yahweh is sovereign over all nations and that sovereignty will be shown in the destruction of the capital of arrogant, violent Assyria.

IV. Outline of the Book.

A. Yahweh is sovereign and in control of world events (1:1-15).

1. God is both gracious and just (1:1-8).

The just side of God is presented in this section. This is a side that must not be ignored: He wreaks vengeance on His enemies. Even though He is slow to anger (1:3), His anger will eventually be aroused against those who hate Him. It has been a century since Assyria first began to dominate Judah. Yahweh's ability to carry out His threats is described in cosmic terms. Nature is responsive to His command. None can stand before His indignation (1:6). At the same time Yahweh is good and a refuge to those who trust him, but He will pursue His enemies into darkness (1:7-8).

2. Nahum dramatically weaves judgment on Assyria and blessing on Judah into one piece of cloth (1:9-15).

Assyria's plans will be frustrated by Yahweh. Her defenses will be worthless. The wicked counselor probably refers to a king of Assyria, unnamed. He quickly turns to Judah (1:12b-13) to say that the affliction Yahweh brought upon her through Assyria will come to an end. He will break Assyria's yoke from Judah's neck.[265] He turns back

---

[265]See *NIV* for the insertion of the subjects.

to Assyria (1:14) to say that Yahweh has issued a decree of destruction to Assyria. Finally he turns back to Judah (1:15) to echo the words of Isaiah (52:7) about the beauty of the feet of a messenger of good news. He will announce peace and declare that Judah will be able to keep her feasts again for the wicked one (Assyrian king) will not pass through her again.

B. Nahum in graphic poetry depicts the fall of Nineveh (2:1-13).

    1.   The One who is in charge has come against Nineveh (2:1-2).

As Assyria has scattered Israel (722 B.C.) and Judah (701 B.C. for cities like Lachish), so God will scatter her. He is using the Medes and Babylonians as He once used Assyria. At the same time, Nahum predicts that Yahweh will restore the splendor of Jacob.

    2.   The confusion and distress of the defeat (2:3-7).

The bloody, confused mass of peoples charging back and forth, trying to defend the walls, and marshal the troops is caught by Nahum's prophecy. There must have been a flooding of the river (2:6) that assisted in the breakthrough by the Medes.

    3.   The despoiling of Nineveh (2:8-13).

Nineveh's past greatness is now nothing, as all her people try to flee the tomb that was Nineveh. Her wealth is being plundered by the invaders. The Assyrian army is depicted as a lion that went forth to kill and bring back prey to the lioness and the cubs.[266] Yahweh declares Himself to be against Nineveh: that spells her doom.

---

[266]Cf. *ANET*, pp. 281, 283 for an illustration of Assyrian plunder.

C. A final oracle on the reason for Nineveh's fall (3:1-19).

    1. Nineveh's fall and the reason (3:1-7).

        Nineveh is depicted as a bloody city, that is, full of murder as well as of lies and pillage. Then the fall of the city is taken up again describing the mass confusion and death (3:1-3).

        The reason given is that Nineveh acted the part of a prostitute. She was wealthy and "beautiful," and as such enticed other nations as she enticed Ahaz. Her sorceries (false religion) also attracted people. Judah adopted many of the astral religious deities of Assyria (3:4).

        As a result, God is against her. This beautiful prostitute will be exposed for what she is. God will strip her and throw filth on her (this word is usually used of idols which were especially abominable to Yahweh: *shiqutsim* שִׁקֻּצִים). Nations will be amazed at her when they see her in these straits (3:5-7).

    2. Nineveh is compared to Thebes (3:8-15a).

        No-Amon means the city of Amon and refers to the ancient capital of Egypt located four hundred miles south of Cairo in upper Egypt. Thebes was well-known as the capital of the eighteenth dynasty under such famous pharaohs as Tutmose III. The Nile, referred to as the sea, ran "through" Thebes in that there were two cities—the living and the dead. The mortuary monuments were on the west side of the Nile. Assyria defeated Thebes in 671 B.C., 667 B.C. and finally it was razed in 663 B.C. and never recovered.[267] Why does Nineveh, similarly situated, think she can escape punishment (3:8-10)?

        Nineveh too will be dealt with. The defenses will not hold up, the warriors are like women, the gates will be opened wide to the enemy.

---

[267]Cf.,H. R. Hall, "The Ethiopians and Assyrians in Egypt," CAH 3:285.

Then the commands are given for defense—but it will be of no avail (3:11-15a).

3. Nineveh's demise (3:15b-19).

Assyria has dominated the scene for a long time. Her traders, guardsmen and marshals have been like hordes of grasshoppers. But now the shepherds are sleeping, the nobles are lying down and the people are scattered. There is no hope for Assyria/Nineveh.

Notes on the Book of Ezekiel

I. The Prophet Ezekiel.

Ezekiel went in into exile with Jehoiachin in 597 B.C. Like Daniel a few years earlier, Ezekiel was a godly young man who followed the Law of Moses, including the dietary laws. His wife died in exile, and he was prohibited from mourning for her. Some critical scholars have tried to interpret his message in terms of his personality that exhibited such strange behavior. Childs says that this has met with little success.[268] Ezekiel was probably twenty-five years old at the time of the exile (working on the supposition that the thirty years of 1:1 refers to his age). He lived in his own house in exile, at Tel Abib on the Great Canal (3:15). The location, if the river Kebar can be identified with Babylonian *naru kabari*, was between Babylon and Nippur. He was therefore living in one of the Jewish colonies that the Babylonians had transplanted from Judah.[269]

II. The Historical Context

Ezekiel's dated messages began in the fifth year of the exile which would be July 31, 592 B.C. (1:1-2). The last dated message was the twenty-seventh year or Apr. 26, 571 B.C. (29:17). Thus Ezekiel's ministry covered a span of at least twenty-one years. His message was delivered before and after the destruction of Jerusalem in 586 B.C. He spoke to all Israel, but locally to the exiles whom Jeremiah addressed by

---

[268]B. S. Childs, *Introduction to the Old Testament as Scripture*, 359.

[269]See LaSor, *et al., O. T. Survey,* 461. For Jews at Nippur (south of Babylon) a century later, see M. D. Coogan, "Life in the Diaspora," *BA* 37 (1974): 7-12.

letter (e.g., Jer. 29), as people who continued to listen to false prophets and practice idolatry. The contents of Ezekiel indicate that little had changed in the attitude of the Jewish people who had come to Babylon.

III. The Unity of the Book

Early in the twentieth century S. R. Driver could say: "No critical question arises in connexion with the authorship of the book, the whole from beginning to end bearing unmistakably the stamp of a single mind."[270] It was in 1924 that G. Holscher[271] began to subject the book to the critic's knife. Since that time it has undergone radical surgery, particularly by C. C. Torrey, who viewed it as a pseudograph from the third century B.C.; a literary creation without any real historical roots.[272] Critical scholarship, in the interest of advancing new theories, often abandons common sense in dealing with these biblical books. The approach of B. S. Childs is refreshing. Though he follows W. Zimmerli in attributing some of the book to a "later school," he views the bulk of the book as "Ezekielian."[273] His section on Ezekiel can be studied with profit. He argues that Ezekiel was "radically theocentric," that is, everything was viewed from God's eternal perspective and is not therefore historically particularistic (he does not direct his invective against historical situations as does an Amos or a Jeremiah). Following Zimmerli, he shows how Ezekiel used the pre-prophetic Scriptures as the basis for his teaching. Ezekiel's method was casuistic and priestly in its orientation. Childs' position is summed up in the statement: "particular

---

[270]S. R. Driver, *Introduction to the Literature of the Old Testament*, 297.

[271]G. Holscher, "Hesekiel: Der Dichter und das Buch," *BZAW* 39 (1924).

[272]W. F. Albright attacks Torrey's position in "The Seal of Eliakim and the Latest Pre-Exilic History of Judah, with some Observations on Ezekiel," *JBL* 51 (1932): 77-106. His opinion on the Eliakim seals has since proven wrong.

[273]B. S. Childs, *Introduction to the Old Testament as Scripture,* 364-365.

features within Ezekiel's prophetic role which shaped both the form and content of his message contained important elements which the later canonical process found highly compatible to adapt without serious reworking for its own purpose of rendering the tradition into a corpus of sacred writing."[274]

Finegan argues that all the dates in Ezekiel are to be related to the captivity of Jehoiachin. Consequently, he provides the following list:[275]

Ref.	Year	Month	Day	Subject	From 597/596	From 598/597
1:1f.	5	4	5	First vision	July 1, 593	July 13, 594
3:16	"at end of 7 days"			Appointed watchman	July 7	July 19
8:1	6	6	5	Brought to Jerusalem	Sept 17, 592	Aug 29, 593
20:1	7	5	10	Elders inquire	Aug 13, 591	Aug 24, 592
24:1	9	10	10	Siege of Jerusalem	Jan 15, 588	Jan 26, 589
26:1	11	?	1	Against Tyre	587/586	588/587
29:1	10	10	12	Against Egypt	Jan 6, 587	Jan 17, 588
29:17	27	1	1	Egypt in place of Tyre	Apr 26, 571	Apr 8, 572
30:20	11	1	7	Against Pharaoh	Apr 29, 587	Apr 10, 588
31:1	11	3	1	Against Pharaoh	June 21, 587	June 2, 588
32:1	12	12	1	Lament for Pharaoh	Mar 3, 585	Mar 14, 586
32:17	12	[12] Cf. 32:1	15	Lament for Egypt	Mar 17, 585	Mar 28, 586
33:21	12	10	5	News comes of the fall	Jan 8, 585	Jan 18, 586
40:1	25	1	10	Brought to Israel	Apr 28, 573	Apr 9, 574

"The foregoing may now be seen to constitute a self-contained and consistent chronological scheme. The only essential difficulty is the problem of whether Jehoiachin's captivity began in 597 and [or?] 598, and that is a matter of interpretation of the data in Kings and Jeremiah. Reckoning from either year, the notations in Ezekiel fall into a comprehensible pattern. The most significant point at which to check the figures is with reference to the fall of Jerusalem. Here the dates may be tabulated as follows:

Nebuchad. began siege (Ezek 24:1)   Jan 15, 588 or Jan 26, 589

---

[274]For an excellent summary and evaluation of the critical scholarship in Ezekiel, see D. N. Freedman, "The Book of Ezekiel," pp. 466-71.

[275]Jack Finegan, "The Chronology of Ezekiel," *JBL* 69 (1950): 61-66.

| Jerusalem fell (Kings/Jer) | Aug 15-18, 586 or Aug 26-30, 587 |
| Fugitive came with news of fall of Jerusalem (Ezek 33:21) | Jan 8, 585 or Jan 18, 586 |

"The time required for Ezra to journey from Babylon to Jerusalem (Ezra 7:9) was from the first day of the first month to the first of the fifth month, or four full months. The time required here for the fugitive to come from Jerusalem to Ezekiel in Babylonia was from the tenth day of the fifth month to the fifth day of the tenth month, less than five months. The sequence and time of events, compared with the independent data of other Biblical passages, works out with exactitude."[276]

Finegan includes the "seven day" phrase in 3:16 as one of the chronological points. Most people would not include it. If it belongs, there are fourteen chronological references, as one might expect. The problem with including it is that it seems to be a sub point under the first main reference in 1:2.

IV. The Structure and Synthesis of the Book of Ezekiel.

The unifying feature in the book of Ezekiel is the Glory of the Lord. The opening vision during which Ezekiel is called to the prophetic ministry centers on the visible presence of the throne of God. This overwhelming presentation is to show the theocentricity of the book: God is the center of this unfolding drama.

The first vision concludes with the statement, "Such was the appearance of the likeness of the glory of the Lord. And when I saw it, I fell on my face and heard a voice speaking" (1:28). The "call" unit returns to the theme of the glory of the Lord in 3:12 and concludes with reference to the Gory of the Lord (3:23) where we are reminded that it is the same glory of the Lord referred to in chapter 1.

---

[276]Ibid., p. 66.

Chapters 4-7 are predictions of the coming siege and fall of Jerusalem. They are to show the necessity of God's judgment because of the sinfulness of the people. The argument, however, moves back to Jerusalem in 8-11. The exiles kept arguing that God would not destroy the holy city. The same obtuseness with which Jeremiah deals ("the temple of the Lord will prohibit the fall of this city"—Ch. 7) is faced by Ezekiel in the exile. This unit shows the continued perverse pagan practices that deserve and will receive the judgment of God. Furthermore, these perverse practices led to the removal of the glory of God (a symbol of the removal of God's protective blessing). Before the glory is removed, we are allowed to see it (8:4) and are reminded that it is the same glory seen in the exile. The glory begins to move in chapter 9 (v.3) to the threshold of the temple. In chapter 10 there are four steps in the removal: (1) from the cherub to the threshold of the temple (10:4), (2) from the threshold to a place over the cherubim (10:18), (3) accompanying the cherubim, it moves to the east gate of the temple, (4) from the east gate it goes out and stands over the mount of Olives. Thus, God was demonstrating the departure of His blessing and protection of Jerusalem.

Ezekiel's visit to the pagan city of Jerusalem in a vision (8:1) occurred in 592 or some six years before the fall in 586. Now (40-48) some twenty years later, he revisits the land in a vision. The temple, so tragically destroyed in 586, is being rebuilt in glorious dimensions.

When the temple is completely measured, he sees the glory of the Lord returning from the way it disappeared in chapter 8 (43:3-4).

The argument of the book is complete: Yahweh, because of His justice, had to punish His people for their sins. However, the future is glorious for Israel, and in that future time, they, their land and their temple will be restored. At that time, the return of God's protective care will take place as the glory of the Lord returns to the temple from which it departed (in a figure) prior to 586.

The *event* on which the book centers is the fall of Jerusalem. One of the signs to the exiled community of the legitimacy of Ezekiel's message is that he will become supernaturally mute (3:26). He will be able to speak only in an official capacity, that is, when God gives him a message. All the messages up to 33 bear on the inevitable siege and fall of Jerusalem and the reasons for that end. However, in 24:2, 25-27, God tells Ezekiel that the siege has begun. He is to write the day down so that everyone will know that he has received the information divinely. Further, when the city falls, Ezekiel will be able to speak freely (24:27). When the messenger of the disaster arrives in 33:21, Ezekiel was able to speak without inhibition. All this was a sign to the people.

The messages after the fall, deal with Israel's future, including the restoration of the two nations (36-37), invasion in the Eschaton of Gog and Magog, and the idyllic restoration of people, land, and temple. "Then they shall know that I am Yahweh."

V. The Outline of the Book

A. God pronounces judgment on Israel (1:1—24:27).

1. Yahweh calls Ezekiel to a difficult ministry on July 1, 593 B.C. (1:1-3:27).

The vision of the glory of God (1:1-28).

The time element "thirtieth year" is much debated. It should probably be understood as the age of Ezekiel; the age at which a priest (at least the Levite) began his ministry (Num. 4:3) (1:1-2).

The four living creatures (*ḥayyoth* חַיּוֹת) obviously represent the presence of God. They form the basis for the revelation of God to John as well (Rev. 4:1-11). Each creature has four faces and four wings. The four faces are like that of a man, a lion, a bull, and an eagle. In Revelation 4:7 *each* creature has the characteristics of one of the above. They also have six wings (as in Isaiah 6) while

Ezekiel's creatures have four wings. All kind of lights flash back and forth in Ezekiel's creatures (1:4-14).

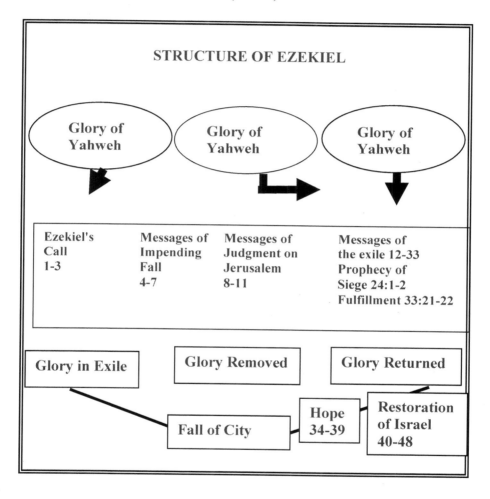

The movement of the living creatures is linked to a series of wheels with a strange configuration (wheel within a wheel). The rims have eyes all around them. The living creatures are linked with the wheels and the spirit of the living creatures is in the wheels (1:15-21).

Structure of Ezekiel
Glory of Yahweh

Glory revealed (1-7)	*Glory removed* (8-39)	*Glory restored* (40-48)
(592) 1-3 Call of Ezekiel 4-7 Prediction of fall of Jerusalem	(591) 8-Sin in Jerusalem 9-Glory=temple 10-Glory=east gate 11-Glory=Olivet 12-Prep exile 13 Prophets 14-Idolatry 15-Wood for fire 16-19-Israel's problem (590) 20-23 Lessons from the past (588) 24-Siege begins	(572) 43 G of Y=east gate 44:4 G filled house 45 Land 47 Water/land Yahweh shammah!!

(587,70,86,86,86,85,85,85)
Nations (25—32) Ammon, Moab, Edom, Phil, Tyre, Egypt
33—Watchman (33:21-22) <u>fall</u>
34—Shepherds
35—Edom
36—39—Eschaton
Restoration
Bones/sticks
Gog/Magog

An expanse is over the heads of the living creatures under which the creatures move, and the sound of their wings is like the sound of the Almighty. The throne of the Almighty is in the expanse. Sitting on it is a figure with the appearance of a man (cf. Daniel's Ancient of Days, Chapter 7:13). A rainbow surrounds the throne (1:22-28).

A comparison of Ezekiel 1 with Revelation 4 yields the following results:

Ezekiel	Revelation
Living Creatures	Living Creatures
(Heb.: ḥawoth)	(Gr.: zon)
Four faces:	Each one like:
Man	Lion
Lion	Calf
Bull	Man
Eagle	Eagle
Four wings	Six wings
Eyes on rims	Full of eyes
One like a man	One sitting on the throne
Throne, lapis lazuli	Like a jasper stone
Rainbow in the clouds	Rainbow around the throne
	Twenty-four elders
	Lightning, thunders
THE GLORY OF THE LORD	HOLY, HOLY, HOLY

Without trying to go into details on the significance of the component parts of the vision, suffice it to say that the entire vision is designed to show the glory of God and to overwhelm Ezekiel (the same thing happened to Isaiah). The end of this vision is to convince Ezekiel of the *theocentricity* of God in the universe. All that happens comes from God. He is the beginning and the end. Ezekiel is the "son of man," the representative of the human race with all its limitations.

The call of Ezekiel to speak to a stubborn people (2:1-7).

Ezekiel is addressed as the "son of man." This is not to be equated with the "son of man" in Daniel 7:13 where it is a messianic title. Throughout the book "son of man" is applied to Ezekiel as the representative of the human race before a holy god. When God addresses him, the Spirit enters him and he hears God speaking (2:1-2).

Ezekiel is told that his task will be difficult. Israel is rebellious, but they will know that Yahweh God has sent a prophet among them. Ezekiel is told not to fear them in spite of the persecution he will receive (cf. Jeremiah's call) (2:3-7).

The place of Scripture in Ezekiel's ministry is illustrated by the scroll (2:8—3:11).

An extensive quote from Childs is appropriate here:[277]

"Surely one of the most important aspects of Ezekiel's message was its dependence upon the activity of interpretation within the Bible itself. Not only was Ezekiel deeply immersed in the ancient traditions of Israel, but the prophet's message shows many signs of being influenced by a study of Israel's sacred writings. The impact of a collection of authoritative writings is strong throughout the book....Thus, for example, in Ch. 20 Ezekiel is not only making use of the great traditions of the Egyptian slavery, exodus, and conquest, but he offers a detailed and radical reinterpretation of the law of the first-born found in Ex. 22:28. Again, the vision of the seventy elders of Israel 'each with a censer in his hand' is not understood unless this cultic abuse is seen in the light of the covenant ceremony in Ex. 24.9ff. and the judgment of Korah in Num. 16.16ff. Or again, in the portrayal of Gog and Magog (Chs. 38-39) one can recognize the influence of Isa. 5.26ff.; Jer. 4.29ff.; and Ps. 46."[278]

---

[277]B. S. Childs, *Introduction to the O. T. as Scripture*, 364.

[278]Cf. also W. Zimmerli, "The Message of the Prophet Ezekiel," *Int* 23 (1969): -131-57.

God tells Ezekiel not to rebel as Israel does, but to accept the order to eat the scroll. The scroll was written on the front and back. Its contents were lamentations, mourning and woe. At God's command he ate the scroll and it was as sweet as honey to his taste (2:8-3:3).[279]

The commission is given to Ezekiel. The scroll represents the message of judgment Ezekiel is to preach. The people will be hard and unwilling to listen, but God has made Ezekiel hard as well so as to respond to their resistance. His message will be "Thus says Yahweh" (3:4-11).

The carrying out of the commission begins as the Spirit lifts him up (3:12-27).

He hears a great noise with a shout of "Blessed be the glory of Yahweh in His place." The Spirit takes him away, and he goes in bitterness of spirit.[280] He comes to the exiles in Tel-abib where he sits in morose silence, meditating on the bitter message for seven days, "causing consternation among them" (3:12-15).

God expands the commission to tell Ezekiel that he is a watchman. This important section on the responsibility of the watchman and his hearers must be understood in the context. The watchman is Ezekiel warning the people of Israel. The death or life spoken of is to be taken literally. They will die by the sword, pestilence or whatever judgment befalls them. This is a similar message to that of Jeremiah (3:16-21).

---

[279]Cf. Rev. 5:1-5; 10:8-11; Jer. 15:16 and Greenberg's discussion on the common biblical motif of God working with a prophet's mouth, *Ezekiel* in AB, 78.

[280]In Rev. 10:9-11, a passage built on the scroll motif of Ezekiel, the swallowed scroll is sweet to the taste but bitter in the stomach. This may be the intent of Ezekiel's bitterness also.

Ezekiel is then told by God to begin his ministry. He was taken out to the plain (the Euphrates Valley—*habiqe'ah,* הַבִּקְעָה). There he saw the same glory of the Lord he saw at the beginning. This links the messages together. God tells him he will be dumb until God speaks to him, and then he will be able to say "Thus says the Lord God." At the same time, people will try to prevent him from speaking (3:22-27). [281]

2. Ezekiel begins his ministry of prophecy to Israel by symbolically acting out the siege (4:1—5:17).

The first symbolic act is the brick (4:1-3).

Ezekiel is to take a brick, draw a map of Jerusalem on it so that it can be identified, and pretend to lay a siege against it. He will do this by making a siege wall, a ramp, and by placing tents and battering rams around it. All Israel is to understand by this that God is going to use Nebuchadnezzar to besiege Jerusalem and capture it.

The second symbolic act is lying on his side (4:4-8).

Greenberg, works from the dedication of the temple in 970 B.C. This brings him to 580 B.C. as the period of time when Israel was sinning. He cites Lev. 26 for covenant curses applied to continual sins. [282] Gardiner suggests that the 430 years in Egypt forms the backdrop (Exod. 12:40-41). Judah is to be punished forty years (as in the

---

[281]See Greenberg, *Ezekiel*, 120-21, who refers it to confinement to his home and prohibition from reproving the people until God speaks though him. See also M. Greenberg, "On Ezekiel's Dumbness," *JBL* 77 (1958): 101-105. He discusses a certain Jesus ben Ananias referred to by Josephus (when Rome besieged Jerusalem) who cried out for seven and one half years "Woe on Jerusalem, etc." He did not speak with anyone except to pronounce the woe.

[282]Greenberg, *Ezekiel*, 125.

wilderness); Israel three hundred ninety years (430-40).[283] Keil agrees except that he believes the 40 years represents Moses' sojourn.[284] It is then an indefinite prediction of judgment. Ezekiel must have lain on his side parts of each day. Using Finegan's data, there are approximately 445 days between vision one and two (1:1 with 8:1).

The third symbolic act is eating rationed food (4:9-17).

The lack of food is illustrated by taking certain staples, making bread from them and eating them for the three hundred and ninety days. He is to take scales so as to ration the food to twenty shekels per day. The water is likewise to be limited, and barley cakes are to be baked over human excrement. This latter will symbolize that the Jews will eat unclean food in captivity. When Ezekiel protests the non-kosher cooking fuel, God allows him to use cow's dung. The first illustration is to represent the fact that food will be limited during the siege.[285]

The fourth symbolic act is the cutting of hair (5:1-12).

The conclusion of the siege is illustrated by what Ezekiel does with his hair. Ezekiel is to shave his head and face with a sharp sword. The hair will then be divided into three parts.

> One part he burns in fire.
> One part he cuts with the sword.
> One part he scatters to the wind, waving a sword.
> A few he puts in the edges of his clothes.

---

[283]F. Gardiner, *Ezekiel* in Ellicott's Commentary on the Whole Bible, 5:214.

[284]C. F. Keil, *Prophecies of Ezekiel*, 1:71-76.

[285]2 Kings 6 and 7 illustrate the horrible problem of starvation when a city is under siege.

Some he throws in the fire.

The reason for this judgment, God says, is that he selected them to be in the center of the nations. However, Israel rebelled and rejected God's ordinances and statutes. They are worse than the nations around them, therefore, God is judging them. The siege will be terrible (fathers eating sons, etc.) and many will be scattered. God will not spare them because they have practiced idolatry in His sanctuary (5:5-12).

The result will be the satisfaction of God's anger (5:13-17).

God's just anger against an ungrateful and rebellious people will be appeased (propitiated). The judgment will be awful, but it will serve as a warning to both the people of God and those who are around them. This is the first full statement of the exile.

3. God gives a series of woe declarations against the people of Judah (6:1—7:27).

O Mountains of Israel (6:1-10).

The mountains of Israel stand for the nation of Israel (included are the hills, ravines and valleys). God decrees that He is going to bring judgment against Israel. The emphasis is placed on the idolatry (high places, altars, incense altars, idols). God will kill His people and let their corpses lie around their altars. Then *they shall acknowledge that He is Yahweh* (this is an important phrase, appearing about 72 times (6:1-7).

A remnant will be left in spite of this devastating judgment coming upon God's people. These will be in the captivity where they will remember Yahweh and the pain their adulterous hearts have caused Him. Then they will know that Yahweh is their God. When that happens it will be clear that His chastisement has not been futile. Then *they shall acknowledge that He is Yahweh* (6:8-10).

Alas because of the evil abominations (6:11-14).

The three-fold judgment of God is promised against Judah: plague, sword, and famine. God pronounces the litany of idolatry seen many times in Isaiah and especially in Jeremiah. Death and the devastation of the land are promised. Then *they shall acknowledge that He is Yahweh.*

An end! An end is coming on the four corners of the land (7:1-4).

God promises that He will bring judgment on the land of Judah because of their idolatrous practices. Then *they will acknowledge that He is Yahweh.*

A disaster, a unique disaster is coming! (7:5-9).

This warning is parallel with the preceding. An end is coming on the land. God's wrath will be poured out on them. They will suffer the results of their idolatrous practices. He will show no pity (as in 7:4). Then *they will acknowledge that He is Yahweh.*

Behold, the day! Behold, it is coming (7:10-13).

This woe oracle is against the materialism of the day. Their evil has grown like trees (the rod has budded, arrogance has blossomed, violence has grown into a rod of wickedness). The buyers and sellers will not make a profit. God's judgment is sure (the vision), and no one will be able by means of his materialistic gain to save his life.

Blow the trumpet; get everything ready (7:14-22).

I have read the imperative (*tiqe'u bataqo'a* תִּקְעוּ בַתָּקוֹעַ and *vhaken* וְהָכֵן). The shout to Israel is to prepare for war. Yet, with all their preparation, no one will go into battle, because that would be futile. Yahweh Himself will be fighting against His people. The evil triumvirate (sword, plague, and famine) will again be active. Even those who escape will be extremely vulnerable. Their material gains will mean nothing (7:19), and God's beautiful things which they turned into idols will become abhorrent to them. God will deliver them over to foreigners and turn His face against them.

Make the chain! (7:23-27).

This Hebrew is difficult, but as it stands, it is telling someone to prepare to take captives. The reason is that the land is full of bloody crimes (judgment of bloods) for which it must be judged. Evil nations will then be brought against Judah as God's instrument, and the pride of Judah will cease. They will look for peace, but not find it. They will seek a vision from the prophet, the law from the priest, and counsel from the elders, but they will all be gone (note Ezekiel's dependence upon Jeremiah for this triad, Jer. 18:18). The royal house as well as the people will mourn in this judgment. Then (notice the repetition) *they will acknowledge that He is Yahweh.*

4. Ezekiel's prophetic ministry is transferred to Jerusalem on September 17, 592 B.C. (8:1—11:25).

The relation of the two visions.

Ezekiel, through a trance, is transferred to Jerusalem where he sees idolatry being practiced in the temple. The purpose of this vision is to give the reason for God's judgment upon the city. The people have given up hope in Yahweh: they fail to recognize that their disobedi-ence is the cause of His absence. They have turned to other gods for help. The references to the Living Creatures in this unit (9:3) are to tie together this vision and the one in chapter 1. The Living Creatures showed the glory of God in exile (Chs. 1-7); now they show the glory of God leaving Jerusalem (Chs. 8-11).

The setting of the vision (8:1-4).

While Ezekiel was sitting among the elders of the exile, God appeared to him again. The spectral, semi-human creature seems to be a theophany. The Spirit lifts him up and brings him *in visions* to Jerusalem. There he comes to the north gate of the inner court. (This could also be "the entrance of the inner gate facing northward" *hap*^e*nimith haponeh tsaponah* הַפְּנִימִית הַפּוֹנֶה צָפוֹנָה). At that spot was located the "idol of jealousy that provokes to jealousy" (*semel hqine'ah hmaqeneḥ* סֵמֶל הַקִּנְאָה הַמַּקְנֶה) This word in Phoenician denotes a statue of a divine or human being. 2 Kings 21:7 speaks of a *pesel* of Asherah which Manasseh set up. 2 Chron. 33:7, 15 (reflecting Ezekiel?) calls it *pesel hassemel*. It is instructive that a Canaanite goddess Asherah should be referred to by the Phoenician/Canaanite word *semel*.[286]

The glory of the Lord appears in the temple as it had appeared to Ezekiel in the plain (3:22). This device is used to tie the visions together (8:4).

The north side of the altar (8:5-6).

Ezekiel sees the idol of jealousy (see above) and the people committing idolatry.

The entrance of the court (8:7-13).

God tells Ezekiel to dig through the wall and there he sees theriomorphic images being worshipped. These would be similar to the art on the Ishtar gate. The seventy elders represent the leadership of Israel and show the pervasiveness of idolatry.

---

[286]See Greenberg, *Ezekiel.*

The entrance of the gate of the temple (8:14-15).

God shows Ezekiel women weeping for Tammuz. This is an ancient Sumerian rite of weeping for the dying and rising God.[287]

The inner court of the temple (8:16-18).

The people are worshipping the sun. Josiah got rid of horses and chariots dedicated to the sun (2 Kings 23:11). Manasseh built altars for the host of heaven (2 Kings 21:5). The "twig to the nose" may be a cultic gesture, but it is unknown.[288]

God brings judgment on the city and temple (9:1-11).

The call for the executioners (lit. appointed ones: *piqudoth*, פְּקֻדוֹת) goes out and six men come from the upper (northern) gate. Each has his weapons of destructions, but one man, clothed in linen has a writing case (ink horn: *qeseth hasopher*, קֶסֶת הַסֹּפֵר). The man in linen is given the task of putting a mark on the foreheads of God's faithful people. The other five are to follow after him slaying all those who do not have the mark, beginning with the elders before the temple. (Note the sealing of the 144,000 in Revelation 7.) As the five men began killing the people in the city, Ezekiel pled for the people. Yahweh's response is that their sin is so bad, drastic measures are called for. His eye will not pity, but their conduct will be rewarded with judgment. The man in linen reports the completion of the task. This entire event probably takes place in a vision or trance.

---

[287]For a description see Greenberg, *Ezekiel*, p. 171.

[288]See ibid., p. 173.

God removes His glory to the east gate (10:1-22).

God, who sits over the expanse above the living creatures, tells the man in linen to bring coals of fire from among the Cherubim (הַכְּרֻבִים). This is the first time the living beings are called Cherubim. They are otherwise known from Gen. 3:24, where they guard the garden, and they sit at either end of the ark of the covenant, where they seem to represent the throne of Yahweh, "who sits above the Cherubim" (1 Sam. 4:4). It is no doubt the Cherubim of the ark that are represented here carrying the glory cloud, a symbol of the presence of God (10:1-5).

The coals of fire are to be scattered over the city (judgment is involved perhaps with the idea of purification). An extended description is given of the Cherubim showing that they are the same as in the vision of chapter 1. The only difference is that instead of an ox, the face of a Cherub is present. Does this indicate that a Cherub normally looked like an ox? (10:6-17).

The glory of Yahweh (*kabod*) then departs from the threshold of the temple, stops over the Cherubim, who move to the east gate of the Lord's house (10:18-22).

God removes His glory from Jerusalem (11:1-25).

At the entrance of the east gate, Ezekiel sees a certain Jaazaniah and a Pelatiah. These, says God, are those who plan iniquity in the city. Their plans seem to include the building of houses, i.e., there is no fear of further judgment. From later verses, it appears that they have taken over land forsaken by those who have gone into captivity. They are "land speculators." They use a proverb that is cryptic to us: "The city is the pot and we are the flesh." This seems to be used in a good sense: "we are the stuff out of which good soup is made, and the city is what produces it" (11:1-4).

God uses the proverb against them. The dead in the city (from 597) were the flesh and the city the pot, i.e., the proverb is used negatively. The city will not be a place of protection; God will bring them out and slay them in the borders of Israel. Then they will *acknowledge that He is Yahweh* (11:5-12).

Ezekiel again protests that Yahweh is going to destroy Israel completely when he sees Pelatiah die. Yahweh's answer is found in the rest of the chapter. These "land speculators" are saying: "They have gone far (read the indicative rather than the imperative) from the Lord (temple in Jerusalem); this land has been given us as a possession." They are growing rich on the misfortune of their fellow Jews. God says: "On the contrary, no matter how far I have removed them, I will bring them back and give them the land of Israel." There will be genuine conversion (Jer. 31:31), idolatry will be over, they will be "My people, and I shall be their God" (11:13-21).

Finally, the Cherubim fly away with the glory of the Lord riding on them and stop over the Mount of Olives. Then the Spirit brought Ezekiel back to the exiles in Chaldea. He then reported this extraordinary vision to the exiles (11:22-25).

5.   Ezekiel, back with the exiles, predicts the deportation of the remaining Jews in Jerusalem (12:1-28).

Ezekiel acts out an escape attempt (12:1-7).

It would appear the people of the *golah* refuse to admit that God is going to punish Jerusalem. God therefore tells Ezekiel to act out the removal of the people from Jerusalem. The first step is to pack a bag and to move from his home to another place in the daytime. Then at night, he is to dig a hole through the wall, cover his face, and try to escape. Ezekiel did all this (12:1-7).

God tells Ezekiel to declare the meaning of his act (12:8-16).

The daytime movement represents the capture of the people in general. The night escapade represents Zedekiah's attempt to escape the Babylonian army. God throws His net over him, and he is captured by the Babylonians, blinded and taken to Babylon. The rest will be scattered, but He will leave a few to spread the news of God's judgment. Then *they will acknowledge that He is Yahweh.*

God tells Ezekiel to act out a life of fear (12:17-20).

Ezekiel is to eat his bread and drink his water with trembling, quivering and anxiety. This is to symbolize the fear of the Jews in the foreign countries into which they will be taken captive.

God rebukes the Jews for discounting the prophetic messages (12:21-28).

The Jews are quoting a proverb: "The things that have been prophesied must be for a distant future, because nothing is happening as prophesied." (They say this in spite of Jeremiah's prophecies.) Yahweh's answer is that the days are drawing near and the vision will indeed be fulfilled. The false prophecies will fail. To those who declared of Ezekiel's visions, "they must be for a distant future," God says "None of My words will be delayed any longer."

6. God tells Ezekiel to speak out against false prophecy (13:1-23).

The practice of false prophets (13:1-7).

False prophets were apparently fairly common in Israel's history from the beginning of the Monarchy on down. Jeremiah encounters them personally and confronts them (Jer. 28, 29). God tells Ezekiel to speak out against them. They prophesy from their own inspiration (lit.: "their heart" *milibam,* מִלִּבָּם). They are foolish prophets (*han^e valim,* הַנְּבָלִים), who are following their own spirit. The proverb "like foxes among ruins" points to selfish prophets: they do not build or maintain the wall, but they run around on it like foxes making dens. Their vision is false, and Yahweh has not spoken through them.

The judgment on the false prophets (13:8-16).

God promises that false prophets will not be allowed in the council of Israel nor written in the register of the temple (census list). Their message is one of peace when there is nothing but disaster ahead. We know from Jeremiah 28 that the false prophets were teaching an early return from the exile. They are "whitewashing" the situation. The wall is dangerously weak, but instead of recognizing that fact, they paint it over with whitewash (false comfort). God promises to fulfill his judgment (symbolized by the falling wall against which He will send a storm).

Ezekiel is to prophesy against the false female prophets (13:17-23).

This paragraph indicates that the men were not alone in their false prophecy. Certain women likewise were misleading the people. These "fortune tellers" instead of submitting to divine providence, try to tell people who will live and die.[289] The bands on the wrists (*kesathoth*, כְּסָתוֹת) and the head coverings were probably some magical garments with which they enticed and ensnared people. The handfuls of barley and pieces of bread may refer to incantations or to offerings. God promises to judge the women for deceiving the people into ignoring Ezekiel's warnings.

---

[289]Greenberg, *Ezekiel*, p. 244.

7. God condemns internal and external idolatry (14:1-23).

God criticizes the elders in the exile (14:1-5).

The elders take their place before Ezekiel, presumably to receive a word from the Lord through him. God tells Ezekiel that the elders have set up idols in their hearts. This surely means that they are still worshipping idols even though it may only be internal. The second thing they are doing is putting "the stumbling block" of their iniquity (*mikshol "vonam* מִכְשׁוֹל עֲוֹנָם) before them. This is another form of mental idolatry "a rubric for an unregenerate state of mind."[290]

God promises punishment on men who do this thing (14:6-11).

Yahweh demands repentance and complains of the audacity of these who would carry on this idolatrous practice and then come to Yahweh for an answer to their inquiry. God says that he will deal directly with such a person. "I Yahweh will by myself oblige him with an answer."[291] God will set his face against that man. Furthermore, any prophet who deigns to answer such an inquiry will be held accountable to God.

God speaks of the irrevocability of His judgment (14:12-23).

God speaks of his four-fold messengers of judgment: famine, wild beasts, sword and plague. Once He has decreed these against a disobedient people, no one will be able to turn Him back. Not even the intercession of Noah, Daniel and Job would change the situation. Daniel is a contemporary of Ezekiel and as such is thought by some to be too young to have such a reputation. Many seek to find this Daniel in a more ancient personage such as the Danel of the Ugaritic

---

[290]Ibid.

[291]Ibid.

epics.[292] This latter has not enjoyed much popular support recently, but few critics believe this could refer to the Daniel known in the Bible. However, Daniel's wisdom must have become quite well known since he interpreted Nebuchadnezzar's dream even before the exile that brought Ezekiel to Babylon (14:12-20).

God applies the principle to Jerusalem. He will indeed carry out His judgment, but at the same time he promises the deliverance of a remnant. This will bring comfort to Ezekiel because he will know that God has a purpose in what He is doing, and it will not be in vain (14:21-23).

8. God likens Judah to a worthless vine (15:1-8).

Vines have their value, but that value is not for woodworking. The vine-wood is virtually worthless. When it has been burned in a fire, it is even less valuable. God then compares the vine to the people of Israel. Like the vine, they are worthless apart from God. The judgment to come upon them, like the fire to the vine, will not improve them any. Apart from God, Israel is worthless both before and after the judgment to be brought upon them. Their land is to be made desolate because of their unfaithful response to Yahweh.

9. God rehearses Israel's inglorious past but her promising future (16:1-63).

Israel's family tree (16:1-5).

God ties Israel's abominable practices into her heritage. Her family tree goes back to the Canaanites: her father was an Amorite and her mother was a Hittite. Amorite is a generic term similar to Canaanite (see Gen 15:16). The Hittites were a proto-Hamitic people who were assimilated into their Indo-European conquerors. The Canaanites

---

[292]*ANET*, pp. 151-53.

epitomized all that God is opposed to. He was constantly trying to keep Israel from entanglements with them. (Note Abraham's determination to keep Isaac from marrying a Canaanite—Gen. 24—and Isaac and Rebecca's unhappiness with their son Esau for marrying one—Gen. 27-28). When God found Israel, she was squirming as a naked little baby with no post-natal care whatsoever.

God's wonderful grace to Israel (16:6-14).

God's grace toward Israel is depicted in His care for this poor abandoned baby. He willed her to live (Patriarchs?), nourished her into adolescence (Egypt), married her and made a covenant with her (Exodus), cared for her, clothed her with ornaments (in the land under kings), so that all the nations heard of her. All of this was because God, in His grace, bestowed His splendor on her (16:6-14).

Israel forgot God's gracious acts (16:15-22).

God speaks in this paragraph of the fact that Israel, as so often happens to people who have received mercy, forgot God's grace and began to take pride in herself. This led to idolatry as she turned all God's gracious gifts into idolatrous practices. The consummating evil was the sacrifice of children in the fire (to the god Moloch). Her worst "abomination" was to forget her awful past and God's grace in rescuing her.

Israel's "adultery" against her husband was heightened by turning from Him to the various nations (16:23-34).

In the fourth year of Zedekiah (593 B.C.) we know that there was trouble in the Chaldean empire that led Judah and her neighbors to conspire against Nebuchadnezzar (Jer. 27-28). This paragraph is to say that Israel, every time she went to other nations for help, was committing adultery against her husband, Yahweh. She should have trusted Him. He specifically mentions Assyria, Egypt and Chaldea. Ahaz was the first to go to Assyria under the threat of the Syro-Ephraimite coalition (Isa. 7). Hezekiah, Ahaz' son, received ambassadors from the newly emerging Chaldean power group (Isa. 38-39), and under Zedekiah, efforts were made to persuade the Egyptians to take on the Babylonians (Jer. 37 cf. also Isaiah 23 which may indicate that Hezekiah was doing the same). By going to the nations for help rather than trusting Yahweh, she was committing adultery against her husband. Judah, however, was an adulteress, not a harlot. A harlot collects pay for her services, but Judah pays her lovers (an allusion to taking the temple gold, etc., to buy off foreign powers).[293]

God's judgment will be to turn her "lovers" against her (16:35-43).

God is going to call together these nations whom Judah has "lusted" after and bring them against her. They will not spare her. She will be stripped naked and treated like an adulteress. Her houses will be burned and the people will be put to the sword. Like an offended husband, Yahweh will find his anger appeased when all this happens. God's purpose in punishing Judah is to bring her to the point where she will stop committing lewdness.

---

[293]Excursus on Judah going to Egypt:

Thompson (*CAH*, 3:213) says: "Yet Judah still believed that Egypt, so much nearer than distant and vague Babylon, could help her. A new Pharaoh, Hophra (Apries), had succeeded Psammetichus II, the son of Necho, and, burning to reconquer the ancient tributaries of the Mediterranean coast, he invaded Palestine. The Babylonian army, doubtless now little more than an army of occupation, where homesickness and boredom at so long a sojourn in a foreign land would militate against discipline, gave way before him and retreated from Jerusalem. Again the Judaean king's spirits rose in expectation that they had gone forever; again did Jeremiah cast them down (xxxvii, 7 *sq.*). 'Behold,' warned he, 'Pharaoh's army, which is come forth to help you, shall return to Egypt into their own land, and the Chaldaeans shall come again and fight against this city, and they shall take it, and burn it with fire.' It was of no avail to say that the Chaldaeans would not return; they would certainly return: even though the Babylonian army had fallen back from Jerusalem, it was only a temporary retreat."

God concludes this discussion of Judah's sordid past by discussing her relation to her sisters (16:44-59).

God quotes another proverb to make His point: "like mother, like daughter." The mother is a Hittite and the father is an Amorite. Judah's conduct is what one would expect from someone who has such a family background. Her sisters also were adulteresses.[294] Her older sister was Samaria and her younger sister was Sodom. These of course represent two groups who have already received God's judgment because of their sin. Judah, however, has not learned from her sisters so that she acts even more wickedly than they. Her conduct is so disgraceful that she makes Samaria and Sodom look good by comparison. God however is going to restore Sodom as well as Samaria and Judah. All three of these groups will return to "their former state" that is prior to their wicked acts (cf. Matt. 11:20-24.)[295] Judah was so proud she would never even mention the name of her sister Sodom, that is, she disdained her. Now that her sin has been uncovered, Edom will mock her. God will judge her in proportion to her sin: she has broken His covenant.

---

[294]The sister motif is put forth by Jeremiah (3:6-9) and is probably adapted by Ezekiel both here and in chap. 23.

[295]Brownlee, *Ezekiel 1-19,* 28:248 says, "The promised restoration of Samaria and of Jerusalem is not surprising, and it accords with 4-6; 37:15-22, but that of Sodom is! Zimmerli has noted that Sodom is supposed to be somewhere near the southern end of the Dead Sea and that this region is to be included in the new Land of Israel (47:18)....More probably, by 'Sodom and her daughters' Ezekiel no longer means the archaic places mentioned in Gen 14:2 but all unassimilated Canaanite communities. He is thus dealing with the threefold character of the land of Israel: (1) the kingdom of Israel, (2) the kingdom of Judah, (3) and Canaanite inhabitants."

God gives a comforting message of restoration (16:60-63).

This paragraph contains a marvelous promise of complete forgiveness and restoration for Judah. Along with Samaria and Sodom, God will make a covenant with Judah and she "shall know that He is the Lord." She will then always remember her shameful fall and will bask in the forgiveness of God. "Not because of your covenant" indicates that He will deal independently with the others.[296]

10. God gives the parable of the two eagles (17:1-24).

The first eagle (Babylon) (17:1-6).

The eagle is quite outstanding. He comes to Lebanon and takes away the top of the cedar tree (top is *tsamereth,* צַמֶּרֶת usually wool, perhaps the wooly appearance of the top of the cedar trees). The cedar trees in the Bible are used to depict pride, because the cedar wood was a very special wood coveted throughout the Middle East. Since the cedars grow in Lebanon, that place name will often accompany the symbol even though the referent is to some other place. Its top or best twig was brought to a land of merchants *kena'an,* כְּנַעַן) and set in a city of traders *rokalim,* רֹכְלִים) (cf. Revelation 17-18). He also took some of the seed of the land and planted it in a fecund place. The branch and the seed turned into a vine which inclined toward the eagle (Babylon as its protector). However it kept roots under it (Jews in Jerusalem).

---

[296]For background on Ezekiel's promises see Leviticus 26.

The second eagle (Egypt) (17:7-10).

The vine begins to reach out toward the second eagle for sustenance. The action seems to be effective because the vine is fruitful. However, God says that He will pull it up and let it wither.

The interpretation (17:11-21).

God's teaching about His place in the events of the last days of the monarchy is very instructive. The royal covenant made with Zedekiah and the oath that goes with it are from God (17:19). The deportation to Babylon is considered to be good (cf. the good figs in Jeremiah 24). In all these tragic events of the last quarter century of the monarchy, God declares Himself to be completely in charge. It is wrong to rebel against Babylon and to go to Egypt or any other nation for help.

The first eagle represents Babylon. The top twig represents Jehoiachin taken to the city of merchants (Babylon). The seed represents Jews deported in 597 B.C. The second eagle represents Egypt to whom Zedekiah and his advisors were looking for help against Babylon. Egypt promised to help and actually fielded an army so that the Babylonians pulled back temporarily. But they did not provide a permanent support.

God declares that He will one day set up a special twig that will rule (17:22-24).

Ezekiel delivers another message of hope. The twigs mentioned so far are being rejected (cf. a similar message in Jeremiah 23 where the kings of Judah are rejected but the Messiah [the branch] is promised). This twig will be put on a high mountain where it will become a stately cedar and a place of refuge for birds (cf. Nebuchadnezzar's kingdom in Daniel 4). Furthermore, the other trees (kingdoms) will learn of the sovereignty of God. "He puts up one and sets down another."

11. God gives a message on human responsibility (18:1-32).

God teaches His sovereignty in human affairs and that He does not discriminate (18:1-4).

The Jews were complaining that their suffering was the result of their ancestors' sin. They quote the parable about sour grapes. God argues that everyone belongs to Him and the He will see to it that individual responsibility is enforced (cf. Deut. 24:16).

God says that the righteous man will live (18:5-9).

It is important to remember the context. Life and death in this chapter refer to physical not spiritual states. It is not clear whether God is saying that He will see that a wicked man dies or whether the community should follow up on the sin, but it is clear that he is teaching individual responsibility. *The righteous man who*:

is righteous and practices the same
does not become involved in idolatry
does not commit adultery
does not violate menstrual laws
does not oppress, but restores pledges
does not rob, but gives bread and clothes to the poor.
does not lend money on interest
keeps his hand from iniquity
sees to justice between people
walks in God's statutes and ordinances
             will live!

God says that the unrighteous man will die (18:10-13).[297]

---

[297]See Brownlee, *Ezekiel 1-19,* 28:293 for an important discussion. It is important to distinguish between eternal life as Christians understand it and physical life as is

The righteous man may have a son whose conduct is opposite that of his father. That man will not live, says Yahweh. His blood will be on his own head when he is put to death.

God says that the righteous grandson will not be punished for his father's sins (18:14-20).

Apparently, their popular theology did not teach that a father's good deeds would compensate for a wicked son's bad deeds, but it did hold that a father's wicked deeds would be passed on to his son. God emphatically denies that dictum. The grandson, who lives a godly life as his grandfather did, will live regardless of what his father was like.

The people insist that the son should bear the sins of the father.[298] That passage is probably talking more about the natural consequences of a father's sins being passed onto succeeding generations). However, God insists that each will be judged by his deeds (See Exodus 20 for further discussion).

God says that changed conduct will change divine attitude toward the person (18:21-32).

God's grace responds to repentance. The wicked man who turns away from his sin, will encounter God's forgiveness, and his sinful past will not be held against him (18:21-23).

---

often in view in the Old Testament. See Ellison, *EBC*, p. 828 where he discusses physical death in this context.

[298]This fallacious idea apparently came from a misunderstanding of Exodus 20:5 (cf. also 34:6, 7). The idea is denied by Jeremiah (31:30, note that he even cites the law in 32:18), and Deuteronomy (24:16). The "visitation" of the fathers' sins is on children who *hate* God.

Conversely, the righteous man who abandons his good conduct will encounter God's judgment, and his past goodness will not avail him God's favor (18:24).

Regardless of human opinion, God says that his ways are the right ways, and the people are wrong in their philosophy. God does not take pleasure in the death of the wicked, but he is just and will deal justly (18:25-29).

This true philosophy applies to Israel. God calls upon her to repent, to turn back to Him. They are to make themselves a new heart and spirit lest they die. God takes no pleasure in anyone's death—therefore, He exhorts them to repent (18:30-32).

12. Yahweh gives Ezekiel a lament against the royal leadership of Judah (19:1-14).

The form of this prophecy is a lament (*qinah*, קִינָה). It is directed to the princes of Israel. Their mother is described as a lioness with cubs. The first cub was reared to be a leader but was deported to Egypt (this would have to be Jehoahaz since he is the only one to go to Egypt). The second "cub" was taken to Babylon (this one must be Jehoiachin, since he is the first one who went to Babylon. Jehoiakim is being passed over). Finally the "mother" (Judah) is referred to as a vine which in spite of its once fruitful condition, has been plucked up and thrown into the desert where it cannot produce. In other words, there will be no more leaders in Judah to deliver her.

13. On August 13, 591 B.C. Yahweh speaks to the elders who come to inquire of Him (20:1-44).[299]

Yahweh takes the opportunity of the elders' visit to challenge them with the lessons of the past. He refuses to respond to their request, but rather calls upon Ezekiel to judge them for their conduct. The elders are representing the nation of Israel, therefore, this message transcends the *golah* of Babylon and applies to all the people of Israel. He recounts Israel's history and shows their sinfulness and His grace up to the present time (20:1-4).

The first stage is the sojourn in Egypt. There they disobeyed him (apparently when Moses approached them about bringing them from Egypt) and refused to put away their idolatry. God considered pouring out His wrath upon them, but chose not to "for His name's sake" lest it be profaned among the nations (20:5-9).

The second stage is in the wilderness. God gave them His covenant (Exodus 20) and His Sabbaths as a sign. However they rebelled against Him (Exodus 33), and He again considered annihilating them. Again, He restrained Himself because of His name (note in Exodus 32 that Moses interceded for Israel with the same argument about the inviolability of God's name). However, as punishment, He told them they would not go to the land, but die in the wilderness (20:10-17).

The third stage is the offspring of the wilderness rebels. These children who were allowed to live even though their parents died in the wilderness did not learn the lesson God gave them. They also became involved in idolatry. God again considered annihilating them, but held back His hand because of His reputation among the

---

[299]Hananiah's prophecy of the return of the captives within two years (Jer. 28:3), if it had been true, would have been fulfilled at this time.

nations. He did give them the Deuteronomic covenant containing curses for disobedience (statues not good; ordinances not resulting in life, 20:25) (20:18-26).

The fourth stage is in the land. Once in Canaan, they began to adopt the pagan practices around them. They learned of the "Bamah's" or high places. They determined to be like the other nations around them. In light of this, should Israel seek to inquire of Yahweh (as the elders are doing)? (20:27-31).

The final, eschatological stage is when Yahweh restores His people. This paragraph is an extraordinary statement of God's future grace in behalf of His people. While the Jews may think they can act like all the other nations, Yahweh will not allow them to. He will be king over them. Two things must happen: He will regather the people and purge them of sinners. They must "pass under the rod" and be brought into the bond of the covenant. In the present time, they may indeed serve their idols (20:39), but in the future time they will be gathered on the mountain of Israel where they will serve Yahweh and He will accept them. They will hate their past life and "know that He is Yahweh and that He has dealt with them in accordance with His reputation" (20:32-44).

14. Yahweh speaks through Ezekiel a prophecy of the imminent fall of Jerusalem (20:45—21:32).

The last five verses of chapter 20 are included in chapter 21 in the Hebrew where they belong. The first unit (20:44-49) is a "parable" against Jerusalem, the second unit is an explicit statement (responding to the cynical statement "he is just speaking parables").

There is no forest in the Negev. Therefore, "the southland" (Teman), "the south" (Negev), "against the south" (*darom,* דָּרוֹם) are all terms for Judah.[300] God predicts an unquenchable fire in Judah. Perhaps the south is viewed as the starting point of the conflagration. From there it will spread northward as does the sword in the following paragraph. Everyone will know that it is Yahweh who has done it (20:44-49).

Yahweh states explicitly that this prediction is against Jerusalem. Both righteous and wicked will suffer when Yahweh's sword goes forth (again "all flesh will know that the drawn sword is from Yahweh"). The sword will cut from *south* to north. Ezekiel is told to groan with breaking heart and bitter grief. The people of the *golah* will ask him what he is groaning about, and he will reply that it is because of the news coming imminently about the disaster. This refers to the soon to be announced fall of Jerusalem (21:1-7).

This message is against the people of God and the officials of Israel (21:12). Therefore, Ezekiel is to show signs of grief (strike your thigh). But it will get worse as the sword multiplies its efficiency against the people. But God will appease His wrath by bringing judgment on His disobedient people (21:8-17).

The phrases "Or shall we rejoice, the rod of My son despising every tree?" (21:16) is virtually impossible to translate. It makes some sense if we assume it means that "My son" refers to Nebuchadnezzar attacking the people of Judah (trees). 21:18 has a phrase with several of the same words: "for there is testing [Babylonian invasion?]; and what if even the rod [Zedekiah?] which despises will be no more." The difficulty in the text leaves the translation tenuous.

The sword imagery continues through the symbolic word: Ezekiel is to mark out two roads with a sign post. One sign will read "Rabbah

---

[300]Cf. Josh. 15:1 where "Negev" and "Teman" are used of Judah's boundaries.

of Ammon"; the other will read "Jerusalem." Nebuchadnezzar will stand at the crossroads trying to decide which way to go. He will practice divination (arrows, idols, liver) and the answer comes: "Jerusalem." However, the elders in the *golah* cannot believe it. They declare it to be a false divination (Nebuchadnezzar has made a mistake? or Ezekiel has made a mistake in interpretation?). Yet, God is reminding them of their sin and delivering them into the hand of Nebuchadnezzar. Furthermore, Zedekiah is looked upon as a slain, wicked one. His royal dignity will be removed. Jerusalem will be a ruin, and yet there is hope: One is coming whose right it is to rule and God will give it to him (21:18-27).[301]

Ammonites (the other road sign) will not escape even though the divination of Nebuchadnezzar led him to Jerusalem. He will come back against the Ammonites and judge them severely (21:28-32).

15. Yahweh calls on Ezekiel to judge Jerusalem for her sinfulness (22:1-31).

Jerusalem first is attacked for her idolatry and the shedding of blood. They have become a reproach to the nations as God's judgment on her (22:1-5).

The rulers are next singled out because as God's representatives, they are expected to live exemplary lives. Instead they:

treated father and mother lightly.
oppressed the alien.
wronged the widow and the orphan.

---

[301]W. L. Moran, "Genesis 49:10 and Its Use in Ezekiel 21:32," *Bib* 39 (1958):405-25. For, just as in Gen 49,10 'until Shiloh comes' indicates, in some sense, a terminus to Judah's history, so in Ez 21,32 the *'ad bo 'aser lo hammispat* terminates, in some sense, the history of Judah's kingdom. Structurally, there is the similarity of the 'until. . ."—clause being preceded by a negative clause (a point to which we shall return). Lexically, we have the same elements in *'ad* and *bo/yabo.* " (p. 417)

despised God's holy things.
profaned God's Sabbaths.
shed blood.
ate at mountain shrines.
committed acts of lewdness.
uncovered their father's nakedness.
violated the menstrual laws.
defiled daughters-in-law.
humbled step-sisters.
took bribes for murder.
took interest.
injured neighbors for gain.
forgot God.

Their sin will be punished by dispersion among the nations (22:6-16).

Judah is compared to dross. God must smelt the metal and remove the dross. Jerusalem will be the pot and he will set a fire under her, and then they will know that Yahweh is the one who has poured our His wrath (22:17-22).

Judah is compared to a polluted land that needs cleansing by rain. The prophets conspire for their own ends (23-25); the priests profane holy things (26); the princes are like wolves (27); the prophets whitewash everything, and the people practice all kinds of sin (28-29). God searched for a man to stand in the broken down wall to stave off His judgment, but He could find no one. God therefore must judge them (22:23-31).

16. Yahweh gives Ezekiel a tale of two sisters (23:1-49).

There were two women, named Oholah (tent = אָהֳלָה) and Oholibah (a tent in her = אָהֳלִיבָה, cf. Jer. 3:6-10 for the same motif). These names are apparently linked to the Tent of Yahweh (= the tabernacle, *'ohel mo'ed,* אֹהֶל מוֹעֵד), i.e., these people were related to the Lord.

They were sisters and while in Egypt committed harlotry. Harlotry and adultery have two significances, both of which are found in this chapter: religious apostasy and political dependence on other nations rather than on God (23:1-4).[302]

Oholah (Samaria) committed harlotry with Assyria. In graphic terms God depicts the sin of Samaria in pursuing Assyria. Finally, God turned them over to the Assyrians who took them into captivity (23:5-10).

Her sister Oholibah should have known better, but she also pursued lovers: (Ahaz) went after the Assyrians (Isa. 7:14); then (Hezekiah) went after the Chaldeans (Isaiah 38-39); now (Zedekiah) is going after Egypt (23:11-21).

It remains that the same fate that befell Samaria must also befall Jerusalem. God will bring all Jerusalem's lovers against her: Babylonians, Chaldeans (viewed as a sub-group), Pekod, Shoa, and Koa (these three are usually considered peoples in southern Mesopotamia allied with Babylonia), Assyrians (conquered and now in Babylonia's army). These will come against Jerusalem and strip her bare. When God does this through her enemies, he will remove her harlotry which she has been practicing since Egypt. They will be made to drink the cup of Samaria (23:22-35).

The second aspect of harlotry is stressed in this paragraph. Jerusalem (Oholibah) has become involved in the religious practices of all these nations. He lists all the profane things they have done: idolatry, child sacrifice, defiled His sanctuary, and profaned the Sabbaths. He then turns back to the political alliances (40-44). However, she will be judged as a harlot and will be stoned to death by righteous men. Then they will know that He is Yahweh God (23:36-49).

---

[302]Greenberg, *Ezekiel, loc. cit.* says both chapters 16 and 23 are adapted from Jeremiah 3:8-11.

17. Yahweh gives a final prophecy of judgment against Jerusalem to Ezekiel on January 15, 588 B.C. (cf. 2 Kings 25:1) (24:1-27).

The siege against Jerusalem began on the tenth day of the tenth month of the ninth year of the captivity. God gave Ezekiel prescience of this event so that he could speak to the people of the *golah* with authority (24:1-3).

Through the parable of the stew-pot,[303] Ezekiel depicts the awful judgment about to fall on Jerusalem after a siege of just under two years. The judgment of God will result in cleansing of the filthy city. God has decreed it, and it will come to pass (24:4-14).

Yahweh illustrates the horrible suffering to come upon Judah through the drastic symbolism of Ezekiel losing his wife. When his beloved dies, he is not to show any signs of mourning. He dutifully went to the people of the *golah* and told them what would happen. That evening his wife died (24:15-19).

When they asked him about the significance of this awful event, he explained that he was a sign: what had happened to him would happen to the people of Judah and their temple (vv. 21, 25) (24:20-24).

Yahweh speaks to Ezekiel and tells him that He is going to remove Judah's stronghold (the temple), their joy, the desire of their eyes, etc.: family members who will be lost in the captivity of the city. When the siege ends, a messenger will come to Babylon with the news and Ezekiel will be released from his "dumbness," i.e., being able to speak only when God directed him to do so (24:25-27).

---

[303]This is a play on the pot motif in chap. 11. The Jews in Jerusalem thought they were in a good position to prosper, but Yahweh says the pot will actually boil *them*.

B. Prophecies against the nations (25:1—32:32).

The theology of the Book of Ezekiel is centered on the glory of God. He

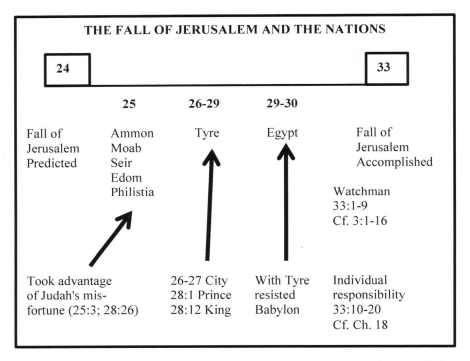

is willing to let His own name be blasphemed by the nations to bring justice on His covenant people. At the same time, the nations are under His control and cannot mistreat His people with impunity. These chapters are to show that the time of the nations has come. The narrative of the fall is interpreted in Chapter 24 to be resumed in Chapter 33.

1. Prophecies against the nations that have mocked Jerusalem (25:1-28:26).

   Ammon (25:1-7).

   In chapter 21, God told Ezekiel to draw crossroads and put up two road signs: To Jerusalem and To Ammon. Nebuchadnezzar then came to the crossroads and used divination to decide which way to go. The omens read "Jerusalem," and he went in that direction. The fact that Nebuchadnezzar came to Jerusalem caused consternation to Jerusalem but rejoicing to Ammon. Now in chapter 25, God tells Ammon that they will not escape.

The sons of the east who will come against Ammon are the Babylonians, but they may include other people whom Nebuchadnezzar hires to fight for him (cf. 2 Kings 24:2).

Moab and Seir (25:8-11).

The traditional enemies of Judah (Moab and Seir=Edom) were delighted to find that Jerusalem could fall to her enemies as any other people. They of course rejoiced in that fact. Therefore, God will treat their cities as Jerusalem has been treated. Again they will be given to the "sons of the east" for destruction. They will know that God is Yahweh.

Edom (25:12-14).

Edom has not only mocked Jerusalem, they have in some way become actively involved in persecuting the distressed Jews. This is more explicitly dealt with in Obadiah who is probably dealing with this same event (see my notes on Obadiah and the comparison with Jeremiah). God will take vengeance on Edom through Israel. (Edom was subjugated by the Jews under the Maccabees.)

Philistines (25:15-17).

The Philistines also suffered at the hands of Nebuchadnezzar, but they have, like the Edomites, taken an active hand in the suffering of the Jews. Therefore, God is going to destroy the Philistines (Cherethites is another, older name. See also Gen. 10:14).

Tyre (26:1—28:23).[304]

One must wonder why such an extensive amount of material is devoted to Tyre when she played a relatively insignificant role in the fall of Jerusalem. During David and Solomon's time, Hiram king of Tyre was a friend of Israel. Jezebel, Ahab's wife, was a Tyrian princess. Later, Tyre's interests were strictly mercantile and not in an empire. It seems to me that Tyre has become such a symbol of arrogance and independence that God uses her to represent the rebellion and hostility exhibited by the nations against Him. Zimmerli says: "In 587, however, apart from Jerusalem, only Egypt and Tyre were in a state of rebellion against Nebuchadnezzar. In the case of both of these, the rebellion continued for some years.[305] It thus follows inevitably that the prophetic message must be concerned in a quite special way with Yahweh's judgment on these two powers."[306]

The time given in 26:1 is the eleventh year, but the month is not given. Consequently, the date can only be approximated at 587/6. However, this is during the siege and probably not too long before the capitulation because Tyre is rejoicing that the gateway has been broken. She (Tyre) believes this will be a great opportunity for her to prosper at Judah's expense. However, God promises Tyre that she

---

[304]For the definitive work on Tyre to date see, S. Moscati, gen. ed., *The Phoenicians*. There is his discussion on temple prostitution to Astarte (Herodotus says that Babylonian and Cyprian women had to submit to this ritual once in their lives. The practice was not only for fertility, it also brought money into the temple treasury). Child sacrifice was probably only practiced in extreme cases. Molk is the process of this offering. Perhaps "passing through the fire" was only an initiation rite (pp. 117ff).

[305]Josephus (Antiquities, X., 11, 1 [Loeb, p. 285]) cites Philostratos (otherwise unknown) to the effect that "this king (Nebuchadnezzar) besieged Tyre for thirteen years at the time when Ithobalos was king of Tyre."

[306]W. A. Zimmerli, *Ezekiel,* 2:24.

will be defeated and will become a place for the spreading of nets and spoil for the nations. The daughters on the mainland refer to the towns and villages on the shore as opposed to the island Tyre. This first unit is stated in general terms: many nations (plural) will come against her (26:1-6).

The destruction becomes particularized as he describes one of the agents of destruction: Nebuchadnezzar, King of Babylon. He will slay people on the mainland and set a siege against the island fortress. Nebuchadnezzar will enter her gates and spoil her people. There will be desolation in Tyre as the harps are silenced and the Island fortress will return to its original status as a bare rock where fishermen will spread their nets (26:7-14).[307]

---

[307]Excursus on Nebuchadnezzar and Tyre:

Thompson, "The New Babylonian Empire," *CAH* 3:214) says: "Tyre, safe-guarded by the sea, appears always to have clung to her independence, both against Egyptian and Babylonian. Josephus says that a few years after the battle of Carchemish Tyre led a Phoenician revolt; according to Menander, Nebuchadrezzar besieged the city for thirteen years in the reign of Ithobalus (Ethbaal), and Ezekiel (ch. xxix) refers to the great difficulty of the operations: 'Nebuchadrezzar, king of Babylon, caused his army to serve a great service against Tyre: every head was made bald and every shoulder was peeled: yet he had no wages, nor his army, from Tyre, for the service that he had served against.' Presumably Nebuchadrezzar was compelled to recognize that he must 'contain' it only, which he could do with a small force."

Some 250 years later, Alexander the Great conquered Tyre. Tarn (*CAH* 6:374-75) says: "Leaving Marathus, he [Alexander] received the surrender of Byblus and a hearty welcome from Sidon. Envoys from Tyre met him and offered a general form of submission; as a test, he asked leave to enter the island city and sacrifice to his ancestor Heracles (Melkart). The Tyrians were really loyal; they were not yet satisfied that Alexander would ultimately be victorious, and they were satisfied that Tyre was impregnable, as after its thirteen years' siege by Nebuchadrezzar they had a right to think . . . . Alexander at once prepared for a siege . . . The city stood on an island half a mile from the coast, and Alexander set about building a mole to it from the mainland. Progress at first was easy; it was when the deep water near the island was reached and the workers came within shot of the walls that trouble began, while

How are we to reconcile the account of Ezekiel 26 attributing the disastrous fall to Nebuchadnezzar with Ezekiel 29:17-20 and the extra-biblical accounts that indicate Babylon's apparent inability to capture Tyre? Jerome says that the Tyrians carried off all wealth

---

winter gales and the Tyrian warships alike hindered the work. Alexander got two siege-towers out to the end of the mole, their sides protected against blazing arrows by coverings of skins; but the besieged prepared a fire-ship, fitting long yards to the masts with baskets of inflammable matter depending from the ends. They weighted down the stern to raise the bows above the mole, grounded her successfully, and set her on fire; the crew swam away, and the yards burnt through and discharged their cargoes on to the towers, which also took fire. The arrows from the Tyrian warships prevented any rescue, and the besieged, swarming out in boats, tore down the mole. Alexander began to build it again much broader, to avoid a similar mishap; but he saw that without a fleet he must fail, and went personally to Sidon to collect ships...

"The Tyrians however were ready for him. They had raised towers on the walls, whose fire worried the ships, and had made near approach to the island impossible by dropping rocks into the sea. Alexander brought up merchant ships to sweep for the obstacles; the Tyrian warships attacked them and cut their anchor-cables. He covered the sweepers with warships; Tyrian divers cut the cables under water. Then he anchored the sweepers by chains; the Tyrians had no reply, and he got the rocks out. As a last resource, the Tyrians manned 13 warships, attacked the Cyprian fleet when the crews had landed for dinner, and destroyed Pnytagoras' flagship and other vessels; but Alexander, who was watching, manned some Phoenician ships, rowed round Tyre, and cut off two of the returning squadrons. The way was now open for a great combined assault. Part of the wall fell, and Alexander brought up the two transports which carried the storming party and bridges; on one was Coenus' battalion of the phalanx, on the other himself with a battalion of the hypaspists; their operations were covered by fire from the fleet. Both ships got their bridges placed successfully, and Alexander and Coenus captured their sections of the wall, while the Phoenicians and Cyprians forced the two harbours. Then the Tyrians broke; the Macedonians, embittered by the Tyrians having murdered their comrades taken prisoners, could not be held in; and the rest was massacre. Eight thousand fighting men were killed, and, as at Thebes, many men, women and children sold as slaves. Some were saved by the other Phoenicians, and a few found asylum in the temple of Melkart...Tyre fell in July 332, after holding out for seven months. Its capture was possibly Alexander's greatest feat of arms; and he offered his sacrifice to Melkart after all, surely the most costly that deity had ever received. Tyre became a Macedonian fortress, and Sidon again took the lead in Phoenicia, which dated a new era from Issus."

when it became apparent the city would fall.[308] Thompson,[309] argues for a general interpretation of Scripture (Tyre will fall) and not a specific fulfillment. Lawhead[310] argues for a negotiated surrender.[311]

Some would argue that the destruction of Tyre refers to a mainland city with that name, while the failure to gain pay (Ezekiel 29) refers to the island fortress. An Egyptian reference,[312] from the thirteenth century B.C. indicates two cities: "Let me tell you of another strange city, named Byblos. What was it like? And its goddess? Once again—[thou] hast not trodden it. Pray instruct me about Beirut, about Sidon and Sarepta. Where is the stream of the Litani? What is Uzu [ed. note="old Tyre on the mainland"] like? They say another town is in the sea, named Tyre-the-port. Water is taken (to) it by the boats, and it is richer in fish than the sands."

More likely, however, the prophecy has both general and specific implications. Having begun in a generalized way: nations (1-6), he became particular with Babylon (7-11), but he became general again in v. 12. "They" (the nations) will despoil her. At this point we are

---

[308]Cited by Keil, *Ezekiel*, 1:421-22. Keil agrees and gives a cogent argument for the defeat of Tyre, but not its despoliation. The thirteen year siege is preserved in Josephus, *Ant.* x, 11, 1 and *Contra Apion* i, 21.

[309]D. L. Thompson, "A Problem of Unfulfilled Prophecy in Ezekiel," *WTJ* 16 (1981): 93-106.

[310]See A. S. Lawhead, "A Problem of Unfulfilled Prophecy in Ezekiel: A Response," *WTJ* 16 (1981): 15-19 and J. Bright, *History of Israel*, 333 (he says they were obliged to acknowledge Babylonian suzerainty). See also D. J. Wiseman, *Nebuchadrezzar and Babylon,* 27ff, who shows Babylonian control of Tyre.

[311]For an overall discussion, see John C. Beck, "The Fall of Tyre According to Ezekiel's Prophecy," Th.M. thesis, DTS.

[312]*ANET,* p. 477.

looking to the subsequent devastating calamity under Alexander the Great (26:12-14).

The fall of Tyre, seemingly impregnable, will strike fear into the hearts of other Mediterranean powers. They will sing the lament song about this unexpected fall. Tyre personified will go down to Sheol, terrified. The earlier part of the chapter speaks in historical terms of the defeat of Tyre. Only in the last unit (15-18; 19-21) is a lament taken up using the stereotypical phrases found also in Isaiah 14 (26:15-21).

A long and beautiful description is given of Tyre's greatness as a maritime power in chapter 27. Her ships, sail, awning, rowers, pilots, seam repairers and sailors are described as a vast force necessary for Tyre to carry on her trade. Tyre controlled the southern part of the Mediterranean all the way to the pillars of Hercules (27:1-9).

Tyre's army consisted of mercenaries from as far east as Persia and south to Lud and Put. This was an army to defend the island fortress as well as Phoenician trade in general (27:10-11).

The world-wide trade carried on by Tyre was astounding: Tarshish (Spain; known for silver mines), Javan (Greeks), Tubal and Meshech (Black Sea), Beth-Togarmah (north) and Dedan (southeast), Islands, Aram, Judah and Israel (bought food stuffs), Damascus, Vedan and Javan, Arabia, Shebah, etc. Tyre was truly an international conglomerate! (27:12-25).

This greatness, however, must come to an end. God will judge Tyre, and all her might will not prevent it. Nations will be amazed at her fall. (Note Revelation 17-18 for a similar description of "Babylon") (27:26-36).

The first ten verses of chapter 28 are a judgment oracle on the Prince of Tyre. He is called the prince or ruler (*nagid* נָגִיד). Clearly here

Ezekiel is speaking of a human being who has declared himself a god. S. Ribichini says "that the kings of Sidon, Byblos and Tyre were also high priests of Baalath, Astarte and Melqarth. In fact, for Phoenician kings at the time of the Persians, their religious role was more important than their royal title: in the Tabnith inscription the title 'priest of Astarte' comes before the attribute 'King of the Sidonians' in the description both of the king and of his father Eshmunazar."[313] The prince's wisdom has brought him great wealth, and the ensuing pride has caused him to refer to himself as a god. Therefore, God will judge him and bring him down to death (28:1-10).

Chapter 28:11-19 is one of the most difficult units in the Bible. It is cryptic, full of symbolism, and highly poetic. We must be careful not to divorce it from the context. The use of "King" instead of "Prince" may indicate two different referents or it may only be due to two different oracles from different periods. "Your trade" (28:16, 18) ties the unit to the others.[314]

Zimmerli cites some older critical scholars who see in the "King" some angel of Tyre, or gods of the nation.[315] Some evangelicals argue that the unit refers to Satan. Feinberg struggles with the issue and tries to maintain both historical referent (Tyre) and supra historical referent (Satan).[316] Keil does not even mention Satan in his discussion. "Created" means he became king; the garden of God refers to the ideal situation of Tyre, etc. The king is compared with

---

[313]S. Moscati, gen. ed., *The Phoenicians*, p. 116.

[314]Root רכל *rakal* (14 times, all Ezekiel: 26:12, 27:3, 13, 15, 17, 20, 22, 23, 24).

[315]W. Zimmerli, *Ezekiel* in Hermeneia, Philadelphia: Fortress Press, 1983, 2:90.

[316]C. Feinberg, *The Prophecy of Ezekiel*, Chicago: Moody Press, 1969.

Adam who was placed in ideal circumstances and yet rebelled against God. Alexander has moved toward this interpretation.[317]

There are problems in interpreting this unit as referring to Satan:

1. He is called the king of Tyre.
2. The garden of Eden language sounds like Adam.
3. The garden of Eden is parallel to the Mountain of God (cf. 31:7-9).
4. V. 13 sounds like Adam.
5. Trade (16) sounds like Tyre.
6. Beauty (12,17) parallels the same idea in 27:4 where it is Tyre.
7. Wisdom (12,17) parallels 28:4,5 of the Prince of Tyre.
8. He is cast to the ground and put before kings (17). When?
9. What are Satan's sanctuaries? (v. 18)
10. When/how was Satan turned to ashes? (v. 18).
11. You will be no more (19) sounds like Tyre in 26:21.

I am moving toward the opinion that we must begin with the historical referent of the king of Tyre (Ethbaal?). If this is the primary referent, then we must understand the language to be used metaphorically to refer to the position of excellence and glory held by the Tyrian king at God's disposal. He, like Adam, would have been in an ideal situation from which he fell because of rebellion and was judged. On the other hand, the highly symbolic language is surely telling us more than what happened to the king of Tyre; it may at least allude to the force behind the throne as in Isaiah 14.[318]

---

[317]See Ralph Alexander, "Ezekiel," *EBC,* p. 883, for a different discussion. "Eden" may refer to the large garden enclosure of ancient temples. So "Eden garden of God" may refer to the temple complex of Melkart, King of the City.

[318]See U. Cassuto, *A Commentary on the Book of Genesis,* I:75-82 for an important discussion. He believes there was a pre-Torah saga of a fall of a cherub and that Ezekiel refers to it as analogous to the King of Tyre's fall.

Sidon (28:20-23).

Sidon the elder sister of Tyre, was eclipsed by the island city. She also is promised judgment from God that will lead her to the conclusion that Yahweh is God.

Conclusion (28:24-26).

In this section we learn that the reason for the judgment on the nations was their attitude toward the Jews (28:26, cf. 25:3, 6, 8, 12, 15 and Matthew 25), and Tyre and Egypt possibly represent an arrogant rejection of Yahweh's purpose for Nebuchadnezzar. God will remove that cause of suffering by His judgment on these various nations. Furthermore, God promises to regather Israel from all the nations and bring them back to the land. Then they will live securely and they shall know that He is Yahweh their God. This is the promised kingdom.

2. Prophecies against Egypt the ancient nemesis of Israel (29:1—32:32).

The time is January 6, 587.

Jerusalem is under siege and only eight months away from collapse. She still hopes desperately for some assistance from Egypt. There is no other place to look except to Yahweh, and they are unwilling to listen to Him. This first oracle is given to discourage going to Egypt for help. (There are at least six oracles here and perhaps more. The dates, from the 597 exile, are: 10/12/10 [29:1], January 6, 587; 1/1/27 [29:17], April 26, 571; 1/7/11 [30:20], April 29, 587; 3/1/11 [31:1], June 21, 587; 12/1/12 [32:1], March 3, 585; 12/15/12 [32:17], March 17, 585. This makes three in 587, two in 585, and one in 571.)

Under the imagery of a crocodile languishing in the Nile, Egypt is promised judgment by Yahweh.

To Israel they have been "a staff made of reed" which will only break and pierce the hand.[319] The land of Egypt will become desolate, and then they shall know that Yahweh is God (29:1-9).

Egypt will be judged (29:10-16).

God promises such devastating judgment on Egypt that they will be laid waste for forty years. This devastation will extend from the Delta (Migdol) to the first cataract (Syene, Asswan). This is like saying "from Dan to Beersheba." The Egyptians will be scattered for forty years, but will be returned after that to form a lowly insignificant nation. As a result Israel will never again be tempted to put her trust in Egypt. (Note the history of Egypt from that time to this).[320]

---

[319]Cf. 2 Kings 18:21 where the same statement is made by Rab Shakeh to Hezekiah.

[320]Excursus on Babylon/Persia and Egypt

Ezekiel's prophecy seems to contradict what is known of Egyptian history during the Babylonian period. The usual point made is that Nebuchadnezzar did not invade Egypt, but Persia did. During the Babylonian period, it is said, Egypt prospered. For an excellent presentation of an alternate view, see J. B. Reilly, "The Historicity of Nebuchadnezzar's Invasion of Egypt." He argues three basic points:

1. Amasis (Egyptian ruler during Nebuchadnezzar's time) was confined to the western part of the delta with Greek mercenaries. Any discussion of prosperity for Egypt should be confined to that area.

2. Cambyses (the Persian ruler who invaded Egypt) did not destroy Egypt (The ancient writers say he did, but Olmstead argues cogently against them [*History of the Persian Empire*, pp. 89-93]. See also Smith, "The Foundation of the Assyrian Empire," *CAH* 3:17-25). The Elephantine papyri should read, "They [Babylon] *had* destroyed the temples of Egypt, but not the temple of Yaho" (this would require that the temple have been built by 567 B.C. or 42 years earlier).

The oracle coming from 571 (the latest in the book) is placed here to show the fulfillment of the first prediction against Pharaoh (29:17-21).

God will use Nebuchadnezzar, coming from Tyre with some frustration, to attack and defeat Egypt. God will "pay off" Nebuchadnezzar as his hired soldier with Egyptian spoil, since Tyre yielded so little. Thompson says: "The great campaign of Nebuchadrezzar's later years was directed against Egypt in retaliation for the trouble caused by Hophra. Doubtless the Palestinian wars had resulted in many small expeditions, (Jer. xlix, 28 would show, for instance, that Arab nomads of Kedar gave him trouble at one time), but it was Egypt which bore the brunt of his warfare. Hophra, the Egyptian king, who so basely left the cities of Palestine to their fate, brought nothing but evil to his own country and after his disastrous expedition against the Greeks in Cyrene, a revolution broke out at home, where the people were utterly weary of his incapacity. He sent his general Amasis to deal with the revolutionaries, but they merely elected him as king, and in the end Hophra was practically dethroned, Amasis being elected co-regent about 569 B.C. The small fragment of a Babylonian Chronicle first published by Pinches shows that Nebuchadrezzar launched an expedition against Egypt in his thirty-seventh year, *i.e.* about 567 B.C. . . . the very distance to which he penetrated is a matter of dispute. One tradition says he made Egypt a Babylonian province, another that he invaded Libya, while Jeremiah 'foretold' that he would set up his throne in Tahpanhes, but there is no proof that he did so." [321]

---

3. The period from 567 B.C. (Nebuchadnezzar's invasion) to 525 B.C. is the forty years of destruction spoken of by Ezekiel. After Persia's entrance, Egypt began to prosper.

[321] R. C. Thompson, "The New Babylonian Empire," *CAH* 3:215.

God promises that a horn will sprout for the house of Israel (29:21).

This prediction may be messianic, but it could also refer to the power (Nebuchadnezzar) that God will use against Egypt and in so doing, Ezekiel's message will be authenticated.

The word of the Lord indicates that the Day of the Lord is coming to pass on Egypt (30:1-26).

This phrase "Day of the Lord" often has eschatological implications, but in this context it refers to Nebuchadnezzar's invasion of Egypt. Egypt will be totally defeated, regardless of her help, and her people will go into captivity. Egypt's arms will be broken by the Yahweh-strengthened arms of Babylon (cf. also Jeremiah 37:5).

Two months after the oracle of chapter 30, God compares Egypt to Assyria (31:1-9).

The imagery is trees and forest. Assyria was a great tree; the birds of heaven nested in its boughs. No tree in God's garden could compare with it.

However, the tree became very proud and God delivered it into the hands of a "despot" (*'el goyim,* אֵיל גּוֹיִם), who will deal with it appropriately (31:10-18).

The tree will be felled and the birds will roost on its ruins. When the "tree" went down to Sheol, Yahweh caused a lamentation to be sung. Nations shook at the idea that it would go to Sheol. What makes you think, O Egypt, that you are any better? God's judgment will come upon you in the same way.

Almost two years later (March 3, 585) Ezekiel is given another lament for Egypt (Jerusalem fell the preceding August) (32:1-10).

This time Egypt is compared to a lion and a water monster. God promises to ensnare her with many people. Egypt will suffer horribly and nations will be astounded at her devastation.

A further oracle declares that the devastation is to be wrought by the King of Babylon (32:11-16).

The cattle will be destroyed, and the Nile will be made low. This poem of Egypt's destruction, reminds us of the ten plagues that came in the days of Moses. Then they will know that Yahweh is God. This is a lament, chanted over one who has fallen and died.

A final oracle is given on March 17, 585 (32:17-32).

Egypt as an outstanding enemy of Israel will be brought to a final end in Sheol. However, she is not alone. The Gentile powers, so hostile to God's purposes, and so arrogant against Him will also be there: Assyria, Elam, Meshech, Tubal, Edom, and Sidon. Pharaoh will be "comforted," that is he will not be alone in his misery. He will see that he is not the only one who once had great power who has now been reduced to Sheol. This vignette is similar to that of the King of Babylon in Isaiah 14.

D. Messages of warning and encouragement in light of the fall of the city (33:1—39:49).

The oracles against the nations (OAN) were placed between God's promised judgment and the fall of Jerusalem to show that God will deal with the nations who punished Judah and rebelled against Yahweh's agent, Nebuchadnezzar. He will bring about ultimate equity: judgment of the Gentiles and restoration of Judah. With that out of the way, God can then show the fall of the city to Babylon. The fall of Jerusalem is a turning point in the argument of the book. After admonishing those in Jerusalem who believe they can hold on without God and those in the *golah* who refuse to listen to Ezekiel, God denounces the false shepherds of Israel.

Then as in Jeremiah 23, he promises a great shepherd to come. Chapter 35 is a prophecy against Seir (Edom) because of their activity in connection with the fall of Jerusalem.[322] Ezekiel is now ready to turn his attention to the restoration of God's people.

1. God prepares them for the message of the fall (33:1-20).

The commission of Ezekiel (Chs. 1-3) included the fact that he was to be appointed a watchman to his people. This reiterated statement about the watchman is to impress upon the people the place and purpose of Ezekiel and to encourage the people to listen to what he has to say, particularly when they get the message of the collapse of Jerusalem.

The imagery of the watchman (33:1-6).

The same basic description as in chapter 3 is repeated here. The watchman has an unbelievably important task of protecting his people. In such a situation, the consequence of negligence is of a capital nature. The blood of the people will be required of him—that is, he will die. On the other hand, when the watchman does all that is expected of him, the responsibility for refusing to make a proper response rests with the people. So Ezekiel speaks as God's watchman. He has clearly warned the people; it is left only for them to repent or to harden their heart. The responsibility is theirs.

The issue of responsibility again (33:10-20).

God dealt with the issue of individual responsibility in almost identical terms in chapter 18 in response to the "sour grapes" parable. It is being repeated for the same reason as the watchman parable. The news of the fall of the city is about to come; the people will say in despair: "Surely our transgressions and our sins are upon

---

[322]Cf. Jeremiah 49:7-22 and Obadiah.

us, and we are rotting away in them: how then can we survive?" The answer is to repent. They cannot rely on any past righteousness they may have had, but even if they have been unrighteous, God will accept their repentance and forgive them. The Jews of that day felt that the righteous acts should balance out sin. They argue, therefore, that God is unfair. He responds that He is fair, but their way is not right. He will deal with each one according to his ways.

2. The message comes that Jerusalem has fallen (33:21-33). (January 8, 585 B.C.) THE NEXUS OF THE BOOK

    When the news comes about the fall of the city, Ezekiel is relieved of his "dumbness" and permitted to speak normally. This would mean that he was able to speak at will and not be limited to the times Yahweh spoke through him (33:21-22).

    Yahweh speaks against those left in the land (33:23-29).

    In spite of the fall of the city, the people still have the audacity to believe that they will retake the land. After all, they say, Abraham was only one and he possessed the land. Why cannot we who are many do the same? They are incurable optimists. In answer Yahweh tells Ezekiel to tell them that no matter where they go, they will be pursued by the relentless hand of God and killed. The land will be desolated and they will know that He is Yahweh.

    Yahweh speaks a word of encouragement to Ezekiel (33:30-33).

    The people of the *golah* were quite willing to listen to what Ezekiel had to say, but they were unwilling to pay any attention to him. He is like a beautiful song that people listen to and appreciate as music, but it has no lasting impact on their lives. However, when they see that all the things Ezekiel has prophesied have come to pass, they will know that a prophet has been in their midst. This latter promise was given to Ezekiel seven years before when Yahweh called him to the prophetic ministry (2:5).

3. Yahweh speaks to the shepherds and sheep (34:1-31).

Yahweh speaks against the hireling Shepherds (34:1-10).

Ezekiel is dependent upon Jeremiah in this discussion of the leadership of Israel. Jeremiah 21--23 denounces Jehoahaz, Jehoiakim, and Jehoiachin, the prophets, and the priests. Then the promise is given of the "Branch" who will shepherd the people properly. It is important to realize that Jeremiah's prophecies (this one given in 597 B.C.) have reached the *golah* in written form and are being utilized by Ezekiel. For both prophets, a reason for the fall is being given, followed by hope for the future.

The imagery of the sheep and shepherd pervades Scripture, e.g., Zechariah 11, John 10 as well as the passage in Jeremiah cited above. These bad shepherds (hirelings, Jesus calls them) have no personal interest in the sheep; they are only concerned with their own financial gain. Consequently, the sheep suffer and are scattered with no one seeking their welfare. Because of this terrible performance on the part of the leaders, God is going to call them to account for their behavior. These statements against the leadership encompass higher echelons from the King to the priests to the prophets.

Yahweh promises to tend the Flock (34:11-16).

Yahweh promises to take over the shepherding job Himself. He will seek the flock that has been scattered among all the nations and will restore them to the land of Israel in peace and security. He will look after them himself. What an idyllic picture He presents of that future time when Israel will be restored and cared for by a loving God.[323]

Yahweh promises to judge the flock properly and to put "David" over it (34:17—24).

God makes a distinction between the leaders (who are bad) and certain members of the flock (who are equally bad). This refers to Jews who, though they may not be in the higher echelons of leadership, take advantage of their fellow Jews (they muddy the water with their feet so that other sheep may not drink). The Jews who are being mistreated are referred to as "His flock." The imagery is continued in "fat sheep and lean sheep." God will judge between them so that equity is done. Furthermore, a shepherd by the name of David will be set over them: David who delivered his sheep from the bear and the lion, who delivered his people from the enemies around them, of whom Yahweh said, "You will shepherd my people Israel, and you will be a ruler over Israel" (2 Sam. 5:2). Who is this "David"? Rather than argue for the resurrection of the historical David, we should see David as a type of the coming Messiah who will sit upon the throne of David and rule over the house of Israel. I would take this to be a typological use of David as a prefigurement of the Messiah. Along with the rule of David will be God Himself in their midst.

Yahweh promises a covenant with his flock and peaceful and prosperous living (34:25-31).

Yahweh promises a situation in which there will be freedom from the prey of animals, showers in their seasons, fruitful fields, and freedom from other nations. God will plant them in a fertile place, and they

---

[323]Cf. John 10 for the imagery of the good shepherd who gives his life for the sheep.

will then know that Yahweh God is with them and that they are His people.

4. Yahweh speaks against Edom for taking advantage of Judah's defeat (35:1-15).

    This prophecy should be compared with Isaiah 34 and 63, Jeremiah 49:7-22, Obadiah, and Ezekiel 25:8-14. This oracle against Edom is included here as well as in the section on oracles against the nations to show a contrast between them and Judah when the latter will be restored.

    Yahweh predicts judgment against Seir in similar language to that of the previous oracles against her. She will be utterly devastated (35:1-9).

    The reason for the judgment is that they decided to take advantage of Judah's calamity. They were beginning to move into the southern part of Judah and to take over their land (the Edomites—Idumeans— were settled in the Negev in the time of Christ). By their reproach of Israel they were rebelling against God. Therefore, He promises to make their land desolate as they have rejoiced in the desolation of the land of Judah (35:10-15).

5. Yahweh promises a good future to Israel (36:1-38). GREAT APOLOGETIC CHAPTER

    Israel's pathetic situation in the eyes of the nations (36:1-15).

    The message of chapter 35 was against the Mountain of Seir because of their mockery of Judah and their usurpation of Judah's land. This message is to the Mountains of Israel to promise them restoration in God's future plan. Edom thought they had possessed Israel, but in the future the reverse would be true.

The enemy says, "The everlasting heights (*bamoth,* בָּמוֹת) have become our possession." God reminds Judah that it was for a "good cause" that they were judged. God found it necessary to judge His elect people because of their sin against Him. At the same time, those nations who have expropriated the possession of Israel will have to endure the fire of Yahweh's wrath (36:1-5).

Yet, God is not finished with His people. He will repay the nations for abusing His chosen people, and he will bring great blessing on the Mountains of Israel. These "mountains" will be fruitful (better than at the first), and will not "bereave God's people of children."[324] (36:6-15).

Israel's plight is because God judged and scattered her (36:16-21).

God judged Israel because she polluted the land. By their idolatry which included shedding the innocent blood of children, she made the land abominable. As a result God scattered her among the nations (Ezekiel is viewing the whole process from 722 B.C. to the present). They could not understand why as "the people of the Lord" they could be driven from the land (v. 20), but the answer Yahweh gives is that they profaned God's holy name (36:16-21).

God will restore Israel only for His own name's sake (36:22-32).

Yahweh's name has been profaned among the nations as they say that Israel, His chosen, is really no different from all the nations. Consequently, He will bring them from the nations and gather them from all the lands and bring them to their own land. He will purify them (sprinkle clean water: see Num. 19:17-19 for the sprinkling of the ash-water of the red heifer). They will be cleansed from their

---

[324]The mountains are being personified as a malevolent person who kills her own children, i.e., Israel.

filthiness and idolatry. There will also be conversion as He gives them a new heart and a new spirit (cf. again Jeremiah 31:31). God's Spirit will be within them and, they will walk in obedience to His Torah. They will live in the promised land and Yahweh will be their God and they will be His people.

God will rebuild the cities and restore Israel (36:33-38).

It is essential to note that in the restoration of the people of God the land is included. We cannot simply transfer this promise to the Church without doing a disservice to the simple language of Scripture. The land of Palestine must be rejuvenated as well as the people. The land will be fertile, the waste places will be restored and the people will be multiplied like a flock of sheep.

6. Yahweh promises restoration for Israel and Judah (37:1-27).

The vision of the valley of dry bones (37:1-14).

Yahweh brings Ezekiel by the Spirit to a valley (*habiqe'ah,* הַבִּקְעָה) that is full of bones. The bones were very dry (they had been there for a long time). He asks him whether the bones can live, and Ezekiel responds that he does not know. Ezekiel is to prophesy over the bones and tell them that they will have flesh, muscle and breath— they will live (37:1-6).

Ezekiel carried out his orders and prophesied over the bones. The four winds are commanded to come and fill the bones. They turn into live human beings and stand on their feet. They are a great army (37:7-10).

The vision is interpreted by Yahweh as referring to the *whole* house of Israel. It is in direct response to the lament of the people of Judah: "Our bones are dried up." Yahweh promises to open their graves and to bring them to the land of Israel. Then He will put His Spirit in them, and they will know that He is Yahweh. Some interpret this to mean that the Jews will come back to the land unregenerate and only later (decades or centuries?) will be saved. I suspect that Ezekiel saw only one action, and even though we are accustomed to seeing gaps in prophecy, this restoration should be seen as the great eschatological act of God in bringing Jews from all over the world to Israel and regenerating them. The "Aliyah" or return now going on is a prelude to this world-wide regathering, but it is not the same thing (37:11-14).

The message of the two sticks (37:15-28).

Ezekiel is told to take two sticks and write on them. One is for Judah and the Israelites belonging to her; the other is for Joseph (Ephraim) and all the Israelites belonging to him. He is then to join the two sticks in his hand. When the Jews in the exile ask him what all this means, he is to say: God is going to rejoin the two groups of Israel (37:15-20).

The message of this symbolism is one of the clearest and most emphatic in the Old Testament on the eschatological work of God in restoring the people of Israel. (1) All the Jews will be regathered from the nations. (2) There will be one nation instead of the two that resulted from the split in the days of Rehoboam. (3) There will be one king over them. (4) They will be purified from idolatry. (5) They will be God's people and He will be their God (37:21-23).

When they shall have been restored to the land, (1) they will have David to rule over them as shepherd, (2) they will keep the Torah of God, (3) they will live in the land with David as their prince, (4) God will make a covenant with them so that they can multiply, (5) His temple will be in their midst as well as His dwelling place. Then they will be His people and He will be their God and the nations will know that it is Yahweh who sanctifies Israel when the temple is in their midst (37:24-28).

7. The prophecy against the hordes of the north (38:1—39:29).

This is a very mysterious prophecy concerning an attack against the people of Israel in the last days when Yahweh shall have restored them to the land. There are seven "Thus says Yahweh" statements in the two chapters, and we will build the outline around them.

The presentation of the combatants (38:1-9).

The peoples involved in this scenario are Gog (of Magog), prince of Rosh, Meshech, and Tubal. The relationship of this list to Genesis 10 is obvious. These groups are descendants of Japheth and represent remote peoples of the earth. In the last days, God will bring these people against Israel and destroy them. They will be joined by Persia, Ethiopia, Put, Gomer, and Beth-Togarmah. They will come to the peaceful and restored Israel.

The plan of the combatants (38:10-13).

The greed of these people will lead them to attack what seems to be a peaceful, prosperous, and defenseless people. They will come from the remote parts of the north to attack Israel. God's purpose in this activity is to sanctify His name among the nations when they see His protection of Israel.

The battle of the combatants (38:14-16).

This prediction is similar to the one in the preceding paragraph. People will come from the remote parts of the earth to attack Israel. Their army will be so large it will seem like a cloud covering the earth. Then God will be sanctified through these people as He delivers Israel.

The frustration of the plan of the combatants (38:17-23).

When this coalition comes against Israel, God will attack it. They will see His fury and anger. God will bring a great earthquake in the land that will have devastating results. He will send a sword, the pestilence, rain, hailstones, fire, and brimstone against him. Thus God will magnify His name (as He did in delivering Israel from Egypt).

The complete defeat of the combatants (39:1-16).

There are four "declares Yahweh" statements in this unit. God will bring the nations up and defeat them on the mountains of Israel. He will send fire on Magog and others. He will make His name known in their midst. The weapons will be gathered over a period of seven years, and they will make fires of them. The dead from the battle will be buried. Israel will spend seven months burying them to cleanse the land. A burying crew will go looking for bodies until they shall have collected all the corpses.

The call for fowls to devour flesh—the glory of God in returning Israel (39:17-24).

The devastation of the armies of the north is illustrated by God calling for the fowls of the air to come and eat the flesh. The corpses are referred to as sacrifice. At that time God will be glorified because the nations will see His judgment and recognize that He punished Israel for their sin. He hid His face from them and sent them into exile. It was not because the other nations were greater—it was because of the holiness of God.

The complete restoration of Israel and filling with the Spirit (39:25-29).

The final "thus says Yahweh God" concerns the restoration of the whole house of Israel. Upon their restoration, they will forget their former disgrace and their sinfulness. God will bring them back from the peoples and will be sanctified through them. Then He will pour out his Spirit upon them. Israel has been judged by God through the nations who have in turn blasphemed God and His people. The Glory of God has moved from Israel. Chapters 38-39 show that God will be glorified in the restoration and protection of His people.[325]

---

[325]Excursus on Gog and Magog:

There are three other references to great cosmic battles involving Israel in the "latter times":

Zechariah 14 speaks of the nations gathered against Jerusalem and God's coming to fight against them. His feet will stand on the Mount of Olives, and the mountain will split north and south. Then the Kingdom will be ushered in.

Revelation 19 describes a great battle (usually linked with Rev. 16:16 as the battle in Har-Megiddo: Armageddon). A huge assembly is gathered against "Him who sat upon the horse" and led by the "beast." The King of Kings attacks them and destroys them after an angel has called for the fowls of heaven to come to the "great supper of God" to eat the flesh of kings, etc.

Revelation 20 tells of a great battle at the end of the one thousand years when Satan, released from the abyss, goes out to deceive the earth. Gog and Magog are included, and they will be gathered together for battle as a great multitude. They will surround the camp of the saints, but fire will come down and destroy them.

Zechariah 14 and Revelation 19 are usually linked as the same battle at the end of the tribulation and preparatory for the Millennium. Revelation 20 obviously takes place at the end of the Millennium when people born during the ideal time of God's great peace and blessing on earth will be deceived into rebelling against God.

The question is: where should Ezekiel 38 and 39 be placed? Because the Anti-Christ will make peace with Israel for one heptad (Dan. 9:24-27, he will break the covenant in the middle of the heptad) this seems to be the time of peace spoken of in Ezekiel 38. Therefore, most people will put this great battle in the middle of the tribulation. Similar terms are used of different events because Gog and Magog,

D. Worship in the Kingdom (40—48).

This section of Ezekiel is the most difficult in the book. It is somewhat different in terms of the type of material, but more importantly it projects into the eschatological future a revised worship system that includes a new temple, a revised priesthood, and the offering of sacrifices. It is clear in Ezekiel that he speaks of the restoration of Israel in the future in language that cannot be reinterpreted to apply to the church without doing it serious damage. If then in the future there will be a rebuilt temple and a reinstitution of priesthood and sacrifice, how is this to be related to the finished work of Christ so articulately defended in Hebrews 8? We will have to deal with this issue.

1. The new temple (40:1—42:20).

The time is 572 B.C. This is not the latest vision of Ezekiel (cf. 29:17), but it is late in his prophetic career. This is the only reference to the number of years after the destruction of the city and temple in 586 B.C. This vision occurs in the fourteenth year of that destruction. The vision is directly related to that devastating loss. The Solomonic temple was destroyed, but God is not finished with His people—the temple will be rebuilt, and God's people will worship in purity. God brings Ezekiel to the land of Israel (this is the second time—the first time he saw idolatry and the glory of the Lord left the temple). Here

---

though literal designations of geographical areas, also represent remote parts of the world.

Ezekiel 38-39 (Gog and Magog)	Rev. 19 Zech. 14	Rev. 20 (Gog and Magog)
Tribulation		Millennium

he sees a structure like a city and a man with a measuring line and a measuring rod in his hand. Further, he sees the glory return. God instructs Ezekiel to tell Israel all that he sees.[326]

2 Thessalonians 2 indicates that there will be a temple in the tribulation (as does Revelation 11). The rebuilding of the temple by God during the kingdom age simply indicates that God will use it as an external symbol of His presence, a theme he reiterates in the book of Ezekiel.[327] The Old Testament sacrifices were not efficacious in and of themselves ("the blood of bulls and goats can never take away sin"). When the people made their offerings by faith, God forgave them on the basis of Christ's finished work which was already completed in the mind of God. Since the Hebrew Christians in the Book of Hebrews were going back to the sacrificial system and turning their backs on the finished work of Christ, they were reprimanded for doing so. However, in the Millennium, they will apparently be able to offer sacrifices and still be fully aware that they are only symbolic in the same sense that the Lord's supper represents the finished work of Christ.[328]

We must be aware of the fact that the Church is not the only or final agency through which God works. The restoration of the Jewish people, so clearly taught in Ezekiel, demands a willingness to see

---

[326]The medieval Jewish scholar, Saadyah Gaon (882-942) says that Ezekiel speaks of the <u>third</u> temple (Driver and Neubauer, *The Fifty-third Chapter of Isaiah according to its Jewish Interpreters*, pp. 202-204).

[327]For a good general discussion of the issue of the temple and sacrifices during the Millennium, see Feinberg, *The Prophecy of Ezekiel*, 233-239. See also Whitcomb, "Christ's Atonement and Animal Sacrifices in Israel," *GTJ* 6 (1985): 2:212.

[328]Cf. Acts 21:17-26 where some Christians took a Nazirite vow (involving sacrifice) and it was apparently condoned by the Jerusalem elders as well as by Paul himself.

God working somewhat differently during the Millennium, even though some things are universal, e.g., the finished work of Christ as the basis of the new covenant.[329]

---

[329]Some Remarks on the Issue of Sacrifice in the Millennium.

1. The Old Testament speaks extensively of the temple in the Eschaton. This implies the presence of animal sacrifices during that time. Isaiah 60, a clearly eschatological passage, speaks of the "flocks of Kedar" going up with acceptance on his altar (v. 7); his "glorious house" (temple); and the place of his sanctuary (vv. 7, 13). These references are interleaved with mention of the walls of the city (vv. 10, 14, 18, 19). Jeremiah 33:11, 18 indicate that both offerings and Levitical priesthood will be present in the Eschaton. Cf. also Isaiah 2:2, 3, 5 (Parallel with Micah 4:1-3); Isaiah 66:20-21; Joel 3:18; Haggai 2:7, 9; Zech. 14:20-21.

2. The New Testament indicates that there will be a temple in the Tribulation (2 Thes. 2; Rev. 11).

3. The Jerusalem elders and Paul himself condoned animal sacrifice at the completion of a Nazirite vow (involving sacrifice) (Acts 21:17-26).

4. Not all sacrifice was propitiatory. It was used to purify the altar, and it was used to cleanse the sanctuary and thus to allow the Jewish believer to fellowship with God.

5. Most of the objection to the idea of reinstituted sacrifice comes from the concern that the old system is being reintroduced when it was condemned by Hebrews. All that Hebrews is saying is that the old system could not take away sin—only the sacrifice of Christ could do that. Hebrews does not, however, indicate that it would be impossible to have sacrifices under the conditions of the Millennium. There may be a more subtle reason for objection: the very idea of animals being sacrificed is so repugnant that people do not want to contemplate it.

6. Sacrifices in the Millennium will be there to give a visible ritual of sanctification and to remind the believers of the kind of sacrifice that brought their redemption. It is symbolical as a memorial and as an act of worship.

2. The glory of the Lord returns to the temple, and sacrifice is offered (43:1—46:24).

    Ezekiel began with a vision of the glory of the Lord. The mysterious vision of the four living creatures was designed to demonstrate the sovereignty and greatness of God. The cherubim's task was to be a dwelling and a transporter for God's glory. The cherubim removed the glory of God from the polluted sanctuary in chapter 10; they will restore it in the new temple (43:1-5). A key verse is 43:7: "And He said to me, 'Son of man, this is the place of My throne and the place of the soles of My feet, where I will dwell among the sons of Israel forever. And the house of Israel will not again defile my holy name, neither they nor their kings, by their harlotry and by the corpses of their kings when they die." The theme of the book is vindicated: God is the sovereign of the universe, and His glory He will not give to another. He has chosen Israel as His people among whom He wants to dwell. Their sin has prevented a holy God from dwelling in their midst, but His restoration of His people in a converted state makes that dwelling possible. Consequently, the glory of God can return to the sanctuary, and the message of Ezekiel is completed.

    There will be a prince appointed over the people. This is not the Messiah, for he must offer sacrifice for himself (45:22). The Zadokites (a priestly family ministering in the time of David) will have a special place of responsibility in the worship.

3. The River of flowing water and the division of the land (47:1-35).

    There will be a geographical reconfiguration as the fresh water river flows from under the temple to the Arabah where it freshens the Salt Sea and produces all kinds of fruitfulness.

    The land will be divided in equal proportions to the tribes of Israel for occupation during the kingdom (48:1-35). The settlement in the land under Joshua and this settlement look like this:

Naphtali	Dan
Asher	Asher
Zebulun	Naphtali
Issachar	Manasseh
Manasseh	Ephraim
Ephraim	Reuben
Benjamin	Judah
Dan	Restricted area
Judah	Restricted area
Simeon	Restricted area
Benjamin	
Manasseh	Simeon
Gad	Issachar
Reuben	Zebulun
	Gad

The book of Ezekiel closes appropriately with the name of the city:

THE LORD IS THERE.

Notes on the Book of Daniel

I. The Prophet Daniel

Daniel went into exile as a young man in 605 B.C. when Nebu-chadnezzar forced Jehoiakim to submit to the new Babylonian kingdom. Daniel's ministry continued into the third year of Cyrus (10:1) (about 536 B.C.). Daniel therefore ministered for a period of about sixty-nine years. If he were about sixteen at the time of captivity, he would have been eighty-five when he made his last prophecy.

When one considers the religious climate during which Daniel grew up, his strong spiritual character stands out even more. The Josiah's, Daniel's and Ezekiel's may have been rare, but they did exist and bear testimony to the fact that God always had a faithful remnant that did "not bow the knee to Baal."

II. The Apocalyptic genre

Daniel is considered by critical scholars to be a second century work,[330] responding to the critical and traumatic situation of the Syrian persecution of the Jews. Consequently, they place Daniel in the same category as the Book of Enoch and other such materials where the author is anonymous but assumes a name of an ancient, well-known person.[331]

---

[330]The Book of Daniel as found at Qumran and dated, paleographically, at 100 B.C. This would place the text within 65 years of the autograph, a thing unheard of in textual history.

[331]See John J. Collins, *Daniel, with an Introduction to Apocalyptic Literature.*

Ford lists four chief characteristics of apocalyptic literature: pseudo-nymity, rewritten history, determinism, and ethical passivity. However Daniel is not pseudonymous, the New Testament regards it as prophecy (Matt 24:15), other prophecies seem deterministic but were even so conditioned on repentance (Jer. 18:7-10; Jonah), Daniel has strong ethical emphasis (4:27; 5:20-23; 6:4; 9:1-20; 11:32-35; 12:10).[332] The problem with the authorship issue is that there is no venerable person prior to the fifth century with the name Daniel. Efforts to link this Daniel with the Danel of the Ugaritic texts have not proven successful. The form the book of Daniel assumes has indeed many of the characteristics used to denote apocalyptic literature (as does its New Testament counterpart, Revelation), but this book set the pace emulated by the later writers.

III. The Historical Context

Daniel more than any other prophet demands a knowledge of the historical background of the people and culture of which he speaks. Not only does he make the normal historical allusions to people and events, he predicts details about a coming period, so vivid and verifiable, that critics refuse to accept the possibility they are prophetic. Daniel prophesied during the dominion of two different empires: Babylon and Persia. He prophesied *about* the Greeks, Romans, and coming eschatological events.

The Neo-Babylonian Empire (625 B.C.--539 B.C.)

The Neo-Babylonian Empire began with Nebuchadnezzar's father, Nabopo-lassar. He was a Chaldean who managed to take over Babylon and to harass the Assyrians. The date of the beginning of his rule is 625 B.C.

Nebuchadnezzar was the greatest of the Babylonian kings. He was com-mander of the army attacking Egypt in Syria when his father died. He

---

[332]Desmond Ford, *Daniel*, p. 61. For further discussion on this issue, see J. Baldwin, *Daniel*, pp. 46-59.

became king in 605 B.C. and ruled until 562 B.C. He was noted for his great building projects in Babylon and figures largely in the book of Daniel.

Evil-Merodach (Amelu-Marduk), Nebuchadnezzar's son, ruled only a short time (562-560 B.C.). He is noted in Scripture as the one who elevated Jehoiachin and gave him provisions.[333]

Nergal-Sharezer (Neriglissar) is the son-in-law of Nebuchadnezzar. He assassinated Evil-Merodach and ruled from 560 B.C. to 556 B.C.

Labashi-Marduk, his son, was murdered after ruling only his accession year.

Nabonidus, not from the royal family and perhaps from north Syria, ruled from 556 B.C. to the Persian conquest in 539 B.C. For some reason Nabonidus retired to Teima and made his son Belshazzar (Bel-shar-usur) regent. This may have resulted from his support of the moon goddess at Haran (where he rebuilt the temple and his mother may have served as priestess). He returned after nine years to view the overthrow of Babylon.[334]

The Persian Empire ([550] 539—330 B.C.)

Cyrus ruled after the capture of Babylon until 530 B.C. Gobryus ruled as governor of Babylon (is this Darius the Mede?).[335] Wiseman/Kitchen argue that Darius the Mede is really Cyrus who was half Mede).[336]

---

[333]See J. B. Graybill, "Evil-Merodach," in ZPBD, 264, where Graybill says the tablets in *ANET* come from Nebuchadnezzar's time and hence Amelu-Marduk merely increased the allowance.

[334]See R. C. Thompson, "The New Babylonian Empire," *CAH* 3:212-225.

[335]See John Whitcomb, *Darius the Mede* for a defense. See Wiseman/Kitchen, *Notes on Some Problems in the Book of Daniel.*

[336]Greek authors say that Cyrus was 40 in 560 B.C. when he became King of the Persians. This would make him 61/62 in 539 B.C., but Cook, *History of the Persian Empire,* p. 256, believes he was younger.

Cambyses (530-522 B.C.)
Darius I the Great (522-486 B.C.)
Xerxes I (486-465 B.C.)
Artaxerxes I (465-424 B.C.)
Undistinguished rule for the next century.

Hellenistic Empires (330—64 B.C.)

Alexander the Great conquers the east (334-323 B.C.)

The Ptolemies rule Egypt and the Seleucids rule Syria until the Romans interfere in 64 B.C.

IV. Problems in Daniel

Daniel has been the center of much debate and discussion. Critical scholars assume that the "Daniel Cycles" are fairly early, but since chapters 8 and 11 refer to the Greeks and the latter refers to the Maccabean period, they argue that it is prophecy "*ex eventu*" that is, it was written during or after the events and presented as prophecy. The third year of Jehoiakim is taken by most critics to be inaccurate in spite of D. J. Wiseman's defense in *The Babylonian Chronicle*. The rule of Belshazzar has long been debated. We now have Babylonian records using his name. He was the *de facto* if not the *de jure* king when Babylon fell to the Persians.[337]

V. The Language of the Book

Daniel is notable in that it has more Aramaic than any other book of the Bible (Ezra being the only other book with a substantial amount). The Aramaic section begins at 2:4 and continues through chapter 7. Many

---

[337]See R. D. Wilson, *Studies in Daniel* and D. J. Wiseman, *et al., Notes on Some Problems in the Book of Daniel* for an excellent discussion of all these issues.

Chronological Chart for the Prophets

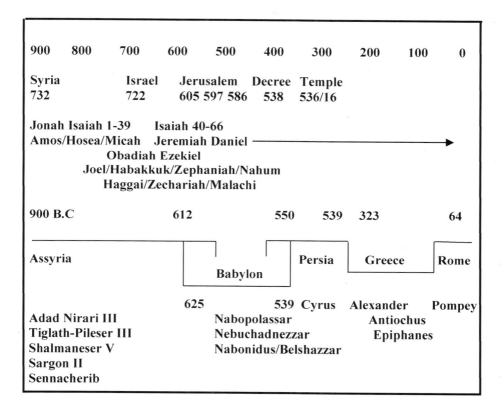

reasons are conjectured for this, but the most plausible is that the subject content is primarily devoted to the Gentile powers, and, therefore, the trade language of the world was used. Aramaic had been used since the Assyrian period (cf. Isaiah 36:11-12). It was also used by the Persians who succeeded the Babylonians.

VI. The Structure of Daniel

The retention of Daniel 7 in Aramaic serves as an interlocking device between the two halves of the book. Chapter 7 belongs with the visions by genre, subject matter, and dating (since it begins a new sequence of

Babylon-Media-Persia). It is linked to the tales by language and by the obvious parallelism with the four-kingdom prophecy of Chapter 2. As Lenglet has noted,[338] Chapters 2-7 form a chiastic structure in which 2 and 7 are related by the four-kingdom schema, 3 and 6 are tales of deliverance, and 4 and 5 offer critiques of the kings. This formation does not disprove that the Aramaic chapters originally formed an independent book, but it does testify to careful editorial arrangement.

2-7 Kingdoms
3-6 Deliverance (furnace/den)
4-5 Judgment on two kings

VII. Outline of the Book

The book is usually divided 1-6 and 7-12, but we will follow the pattern of (1) Introduction—1 (2) Emphasis on the Gentiles (Aramaic)—2-7 and (3) Emphasis on the Jews as related to the Gentiles (Hebrew)—8-12.

A. Introduction, Daniel in Babylon (1:1-21).

1. Historical introduction (1:1-2)[339]

Suffice it to say here that Jehoiakim submitted to Nebuchadnezzar, and temple vessels were carried to Babylon and placed in the pagan

---

[338]A. Lenglet, "La Structure Littéraire de Daniel 2-7," *Bib,* 53, 1972, pp. 169-190.

[339]See Wilson, *Studies in the Book of Daniel* for a detailed discussion of the historical issues raised in these two verses. Also D. J. Wiseman, *Nebuchadrezzar and Babylon,* p. 18, on Hatti Land.

temple (2 Kings 24:1). Hostages were also taken, and Daniel was among them (Jehoiakim himself may have been taken to Babylon to participate in the victory parade, cf. 2 Chron. 36:6).

2.   Choice young men are selected to be in the king's service (1:3-7).

These young men were to be trained in the literature and language of the Chaldeans. They were to be cared for and trained for three years. After that time they were to enter the king's service. Their names were changed to Babylonian ones.

3.   Daniel chooses to follow the Lord regardless of the consequences (1:8-16).

Daniel chose to follow the Levitical dietary laws as an outward symbol of obedience to God. God granted him favor with the overseer who allowed him to test the different food. At the end of the ten day trial, it was shown to have worked, and Daniel and his friends were allowed to continue the regimen.

4.   God honors Daniel's obedience and blesses him and the three friends as they enter the king's service (1:17-21).

B.   Emphasis is placed on the Gentiles (the language is Aramaic) (2:1—7:28).

1.   Nebuchadnezzar dreams of a great image which Daniel interprets in terms of coming kingdoms (2:1-49).

Nebuchadnezzar dreams (2:1).

The setting is the second year of Nebuchadnezzar. In view of the fact that Daniel's training was to last three years, we need to ask how Daniel could stand before the king in the second year of his training. A similar chronological situation exists to that in 1:1. The Babylonian system does not count the accession year as the first year, hence, the second year is actually the third. The idea of dreams as a revelation from God is rather common.[340] The king, having had the dream, calls for the various groups who "divine the seasons" to come to him.

The wise men cannot tell the dream (2:2-13).

The various groups begin to speak to the king (in Aramaic) and ask him to tell them the dream. There were obvious methods of interpreting dreams. The problem is that the king will not tell them the dream, but demands that they give him both the dream and its interpretation. When they declare their incompetency to do such a thing, he demands their heads and those of all in the king's service as wise men. This included Daniel and his friends.

God reveals the dream to Daniel (2:14-24).

Daniel requests from Arioch the king's executioner a reprieve long enough to ask God for the interpretation of the dream. This is granted, Daniel and his friends pray to God for the interpretation, they get it, and Daniel gives thanks to God. He then goes to Arioch and requests an audience with the king.

Daniel reveals the source of his interpretation (2:25-30).

Daniel makes sure that Nebuchadnezzar understands the source of the revelation about the mystery. It is not Daniel's wisdom that produced it, but God has revealed Himself to Nebuchadnezzar and the interpretation to Daniel. God, says Daniel, has revealed things to take place in the future (2:25-30).

---

[340]Cf. Jeremiah 29 as well as the Joseph accounts in Genesis.

Daniel reveals the dream (2:31-35).

The dream consists of two parts: the image and the stone. The image has six components: Head (gold), chest and arms (silver), stomach and thighs (bronze), legs (iron), feet (part clay, part iron). A stone appeared cut out of a mountain but not by human hands, and it struck the statue on its feet and crushed them. The entire image was crushed and became like chaff. However, the stone became a great mountain and filled the earth.

Daniel reveals the meaning of the dream (2:36-45).

First, the head of gold represents Nebuchadnezzar's kingdom. This kingdom is presented as the best of all, not because of size, but because of its position as the first of the Gentile dominions to carry off Israel and bring her under their complete control. Second, the silver chest and arms represent Persia (passed by quite quickly). Third, the bronze stomach and thighs represent Greece. Fourth, the iron legs represent Rome and the feet and toes represent some aspect of the Roman Empire. The critics want the four kingdoms to be: Babylon, Media, Persia and Greece, because they believe the farthest point in the "prophecy" is the Maccabean period.[341] However, Daniel does not view Media as a separate kingdom (Media was co-terminus with Babylon and did not succeed it as the dream requires. Cf. also 5:29-31: Medes and Persians). In 8:3 Daniel sees a Ram with two horns. The Ram represents the Medo-Persian kingdom in two aspects. There are two horns, but the second one (Persia) came up last and was taller. Consequently, the iron legs must represent the Roman Empire.

The most striking aspect of the interpretation of the dream is the stone from the mountain. Daniel is referring to the messianic kingdom to be set up by the God of heaven. God's purposes will

---

[341]See, e.g., Hartman and Di Lella, *Daniel,* AB.

triumph over all of Satan's activities and his kingdom will endure forever.

Daniel is rewarded (2:46-49).

Nebuchadnezzar acknowledges that Daniel's God is supreme. He promotes Daniel and rewards him monetarily. Daniel remembers his friends and asks that they be assigned to responsibilities as well.

2. Daniel's three friends are forced to stand for their faith at the risk of death (3:1-30).

Nebuchadnezzar sets up a great image (3:1-7).

Apparently the dream of chapter 2 inspired the king to set up an image similar to the one he had dreamed about. Daniel is not mentioned in this story for some reason. He must have been away or indisposed in such a way that he was not involved. The king calls all his important officials and demands that everyone worship his new idol.

Jealous Chaldeans charge the Jews with impiety (3:8-12).

They established first the king's rule that anyone who does not fall down to worship will be thrown in a furnace of fire. They then charged the three Jews with refusal to do so. (Jeremiah 29 gave an example of this horrible kind of death by saying that Koliah would be roasted in fire by Nebuchadnezzar.)

The three young men testify of their faith in God (3:13-18).

Nebuchadnezzar demanded a response from the men. They testified of a God who was able to deliver them. However, even if He should choose not to deliver them, the king must understand that they still trust Him and will not worship the image.

The men are punished (3:19-23).

The king became furious, had the furnace heated even more and threw the three men into it. The fire was so hot that it killed the men who threw the Jews in.

God vindicates His servants (3:24-30).

The king was amazed that he was able to see four men walking about. The fourth looked like a son of the gods. (Plural is probably better here than singular. There is no way Nebuchadnezzar would have had any inkling of the coming "son of God.") The men were released unharmed, and Nebuchadnezzar responded with a word of praise to the God of these men. Any future accusers were promised the worst sort of reprisal, and the men prospered in the province of Babylon.

3.   Daniel interprets another of Nebuchadnezzar's dreams (4:1-37).

Nebuchadnezzar's testimony (4:1-3).

In a very unusual move, Nebuchadnezzar sent a letter to his entire kingdom proclaiming the praise of the Most High God for his greatness and goodness. The letter was an explanation of the most significant and unusual period in his life.

Nebuchadnezzar tells of his dream (4:4-18).

As in chapter 2, the magicians and wise men were unable to interpret the dream, but Daniel was able. The king told him the dream. The first part is positive: a large tree is in the midst of the earth. It provides food and shelter to all the beasts and birds. The second part of the dream is negative: a "watcher," a holy one comes down from heaven (as in Revelation) and shouts a command. The tree is to be cut down, but a stump is to be left with a band of iron and bronze around it. Now the tree stump is personified: let him be drenched with the dew of heaven. He will have a disease called *theriomania*, meaning "to act like beasts." Then seven times (*shiv^e 'ah 'idanin* שִׁבְעָה עִדָּנִין) passed over him. This is probably seven years although it could be less. The purpose of this dream was to teach Nebuchadnezzar that the God of Heaven is in charge of the universe and to humble Nebuchadnezzar.

The interpretation of the dream (4:19-27).

Daniel told Nebuchadnezzar that the dream pertained to his enemies (or as in NASB: "would that it applied to your enemies"). Nebuchadnezzar was the tree; the chopping down of the tree referred to Nebuchadnezzar being driven from mankind until seven "times" passed over him. The stump indicated that the kingdom will endure and be restored to Nebuchadnezzar, but all of this was to force Nebuchadnezzar to acknowledge the lordship of the Most High God. Daniel concluded boldly urging the King to repent of his sins.

The fulfillment of the dream (4:28-33).

Everything happened as predicted. The judgment came as the king was gloating over the greatness of his kingdom for which he was taking all the glory. He acted like an animal and had long hair and finger and toe nails.

Nebuchadnezzar's restoration (4:34-37).

After the seven "times" passed over him, Nebuchadnezzar's sanity returned, and his counselors again sought him out and restored him to the throne. As a result Nebuchadnezzar acknowledged the lordship of the Most High God and humbly pro-claimed that He was to receive honor and glory.

Excursus:

Is there anything in the extra-biblical record to support the biblical statements on Nebuchadnezzar's madness? Thompson says: "The name of Nebuchadrezzar became the centre of much romance, notably the story of his madness in the book of Daniel. 'His own inscriptions speak only of a four-year-long suspension of interest in public affairs, which may not be a reference to his malady, though tradition of something of the kind may have lent verisimilitude to the account of it in Daniel' (C. H. W. Johns, *E.Bi.*, col. 3371). His religious character is illustrated above; like Ashurbanipal he may have suffered some mysterious affliction (p. 127), and this might have been ascribed to a divine visitation (cf. also p. 425 and note)."[342]

Wiseman[343] gives a broken text that may indicate mental problems. "Nebuchadrezzar pondered . . . his life was of no value to him . . . he was angry (or stood) and a favourable path (he took . . . and) Babylonia (. . . .). To Amel-Marduk he speaks what was not . . . he then gives a different order but . . . he does not heed the mention of his name (or pronouncement), a courtier . . . . Concerning the fortunes of Esagil and Babylon and . . . the cult-centres of the great gods they considered....He does not have in mind (any concern) for son or daughter, for him there is no family and clan does not exist....In his heart for everything that was abunda(nt. .) His attention was not set to promoting the welfare of Esagil (and Babylon). With ears pricked up (eagerly?) he went in through the Holy Gate...he prays to the lord of lords, his hand raised (in supplication). He weeps bitterly to his god, the great gods.... His prayers go forth to...." Wiseman interprets this entire text as referring to Nebuchadnezzar. Others apply the latter part to Nebuchadnezzar's son, Amel-Marduk.

---

[342]R. C. Thompson, "Assyria," *CAH*, 3:217.

[343]Wiseman, *Nebuchadrezzar and Babylon,* p. 102.

Because of Nabonidus' long stint in Teima, the hostility of the Babylonian priesthood to him[344] and a fragment from Qumran attributing a sickness of seven years to Nabonidus through which he was instructed by a Jewish soothsayer, some want the Nebuchadnezzar story to be transferred to Nabonidus. However, there is no reason why the problem could not have happened to Nebuchadnezzar, and one surely would not expect to find a record of it in the accounts. If Nebuchadnezzar "withdrew from public life for four years," a seven year hiatus should not be considered improbable.

Excursus two:

Was Nebuchadnezzar a believer in the sense of an Old Testament saint? Certainly, he acknowledges the existence, position and power of the Most High God. However, the acknowledgement of the person of God in chapter two does not prevent him from trying to kill the three Jewish men for worshipping the same God in chapter three. Furthermore, in chapter four the same lesson has to be learned again. It seems unlikely to me that he was ever more than a polytheist.

4.   Daniel is involved in the last days of the Babylonian empire which falls under the *de facto* king Belshazzar (5:1-30).

Belshazzar's feast (5:1-4).

The last days of Babylon were characterized by internal weakness. The real king, Nabonidus, was gone and his son was ruling as regent. The people were disaffected and the priesthood was hostile. In spite of all this tenuousness, Belshazzar threw a sumptuous feast and arrogantly drank from the holy vessels of the temple of Jerusalem.

The handwriting (5:5-9).

[344]See *ANET*, pp. 312-314.

A man's fingers came out and began to write on the wall. The king was completely disconcerted and called for the wise men, etc. As on two previous occasions they were unable to read (interpret) the writing on the wall.

Daniel is again brought in (5:10-16).

Daniel would now be in his early eighties. The queen mother remembered Daniel and suggested that he be brought in. (Nebuchadnezzar [5:11] was not Belshazzar's father in actuality. It is a convention to say that Nebuchadnezzar was a predecessor of Belshazzar, though he may have been a grandson through the marriage of his father to a daughter of Nebuchadnezzar.)[345] Belshazzar brings Daniel in and offers him great bribes to interpret the handwriting.

Daniel interprets the dream (5:17-28).

Daniel gave a daring preamble to his interpretation. He reminded Belshazzar of the way God dealt with Nebuchadnezzar. He told Belshazzar that he had not repented but conversely was drinking out of the holy vessels of the temple of the Most High God. Therefore, the hand was sent with the inscription. One knows that the interpretation is going to be very negative before it is even given. The writing consists of four words: *m^{e}ne, m^{e}ne, t^{e}kel, upharsin.* These are Aramaic words: מְנֵא מְנֵא תְּקֵל וּפַרְסִין *Mene* means that God has numbered the kingdom and put an end to it. *Tekel* (Hebrew: *shekel*) means weighed (and found deficient). *Peres* your kingdom has been divided (taken away) and given to the Medes and Persians. The latter word may also be a pun on "Persia." Daniel was appropriately awarded and given the position of *third* ruler in the kingdom since Belshazzar held the *second* position under Nabonidus.

---

[345]See Wiseman, *Nebuchadrezzar and Babylon.*

The fall of Babylon (5:29-30).

We know from extra-biblical material that Babylon fell easily to the Persians probably because of internal rot and dissension. Cyrus was able to win the Babylonians quickly with a benevolent policy toward them and their religion—a policy extended to all people including the Jews. Nabonidus was captured in Babylon and perhaps exiled. Belshazzar, we know from the biblical account, was killed that night. Then the mysterious Darius the Mede took over the province of Babylon.[346]

5. Daniel is exonerated by his God among the Persians (6:1-28).

The Persians appoint Daniel to a high position and jealousy develops among his peers (6:1-9).

It would not be unusual for an incoming power to take advantage of the expertise of a man who had ruled this province before. Consequently, Daniel was one of three supervisors of Babylon under the king.[347] His detractors decided the only way they could get at him was through his religion. As a result, they enticed the king to make a decree that no one might petition any god or man but the king for thirty days. The penalty was to be thrown to the lions and the decree was irrevocable.[348]

---

[346]Cook, *Persian Empire,* p. 25 says Greek writers made Cyrus 40 in 560, so 61/62 in 539.

[347]On Satraps, see Wilson, *Studies in the Book of Daniel,* 175ff. He assumes a local government of 120 rulers.

[348]Diodorus Siculus, *Loeb,* Vol. VIII. 4 At this, Charidemus became angry and made free with slurs on Persian lack of manliness. This offended the king, and as his wrath blinded him to his advantage, he seized Charidemus by the girdle according to the custom of the Persians, turned him over to the attendants, and ordered him put to death. 5 So Charidemus was led away, but as he went to his death, he shouted that

Daniel ignores the decree and prays three times a day as was his custom (6:10-15).

Daniel at his age had already passed the point of worrying about what kings could do to him. He carried on consistently his worship of the Lord as he had been doing since a child. The detractors then pressed for his arrest and reminded a hesitant king that his law was irrevocable.

Daniel's deliverance (6:16-24).

The king's appreciation for Daniel and his words to him are both remarkable. He had apparently been greatly impressed in the past with Daniel's faith, and now encouraged Daniel with the words that his God would deliver him. God protected Daniel from the Lions, and the king, having spent a sleepless night came to the den and rejoiced to find him alive. Daniel gave his testimony to the king. The detractors were thrown into the den with their families.

Darius' testimony to the world (6:25-28).

Like Nebuchadnezzar (4:1-3), Darius sent letters throughout the kingdom to give praise to the living God. Daniel continued to prosper under Darius/Cyrus.

---

the king would soon change his mind and would receive a prompt requital for this unjust punishment, becoming the witness of the overthrow of the kingdom.

Charidemus's prospects had been high, but he missed their fulfilment because of his ill-timed frankness and he ended his life in this fashion. 6 Once the king's passion had cooled he promptly regretted his act and reproached himself for having made a serious mistake, but all his royal power was not able to undo what was done. (For this reference, thanks to Montgomery, *Daniel*, ICC, p. 270.)

6. A vision of beasts (kingdoms), parallel to chapter 2, is given (7:1-28).

Most commentators will conclude that chapters 2 and 7 are parallel.[349] Chapter seven is given in vision form to Daniel whereas chapter two is a dream of Nebuchadnezzar. It is placed here rather than earlier, because it is a part of the visions Daniel saw in his later years. I am keeping it under the second main division of the book (because of its language—Aramaic) though it belongs (stylistically) in the third because the language is still Aramaic. (Chapters 1-6: narratives = God's sovereignty; Chapters 7-12: visions = God's work in the future.)

The contents of the vision. Daniel gives a "summary" of the vision. It is given in apocalyptic terms: fantastic animals and activity, to depict real events (7:1-14).

The four winds and the great sea. Rev. 7:1-3 depicts these same four winds in judgmental terms—that is they represent God's judgment on the earth. Here they symbolize God's control of the world as the four winds were "stirring up the great sea." The great sea in the Bible usually refers to the Mediterranean Sea. Out of the sea Daniel sees four beasts coming (חֵיוָן *ḥeyvan*; Heb.: חַיּוֹת *ḥayyoth*). Each beast is different from the other (7:2-3).

The lion had wings like an eagle, but they were pulled out and the lion was stood up (like a man) and a human mind was given to it. (Cf. Jer. 49:19-22, Lion/Eagle, and Daniel 4 where his "wings were clipped".) (7:4).

The bear had three ribs in its mouth and rose up on one side. It was told to devour much meat (7:5).

---

[349]See, e.g., Archer, "Daniel," *EBC* and Hartman and Di Lella, *Daniel,* AB.

The leopard had four wings on its back and four heads. Dominion was given to it (7:6).

The dreadful beast. This is the most important of the beasts and the one that will occupy the center of the stage in this chapter. It is not likened to any particular animal, but is said to be dreadful, terrifying and strong. It has large iron teeth. It completely dominates and it has ten horns (7:7-8).

Out of the ten horns came a little horn. This little horn pulled out three of the ten. He had eyes and a mouth that bragged (7:8).

The Ancient of Days. This is a depiction of Yahweh sitting on the throne. Revelation 4-5 is patterned somewhat after this section. The emphasis is judgment. "The court sat, and the books were opened" (7:9-10).

Judgment on the beasts. The little horn kept speaking, but the dreadful beast was slain. The rest of the beasts lost their rule, but they were allowed to live for an appointed time (7:11-12).

The Son of Man. Here a very important revelation is given in God's instruction to Israel about the "coming one." He is called "one like a son of man" (*k^{e}bar ' ^{e}nash*, כְּבַר אֱנָשׁ).[350] He comes with the clouds of heaven. (Jesus surely refers to this in Matt. 24:30 and, as a result, is charged with blasphemy). The Son of Man appellation in the Gospels is no doubt based on this verse.[351] The Son of Man receives

---

[350]"Like" is also used of the beast. It is used here to demonstrate that the person who comes to the Ancient of Days has humanness. Consequently, the saints are represented by the one "like" the son of man, and are mentioned exclusively in the following verses. Cf. P. Mosca, "Ugaritic and Daniel 7: a Missing Link."*Bib* 67 (1986) 496-517.

[351]But the concept also figures large in the pseudepigraphal book 1 Enoch. See J. H. Charlesworth, *The Old Testament Pseudepigrapha*, 1:9 for a discussion and texts.

the kingdom. All people, nations, and languages will serve him. His kingdom is eternal. This is one of the clearest messianic statements in the Old Testament (7:13-14).[352]

The interpretation of the vision (7:15-28).

Daniel was deeply troubled by the vision and approached one of the (angelic) beings standing by to ask the meaning of the vision (7:15-16).

The apocopated interpretation. In general, said the angel, the four beasts refer to kingdoms, and the throne scene represents the fact that the saints of the Most High will receive the kingdom (7:17-18).

The focus is on this last (fourth) beast and in particular on the little horn that comes from it. The little horn troubles Daniel, and he is given more information about it in v. 21. Here he is fighting against the saints and overpowering them. The interpretation, says the angel, represents a fourth kingdom on the earth which will be more powerful than any of its predecessors. The ten horns represent ten kings within that kingdom. But from the ten horns will arise a little horn, different from his predecessors who will subdue three kings (7:19-24a).

The little horn is obviously the most important element in the vision. He subdues three kings (of the ten); speaks out against God; wears down the saints; changes times and law. The saints will be delivered into his hand "time, times and half a time" (cf. Rev. 12:14). However, when God's court sits for judgment, the little horn will lose his dominion by destruction (7:24b-26).

God's saints will then rule in the everlasting kingdom with God. All dominions will serve and obey Him (7:27).

---

[352]But see Hartman and Di Lella, *Daniel*, AB, who deny it any messianic meaning except in the most general sense of future deliverance.

Daniel, at the conclusion of the vision and its interpretation, is greatly disconcerted, but he keeps the contents of the vision to himself (7:28).

Fuller interpretation of the vision.

Critical to this discussion is the identification of the kingdoms represented in the idol (cf. Ch. 2) and the beasts. The critics who insist that Daniel seven through twelve was the product of the Maccabean period, must have the silver represent Media and the Iron represent Persia. The same thing applies to the beasts: the bear must represent Media, and the leopard must represent Persia. The reason is that the awful beast for them must represent the Hellenistic empire and the little horn must represent Antiochus IV Epiphanes. There is no question that the Maccabean era is in view in the book of Daniel, but there is also an eschatological reference that grows out of the type. This will be seen in relating the little horn of chapter eight with the little horn of chapter seven.

In response to this argument, it should be noted that in chapter eight, Daniel depicts the Persian Empire as one beast (ram) with *two* horns. The second horn comes up last and is *taller*. The second horn of course is Persia (or Cyrus; Daniel exchanges king with kingdom). Cyrus came out of the Median Empire and dominated it. The text identifies the one ram as the kings of Media and Persia (8:20). The bear rears on one side, probably to show this division of the empire (cf. also 5:28).

Secondly, the leopard has four heads and four wings. Again in chapter eight, the goat that shattered the Persian ram, obviously Greece with Alexander as the "conspicuous horn," grows four horns after Alexander's death. This obviously refers to a four-fold division of Alexander's empire after his death (there were more than four at different times, but Daniel focuses on these four). The number four in connection with the leopard should not therefore be passed off as "four kings of the Persians known to the writer."[353] This identification requires that the "dreadful beast" be the Roman empire that follows the Greeks and leads to the dispensational interpretation that Daniel 2, 7, and 9 all conclude with the eschatological era of a "revived" Roman empire and a time of tribulation where the Antichrist wreaks havoc.

Most everyone agrees that the *lion* represents Nebuchadnezzar and therefore the Babylonian empire.[354] The description of the lion (wings plucked; heart of man) may refer to the humbling and restoration of Nebuchadnezzar.

The *bear* as indicated above refers to the Medo-Persian empire; not just Media as the critics must maintain. The higher side indicates a rising of one part of the empire over the other. The three ribs may refer to the three main conquests of Cyrus and his son Cambyses (Lydia, Babylon, and Egypt), but this is uncertain.

The *leopard* refers to the Hellenistic empire established by Alexander the Great and succeeded by his generals (seen by Daniel to be four as in chapter eight: Greece and Macedon, Antipater then Cassander; Thrace and Asia Minor, Lysimachus; Asia except Asia Minor and Palestine, Seleucus; Egypt-Palestine, Ptolemy).

Finally, the *awful beast* must be Rome (legs of iron of chapter two), but as in chapter two (feet/toes of iron/clay) there will be an eschatological form of that empire that will have ten horns simultaneously ruling (some kind of federation). From them a blasphemous little horn will arise that will destroy three of the ten horns. He will then rule disastrously.

---

[353]Hartman and Di Lella, *Daniel,* AB.

[354]For a different view: Assyria, Media, Medo-Persia, Greece, see J. H. Walton, "The Four Kingdoms of Daniel," *JETS* 29 (1986:25-36).

These kingdoms and all they represent will be brought to a conclusion by the Almighty God. He will establish His kingdom and His people (the Jews) will rule and reign with Him. There will be an awful time of tribulation for the Jewish people, however, before they will triumph. This tribulation is shown typically in the Maccabean period when Antiochus IV Epiphanes persecutes the Jewish people as the first little horn.

C. Emphasis on the Jews as related to the Gentiles (8:1—12:13).

This division is a bit arbitrary since Jews are the centerpiece of the discussion in chapter seven, but it is being maintained because chapter seven is in Aramaic and therefore should be related to the Gentile emphasis of chapters two through seven.

1. The setting for the conflict between Antiochus and the Jews (8:1-27).

The setting of the vision (8:1-2).

This vision takes place two years later. Daniel is in Susa, the capital of the province called Elam, by the Ulai Canal. Elam maintained her independence from Babylon. Daniel, was therefore either there on official business of some kind or he was there *in the vision.*

The contents of the vision (8:3-14).

Daniel first of all sees a ram with two horns. The second comes up higher than the first. The ram dominates the world (8:3-4). He then sees a goat. The goat moves fast and has a conspicuous horn. The goat fights and defeats the ram. The goat magnifies himself, but the horn is broken and four horns take its place (8:5-8).

A small horn arises that will attack in all directions including the "beautiful land," i.e., Israel. He will attack the host of heaven and bring some stars to the earth. He will equate himself with the commander of the host. He will remove the regular sacrifice and damage the place of the sanctuary. The army and the regular sacrifice will be stopped. The suspension of the regular sacrifice along with the sin that causes horror (*hapesha' shomem* הַפֶּשַׁע שֹׁמֵם) will last for 2300 evenings and mornings. Then the holy place will be restored (8:9-14).

The interpretation of the vision (8:15-26).

Now the vision bypasses Babylon. The images are: ram = Medo-Persia; goat = Greece; four horns = Alexander's successors; little horn=a king who shall arise in the latter part of their reign. His work against the people of God has already been presented. Here the little horn must be Antiochus IV Epiphanes who comes from Alexander's successors. "The time of the end" (17-18) normally means the eschatological future, but how is that to be applied to 165 B.C.? It seems to me with Wood (*Daniel*) that this phrase is used because of the fact that Antiochus is presented as a type of the Antichrist. Therefore, while chapter eight refers primarily to the Maccabean era, it is also typical of the "end times" when the Antichrist will be active (cf. also v. 13: "How long . . .")[355]

"This evidently refers to the career of Antiochus IV Epiphanes …who usurped the Seleucid throne from his nephew (son of his older brother, Seleucus IV) and succeeded in invading Egypt 170-169 B.C. His expeditions against rebellious elements in Parthia and Armenia were initially successful 'to the east' as well, and his determination to impose religious and cultural uniformity on all his domains led to a brutal suppression of Jewish worship at Jerusalem and generally throughout Palestine (here referred to as 'the Beautiful Land') …. This suppression came to a head in December 168 B.C.,

---

[355]Baldwin, *Daniel*, p. 159, believes that "end" refers to historical end of rebellion when God intervenes in Judgment. She refers to Amos 8:2; Ezek. 7:2-6 to point out that there are intermediate "ends" and final "ends."

when Antiochus returned in frustration from Alexandria, where he had been turned back by the Roman commander Popilius Laenas, and vented his exasperation on the Jews. He sent his general, Apollonius, with twenty thousand troops under orders to seize Jerusalem on a Sabbath. There he erected an idol of Zeus and desecrated the altar by offering swine on it. This idol became known to the Jews as 'the abomination of desolation' ... which served as a type of a future abomination that will be set up in the Jerusalem sanctuary to be built in the last days (cf. Christ's prediction in Matt 24:15)."[356]

The interpretation of the little horn given by the angel is rather general and does not give us the answers we need to understand 8:9-14. Interpreters are left to struggle with the fulfillment of these verses and everyone has some trouble with them.

The language of 8:10-11 should be understood figuratively of Antiochus' attacks on the Jewish people. The Prince of the Host (Host referring to the army of God's people) refers to God, and the stars must refer to God's people.

Antiochus defiled the temple in 167 B.C. It was restored exactly three years later.[357] The 2300 days are the most difficult part of the interpretation. No one is comfortable with the meanings they try to attach to them. Some divide them in half (1150 mornings and 1150 evenings). This would approximate the three year desolation. It is not at all normal for the Hebrew to state time in this fashion, however. Others take the time to be 2300 twenty-four hour days, but struggle to find a terminus a quo. This is usually taken to be 171, when Onias the legitimate high priest, was murdered. The six plus years would

---

[356]Archer, "Daniel," p. 98. On the Hellenization attempts of Antiochus IV Epiphanes as a desperate attempt to maintain Greek dominance in the face of growing orientalism. See also M. Rostovtzeff, "Syria and the East," *CAH* 7:188-89.

[357]Josephus, *Jewish Antiquities XII*, 319.

terminate with the death of Antiochus in 164 B.C. when the temple was cleansed.

The effect of the vision (8:27).

Daniel is told to keep the vision secret. This may help account for the reason it is in Hebrew. It of course is to be read in the time of tribulation as an encouragement to the people of God. Daniel was exhausted and sick for days. That "there was none to explain it" means only that the fulfillment of the prophecy is unknown. The general meaning is clear, the time and specific events are not.

Why would a sixth century prophet be so concerned with second century events? One facet of prophetic utterance is to provide comfort for the future. The Jewish persecution of the second century was so similar to events of the Eschaton that God apparently wanted to provide comfort for the second century saints as well as to provide a paradigm for the events of the last days.

2.   Daniel meditates on Jeremiah's prophecy of seventy weeks and is given the prophecy of seventy heptads in answer to prayer (9:1-27).

The time is the first year of Darius the Mede which ought to be 539 when Cyrus came into Babylon (or 538 on the non-ascension system). This would be in conjunction with the decree to return given to the exiles. Daniel has been reading Jeremiah 29 and working from 605 B.C. concludes that the 70 years are almost up (605-70=535) (9:1-2).

The result of this meditation was that Daniel prayed for his people and his city (9:3-19).

He appeals to the Lord as the great and awesome God and to His work revealed in covenant and loving kindness. These are two very significant words we have encountered before. Covenant (*b^erith*, בְּרִית) reminds us of the Abrahamic covenant as well as the Mosaic covenant to which he refers directly in this verse (Exod. 20:5,6). Loving kindness (*ḥesed,* חֶסֶד) is that oft-recur-ring word describing God's grace to His people (9:3-4).[358]

Daniel identifies with his people in their sin even though he was not personally involved in it: sinned, committed iniquity, acted wickedly, rebelled, forsaking God's commandments, and as though that were not enough, they have refused to listen to the prophets (9:5-6).

Daniel contrasts the holiness of God with the shame of Israel. He argues that the present calamity of Israel in exile is due to their disobedience of this holy God. He indicates that this disaster is a fulfillment of the curse in Deut. 27:15-26 (9:7-16).

Daniel appeals to God's historical compassion in bringing Israel out of Egypt. He prays for God on the basis of His compassion to forgive Israel and to take action on her behalf (9:17-19).

God sends His angel Gabriel with a message to Daniel in answer to his prayer about the restoration of Israel (9:20-23).

God answered Daniel's prayer while he was praying and confessing and presenting his supplication in behalf of Israel and the "holy mountain of God." The answer came through the angel Gabriel late in the day while Daniel was extremely weary (9:20-21).

The purpose of the instruction is to give Daniel insight *haskil,* הַשְׂכִּיל) with understanding (*binah,* בִּינָה). Gabriel was sent out as soon as Daniel began to pray because of the spiritual stature to which he has attained (9:22-23).

God reveals his plans in behalf of Israel through the seventy heptads (9:24-27).

---

[358]See my Hosea notes, page 26, for this word.

The overview is given first: Seventy heptads (*shavu'im shive'im*, שָׁבְעִים שִׁבְעִים) are determined (*nehtach* נֶחְתַּךְ, a hapax meaning in later Hebrew, "to cut" or "divide" and then "to decide") upon *your people*, that is the Jewish people and upon your holy city, that is Jerusalem. It is important to note the objects of the fulfillment of the seventy heptads (9:24a).[359]

Six things are to be accomplished during these seventy heptads. They are divided into two groups. The first group deals with sin.

Finish transgression	End sin	Atone for iniquity
(*lekala' hapesha'*	(*lehatem hatta'th*	(*lekapper 'awon*
לְכַלֵּא הַפֶּשַׁע)	לְחָתֵם חַטָּאוֹת)	לְכַפֵּר עָוֹן)

Note that in Hebrew each statement is a terse two word phrase.

The second group of accomplishments also has three units, but the phrases are longer: three words each.

To bring in everlasting righteousness (lehabi' tsedek 'olamim, לְהָבִיא צֶדֶק עוֹלָמִים).

To seal up the vision and prophet (*lahtom hazon venabi'*, לַחְתֹּם חָזוֹן וְנָבִיא).

To anoint the holy of holies (*limshoah qodesh qodashim*, וְלִמְשֹׁחַ קֹדֶשׁ קָדָשִׁים).

The first group deals with the sin problem. Israel must have redemption. The prayer of Daniel was for the forgiveness of sin. This is the answer to that prayer. God's purpose for Israel during the

---

[359]Montgomery *Daniel* in ICC, p. 397, cites Jerome that the Jews of his day interpreted the seventieth week as applying to the destruction of the temple in 70 A.D. See the text in J. Braverman, *Jerome's Commentary on Daniel,* pp. 103-104.

seventy heptads is to deal with sin. Finish transgression means to cut it off to terminate it. Sin will be dealt with, and atonement will be made for iniquity. This refers to the work of Christ at the cross, but the application of that work to national Israel will take place in the future.

The second group deals with the effect of Christ's redemptive work for Israel. Everlasting righteousness will be brought in, there will be no further need for a prophet or a vision,[360] and the temple will be reconstructed and anointed for service.

The termini of the periods must be observed carefully: the first element is the decree to rebuild Jerusalem. This should be linked with Nehemiah who was permitted by Artaxerxes to come to Jerusalem to rebuild it in 445 B.C. The *terminus ad quem* is Messiah the Prince and the time between the termini is 69 heptads (why it is 7 + 62 is not really clear. Some try to find a historical event after the seven, but there is nothing known that would be significant). Working on the presupposition that these are heptads of years, we would be talking about 483 Julian years. These are adjusted through the lunar system, etc., to bring us to the time of Christ.

The sixty-nine heptads are terminated with the cutting off of the Messiah (we believe Christ). Then the city and the temple will be destroyed (*yashḥith*, יַשְׁחִית—corrupted) by the coming people of the prince. The question is "what prince, what people?" If the people refers to the Romans who destroyed Jerusalem in 70 A.D., who is the prince? The revived Roman empire theory would argue that this represents a latter day Roman (the Antichrist).

The Prince will strengthen (*higbir*, הִגְבִּיר) a covenant with the many for one heptad. In the middle of that heptad, he will terminate the

---

[360]Baldwin, *Daniel*, believes the sealing refers to the fulfillment of Jeremiah's prophecy.

sacrifice and the minḥah. All of this is some way connected with idolatry (*shiqutsim,* שִׁקּוּצִים). Since the book of Revelation speaks of "time/times/ and a half of time, twelve hundred and sixty days and forty two months," we conclude that the last heptad and particularly the last half of it is being referred to in Revelation 6-19 as the great tribulation.

3. Daniel prays for wisdom about the future of his people and has his prayer answered by an angel (10:1-21).

The setting of the vision (10:1-9).

Daniel relates that after three weeks of fasting and praying, God sent a messenger to him to reveal to him things about the future. The detailed description of the angel (10:5-6) is unique in Scripture. This vision took place in the third year of Cyrus (about 536 B.C. since Daniel is reckoning from the fall of Babylon). Daniel's response to the angel is to fall into a deep sleep.

Daniel is prepared to receive the instruction (10:10-17).

Some very unusual information is given about angelic warfare in this section. This angel was apparently sent by God to answer Daniel's prayer as soon as it began (three weeks before), but he was hindered by the "prince of the kingdom of Persia." This suggests that nations are influenced by evil forces. This fallen angel attacked the angel sent to Daniel and held him up until Michael the Archangel came to help him. The message pertains to the latter days; the days yet future (10:14). The angel touched Daniel's lips, and Daniel began to speak.

The angel strengthens Daniel and begins to give him the mystery (10:18-21).

The angel says he must return to take up battle with the "Persian prince" and mentions that a "Greek prince" is coming. Only Michael (Israel's angel) stands with him against these evil forces.

Comparison of chapters two, seven, eight, nine, and Revelation thirteen

Chap. 2	Chap. 7	Chap. 8	Chap. 9	Chap.11	Rev. 13
Head of Gold (Babylon)	Lion				Leopard
Silver Breast (Medo-Persia)	Bear	Ram (2horns)	Decree to build the city 11:2		Bear
Bronze Belly	Leopard	Goat (one horn)	69	11:3-35	Lion
Iron Legs	Awful beast	Little horn	SEVENS		Beast

Messiah the Prince

CHURCH AGE—UNKNOWN IN THE OLD TESTAMENT

Seventieth Seven

Feet/toes of Clay/iron (Last days)	Ten horns Little horn	Covenant Broken		11:36
Stone from mtn (God's kingdom)	Thrones set (God's judgment)			
	Son of Man			
Kdms. Destroyed Kingdom est.	Beasts killed Kingdom established			

4. The angel tells Daniel about events of the future during the Maccabean period (*a* time of tribulation) and during the last days (*the* time of tribulation) (11:1-45).

The text of Daniel 11 is laid out with interpretative comments in the second column. The chapter may be divided into four units.[361]

First period: Persia to Alexander, 539 B.C. to 323 B.C. (1-4).

Second period: Struggle of the Ptolemies and Seleucids, 323 B.C. to 175 B.C. (5-20).

Third period: Antiochus IV Epiphanes, 175 B.C. to 164 B.C. (21-35).

Fourth period: Eschatological period called the Great Tribulation (36-45).

Daniel 11 (NASB)	Interpretation
1 And in the first year of Darius the Mede, I arose to be an encouragement and a protection for him.	
2 And now I will tell you the truth, Behold, three more kings are going to arise in Persia. Then a fourth will gain far more riches than all of them; as soon as he becomes strong through his riches, he will arouse the whole empire against the realm of Greece.	Cambyses II (529-522), Gaumata (522-521), Darius I Hystaspes (521-486) Xerxes (486-465)
3 And a mighty king will arise, and he will rule with great authority and do as he pleases.	Alexander the Great (d. 323 B.C.)
4 But as soon as he has arisen, his kingdom will be broken up and parceled out toward the four points of the compass, though not to his own descendants, nor according to his authority which he wielded; for his sovereignty will be uprooted and given to others besides them.	Alexander's death Four ultimate divisions (Hellenistic empires) His generals
5 Then the king of the South will grow strong, along with one of his princes who will gain ascendancy over him and obtain dominion; his domain will be a great	Ptolemy I Soter (323-285) Seleucus I Nicator (312-281) joined with Ptolemy against Antigonus and took over

[361]See "DSS, Part I: Archaeology of Biblical MSS," *BA* 49 (1986): 140-154 for a chart from 200 B.C. to A.D.

dominion indeed.

6 And after some years they will form an alliance, and the daughter of the king of the South will come to the king of the North to carry out a peaceful arrangement. But she will not retain her position of power, but she will be given up, along with those who brought her in, and the one who sired her, as well as he who supported her in those times.

7 But one of the descendants of her line will arise in his place, and he will come against their army and enter the fortress of the king of the North and he will deal with them and display great strength.

8 And also their gods with their metal images and their precious vessels of silver and gold he will take into captivity to Egypt, and he on his part will <u>refrain</u> from attacking the king of the North for some years.

9 Then the latter will enter the realm of the king of the South, but will return to his own land.

10 And his sons will mobilize and assemble a multitude of great forces; and one of them will keep on coming and overflow and pass through, that he may again wage war up to his very fortress.

11 And the king of the South will be enraged and go forth and fight with the king of the North. Then the latter will raise a great multitude, but that multitude will be given into the hand of the former.

12 When the multitude is carried away, his heart will be lifted up, and he will cause tens of thousands to fall; yet he will not prevail.

13 For the king of the North will again raise a greater multitude than the former, and after an interval of some years he will press on with a great army and much equipment.

14 Now in those times many will rise up against the king of the South; the violent ones among your people will also lift themselves up in order to fulfill the vision, but they will fall down.

15 Then the king of the North will come, cast up a siege mound, and capture a well-fortified city; and the forces of the South will not stand their ground, not even their choicest troops, for there will be no strength to make a stand.

his territory.

Ptolemy II Philadelphus (285-246) Berenice married Antiochus II Theos (261-246)
Antiochus II divorced his wife Laodice to marry Berenice. Two years later Ptolemy II died. Antiochus II took back Laodice who murdered Antiochus, Berenice and their infant son.

Ptolemy III Euergetes (246-221)
(Brother of Berenice)
Seleucus Callinicus (247-226)

Heb: "stand from"

Heb: "And he (Seleucus Callinicus) shall come into the kingdom of the south (unsuccessfully) and return home"

Seleucus' "sons" or successors waged war against Egypt. Seleucus III (226-223) and Antiochus III the Great (223-187) took land as far south as Gaza.

Ptolemy Philopater (221-203) assembled an army and routed the Syrians.

However, Ptolemy did not pursue his advantage.

Antiochus III comes back fourteen years later against a new and young Ptolemy (201).

Jewish people who join with the Syrians against Egypt and thus pave the way for their own future disaster. Thus they "establish the vision."

Antiochus III defeated Egypt twice. Sidon is the fenced city where the Egyptians were forced to surrender.

16 But he who comes against him will do as he pleases, and no one will be able to withstand him; he will also stay for a time in the Beautiful Land, with destruction in his hand.

17 And he will set his face to come with the power of his whole kingdom, bringing with him a proposal of peace which he will put into effect; he will also give him the daughter of women to ruin it. But she will not take a stand for him or be on his side.

Rome forced Antiochus' hand, and he made a treaty with Egypt, giving his daughter, Cleopatra, to Ptolemy V Epiphanes (192). "It" may refer to the land of Egypt which Antiochus hoped to destroy through his daughter. However, she always sided with her husband.

18 Then he will turn his face to the coastlands and capture many. But a commander will put a stop to his scorn against him; moreover, he will repay him for his scorn.

Coastlands: Greece; Antiochus III tried to defeat Greece and lost, thus opening an opportunity for Rome (commander) to intervene. Rome declared war (190 B.C.)

19 So he will turn his face toward the fortresses of his own land, but he will stumble and fall and be found no more.

Antiochus III dies.

20 Then in his place one will arise who will send an oppressor through the Jewel of his kingdom; yet within a few days he will be shattered, though neither in anger nor in battle.

Seleucus Philopater had to raise taxes from the Jews to pay the Romans tribute.

21 And in his place a despicable person will arise, on whom the honor of the kingship has not been conferred, but he will come in a time of tranquility and seize the kingdom by intrigue.

Antiochus IV Epiphanes (175-164), the little horn of Daniel 8.
Onias III (high priest, orthodox)
Jason (brother, liberal, bought high priesthood)

22 And the overflowing forces will be flooded away before him and shattered, and also the prince of the covenant.

Several battles with Egypt, won by Antiochus IV
Probably refers to the High Priest, Onias, deposed by Antiochus in 172 B.C.

23 And after an alliance is made with him he will practice deception, and he will go up and gain power with a small force of people.

Intrigue by Antiochus in the internal power struggles of Egypt.

24 In a time of tranquility he will enter the richest parts of the realm, and he will accomplish what his fathers never did, nor his ancestors; he will distribute plunder, booty, and possessions among them, and he will devise his schemes against strongholds, but only for a time.

Antiochus was eventually able to defeat the Egyptians.

25 And he will stir up his strength and courage against the king of the South with a large army; so the king of the South will mobilize an extremely large and mighty army for war; but he will not stand, for schemes will be devised against him.

The Egyptian king will not be able to continue in his office.

26 And those who eat his choice food will destroy him, and his army will overflow, but many will fall down

Even the Ptolemy's supporters conspired against him.

slain.

27 As for both kings, their hearts will be intent on evil, and they will speak lies to each other at the same table; and it will not succeed, for the end is still to come at the appointed time.

Various treaties between Antiochus and Ptolemy will not be honored by either.

28 Then he will return to his land with much plunder; but his heart will be set against the holy covenant, and he will take action and then return to his own land.

Antiochus will turn to persecute the Jews.

29 At the appointed time he will return and come into the South, but this last time it will not turn out the way it did before.

Appointed by God.
He will not have as much success as previously.

30 For ships of the Kittim will come against him; therefore he will be disheartened, and will return and become enraged at the holy covenant and take action; so he will come back and show regard for those who forsake the holy covenant.

From the islands; in this case Rome.
The Roman Consul, Gaius Popilius Laenas, met Antiochus and ordered his return to Syria. He reportedly drew a circle around him and told him to decide while in the circle. He returned and made a pact with renegade Jews (1 Mac. 2:18). 1 Mac. 1:44-54 says he offered a sow on the altar and erected an idol in the holy place (cf. Matt. 24:15; Dan. 8:23-25) 167 B.C.

31 And forces from him will arise, desecrate the sanctuary fortress, and do away with the regular sacrifice. And they will set up the abomination of desolation.

32 And by smooth words he will turn to godlessness those who act wickedly toward the covenant, but the people who know their God will display strength and take action.

Believing Jews reacted to the persecution and fought.

33 And those who have insight among the people will give understanding to the many; yet they will fall by sword and by flame, by captivity and by plunder, for many days.

Believing Jews will suffer much for their faith.

34 Now when they fall they will be granted a little help, and many will join with them in hypocrisy.

35 And some of those who have insight will fall, in order to refine, purge, and make them pure, until the end time; because it is still to come at the appointed time.

Suffering purifies the saints.

36 Then the king will do as he pleases, and he will exalt and magnify himself above every god, and will speak monstrous things against the God of gods; and he will prosper until the indignation is finished, for that which is decreed will be done.

From this point on, the correspondence to Maccabean history ceases. Consequently, this section is assumed to point to the future. It must have reference to the Antichrist.* Antiochus IV was typical of the great persecutor to come. This section speaks of the actual Antichrist.

37 And he will show no regard <u>for the gods of his fathers</u> or for <u>the desire of women</u>, nor will he show regard for any other god; for he will magnify himself above them all.

38 But instead he will honor a god of fortresses, a god whom his fathers did not know; he will honor him with gold, silver, costly stones, and treasures.

39 And he will take action against the strongest of fortresses with the help of a foreign god; he will give great honor to those who acknowledge him, and he will cause them to rule over the many, and will parcel out land for a price.

40 And at the end time the king of the South will collide with him, and the king of the North will storm against him with chariots, with horsemen, and with many ships; and he will enter countries, overflow them, and pass through.

41 He will also enter the Beautiful Land, and many countries will fall; but these will be rescued out of his hand: Edom, Moab and the foremost of the sons of Ammon

42 Then he will stretch out his hand against other countries, and the land of Egypt will not escape.

43 But he will gain control over the hidden treasures of gold and silver, and over all the precious things of Egypt; and the Libyans and Ethiopians will follow at his heels.

44 But rumors from the East and from the North will disturb him, and he will go forth with great wrath to destroy and annihilate many.

45 And he will pitch the tents of his royal pavilion between the seas and the beautiful Holy Mountain; yet he will come to this end, and no one will help him.

This phrase leads some to believe that this ruler is an apostate Jew in the latter days. It probably means only that he ignores all deities. Cf. 2 Thes. 2, Rev. 13:1-10; Daniel 7 (little horn). "Desire of women": Either a deity (Tammuz/-Adonis) or (Jewish) women's desire, viz., the Messiah. "God of fortresses" militarism.

The Antichrist is being attacked from the north and south (Russia/Egypt?).

"Beautiful land" refers to Israel.

Rev. 9:13-21?

His royal pavilion: Jerusalem between the Mediterranean and Dead Seas.

The Antichrist will come to an end with the advent of Christ (Revelation 19).

*Hartman and DiLella, *AB* Daniel, p. 303, say of 36-45, "The present section contains no historical information at all, but purports rather to be a genuine prediction of events to happen after this apocalypse was composed and presumably circulated among the faithful. The trouble is that nothing in these verses matches the actual course of history as it is known from other sources . . . In addition to this exegesis of 11:40-45, which is shared by most modern authors except the fundamentalist, ... (3) the entire section, 11:36-45, deals not with Antiochus but with the future Antichrist and his death."

Excursus: Texts on the events of
The Year 13-169 B.C.

Daniel (NASB)	1 Mac 1, 4 (AB)	Wars I 33 (Loeb)
11:28 Then he will return to his land with much plunder; but his heart will be set against the holy covenant and he will take action and then return to his own land. At the appointed time he will return and come into the South, but this last time it will not turn out the way it did before. 30 For ships of Kittim will come against him; therefore, he will be disheartened, and will return and become enraged at the holy covenant and take action;	20 While returning from his conquest of Egypt in the year 143, Antiochus marched against (Israel and) Jerusalem with a strong army...21 Arrogantly entering the temple, he took the golden altar and the candelabrum with all its furnishings 22 and the table for the showbread and the libation jars and the bowls and the golden ladles and the curtain. He stripped off all the cornices and the ornamentation of gold from the front of the temple 23 and took the silver and the gold coin and the precious articles, whatever he found of the treasures on deposit. 24 With all this loot he returned to his own country, having polluted himself with massacres and uttered words of great arrogance.	Onias, one of the chief priests, gaining the upper hand expelled the sons of Tobias from the city. The latter took refuge with Antiochus and besought him to use their services as guides for an invasion of Judaea. The king, having long cherished this design, consented, and setting out at the head of a huge army took the city by assault, slew a large number of Ptolemy's followers, gave his soldiers unrestricted license to pillage, and himself plundered the temple and interrupted for a period of 3 years and 6 months the regular course of the daily sacrifices
	44 The king sent letters by messengers to Jerusalem and the towns of Judah...to put a stop to	Antiquities XII (Loeb)
so he will come back and show regard for those who forsake the holy covenant. 31 And forces from him will arise, desecrate the sanctuary fortress and do away with the regular sacrifice. And they will set up the abomination of desolation.	burnt offerings and meal offering and libation in the temple...47 to build illicit altars and illicit temples and idolatrous shrines, to sacrifice swine and ritually unfit animals, 52 Many from among the people gathered around the officers, every forsaker of the Torah, and they committed wicked acts in the	248 Two years later, as it happened in the 145th year [167 B.C.] on the 25th day of month Casleu...the king went up to Jerusalem and by pretending to offer peace, overcame the city by treachery... 252 The king also built a pagan altar upon the temple altar, and slaughtered swine thereon, thereby practicing a form of sacrifice neither lawful nor native to the religion of the Jews. And he compelled them to

land.

54 On the fifteenth day of Kislev in the year 145 the king had an abomination of desolation built upon the altar...59 as on the twenty-fifth day of the month they would offer sacrifices on the illicit altar which was upon the temple altar.

give up the worship of their own God...

319f They kindled the lights on the lamp stand and burned incense on the altar and set out the loaves on the table and offered whole burnt-offerings upon the new altar. These things, as it chanced, took place on the same day on which, 3 years before, their holy service had been transformed into an impure and profane form of worship. For the temple, after being made desolate by Antiochus, had remained so for 3 years; it was the 145th year that these things befell the temple...And the temple was renovated on the same day, in the 148th year...in accordance with the prophecy of Daniel.

[Since the rededication is not mentioned in Daniel, critics assume the date 165 (169-3.5=165.5) for the date of the book.]

4:52 They rose early on the morning of the twenty-fifth day of the ninth month (that is, the month of Kislev), in the year 148 [164 B.C.] 53 and they brought a sacrifice according to the Torah upon the new altar of burnt offerings which they had built. 54 At the very time of year and on the very day on which the Gentiles had profaned the altar, it was dedicated.

5. The climax of the vision is given (12:1-13).

The great tribulation (12:1).

Michael, who seems to have a special assignment to the people of Israel will arise (probably in protection) because there will be an unprecedented time of tribulation coming upon the Jewish people. Yet those whose names are "written in the book" will be rescued. This tribulation is tied in with the seventieth seven of 9:24-27. Its most intense form is in the second half of the seven year period. This period is called "time, times, and a half of time," "twelve hundred and sixty days," and "forty-two months" (see Revelation 11, 12).

There will be a resurrection of the Old Testament saints at the end of the tribulation according to 12:2.

The life of these saints will be rewarded in their eternal state. Daniel is told to hide the words and seal up the book until the end of time. These words will become significant in that distant time of trouble.

Time elements in the Tribulation period (12:5-13).

Daniel overhears two men talking about the time frame for these amazing events. One swears that it will be for time, times and half a time (three and one half years). Daniel asks about the outcome of these events. He is told to go his way because these things are for a future time. During that time, many will be purged and they will understand the significance of the events at that time. Twelve hundred and ninety days will expire from the time of the abolition of the regular sacrifice and the setting up of the abomination of desolation (horrible idol). The second half of the tribulation will be twelve hundred and sixty days. What the other thirty days are for is not clear. Jesus speaks of this abomination in Matt. 24:15 where he is speaking of the coming tribulation period. It is therefore yet future for Israel. It would appear (see the discussion in chapter 9) that the Antichrist (man of sin, 2 Thes. 2) will make a covenant with the Jews for a seven year period. He will probably be instrumental in allowing them to build the temple. In the middle of the seven year period, he will break the covenant (as the new temple is being dedicated?) and will enter the temple and sit as god. He will then vent his rage on the Jewish people (Rev. 12).

Verse 12 speaks of the blessedness of those who come to the thirteen hundred and thirty-fifth day. These additional days will no doubt be used in the preparation for the millennium. Those who participate in the inauguration of that glorious age are blessed indeed!

Chronology of the Hellenistic Period

334-323 Alexander the Great conquers the East.

330 Macedonian conquest of Palestine.

311 Seleucus conquers Babylon. Beginning of the Seleucid dynasty.

223-187 Antiochus III, the Great, Seleucid ruler of Syria.

202 Rome defeats Carthage at Zama.

198 Antiochus III defeats Egypt, gains control of Palestine.

175-163 Antiochus IV, Epiphanes, rules Syria-Palestine. Proscribes Judaism. Persecution of the orthodox Jews.

168 Battle of Pydna. Romans defeat the Macedonians.

167 Mattathias and his sons rebel against the Syrians. Beginning of the Maccabean Revolt.

166-160 Leadership of Judas Maccabeus.

160-142 Jonathan the High Priest.

146 Scipio Africanus destroys Carthage. Rome controls western Mediterranean.

142-135 Simon, the High Priest.

134-104 John Hyrcanus, son of Simon, High Priest and King.

103 Aristobulus.

102-76 Alexander Jannaeus.

75-67 Salome Alexandra ruler; Hyrcanus II High Priest.

66-63 Aristobulus II. Dynastic battle with Hyrcanus II.

64 Pompey invades Palestine. Arbitrates fate of Hasmoneans and Judeans. Roman rule begins.

63-40 Hyrcanus II rules, subject to Rome. Antipater exercises increasing power.

40-37 Parthians conquer Jerusalem. Establish Antigonus as High Priest and King.

37-4 Herod the Great, son of Antipater, rules as king, subject to Rome.

31 Battle of Actium. Octavian emerges as ruler of the Roman world.

Notes on the Book of Haggai

I. The Prophet Haggai.

Nothing is known about Haggai the prophet beyond what is recorded in his own prophecy and in Ezra 5:1-2. The name has something to do with "festival," but the significance is obscure. Haggai was raised up by Yahweh two months prior to Zechariah for a short ministry in connection with the rebuilding of the temple. This task he shared with Zechariah. He, also like Zechariah, was instrumental in encouraging Zerubbabel the governor and Joshua (this spelling is adopted rather than Jeshua[362] since the Hebrew is the same for this priest as Moses' successor) the high priest.

II. The Historical Context.

Cyrus became the ruler of the Medes and the Persians and conquered an empire that stretched to India in the East and to the western edge of Anatolia. This vast empire, with its disparate peoples could only have come about through a policy of the Persians that differed immensely from their predecessors. Cyrus allowed a measure of local autonomy and allowed the return of various gods, the rebuilding of temples, and the recognition of local cultures. Isaiah (40-45) tells us that God raised him up as His anointed (Isaiah 45:1-2). The Jews benefited from the policy in that they were allowed to return to their land, rebuild their temple, and restore their worship system. The decree of Cyrus, found on the Cyrus Cylinder is as follows: "All the kings of the entire world from the Upper to the Lower Sea, those who are seated in throne rooms, (those who) live in other [types of buildings as well as] all the kings of the West land living in tents, brought their heavy tributes and kissed my feet in Babylon. (As to the

---

[362]Jeshua in Ezra/Nehemiah.

region) from . . . as far as Ashur and Susa, Agade, Eshnunna, the towns Zamban, Me-Turnu, Der as well as the region of the Gutians, I returned to (these) sacred cities on the other side of the Tigris, the sanctuaries of which have been ruins for a long time, the images which (used) to live therein and established for them permanent sanctuaries. I (also) gathered all their (former) inhabitants and returned (to them) their habitations. Furthermore, I resettled upon the command of Marduk, the great lord, all the gods of Sumer and Akkad whom Nabonidus has brought into Babylon to the anger of the lord of the gods, unharmed, in their (former) chapels, the places which make them happy."[363] Cyrus issued his famous edict in 538 B.C. allowing the Jews and other expatriates to return to their homelands and rebuild their temples.

The first return under Sheshbazzar and Zerubbabel to build the temple (538 B.C., Ezra 1-6) saw only the foundation laid. Opposition from surrounding neighbors resulted in a letter to the King and an interruption of the work. Under the leadership of Zerubbabel, Haggai and Zechariah, the work was resumed 16 years later and completed in 516 B.C. The chronology of this period is as follows:

A. Events under Cyrus, first king of Persia (539-529 B.C).

1. Edict issued returning people and temple contents (538 B.C.).

2. Temple foundation laid (536 B.C.).

B. Events under Cambyses, Cyrus' son (529-522 B.C).

No biblical events. Cambyses conquered Egypt (referred to in the Elephantine papyri).

---

[363] *ANET*, p 316.

C. Events under Darius, the great, Persian general (522-486 B.C.).

    1. Darius defeats an alleged usurper to throne (Gaumata) and struggles to put down rebellions (done by 520 B.C.).[364]

    2. Zechariah begins his ministry in the second year of Darius.

    3. The temple was completed in 516 B.C.

    4. Darius was defeated at Marathon by Greeks in 490 B.C.

D. Events under Xerxes (Ahasuerus) (486-465 B.C.).

    1. Xerxes was defeated at Salamis in 480 B.C.

    2. The events of Esther may have taken place after his return.

E. Events under Artaxerxes I (465-424 B.C.).

    1. Ezra's return to promote religious reform (458 B.C.). Fensham says Egypt revolted in 460 and was suppressed in 456 B.C. Artaxerxes needed loyal people in Judah and may have sent Ezra for this purpose (Ezra 7:8).[365]

    2. Nehemiah's first return (445 B.C.) (Neh. 5:14).

    Fensham says the Persian general who defeated Egypt became angry at Artaxerxes and revolted against him. Later he declared loyalty and was restored, but again Artaxerxes would want loyal leaders in the west and so may have sent Nehemiah.[366]

---

[364]This date is uncertain. It ranges from 520-518.

[365] F. C. Fensham, *The Books of Ezra and Nehemiah*, 149-50.

[366]Ibid.

3. Ezra apparently came back a second time early in Nehemiah's period (Neh. 8-10; 12:36).

4. Nehemiah returns a second time (432 B.C.) (Neh. 13:6).

III. The Structure and Synthesis of the Book.

There are four oracles in the book of Haggai. The first comes on 6/1/2. The admonition is to rise and build the temple. The response is positive and on 6/24/2 the leaders, Zerubbabel and Joshua, along with the people obeyed the Lord and began the work on the temple. The second comes on 7/21/2 to encourage them in what seems to be a secondary work. The third comes on 9/24/2 through a legal parable to encourage them to continue in the work with the promise of future blessing. The fourth comes on the same day (9/24/2) to tell Zerubbabel of his choice position as part of the Davidic covenant. The purpose of this book is thus very simple: God wants his temple built, and he encourages Zerubbabel, Joshua and the people to build it. The completion of the temple is not mentioned in Haggai. We learn from Ezra that it was finished on the third day of the month Adar in Darius' sixth year. This would be 516 B.C.

IV. The Outline of the Book.

A. Oracle #1—Build the Temple (1:1-15).

The foundations of the temple, laid in 536 B.C., had lain untouched for sixteen years. The people, roundly discouraged by the "people of the Land," had decided it was not worth the effort to rebuild the temple. God then raised up Haggai and Zechariah to challenge the people to resume the building process (Ezra 4:24—5:2). Since the people have decided that the time must not be right to build the temple, God asks them through Haggai whether it is right for them to be living in their own nice homes while the temple lies desolate. One is reminded of David's statement to Nathan (2 Sam 7:2) that it was improper for him to live in a nice home while the ark sat in curtains. The people have suffered poor harvests and an overall poor economic state because of their refusal to build the temple. This situation can only be rectified by restarting the process of building the temple interrupted so long ago.

Zerubbabel, Joshua and the people responded positively to Haggai's exhor-tation, and they began the work on 6/24/2. Yahweh encouraged them by telling them he was with them (1:13 cf. 2:4).

B. Oracle #2—The leaders are to take courage (2:1-9).

Zerubbabel was admonished by Zechariah not to despise the "day of small things," i.e., the relatively insignificance of the second temple (Zech 4:10). Haggai brought a similar message to the people who were building. The beginning of the nation (Exodus) and its eschatological fulfillment are tied together in 2:5-9. The Day of the Lord is in view when he speaks of shaking the heavens, earth, sea and dry land. In that eschatological future all the nations will come to this temple, and the *shekinah* glory will fill the temple. Then the greater glory will be in place, and there will be peace. This should be related to Isaiah 2, Micah 4, and Ezekiel 40-48.

C. Oracle #3—God promises blessing for obedience (2:10-19).

The rules of uncleanness indicated that something unclean would pollute a clean item, but the reverse was not true. So, says Yahweh, is the people of Israel. Everything they touch becomes unclean. Consequently, their sinfulness has resulted in crop failures. However, from this day of obedience forward, they will enjoy the blessing of Yahweh because they are rebuilding the temple.

D. Oracle #4—God gives a special word to Zerubbabel (2:20-23).

Zerubbabel was a descendant of David (Jehoiachin—Shealtiel—Zerub-babel).[367] The general message is clear: David, the founder of the dynasty,

---

[367]First Chronicles 3:19 indicates that the order was Jehoiachin—Pedaiah—Zerubbabel. Since Pedaiah and Shealtiel were brothers, there may have been a levirate

was given a covenant that his seed would build the temple David wanted to build. Now the returned community includes a Davidic descendant who is the governor (not the king).[368] It is his responsibility, therefore, to build the second temple. Zerubbabel has been chosen for this task, but as a representative of the Davidic dynasty, he will be the signet ring (special authority) on God's hand when the Day of the Lord takes place. Thus in Haggai as in Zechariah, Zerubbabel becomes a type of the ultimate seed of David who will effect God's purposes on the earth.[369] He has been elected as God's servant just as David was. And just as David's descendants were encompassed in God's covenant with him, so Zerubbabel's descendants must be included with him. Thus the house of David continues and will continue to the Eschaton when God overthrows the nations.

---

marriage involved.

[368]Verhoef , *The Books of Haggai and Malachi,* 37-39, essentially agrees with this position.

[369]This passage needs to be related to Jeremiah 22:30 where God says that no one of Jehoiachin/Jeconiah/Coniah's descendants will prosper sitting on the throne of David or ruling again in Judah. Zerubbabel did not rule as king, but as a governor under Persian rule. Perhaps this is the reason Luke's genealogy is traced back to Nathan, son of David, while Matthew's goes through Jeconiah to Solomon.

Notes on the Book of Zechariah

I. The Prophet Zechariah.

Zechariah is mentioned in Ezra (5:1; 6:14) along with Haggai as the prophet who aroused the returned Jews to rebuild the temple. Nehemiah 12:16 lists him in the genealogy. There he is the son of Iddo; here he is the son of Berechiah son of Iddo. These are surely the same persons, even though the name Zechariah (זְכַרְיָה "Yah remembers") is quite common. The Iddo in Nehemiah was the head of a "house" and hence possibly not the immediate ancestor.[370]

II. The Historical Context.

See the same point under Haggai.

III. The Composition of the Book.

Zechariah falls clearly into two disparate parts. Chapters 1-8 are dated and refer to circumstances and events in the second and fourth years of Darius and chapters 9-14 are undated and from a literary point of view are quite different from the first half of the book. This leads many to conclude that there are two different books combined into one. Joyce Baldwin[371] has built upon the work of P. Lamarche,[372] and has clearly demonstrated

---

[370]LaSor, et al., *Old Testament Survey*, 489.

[371]Joyce Baldwin, *Haggai, Zechariah, Malachi*.

[372]P. Lamarche, *Zacharie IX-XIV, Structure Littérarie et Messianisme*.

literary unity for the book. We will assume that the sixth century prophet, Zechariah, produced the entire work.[373]

IV. The Structure and Synthesis of the Book.

The first eight chapters contain an introduction and seven night visions (I am combining the two visions in chapter 5). It should be the first order of business to search for a relevance of the visions for the sixth century groups of Jews who have returned from the exiles. They have returned to meet the Jews left in the land in 586 B.C. who have changed very little spiritually. The returning Jews, under the leadership of such men as Zerubbabel and later Ezra and Nehemiah, had given up idolatry and were seeking to please the Lord. The circumstance of the returnees including strong political opposition led them to begin to slip into the old ways of life. The city and temple were lying in ruins, with the temple foundation a mute witness to the spiritual failure of the returnees. It was Zechariah's and Haggai's task to shore up the diminished enthusiasm of these people to trust the Lord for the present and the future. Baldwin captures the essence of the prophecy when she says "The rebuilding of the Temple was the condition on which the dawning of the Messianic age depended. Haggai implied as much (Hg. 2:6-09) and Malachi proclaimed that the Lord would suddenly come to His Temple (Mal 3:1). The rebuilding of the Temple was at once an act of dedication and of faith. It was a symbol of the continuity of the present with the past, and expressed the longing of the community that, despite the exile, the old covenant promises still stood."[374] The messianic age is then presented apocalyptically in the last six chapters.

---

[373]See the standard introductions for the many and complex issues.

[374]Baldwin, *Haggai, Zechariah, Malachi*, 21.

V. The Outline of the Book.

A. Messages of hope and challenge in connection with the rebuilding of the temple (1:1—6:8).[375]

1. Zechariah challenged the people to repent (1:1-6).

    The date for this message is given as the eighth month of Darius' second year or 520 B.C. The Jews have been back in the land since 536 B.C. or some 16 years. Yahweh challenges them to return to him. This is the language of repentance. They are challenged to remember the sins of their ancestors who, because of their sins, were driven into exile. They, said Yahweh, listened and learned. They recognized that their punishment was just.[376] Now, the returnees should recognize the same situation. The response of the people is not given in this context.

2. Visions of God's concern for his people (1:7—2:13).

    The first vision—God's watchful care (1:7-17).

    Three months later the visions began. Since no other dates are given for the visions, the assumption can be made that they were all given in a relatively short time. The visions begin with horses and end with horses and chariots.

    The horsemen in the vision represent God's vigil over the whole earth. They have been going back and forth checking up on it and discover that the entire world is at peace (by the second year of Darius, he had established his rule in the land and put down resistance). However, the Jewish people cannot be at rest for God's indignation continues as it

---

[375]See R. E. Brown, *The Gospel According to John I-XII*, 29:326 for a discussion of the Book of Zechariah on the New Testament.

[376]The book of Lamentations is instructive in this connection.

has been for some seventy years. This seventy year period probably refers to the time from the destruction of the temple until its completion. From the spiritual point of view, the fact that the temple as the symbol of Yahweh's presence in Jerusalem, is still in ruins indicates a failure of the returning community to achieve what God intended for them.

Yahweh's response is strong and encouraging: "I am exceedingly jealous for Jerusalem and Zion." On the other hand, the nations which he used to punish his people, now at peace, will receive the butt of his anger. But as for Jerusalem, he will again have compassion on her, his house will be built within her, and he will stretch out a line over the city of Jerusalem. The measuring line probably indicates ownership and protection. The pitiable state of Jerusalem would be remedied and would again be prosperous, and the temple would be rebuilt.

The second vision—the horns/craftsmen (1:18-21).

The second vision relates to Yahweh's vindication of his people: having scattered them in judgment, he will punish the nations which scattered them. Who are these nations? Efforts to identify them are fruitless (since there is no logical sequence of four nations fitting this description). Therefore, we should think of the four horns as nations from the four quarters of the earth: all nations who have hurt Israel will be hurt by God.

The third vision—the measuring line (2:1-13).

We have encountered the measuring line before (1:16). There it pertains to Yahweh's compassion on Jerusalem. It probably denotes God's protection of the city and so should be understood in Chapter 2. (God measures in Ezekiel 40-48 and Revelation 11. The latter seems to clearly indicate protection since the court was omitted in the measuring and turned over to the Gentiles.)

SEVEN NIGHT VISIONS OF ZECHARIAH 1-6

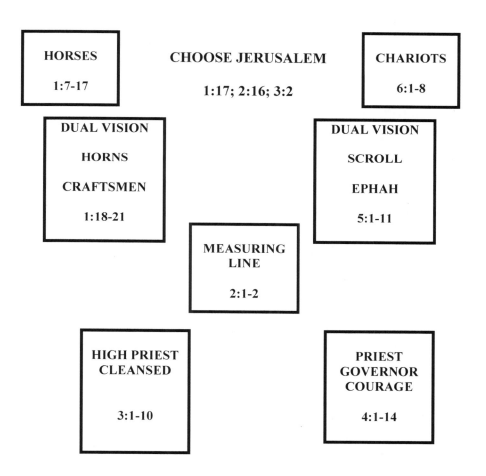

HORSES 1:7-17	**CHOOSE JERUSALEM** 1:17; 2:16; 3:2	**CHARIOTS** 6:1-8

DUAL VISION

HORNS

CRAFTSMEN

1:18-21

DUAL VISION

SCROLL

EPHAH

5:1-11

MEASURING LINE

2:1-2

HIGH PRIEST CLEANSED

3:1-10

PRIEST GOVERNOR COURAGE

4:1-14

Some phrases in this vision need special attention. "Flee from the land of the north …Escape, you who are living with the daughter of Babylon" sounds like Jer 50:8. In that context, it seems to refer to God's judgment of Babylon (Chaldea) by the Persians. At that time the Jews were urged to flee Babylon. This warning may have relevance to the sixth century in urging Jews to come to Jerusalem, but the overall tone of this unit appears to be eschatological. God's great work in behalf of his own people, Israel, is yet to come. He will be "aroused from His holy habitation" in Israel's behalf, and woe to the nation that touches Israel, the apple of God's eye. At that time (2:11) Yahweh will dwell in the midst of his people and many nations will join themselves to him.

3. Visions of cleansing and service (3:1—5:11).

    The fourth vision—the cleansing of Joshua (3:1-10).

    One of the main issues facing the Jews when they returned from the exile was the restoration of the temple and the priesthood. The books of Ezra, Nehemiah and Chronicles spell out this concern in considerable detail. Chapter 3 is not concerned primarily with Joshua's personal cleansing, but with the purification of the priesthood to function in the new temple. The role of the Accuser is to thwart the people of God in their attempt to gain access to him. This effort is interdicted by the Angel of Yahweh who wants all to know that Yahweh has chosen Jerusalem. Here Jerusalem (= Zion) represents the place of the temple. God cleanses Joshua and informs him that an obedient life will allow him to perform his service (as priest in the temple) and govern his house (the temple). Since Joshua and "his friends who are sitting there" were symbols (*mopheth*, מוֹפֵת), this must in some sense apply to the whole priesthood.

    Now for the first time the astounding prophecy of the "Branch" (*zemaḥ*, זֶמַח) is given. Jeremiah 23:5-6 speaks of this same individual in a context of a time when God would provide good leadership for his people. Later Judaism will take his passage in a messianic sense. Isaiah spoke of a "branch" (*ḥoter*, חֹטֶר) from the stump of Jesse (Isaiah 11:1) and of a "branch" (*netzer*, נֵצֶר) from the dry ground (speaking of the servant, Isa 53:2). Ultimate cleansing for Israel must come from this Branch. The idea of "removing the iniquity of the land in one day" (3:9) indicates an eschatological cleansing of Israel.

The stone with seven eyes is the most difficult concept to interpret in the chapter. The word eyes is the Hebrew word *'ayin* (עַיִן) which is ambiguous. It can mean "the eye" or a "fountain" (water flowing from a socket) or "aspect" or "facet." Consequently, Baldwin, following Lipinski, takes the secondary meaning of "fountain" and identifies it with the rock Moses struck from which water flowed and would thus be a metaphor of the cleansing of Israel.[377] This interpretation is attractive, but the seven eyes of 4:10 are eyes which "see" the plumb line in the hand of Zerubbabel and are representative of God's omniscience. Consequently, we probably should see them in a similar sense in 2:9. God sees all things: the nations who judged Israel; Israel's need of restoration and cleansing. In that (eschatological) day, all will sit under vine and fig trees. This is a symbol of eschatological restoration of Israel to her land (Micah 4:4, 5).

The fifth vision—the Lampstand (4:1-14).

Since one of the primary concerns of this book is with the rebuilding of the temple, it should not surprise us to see a chapter devoted to the subject. The obstacles encountered by the returnees are recounted in Ezra 4-5. This chapter is to encourage the governor, Zerubbabel and the high priest, Joshua, to complete the task. The lamp stand (ever a symbol of the light in the temple) is here a symbol for God's provision for protection and strength to finish the temple. The "two sons of oil" or NASB "anointed ones" represent Zerubbabel (4:6) and Joshua, who though unmentioned, should be assumed.

---

[377]Baldwin, *Haggai, Zechariah, Malachi*, 117.

The sixth vision—the Scroll and the Ephah (5:1-11).

Most people see two visions here, but I have chosen to combine them (as the horns and craftsmen were combined). The first part (scroll) speaks of judgment on God's people who break the commandments (the middle commandment in each half of the two tables is given as typical of all), and the second part speaks of dealing with the sin of the people. This much of the interpretation is fairly clear; the difficulty comes with the last verse. "Wickedness" is being removed from Judah and transported to the "Land of Shinar." This is an ancient name for the Babylonian region (Gen 10:10). It was used in later times only in Isaiah 11:11 and Daniel 1:2. The use of this word should alert the reader to a special meaning. It is the symbol of the beginning of rebellion against God. God is taking "wickedness" back to its origin where he will build it a temple (house) where it will be worshipped. "Revelation 17-18 speaks of 'Mystery Babylon,' that embodiment of all evil that God will judge. This concentration of evil in the place of its origin will take place in the last days before the Battle of Armageddon and the establishment of the millennial kingdom. Thus, God will remove evil from the people of Israel as he prepares them to be his people. He will also judge those nations who will become even more wicked in the last days."[378]

4. Vision of Judgment (6:1-8).

The night visions end as they began, with horses (chariots) who are involved with all the earth. In the first vision the problem is that all the nations are at peace while Jerusalem is troubled. God at that time promised that the nations would be judged (1:11,15, 18-21). The visions close with the symbolic prediction that the nations will be judged. The four chariots represent the four winds (or spirits, the Hebrew *ruaḥ* רוּחַ means both) of heaven. These winds/spirits have

---

[378]H. Heater, *Zechariah*, 43.

stood before God (reporting to him) and are now coming forth (as was the Ephah). Thus they have a task to perform.[379] They are to patrol the earth and to appease God's wrath in the land of the north. The word "appeased" can also mean to give rest to. It must mean that God's anger against the nations (alluded to in Chapter 1) will be given rest or appeased when it has run its course against the nations. Thus the vision means that God will eventually vindicate his people Israel when the Day of the Lord brings judgment on them, but also on the nations who have persecuted them.

B.   Special messages to the returnees (6:9—8:23).

1.   Message to the Babylonian Jews: the crowning of Joshua (6:9-15).

Messengers have come from Babylon probably with a gift for the newly rebuilt temple. This visit prompts another message. Zechariah makes a crown of silver and gold. (The word for crown is plural, indicating some kind of complexity.) The dual crown is to be placed on Joshua's head. Because this act was associated with the building of the temple, critics want to substitute the name of Zerubbabel for that of Joshua, but there is no warrant for such action. Joshua, the center of the vision in Chapter 3 and one of the sons of oil in Chapter 4, is more important than Zerubbabel in the restoration of the temple and its ritual than Zerubbabel. Once again we encounter the name "branch." Here it is applied to Joshua, but strangely it says that Joshua will sit on a throne and that the counsel of peace will be between the two offices. This symbol now creeps into the Eschaton where one will rule as both priest and king. Joshua will be involved in building the sixth century temple (6:12), but so will be the latter day successor who will rule as priest and king (6:13).[380]

---

[379]See *Ibid.* for a discussion of the details of the vision.

[380]Baldwin, *Zechariah*, 135-37.

2. Instruction on true religion: the fast question (7:1-14).

    Another situation developed on 9/4/4 when certain pilgrims came to Jerusalem to seek the Lord. They asked the teaching priests whether they should continue fasting on the fifth month as they had been doing for a long time. Apparently because the temple was well under way, they decided they should probably stop remembering the fall of the temple (fifth month) by fasting. Zechariah seizes the opportunity to warn them about the futility of ritual with reality. Their ancestors had plenty of the former, but God judged them for failing to carry out the requirements of the covenant by treating properly the vulnerable people in the land. The result was the exile. Now the word is, "learn from the past."

3. Instruction on future Zion: the fast question continued (8:1-23).

    The message of Chapter 8, in contrast to Chapter 7, is encouraging. This chapter is replete with promises, some of which are among the most marvelous in the Old Testament. As if to assure the reader of the integrity of the promises, Zechariah speaks in the name of Yahweh of hosts. This title for God appears fifty-four times in Zechariah, and eighteen of those are in Chapter 8. This name is a favorite title for God in the prophets, especially Isaiah, Jeremiah, and Zechariah. The stress is on God's omnipotence as the head of the armies of heaven fighting on behalf of God's people.[381] The chapter may be divided into two major sections. The first is 8:1-18 ("and the word of the Lord of hosts came"); the second, 8:19-23 ("and the word of the Lord of hosts came to me"). There are ten "oracles" or "sayings" introduced by the phrase "thus says the Lord of hosts" (vs. 3 is included even though it has only "Thus says the Lord" because it seems to be the same introductory clause).

---

[381]H. Heater, *Zechariah*, 63.

First segment: Encouragement to the returnees (8:1-17). There are several parallels between this chapter and chapters 1-2: 8:2=1:14; 8:3=2:10; 8:4-5=1:17; 8:7=2:6. This lends weight to the argument for chiastic structure in the first half of the book. It is important to understand that while some of Zechariah's prophecies had application in the sixth century, many of them find their ultimate fulfillment in the future. Any Jew of that day would have known that the scenes depicted by Zechariah (8:3-4) were not yet in effect (cf. Ezra-Nehemiah for the actual conditions). But they could take heart in the fact that the work begun by God in their day would come to glorious fruition in "the latter days."

The first segment speaks of ideal conditions to prevail in the future. Blessings are promised in Zechariah's day as a reward for resuming the temple, but the description given in this unit takes us into the Eschaton. God has purposed to do good to Jerusalem; this good began in the sixth century, but it will culminate in the golden age of the future.

Second segment: Kingdom promises (8:19-23). In that beautiful age, all fasting will turn to joy.[382] The beautiful picture of the restored Jews entreating the favor of Yahweh, a favorite with the prophets, concludes the oracles. Ten men from the Gentiles will grasp the garment of a Jew saying, "Let us go with you, for we have heard that God is with you."

C. The First Burden of the Lord (9:1—11:17).

We now enter the second part of the book commonly known as the apocalyptic section. Here the cryptic predictions of the culmination of the

---

[382]The siege of Jerusalem began in the tenth month; the city fell in the fourth month; the temple was destroyed in the fifth month; and Gedaliah was assassinated in the seventh month (1 Kings 25:1, 8, 25).

age, the deliverance and triumph of Israel, the establishment of God's rule on earth and the ensuing golden age are presented. The great emphasis on God's intervention in the affairs of men no doubt affected the extensive reference to these two units in the New Testament.

Smith points out a number of connections between Chapters 9-14 and 1-8. "(1) The significant role of Jerusalem and Zion (1:12-16; 2:1-13; 9:8-10; 12:1-13; 14:1-21). (2) The cleansing of the community as part of God's final act (3:1-9; 5:1-11; 10:9; 12:10; 13:1-2; 14:20-21). (3) The place of all the nations in the kingdom of God (2:11; 8:20-23; 9:7, 10; 14:16-19). (4) The use of the work of the former prophets (Amos 1:9-10, 5:27-62 in 9:1-8; Jer 25:34-38 in 11:1-3; Ezek 38-48 in 14:1-4). Practically all of Zech 9-14 is an interpretation or an application of earlier prophecies."[383]

1. The coming king and the kingdom (9:1-17).

    The first eight verses speak of the reclamation of the coastal plain for Israel. A conversion of the Philistine states is indicated in the removal of idolatry (9:7) and the description of Ekron as a Jebusite (one incorporated into Judah). Hanson is probably right that the emphasis of the passage is not on the historical past, but upon the eschatological future.[384] Several events could be pointed to as possible fulfillments of this prophecy, but ultimately, the reference is to the restoration period yet in the future (9:1-8).

    One of the most dramatic prophecies in the Old Testament, the picture of the warrior king coming to deliver Zion stands out as a representative of the hope of God's salvation in behalf of his people. This reference should be related to Gen 49:10; 2 Sam 5:2; Micah 5:2;

---

[383]Ralph L. Smith, *Micah to Malachi*, p. 242.

[384]P. Hanson, "Jewish Apocalyptic against Its Near Eastern Environment," *RB* 78 (1971): 31-58. Baldwin, *Haggai, Zechariah and Malachi*, 157-58, generally agrees. She argues that past events typify the future.

Isaiah 9:6; 11:1-5 and Matt 2:5-6. The indication of verse 10 is that the fulfillment is in connection with the establishment of the glorious kingdom of Old Testament hope. However, its use in the Gospels shows that its initial thrust has to do with Jesus' first coming (9:9-10).

The final unit continues the theme of holy war and deliverance of Israel, the people of God. Smith argues that the reference to the war between the Greeks and Zion in 9:13 should not be pressed as to date. It represents the holy war concept which is eschatological.[385] Baldwin believes that the references to Greeks in Gen 10:2, 4 and Isa 66:19 indicate that they represent a distant people.[386] In any event, the tendency of some scholars to link the battle with the Maccabean wars should be rejected.

2.   The first shepherd pericope—protection of Israel (10:1-12).

A transition is presented in 10:1 as the account moves from the glorious future to problems of the fifth century. The rain and all it represented (vegetation, etc.) comes from Yahweh. Some people of Zechariah's day had failed to learn the lesson of Baalism (here *teraphim*). "In spite of the fact that most Jews gave up polytheism in the Exile, some still clung to the native beliefs. One has to wonder whether these are Jews who did not go to Babylon but stayed in Palestine, never fully renounced their pagan practices" (10:2).[387]

The sheep and shepherd motif, so common to the prophets, is taken up in terms of a suffering flock due to the lack of concern by the shepherds. Consequently, God will punish the leaders,[388] but he will

---

[385]Smith, *Micah to Malachi*, 260.

[386]Baldwin, *Haggai, Zechariah, Malachi*, 168-69.

[387]H. Heater, *Zechariah*, 84.

[388]Shepherds can refer to either Israel's leaders or foreign leaders (Baldwin, *Haggai,*

cause his sheep to be triumphant (this is the basic idea of the various metaphors: majestic horse, cornerstone, tent peg, bow, ruler) (10:2b-5).

When this happens, the result will be great victory and God will bring all his people (both from the old north and the south). There will be a great prosperity when the regathering takes place (cf. Zechariah 2). The old persecuting nations (Egypt, Assyria) will yield up God's people. A second exodus will take place when God strengthens his people and dries up the waters of the Nile (10:6-12).

Chapter 10 is, like chapter 9, an eschatological picture. When God brings his work in the world to a consummation, it will include punishment of Israel's bad leaders (either national or foreign), the strengthening of both the Jews from the north and south, the providing of good leaders, the restoration to the land of Israel, and a triumphant, miraculous work of God in returning them. From a New Testament perspective, we would see this taking place during the Tribulation in preparation for God's rule on the earth, which we call the Millennium.

3.   The second shepherd pericope—the rejected shepherd (11:1-17).

The unit contained in 11:1-3 is to be linked with chapter 10, not the rest of chapter 11. With Baldwin I would say that it represents a song of exultation after the victory granted by Yahweh in chapter 10.[389] Smith believes it could either close chapter 10 or introduce chapter 11.

Zechariah, Malachi, 172).

[389]Baldwin, *Haggai, Zechariah, Malachi,* 177 says "The climax is the arrival of the king to set up his universal kingdom, but first there is opposition to be overcome, hence the darker side of the picture."

He calls it a taunt song.[390] The trees represent powers, and the powers have fallen. God has delivered and restored his people (11:1-3).

The rest of the chapter is so graphic and personified, that interpreters have struggled to find a historical fulfillment of some sort. An individual is hired to tend a flock (though it is God who commanded him to do so), he shepherds the flock with two staffs symbolic of God's work, and he is rejected and paid off (11:4-14).

Who is this person? In actuality it is impossible to find any historical referent. It means at least that God himself is concerned about his flock and though he wants to shepherd it, is rejected from the task. Small wonder that this is shown by the New Testament to be an adumbration of the ministry of the great shepherd of the sheep who gave his life for the flock.

The doomed flock. God's people are being abused by those whose assigned task was to care for them. Both foreign rulers (11:5a) and their own national leaders (11:5b) have used the flock to their own advantage. Furthermore, God himself says that he will punish these people. This could be associated with the Maccabean era, e.g., or A. D. 70, but it would be mistaken to try to pin point any particular time. Since the book is apocalyptic in tone, one should expect the setting to be in the last days (11:4-6).

The pastor of the flock. The phrase "even the afflicted of the flock" (*"niye hats'on,* עֲנִיֵּי הַצֹּאן) is very difficult. There seems to be a subdivision of the large flock, and this does not seem called for by the context. By letting the words "even" and "afflicted" slide together in Hebrew, the word "merchant" appears (*kena'ani,* כְּנַעֲנִי). This makes much better sense in both contexts.[391] The shepherd took two staffs

[390]Smith, *Micah to Malachi*, 267.

[391]Baldwin, *Haggai, Zechariah, Malachi*, 180.

with which to pastor the flock. One was called "favor" (*noam*, נֹעַם),
and the other was called "union" (*ḥobelim*, חֹבְלִים bands, ropes). These
he will explain later. Rather cryptically, the text says that the shepherd
then will annihilate three other shepherds. Much ink has been spilled
trying to identify these three people historically. The effort is futile. I
assume that the genre of material here is live drama. In some way,
Zechariah is acting out this scenario. Rather than try to identify the
three shepherds, we must simply assume that they represent bad
leadership which will come under the judgment of God. The flock
itself apparently was not happy with the shepherd, and consequently,
he decided to break his staff "favor" which represented his contract
with the sheep. He then demanded his wages which were disdainfully
measured at thirty shekels of silver. The Lord recognized the wages as
an insult and told Zedekiah to throw them to the potter in the temple.
Finally, he cut the second staff which symbolized the unity between
Israel and Judah. Is it possible that this in some way summarizes
God's dealings with Israel over the centuries? It surely ultimately
refers to the rejection of the Good Shepherd who was also valued at
thirty pieces of silver (11:4-14).

The wicked shepherd. Zedekiah is then told by the Lord to dress
himself with the equipment of a foolish shepherd. What kind of
equipment would that be?! Perhaps he changes certain items and then
acts out the part of a shepherd who only abuses the flock. God will
ultimately bring judgment on this wicked person. He is usually linked
with the wicked one of the last days spoken of in 2 Thessalonians 2
(11:15-17).

D. The Second Burden of the Lord (12:1—14:21).

We now come to the second unit of the last half of the book of Zechariah.
"The burden of the lord" separates the unit from 9—11. God's dealings
with his people Israel and the Gentile world are taken up and amplified in
this unit.

1. God's great work "in that day"—the pierced one (12:1-14).

   The phrase "in that day," designed to show that God is referring to his work in the Eschaton, occurs 17 times in this unit (12:3, 4, 6, 8, 8, 9, 11; 13:1, 2, 4; 14:4, 6, 8, 9, 13, 20, 21).

   Chapter 12 parallels chapter 9 in teaching that God will miraculously deliver the people of Israel in the last days. A coalition of peoples will gather against Jerusalem, but divine intervention will cause Israel to become "a heavy stone" that will cause injury to those who try to lift it (i.e., attack Jerusalem). Judah and Jerusalem will be strengthened and like Samson's foxes among Philistine wheat, so they will devastate the nations gathered against them. The royal house will triumph over the enemies. "The concluding verse sums up in unambiguous words the main point of the passage: *the Lord will seek to destroy all the nations that come against Jerusalem*"[392] This takes up the first six "in that day" phrases (12:1-9).

   The seventh "in that day" makes an astounding statement, provoking extended discussion and debate (12:10). The idea that God will pour out his spirit (whether technically—the Holy Spirit—or generally—the spirit of grace) is rather common in the prophets (particularly Jeremiah and Ezekiel). However, the phrase, "so that they will look on Me whom they have pierced, and they will mourn for Him, as one mourns for an only son, and they will weep bitterly over Him, like the bitter weeping over a first-born" is strange indeed. Who is the "Me"? Who is the "Him"? Are they the same people?[393] A number of Hebrew manuscripts have "they shall look on *him*" which is what appears in the New Testament. From the text of Zechariah, we can at least

   ---

   [392]Ibid., 190.

   [393]In the New Testament (John 19:37; Rev 1:7) the pronoun "me" in Zechariah is "him."

conclude that some individual was going to be killed and that the people of Israel would mourn (in repentance) *after* Yahweh pours out on them a spirit of grace and supplication. The New Testament is certainly applying this verse to Jesus Christ as the one who was crucified for the redemption of his people. The time will come when they will turn to him (Rev 1:7) in repentance.[394]

2.   The third shepherd pericope—the smitten shepherd (13:1-9).

The eighth "in that day" concludes the mourning section of Chapter 12, with the promise of a cleansing for the house of David and for the inhabitants of Jerusalem (13:1). This fountain will cleanse from sin and impurity (*niddah,* נִדָּה). The piercing of 12:10 resulted in the mourning of 12:11-14. This will be followed by cleansing in the fountain. Israel's sin (emphasis on the house of David/Jerusalem) will take place when God resumes his dealings with the people of Israel in the last days.

The ninth "in that day" turns to false prophets (13:2-6). This was a major issue in the pre and exilic period. However, in the post-exilic era it was not as significant a problem (at least as far as can be discerned from the Scripture accounts).[395] In the eschatological period, however, false prophecy will rear its ugly head once more. When that happens, concomitant with the cleansing from sin, God will remove the false prophets and the unclean spirits from the land. Even parents will assume their responsibility of denouncing their children who are caught up in this satanic movement. Furthermore (the tenth "in that

---

[394]Romans 11:26 is another marvelous verse that indicates a universal turning to the Lord in repentance by the people of Israel.

[395]An exception to this statement should be found in the prophetess Noadiah and the "rest of the prophets" who opposed Nehemiah's work of restoration (Neh. 6:14).

day") the false prophets will be so frightened of the penalty for their perfidy that they will deny that they are prophets.[396]

Once more the motif of the shepherd and the flock appears (13:7-9). This passage should be related to the enigmatic Chapter 11. Here God calls upon the sword to slay the shepherd. This shepherd is, amazingly, God's companion. This word (*gever ᵃmithi*, גֶּבֶר עֲמִיתִי) is otherwise used only in Leviticus (6:2; 19:15, 17; 25:14, 15) where it means "companion," "neighbor," "friend." This shepherd bears a special relationship to Jehovah.[397] It is God who smites the shepherd (cf. Isa. 53:4-5).

The result of the shepherd's death is that the flock will be scattered. Jesus cited this verse in connection with his own death (Matt 26:31; Mark 14:27). However, the ultimate fulfillment goes beyond the crucifixion to a time when great tribulation will come upon the people of Israel. This terrible time of suffering will result in refinement of the Jews resulting in their calling upon the name of the Lord. Then the recurring prophetic theme will come to pass: "He will be their God and they will be His people."

---

[396]Some have argued that 13:6 is a reference to Christ crucified, but the context clearly is one of false prophets. The "wounds between your arms" (Heb.: "hands") refers to chest wounds probably caused by self-flagellation common in Baal worship (cf. 1 Kings 18).

[397]F. C. Keil (*The Twelve Minor Prophets*, vol. 2 in Biblical Commentary on the Old Testament, 397) says, "The shepherd of Jehovah, whom the sword is to smite, is therefore no other than the Messiah, who is also identified with Jehovah in ch. xii. 10; or the good shepherd, who says of Himself, 'I and my Father are one' (John x. 30)."

3. Jerusalem delivered—Holy to the Lord (14:1-21).

This chapter contains seven more "in that day" phrases and is the most apocalyptic of all the chapters. Baldwin points out the chiasm of reversal in the chapter:

a I will gather all the nations against Jerusalem (14:2)
       b Jerusalem despoiled (14:2)
             c The people will suffer (14:3)
             c' All the peoples will suffer (14:12)
       b' Jerusalem despoils the nations (14:14)
a' Any who are left of all the nations . . . will go up to [Jerusalem] (14:16)[398]

This chapter contains the classical description of the Day of the Lord when He shall bring judgment upon the nations who reject him and fight against His people Israel. A unified attack by the nations who have formed a confederacy will be made against the small city of Jerusalem. Were this not a spiritual battle, such an attack would be unnecessary. The strategic position of God's people in this strategic "City of Zion" is what elicits this satanic response to the Jews. God intervenes on Mt. Olivet, a place so significant in Israel's history. From this mountain Jesus ascended back into heaven, and the angels promised that he would return as they had seen him go. This cosmic battle will result in geological changes in the land as well as astronomical changes and there will be a time of unprecedented blessing (14:6-8). Furthermore, the Lord will be acknowledged as the only God; idolatry will be gone and the people will give their undivided allegiance and devotion to the one true God of Israel.

The nations who have chosen to rebel against God and His people will now be judged (14:12-15), and Judah will despoil them as they had planned to despoil Jerusalem. Furthermore, the nations that are left will be required to come to Jerusalem annually to worship King

---

[398]Baldwin, *Haggai, Zechariah, and Malachi*, 199.

Yahweh of hosts and to celebrate the feast of Succoth. Those who refuse to come will be punished.

The final two "in that day" phrases speak of the Holiness of the situation. There will be ceremonial cleanness, but more important, there will be actual redemptive cleanness because Israel will be redeemed. The key phrase is "HOLY TO YAHWEH!" The setting for this scenario is what we call from the New Testament the Millennium—the fulfillment of all the Old Testament promises to Abraham and David in connection with the people of Israel.

Notes on the Book of Malachi

I.   The Prophet Malachi.

The Hebrew word Malachi (מַלְאָכִי) means "my messenger." The Septuagint has translated the word as a common noun: "his angel/messenger"
(ἄγγελος αὐτοῦ). Furthermore, the same word appears as a common noun
in Mal 3:1: "Behold, I am going to send My messenger, and he will clear
the way before Me. And the Lord, whom you seek, will suddenly come to
His temple; and the messenger of the covenant, in whom you delight,
behold, He is coming," says the Lord of Hosts. This fact and the absence
of this name elsewhere in Scripture has led some to question whether it is a
proper name or a common name. Von Orelli's discussion arguing for a
proper name is still valid. It should be considered a reduction of a form
like Malachiah.[399]

II. The Date and Historical Background of Malachi.

Chisholm says, "Internal evidence indicates the book was written in the
post-exilic period. The reference to a governor (*peḥa,* 1:8) points to the
Persian period. This title is used frequently in Nehemiah for Persian
governors. Earlier Haggai applied the title to Zerubbabel (Hag. 1:1, 14;
2:2, 21). Various parallels between Ezra-Nehemiah and Malachi suggest
that the latter dates to the mid-fifth century B.C. Both Ezra-Nehemiah and
Malachi refer to intermarriage with foreign wives (Ezra 9—10; Neh 13:23-
27; Mal 2:11), failure to pay tithes (Neh 13:10-14; Mal 3:8-10), and social

---

[399]C. Von Orelli, *The Twelve Minor Prophets*, pp. 382-83).

injustice (Neh 5:1-13; Mal 3:5). The precise date of Malachi is impossible to ascertain."[400]

III. The Structure of Malachi.

The structure of the book is not altogether obvious. The style is generally considered to be "disputation," that is, question, answer and rebuke. Chisholm,[401] in general agreement with Verhoef,[402] finds six units. It can at least be said that there are seven questions in the book (I am assuming that 1:7 is another facet of the same question in 1:6). The people respond to Yahweh's statement with a question in 1:2,6,7; 2:14,17; 3:7,8,13. Questions 1, 2, and 2a are introduced with the Hebrew "in what" (*bammeh,* בַּמֶּה or בַּמָּה) as are questions 4, 5, and 6. Question 3 begins with "upon what" (*'al mah,* עַל־מָה) and the final question with the simple "what" (*mah,* מָה). The form looks like this:

Chapter 1

1. But you say, How hast Thou loved us? (1:2)

2. But you say, How have we despised Thy name? (1:6)

2a. But you say, How have we defiled Thee? (1:7)

Chapter 2

3. Yet you say, For what reason? (2:14)

4. Yet you say, "How have we wearied Him? (2:17)

---

[400]R. Chisholm, *Introduction to the Minor Prophets*, 278.

[401]Ibid., 279.

[402]P. A. Verhoef, *The Books of Haggai and Malachi*, 164-68.

Chapter 3

5. But you say, How shall we return? (3:7)

6. But you say, How have we robbed Thee? (3:8)

7. Yet you say, What have we spoken against Thee? (3:13)

IV. The Outline of the Book.

A. Heading (1:1).

This message is an oracle (*massa*, מַשָּׂא) as in Zech. 9:1 and 12:1. A heavy, that is, judgmental, message is about to be delivered. It is the word of Yahweh through the prophet Malachi. The recipient of this burden is Israel. The returned exiles are aware that the remnant of Israel has returned from Babylon and thus "Israel" is used here in that sense.

B. Rhetorical question #1: "How hast Thou loved us?" (1:2-5).

The difficulty through which "Israel" has gone since 586 B.C. may have led to a cynical questioning of whether Yahweh's love was valid. After the holocaust of World War II, many Jews asked the same question. The issue of Yahweh's unfailing love for his people is a recurring theme in the prophets. Yahweh's love for Israel is demonstrated negatively: that is he has chosen Jacob over Esau. Love and hate are often used in the Bible to mean "choice" and "rejection." The words should not be understood in a visceral sense. It refers to God's sovereignty, asserted early in Genesis 25:23 (note Paul's use of both these passages in his teaching on the selection of the church over Israel in Rom 9:12-13). At this time in history (400's B.C.) the old Edomite home in Petra has been taken over by Nabatean Arabs and the Edomites have moved into the Negev area. Their original homeland has been devastated and their failure to accept this does not assure them of a future blessing.

C. Rhetorical question #2: "How have we despised your name?" (1:6—2:9).

This unit takes the priests to task. The book of Nehemiah indicates continued problems in getting the priests to perform their ritual with justice and purity. In Malachi Yahweh castigates the priests for despising his name which for them (rhetorical question 2b) means that they are defiling the altar of the temple. In spite of the priests' protestations of innocence, God says that they bring offerings that violate the Mosaic order of sacrifices. They would not even dare give such offerings to their governor (a concept indicating the post-exilic period). There will come a time, says Yahweh, when his name will be glorified among the Gentiles (1:11), but in that time even his own people were polluting his name.

The criticism of the priesthood continues in chapter 2. Yahweh promises that his judgment on them will take the form of reversal of their pronounced blessings (2:2) and the rebuking of their offspring (2:3). Yahweh reminds them of his original covenant with Levi the father of the priesthood. This covenant was one of life and peace. The priest was involved in instruction, rebuke, and his lips were to be filled with knowledge and instruction (these are "wisdom" words found in Proverbs and indicate the post-exilic emphasis on teaching by the priests). In contrast to Yahweh's original plan for the priesthood, these priests have turned from the way and have corrupted the covenant made with their ancestor Levi (2:8-9).

D. Rhetorical question #3: "For what reason" (has Yahweh rejected us)? (2:10-16).

Both Ezra (9:1—10:44) and Nehemiah (13:23-28) dealt with the problem of intermarriage between the Jews and the surrounding (pagan) peoples. Since the latter part of the chapter deals with marriage, it is probable that the first part does as well. The problem is that the "holy seed" (*zera' haqqodesh* זֶרַע הַקֹּדֶשׁ, Ezra 9:2) is being defiled through intermarriage. The "abomination" of Malachi 2:11 is also referred to in Ezra 9:1 in connection with intermarriage. The imagery of this unit, therefore, should be viewed in that light: "the covenant profaned" refers to the Mosaic prohibition against intermarriage with unbelievers; the "sanctuary" (*qodesh*, קֹדֶשׁ), as in Ezra 9:2, refers to God's holy people; and "the daughter of a foreign god" is the "idolatry" committed by this intermarriage. Consequently, Yahweh will not receive their offerings (2:10-13).

On the contrary, these people have been unfaithful to their Jewish wives. The Hebrew of 2:15 is obscure, but the sense should be picked up from the "godly offspring" (Heb: seed of God, *zera' 'elohim*, זֶרַע אֱלֹהִים). This should point to Ezra 9 where the phrase is "holy seed." In other words these returned believers are to produce holy children by staying faithful to their Jewish wives instead of divorcing them, perhaps to marry pagan wives. God hates divorce, even though he permitted it because of "the hardness of their hearts," and even though Jesus permits (but does not require) it in his discussion in the Gospels. It still is not God's ideal (2:14-16).

E. Rhetorical question #4: "How have we wearied *Him*?" (2:17—3:5).

An eschatological tone now comes into the prophecy. Yahweh has become weary of hypocrisy and disobedience. The time will come for rectifying that which is crooked. This is known throughout the prophets as "the Day of Yahweh." God will thrust himself onto the historical scene first with a predecessor or messenger. He will prepare the way before him: *upinna derek l'panai*, וּפִנָּה־דֶרֶךְ לְפָנָי (cf. Isaiah 40:3: "A voice is calling, Clear the way for the Lord (*pannu derek Yahweh* פַּנּוּ דֶּרֶךְ יהוה) in the wilderness; Make smooth in the desert a highway for our God"). Yahweh will suddenly visit his temple, obviously an accountability trip. "The messenger of the covenant" is difficult. Is it the same as the Lord or a different person? The parallelism would point to an identity of the Lord and the messenger.[403] However, the first messenger should be identified with the

---

[403] For a discussion see Chisholm, *Introduction to the Minor Prophets*, 286.

person in Isaiah 40:3 as the forerunner. Furthermore, the phrase "behold I am about to send" appears in 3:23 where it refers to Elijah as the one who will serve as a catalyst in conjunction with the Day of Yahweh.

The coming of the Lord will result in thorough purging (3:2-3). Two stringent purifiers are referred to: refiner's fire (to remove dross from metals) and washer's soap (comparable to lye soap today). This purging will bring certain results (3:4-5). (1) The offerings brought to the temple by God's people will be pleasing to Yahweh and (2) social inequities and religious apostasy will be corrected.

F. Rhetorical questions #5 and 6: "How shall we return?" and "How have we robbed Thee?" (3:6-12).

It is difficult to determine whether 3:6 goes with the preceding (NASB) or the following section (NIV). By taking the "for" as a strong assertion ("indeed"), it may be linked with what follows. Because of God's covenant faithfulness and unchangeableness, God's people will not be destroyed even though they have turned aside from Yahweh's laws (3:7).

Their insensitivity leads them to ask "what wrong have we done that would require us to return (repent)?" Yahweh then gives them a specific: they have failed to support the work of the temple with their tithes to the Lord.[404] A favorable response on their part will result in God's blessings being poured out in such a way that their agriculture will flourish (3:10-12).

G. Rhetorical question #7: "What have we spoken against thee?" (3:13-15).

Yahweh connects the final "disputation" with their arrogant words. They argue that it is of no value to serve the Lord.[405] Because of their attitude

---

[404] A similar situation existed after 432 B.C. in Nehemiah's day (13:10-14).

[405] Job says the same thing in Job 9:29.

they have concluded that those who go their own way and ignore God are the happy ones. The teaching of Ecclesiastes has been taken to a cynical extreme.

H. Concluding message of hope and judgment (3:16—4:6).

Some include this latter section with the final "disputation" unit,[406] but it seems to me that a new thought has begun. A remnant appears in 16-17; those who "fear the Lord" (*yir'e Yahweh,* יִרְאֵי יהוה) or one could say, "God-fearers." In that wonderful, future time, there will be a faithful remnant who will distinguish between the righteous and the wicked. This will come about because of God's faithfulness to them and his love for them (3:16-18).

The purification spoken of in 3:1-3 is taken up again in chapter 4.[407] It is the Day of Yahweh that will bring about the cleansing resulting in a purified remnant. Again this remnant is referred to as those who fear Yahweh's name (*yir'e shemi,* יִרְאֵי שְׁמִי). What a glorious picture of the triumph of righteousness and righteous people. What a contrast to the present immorality and injustice in the world! (4:1-3).

The concluding message to the Old Testament is found in 4:4-6. Rudolph sees Malachi 3:22-24 (4:4-6) as the conclusion of the entire prophetic canon which begins for the Hebrew Bible with Joshua 1:1. The last chapter in the Pentateuch (Deuteronomy 34), the first chapter in the prophetic canon (Joshua 1:1) and Malachi 3:22 (4:4) all refer to Moses as the servant of the Lord.[408] The righteous will be remembered (3:16), but they are also to remember the law of Moses, the law which is being cavalierly broken in

---

[406]See, e.g., Chisholm, *Introduction to the Minor Prophets,* 288-89 (3:13—4:3) and Verhoef, *The Books of Haggai and Malachi,* 312ff.

[407]The Hebrew text has only three chapters and so 4:1-6 are in Hebrew 3:19-24.

[408]W. Rudolph, *Haggai—Sacharja 1-8—Sacharja 9-14—Maleachi,* 4:291.

the post-exilic period. Furthermore, a classical Old Testament figure will come on the scene preparatory to this great period when all things will be made right, Elijah the Tishbite. This prophecy is the subject of much discussion in the New Testament. Zechariah, John the Baptist's father, is told that John will "turn back many of the sons of Israel to the Lord their God. And it is he who will go *as a forerunner* before Him in the spirit and power of Elijah, to turn the hearts of the fathers back to the children, and the disobedient to the attitude of the righteous; so as to make ready a people prepared for the Lord" (Luke 1:15-17). John the Baptist denies that he is Elijah when the Pharisees ask him whether he is Elijah (John 1:21), but he does say that he is the "voice of one crying in the wilderness, Make straight the way of the Lord, as Isaiah the prophet said" (John 1:22). When Elijah appeared in the transfiguration (Matthew 17:1-8), the disciples' curiosity was piqued, and they asked him about the teaching that "Elijah must come first" (17:10). Jesus answers that in one sense John the Baptist was Elijah but both he and the one whom he represented must be rejected and suffer at the hands of the religious leaders. However, in the future, Elijah will indeed come and restore all things (by implication, the Son of Man will also come).

There is a structure beginning with chapter 3 that carries through to the end of the book. It is eschatological in content.

Behold I am going to send my messenger (3:1-6)
  Criticism, three questions (3:7-15)
    Faithful remnant (3:16-18) God-fearers

Behold a day is coming (4:1-4)
    Faithful remnant (4:2-3) fearers of my name
  Remember the law of Moses (4:4)

Behold I am sending Elijah the prophet (4:5-6)
  Faithful remnant (4:6)

The Prophets fittingly come to a close with emphasis on the coming of Yahweh to the earth to establish the equity and justice all the prophets from Amos on down have been writing about. The predecessor, Elijah, is the harbinger of that coming one. Small wonder that the crowds poured into the Jordan valley to hear the one who came "in Elijah's spirit and power" and pointed them to the one who would "baptize them with the Holy Spirit and fire" (Matt. 3:11).

Abbreviations

AB *Anchor Bible*

ABD *Anchor Bible Dictionary*

ANEP *Ancient Near East in Pictures* (Pritchard)

ANET *Ancient Near East Texts* (Pritchard)

BA *Biblical Archaeologist*

BAR *Biblical Archaeology Review*

BASOR *Bulletin of the American School of Oriental Research*

BHS *Biblia Hebraica Stuttgartensia*

Bib *Biblica*

BibSac *Bibliotheca Sacra*

BJRL *Bulletin of the John Rylands University Library*

BKC *Bible Knowledge Commentary*

BZAW *Biblische Zeitschrift fur die Alttestamentliche Wissenschaft*

CAH *Cambridge Ancient History*

CBQ *Catholic Biblical Quarterly*

GTJ *Grace Theological Journal*

DTS *Dallas Theological Seminary*

EBC *Expositors Bible Commentary*

HUCA *Hebrew Union College Annual*

ICC *International Critical Commentary*

IEJ *Israel Exploration Journal*

JBL *Journal of Biblical Literature*

JETS *Journal of the Evangelical Theological Society*

JNES *Journal of Near Eastern Studies*

JSOT *Journal for the Study of the Old Testament*

MNHK *The Mysterious Numbers of the Hebrew Kings*

NASB *New American Standard Bible*

NICOT *New International Commentary on the Old Testament*

NIV *New International Version*

OAN Oracles against the Nations

OROT *On the Reliability of the Old Testament* (Kitchen)

RB *Revue Biblique*

TDOT *Theological Dictionary of the Old Testament*

WTJ *Westminster Theological Journal*

ZAW *Zeitschrift für die Alttestamentliche Wissenschaft*

ZPBD *Zondervan Pictorial Bible Dictionary*

Old Testament Prophets Selected Bibliography
General Works

Avigad, N. *Discovering Jerusalem*. Jerusalem: Shikmona Pub. Co., 1980.

Barkay, G. and A. Kloner. "Jerusalem Tombs from the Days of the First Temple." *BAR* 12 (April 1986): 23-29.

Beale, G. K. *We Become What We Worship—a Biblical Theology of Idolatry*. Downers Grove, IL: Inter-Varsity Press, 2008.

Bright, John. *History of Israel*. Philadelphia: Westminster, 1959.

Brin, Gershon. 'azar and 'azaz," *Leshonenu* 24 (1960): 8-14.

Brinkman, J. A. "Merodach-Baladan II" in *Studies Presented in Honor of Leo Oppenheim*. Chicago: Oriental Institute of the Univ. of Chicago, 1964.

Brown, R. E. *The Gospel According to John I-XII* in the AB.

Browning, I. *Petra*. London: Chatto and Windus, 1982.

Burrows, Millar. ed. *The Dead Sea Scrolls of St. Mark's Monastery*, vol. 1. New Haven: The American Schools of Oriental Research, 1950.

Bullock, C. Hassell. *An Introduction to the Old Testament Prophetic Books*. Chicago: Moody, 1986.

Buttrick, George A. *The Interpreter's Bible*. 12 vols. New York: Abingdon Press, 1951-55.

Charlesworth, J. H. *The Old Testament Pseudepigrapha*. Vols. 1-2. Garden City, NY: Doubleday, 1983.

Childs, B. S. *Introduction to the Old Testament as Scripture.* Phila: Fortress 1979

Cohen A. *Every Man's Talmud,* New York: Schocken Books, 1975.

Coogan, M. D. "Life in the Diaspora," *BA* 37 (1974): 7-12.

Cook, J. M. *Persian Empire.* NY: Schocken Books, 1983.

Dillard, R. B. and T. Longman, *An Old Testament Introduction.* Grand Rapids: Zondervan, 1994.

Driver, S. R. *Introduction to the Literature of the Old Testament.* 1913. Reprint ed. Magnolia, MA, 1972.

Eissfeldt, Otto. *The Old Testament: An Introduction.* New York: Harper and Row, Publishers, 1965.

Fensham, F. C. *The Books of Ezra and Nehemiah,* NICOT. Grand Rapids: Eerdmans, 1982.

Freeman, Hobart E. *An Introduction to the Old Testament Prophets.* Chicago: Moody, 1968.

Goldstein, J. A. *1 Maccabees,* AB. Garden City, NY: Anchor, 1967.

Graybill, J. B. "Evil-Merodach," in ZPBD.

Hanson, P. "Jewish Apocalyptic against Its Near Eastern Environment," *RB* 78 (1971): 31-58.

Kenyon, K. *Digging Up Jerusalem.* NY: Praeger, 1974.

Kitchen, Kenneth. *On the Reliability of the Old Testament.* Grand Rapids, Cambridge: Eerdmans, 2003.

_____. *Ancient Orient and Old Testament.* Chicago: Inter-Varsity, 1966.

_____. *The Third Intermediate Period* in Egypt: (1100-650 B.C.). Oxford: Aris and Phillips, 1986.

Koch, Klaus. *The Prophets, the Babylonian and Persian Periods.* Phila: Fortress, 1982.

LaSor, W. S., D. A. Hubbard, F. W. Bush. *Old Testament Survey.* Grand Rapids: Eerdmans, 1982, 1996.

Longenecker, Richard. *Acts,* in *Expositor's Bible Commentary.* Grand Rapids, Mich.: Zondervan, 1995.

Moscati, S. gen. ed., *The Phoenicians*, New York: Abbeville Press, 1988.

Nestle-Aland. *Novum Testamentum Graece.* Stuttgart: Deutsche Bibelgesell-schaft, 2012.

Podhoretz, Norman. *The Prophets.* NY: The Free Press, 2002.

Provan, Longman, and Long, *A Biblical History of Israel,* Westminster John Knox Press, Louisville, 2003.

Roberts, J. J. "The Old Testament's Contribution to Messianic Expectations," in *The Messiah,* ed. Charlesworth *The Messiah: Developments in Earliest Judaism and Christianity.* Augsburg: Fortress, 2002,

Rogerson, John. *Atlas of the Bible.* New York: Facts on File, 1985.

Rostovtzeff, M. "Syria and the East," in *CAH*, vol. 7.

Schedl, C. *History of the Old Testament.* NY: Alba House, 1973.

Smith, S. "The Foundation of the Assyrian Empire," in *CAH,* vol. 3.

Soggin, J. A. *Introduction to the Old Testament.* Tran. J. Bowden. OTL. Philadelphia: 1976.

Thiele, Edwin. *The Mysterious Numbers of the Hebrew Kings*. Grand Rapids: Zondervan, 1983.

von Rad, G. *The Message of the Prophet*. San Francisco: Harper, 1967.

Watson, W. G. E. *Classical Hebrew Poetry*. Sheffield: Academic Press, 2001.

Young, Edward J. *My Servants the Prophets*. Grand Rapids: Eerdmans, 1952.

Isaiah

Albright, W. F. "The Son of Tabeel [Isa. 7:6]." *BASOR* 140 (1955): 34-35.

Alexander, Joseph. A. *Commentary on the Prophecies of Isaiah*. Reprint. Grand Rapids: Zondervan, 1953.

Barnes, Albert. *Notes on the Old Testament, Explanatory and Practical: Isaiah*. 2 vols. Grand Rapids: Baker, 1950.

Delitzsch, Franz. *Isaiah*. Trans. by James Martin. 2 vols. Reprint ed. Grand Rapids: Eerdmans, 1954.

Driver, S. R. and A. Neubauer, *The Fifty-Third Chapter of Isaiah According to the Jewish Interpreters*, Oxford: Parker & Co., 1877. Reprint 1969 New York: Harmon Press.

Erlandsson, Seth. *The Burden of Babylon*. Lund, Sweden: CWK Gleerup, n.d.

Gray, George B. *A Critical and Exegetical Commentary on the Book of Isaiah: Vol. I: Introduction and Commentary on I-XXVII*. ICC. Edinburgh: T. & T. Clark, 1912.

Hayes, John H. and Stuart A. Irving. *Isaiah, the Eighth Century Prophet; His Times and His Preaching*, Abingdon Press, 1987.

Heater, H. "Do the Prophets Teach that Babylonia will be rebuilt in the *Eschaton*?" *JETS* 41 (1998) 23-43.

Hebert, A. S. *The Book of the Prophet Isaiah: Chapters I-XXXIX.* Cambridge: University Press, 1973.

Janowski, Bernd and Peter Stuhlmacher, eds., *The Suffering Servant; Isaiah 53 in Jewish and Christian Sources*, 2004. Originally: *Der leidende Gottesknecht*, by Mohr Siebeck, 1996.

Jennings, F. C. *Studies in Isaiah.* New York: Loizeaux, 1950.

Jensen, J. *Isaiah 1—39.* O. T. Message. Vol. 8. M. Glazier, 1984.

Josephus. *Jewish Antiquities.* 9 vols. Cambridge, MA: Harvard University Press, 1966.

Joüon, P. *Grammaire de l'Hebrew Biblique.* Rome: Pontifical Biblical Institute, 1923.

Kaiser, Otto. *Isaiah 1-12: A Commentary.* Philadelphia: Westminster, 1972.

_____. *Isaiah 13-39: A Commentary.* Philadelphia: Westminster, 1974.

Kline, M. "Death, Leviathan, and Martyrs: Isaiah 24:1—27:1." *A Tribute to Gleason Archer.* Ed. W. Kaiser and R. Youngblood. Chicago: Moody, 1986.

Knight, George A. F. *Deutero-Isaiah: A Theological Commentary on Isaiah 40-55.* New York: Abingdon, 1965.

Knudsen, Joel. "The Archetypes of Evil in Isaiah 13-27." Th.M. thesis, DTS, 1980.

Leupold, H. C. *Exposition of Isaiah.* 2 vols. Grand Rapids: Baker, 1968.

Luckenbill, D. D. *Annals of Sennacherib.* Chicago: Univ. of Chicago Press, 1926.

MacRae, Allan A. *The Gospel of Isaiah.* Chicago: Moody, 1977.

Martin, Alfred. *Isaiah: The Salvation of Jehovah.* Chicago: Moody, 1956.

McKenzie, John L. *Second Isaiah.* AB. Garden City, New York: Doubleday, 1967.

Mauchline, John. *Isaiah 1-39.* London: S. C. M., 1962.

Millar, W. R. *Isaiah 24—27 and the Origin of Apocalyptic.* Missoula, MT: Scholars Press, 1976.

Motyer, J. Alec. *The Prophecy of Isaiah.* Downers Grove, IL: Inter-Varsity Press, 1993.

North, Christopher R. *The Second Isaiah: Introduction, Translation and Commentary to Chapters 40-55.* Oxford: Clarendon, 1964.

____. *The Suffering Servant in Deutero-Isaiah: An Historical and Critical Study.* Oxford: University Press, 1948.

Oded, B. "The Historical Background of the Syro-Ephraimite War Reconsidered." *CBQ* 34 (1972): 153-65.

Olmstead, A. T. *History of Assyria.* Chicago: Univ. of Chicago Press, 1951.

Oswalt, John N. *The Book of Isaiah--Chapters 1-39.* NICOT. Grand Rapids: Eerdmans, 1986.

Ridderbos, J. *Isaiah.* Bible Student's Commentary. Grand Rapids: Zondervan, 1984.

Schafron, Phillip. "The Importance of Cyrus in the Argument of Isaiah 40—48." Th.M. thesis, DTS, 1981.

Shanks, Herschel. "Assyrian Palace Discovered in Ashdod," *BAR* 33:1 (2006) 56-60.

Skinner, J. *The Book of Isaiah the Prophet.* 2 vols. The Cambridge Bible for Schools and Colleges. Cambridge: University Press, 1898.

Tadmor. "Azarijau of Yaudi," *Scripta Hierosolymitana* 8 (1961): 232-271.

Torrey, Charles Cutler. *The Second Isaiah: A New Interpretation.* New York: Charles Scribner's Sons, 1928.

Von Orelli, C. *The Prophecies of Isaiah.* Trans. by J. S. Banks. Edinburgh: T. & T. Clark, 1889.

Watts, John D. W. *Isaiah 1—33* in Word Biblical Commentary. Vol. 24. Waco, TX: Word Books, 1985.

Westermann, Claus. *Isaiah 40-66: A Commentary.* Philadelphia: Westminster, 1969.

Wolf, Herbert M. *Interpreting Isaiah.* Grand Rapids: Zondervan, 1985.

_____. "The Relationship Between Isaiah's Final Servant Song (52:13—53:12) and Chapter 1—6." *A Tribute to Gleason Archer.*

Wright, G. Ernest. *The Book of Isaiah.* The Layman's Bible Commentary. Richmond: John Knox, 1964.

Young, Edward J. *The Book of Isaiah.* 3 vols. NICOT. Grand Rapids: Eerdmans, 1969-1972.

_____. *Studies in Isaiah.* (Now out of print.)

Jeremiah

Ackroyd, Peter R. "The Book of Jeremiah—Some Recent Studies," *JSOT* 28 (1984) 47-59.

_____. "Two Old Testament Historical Problems of the Early Persian Period," *JNES* 217 (1958) 23-27.

Aitken, Kenneth T. "The Oracles Against Babylon in Jeremiah 50-51: Structures and Perspectives." *TynBul* 35 (1984) 25-63.

Borger, Riekele. "An Additional Remark on P. R. Ackroyd, *JNES* XKVII, 23-27," *JNES* 18 (1959) 74.

Boutflower, Charles. *The Book of Isaiah, Chapters I-XXXIX, in the Light of the Assyrian Monuments.* New York: Macmillan, 1930.

Bright, John. *Jeremiah* in AB, Garden City, NY: Doubleday and Co., Inc., 1965.

_____. "The Date of the Prose Sermons of Jeremiah," *JBL* 70 (1951) 15-35.

_____. *A Commentary on Jeremiah; Exile and Homecoming."* Grand Rapids: Eerdmans, 1998.

Carroll, Robert P. *Jeremiah* in Old Testament Library. London: SCM Press, 1986.

Craigie, Peter. *Jeremiah 1-25.* Word Biblical Commentary. Waco, TX: Word, 1985.

De Roche, Michael. "Is Jeremiah 25:15-29 a Piece of Reworked Jeremianic Poetry?" *JSOT* 10 (1978) 58-67.

Delcor, M. "Le culte de la 'Reine du Ciel'" in From Kanaan bis Kerala, ed. W.C. Delsman, et al., Neukirchen-Vluyn: Neukirchner Verlag, 1982.

Dijkstra, Meindert. "Prophecy by Letter Jeremiah XXIX 24-32," *VT* 33 (1983): 319-322.

Dorsey, David A. "Broken Potsherds at the Potter's House: an Investigation of the Arrangement of the Book of Jeremiah," *Evangelical Journal* 1 (1983) 3-16.

_____. "Recent Commentaries on Jeremiah." *Evangelical Journal* 6 (1988) 37-42.

Erdman, Charles R. *The Book of Jeremiah and Lamentations.* Westwood, New Jersey: Revell, 1955.

Feinberg, C. L. *Jeremiah, a Commentary.* Grand Rapids: Zondervan, 1983.

Finkelstein, J. "Excavations at Shiloh 1981-1984, Preliminary Report," *Tel Aviv* 12 (1985) 159-77.

Friedman, H. *Jeremiah.* London: Soncino, 1949.

Gordon, C. H. *Ugaritic Textbook.* Rome: Pontifical Biblical Institute, 1967.

Gosse, Bernard. "La malédiction contre Babylone de Jérémie 51,59-64 et les rédactions du livre de Jérémie." *ZAW* 98 (1986) 383-99.

Grothe, J. F. "An Argument for the Textual Genuineness of Jeremiah 33:14-26 (MT)," Concordia Journal 7 (1981) 188-91.

Harrison, R. K. *Jeremiah and Lamentations.* Downers Grove, IL: Inter-Varsity, 1973.

Herr, Larry G. "The Servant of Baalis," *BA* 48 (1985) 169-72.

Hobbs, T. R. "Some Remarks on the Composition and Structure of the Book of Jeremiah" in A Prophet to the Nations; Essays in Jeremiah Studies, eds. L. G. Perdue and B. W. Kovacs, Winona Lake, IN: Eisenbrauns, 1984. Originally pub. CBQ 34 (1972) 257-75.

Holladay, Wm. L. "Prototype and Copies: a New Approach to the Poetry-Prose Problem in the Book of Jeremiah," *JBL* 79 (1960) 351-367.

_____. "A Fresh Look at 'Source B' and 'Source C' in Jeremiah," *VT* 25:2 (1975) 394-412.

_____. *Jeremiah 1 and 2* in Hermeneia, Philadelphia: Minneapolis: Fortress, 1986, 1989

_____. "God Writes a Rude Letter (Jeremiah 29:1-23)." *BA* 46 (1983): 145-146.

_____. "Jeremiah 31:22b Reconsidered: 'The Woman Encompasses the Man.'" VT 16 (1966): 236-239.

Hopper, S. R. "Jeremiah" in *The Interpreters Bible*. NY: Abingdon Press, 1956.

Jackson, J. J. "A Vision of Figs: Current Problems." Proceedings Eastern Great Lakes and Midwest Bible Society 7 (1987) 143-157.

Janzen, Gerald. *Studies in the Text of Jeremiah*. Cambridge, MA: Harvard University Press, 1973.

Jones, Douglas R. *Jeremiah* in The New Century Bible, Clements and Black, eds. Grand Rapids: Eerdmans, 1992.

Joüon, P. *Grammaire de l'Hébreu Biblique.* Rome: Pontifical Biblical Institute, 1924, 1993.

Keil, C. F. *The Prophecies of Jeremiah.* 2 vols. Grand Rapids: Eerdmans, 1950.

Laberge, Leo. "Jeremie 25:1-14: Dieu et Juda ou Jeremie et tous les peuples." *Science and Esprit* 36 (1984) 45-66.

Laetsch, Theodore. *Jeremiah.* St. Louis: Concordia, 1952.

Larsson, Gerhard. "When Did the Babylonian Captivity Begin?" *JTS* 18 (1967) 417-423.

Lemke, Werner E. "'Nebuchadrezzar, My Servant,'" *CBQ* 28 (1966) 45-50.

Malamat, A. "The Historical Setting of Two Biblical Prophecies on the Nations." *IEJ* 1 (1950-51) 149-59.

McConville, J. Gordon. "Jeremiah: Prophet and Book." TynBul 42:1 (1991) 80-95.

McKane, William. *Jeremiah*, 2 vols in ICC, Edinburgh: T. & T. Clark, Ltd, 1986.

Oded, B. "When did the Kingdom of Judah Become Subjected to Babylonian Rule?" *Tarbiz* 35 (1966) 104 [Hebrew].

Orr, Avigdor. "The Seventy Years of Babylon," *VT* 6 (1956) 304-6.

Overholt, Thomas W. "King Nebuchadnezzar in the Jeremiah Tradition." *CBQ* 30 (1968) 39-48.

Patterson, Robert M. "Reinterpretation in the Book of Jeremiah." *JSOT* 28 (1984) 37-46.

Payne, J. B. "The Arrangement of Jeremiah's Prophecies." *BETS* (now *JETS*) 7:4 (1964): 120-130.

Plotkin, Albert. *The Religion of Jeremiah.* New York: Bloch, n.d.

Rietzschel, C. *Das Problem der Urrolle*, Gütersloh: Gütersloher Verlagshaus G. Mohn, 1966.

Schenker, Adrian. "Nebukadnezzars Metamorphose—vom Unterjocher zum Gottesknecht," *RB* 89 (1982) 498-529.

Shiloh, Yigal. "Did the Philistines Destroy the Israelite Sanctuary at Shiloh?—the Archaeological Evidence," *BAR* 1:2 (1975): 3-5.

_____. "A Group of Hebrew Bullae from the City of David." *IEJ* 36 (1986) 16-38.

Smith, Ralph L. *Micah to Malachi* in Word Biblical Commentaries. Waco, TX: Word Publishers, 1984.

Smothers, Thomas G. "A Lawsuit against the Nations: Reflections on the Oracles against the Nations in Jeremiah." *RevExp* 85 (1988) 545-54.

Streane, A. W. *The Book of the Prophet Jeremiah Together with the Lamentations.* Cambridge: University Press, 1899.

Taylor, M. A. "Jeremiah 45: the Problem of Placement," JSOT 37 (1987) 79-98.

Thompson, J. A. *The Book of Jeremiah.* NICOT. Grand Rapids: Eerdmans, 1980.

Troth, William A. "A Study of the Termini of the Seventy Year Captivity." Th.M. thesis, Dallas Theological Seminary.

Unterman, J. *From Repentance to Redemption.* Sheffield: JSOT 1987.

Wanke, B. *Untersuchungen zur sogenannten Baruchschrift*, BZAW 122, de Gruyter, Berlin/NY, 1971.

Weippert, H. *Die Prosareden des Jeremiabuches* BZAW 132, de Gruyter, Berlin/NY, 1973.

Whitley, Charles F. "The Term Seventy Years Captivity," *VT* 4 (1954) 60-72.

_____. "The Seventy Years Desolation—A Rejoinder," *VT* 7 (1957) 416-18.

Winkle, Ross E. "Jeremiah's Seventy Years for Babylon: A Re-assessment: Part I: The Scriptural Data." *AUSS* 25 (1987) 201-14.

Wiseman, D. J. *Nebuchadrezzar and Babylon.* Oxford: University Press, 1983.

_____. *Chronicles of Chaldaean Kings.* London: Trustees of the British Museum, 1956.

Zevit, Ziony. "The Use of עֶבֶד as a Diplomatic Term in Jeremiah," *JBL* 88 (1969) 74-77.

Lamentations

Cohen, Abraham. *The Five Megilloth.* London: Soncino, 1946.

Erdman, Charles R. *The Book of Jeremiah and Lamentations.* Westwood, New Jersey: Revell, 1955.

Gordis, Robert. *The Song of Songs and Lamentations.* New York: KTAV, 1974.

Gottwald, Norman K. *Studies in the Book of Lamentations.* London: SCM, 1954.

Harrison, R. K. *Jeremiah and Lamentations.* Downers Grove, IL: Inter-Varsity, 1973.

Heater, H. "Structure and Meaning in Lamentations." *Vital Old Testament Issues.* Ed. Roy Zuck. Grand Rapids: Kregal, 1996.

Hillers, Delbert R. *Lamentations.* AB. Garden City, New York: Doubleday, 1972.

Keil, C. F. *The Prophecies of Jeremiah.* 2 vols. Grand Rapids: Eerdmans, 1950.

Kuist, Howard Tillman. *The Book of Jeremiah, the Lamentations of Jeremiah.* The Layman's Bible Commentary. Richmond: John Knox, 1960.

Pearce, R. A. "Shiloh and Jeremiah VII, 12, 14, & 15." *VT* 23:1 (1973): 105-108.

Plotkin, Albert. *The Religion of Jeremiah.* New York: Bloch, n.d.

Streane, A. W. *The Book of the Prophet Jeremiah Together with the Lamentations.* Cambridge: University Press, 1899.

Ezekiel

Albright, W. F. "The Latest Pre-Exilic History of Judah, with some Observations on Ezekiel." *JBL* 51 (1932): 77-106.

_____. "The Seal of Eliakim and the Latest Pre-Exilic History of Judah, with some Observations on Ezekiel," *JBL* 51 (1932): 77-106.

Alexander, Ralph. *Ezekiel.* Chicago: Moody, 1976.

_____. *Ezekiel* in EBC. 12 vols. Ed. Frank E. Gaebelein. Vol. 6. Grand Rapids: Zondervan, 1979.

Beck, John C. "The Fall of Tyre According to Ezekiel's Prophecy." Th.M. thesis, Dallas Theological Seminary.

Blackwood, Andrew W. *Ezekiel: Prophecy of Hope.* Grand Rapids: Baker, 1965.

Brownlee, W. H. *Ezekiel 1-19* in *Word Biblical Commentary.* Waco, TX., 1986.

Cassuto, U. *A Commentary on the Book of Genesis.* Jerusalem: Magnes Press, 1978 (Reprint of 1944 ed.).

Cook, J. M. *History of the Persian Empire.* New York: Schocken Books, 1983.

Cooke, G. A. *A Critical and Exegetical Commentary on the Book of Ezekiel.* Edinburgh: T. & T. Clark, 1936.

Davidson, A. B. *The Book of the Prophet Ezekiel.* Cambridge: University Press, 1892.

Driver, S. R. and A. Neubauer, *The Fifty-Third Chapter of Isaiah According to the Jewish Interpreters*, Oxford: Parker & Co., 1877. Reprint 1969 New York: Harmon Press.

Eichrodt, Walther. *Ezekiel.* Philadelphia: Westminster, 1970.

Ellison, H. L. *Ezekiel, the Man and His Message.* Grand Rapids: Eerdmans, 1956.

Erdman, Charles R. *The Book of Ezekiel.* Westwood, New Jersey: Revell, 1956.

Fairbairn, Patrick. *An Exposition of Ezekiel.* Reprint ed. Grand Rapids: Zondervan, 1960.

Feinberg, Charles Lee. *The Prophecy of Ezekiel, the Glory of the Lord.* Chicago: Moody, 1969.

Finegan, Jack. "The Chronology of Ezekiel." *JBL* 69 (1950).

_____. *Light from the Ancient Past*, Princeton: Princeton University Press, 1946, 1959.

Fisch, S. *Ezekiel.* London: Soncino, 1950.

Freedman, David N. "The Book of Ezekiel." *Int* 8 (1954): 466-71.

Gaebelein, Arno C. *The Prophet Ezekiel.* New York: Revell, 1918.

Gardiner, F. *Ezekiel* in Ellicott's Commentary on the Whole Bible, Reprint, Grand Rapids: Zondervan, 1959.

Greenberg, Moshe. *Ezekiel 1-20.* AB. Garden City, NY: Doubleday, 1983.

_____. "On Ezekiel's Dumbness," *JBL* 77 (1958): 101-105.

Holscher, G. "Hesekiel: Der Dichter und das Buch." *BZAW* 39 (1924).

Jensen, Irving L. *Ezekiel—Daniel.* Chicago: Moody, 1968.

Keil, C. F. *Biblical Commentary on the Prophecies of Ezekiel.* Grand Rapids: Eerdmans, 1950.

Lawhead, A. S. "A Problem of Unfulfilled Prophecy in Ezekiel: A Response." *WTJ* 16 (1981): 15-19.

Moran, W. L. "Genesis 49:10 and Its Use in Ezekiel 21:32," *Bib* 39 (1958):405-25.

Olmstead, A. T. *History of the Persian Empire*, Chicago: Univ. of Chicago Press, 1948.

Reilly, J. B. "The Historicity of Nebuchadnezzar's Invasion of Egypt," Th.M. thesis, DTS.

Thompson, D. L. "A Problem of Unfulfilled Prophecy in Ezekiel," *WTJ* 16 (1981): 93-106.

Thompson, R. C. "The New Babylonian Empire," in *CAH* 3:215.

Whitcomb, John. "Christ's Atonement and Animal Sacrifices in Israel," *GTJ* 6 (1985): 2:212

Zimmerli, Walter. *Ezekiel*. Hermeneia. Philadelphia: Fortress, 1979.

_____. "The Message of the Prophet Ezekiel." *Int* 23 (1969): 131-57.

Daniel

Anderson, Robert. *The Coming Prince.* Reprint ed. Grand Rapids: Kregel, 1957.

Archer, Gleason. *Daniel*, in EBC. Vol. 7. Ed. Frank E. Gaebelein. Grand Rapids: Zondervan, 1985.

Baldwin, Joyce. *Daniel*. Tyndale Old Testament Commentaries. Downers Grove, IL: Inter-Varsity, 1978.

Barnes, Albert. *Barnes' Notes on the Old Testament: Daniel.* Grand Rapids: Baker, 1950.

Braverman, J. *Jerome's Commentary on Daniel.* CBQ Mongraph Series 7. Washington DC: CBQ, 1978.

Cohen, Simon. "The Political Background of the Words of Amos," HUCA 36 (1965) 158.

Collins, John J. *Daniel with an Introduction to Apocalyptic Literature*, 20 in The Forms of the Old Testament Literature, Grand Rapids: Eerdmans, 1984.

Culver, Robert D. *Daniel and the Latter Days.* Chicago: Moody, 1954.

"DSS, Part I: Archaeology of Biblical MSS." *BA* 49 (1986): 140-154.

Ford, Desmond. *Daniel.* Nashville: Southern, 1978.

Gaebelein, Arno C. *The Prophet Daniel.* Reprint ed. Grand Rapids: Kregel, 1955.

Gaebelein, Frank E., ed. *The Expositor's Bible Commentary.* Vol. 7. Grand Rapids: Zondervan, 1985.

Hartman, Louis and Alexander DiLella. *Daniel* in AB. Garden City, NY: Doubleday, 1977.

Jensen, Irving L. *Ezekiel--Daniel.* Chicago: Moody, 1968.

Keil, C. F. *Biblical Commentary on the Book of Daniel.* Reprint ed. Grand Rapids: Eerdmans, 1949.

Kalafian, Michael. *The Prophecy of the 70 Weeks of the Book of Daniel.* Lanham, MD: University Press, 1991.

King, Geoffrey C. *Daniel.* Grand Rapids: Eerdmans, 1966.

Lang, G. H. *The Histories and Prophecies of Daniel.* Grand Rapids: Kregel, 1973.

Lenglet, A. "La Structure Littéraire de Daniel 2-7," *Biblica,* 53, 1972, pp. 169-190.

Leupold, H. C. *Exposition of Daniel.* Reprint ed. Grand Rapids: Baker, 1969.

Luck, G. Coleman. *Daniel.* Chicago: Moody, 1958.

Montgomery, J. A. *Daniel* in ICC, Driver, et al. editors. Edinburgh: T and T Clark, 1926.

Mosca, P. "Ugaritic and Daniel 7: a Missing Link." *Biblica* 67 (1986) 496-517.

Newell, Philip R. *Daniel, the Man Greatly Beloved and His Prophecies.* Chicago: Moody, 1951.

Perowne, S. *The Life and Times of Herod the Great.* NY: Abingdon Press, 1956.

Pusey, Edward B. *Daniel the Prophet.* New York: Funk, 1885.

Stevens, W. C. *The Book of Daniel.* New York: Revell, 1915.

Talbot, Louis T. *The Prophecies of Daniel.* Wheaton, IL: Van Kampen, 1940.

Tregelles, J. P. *Remarks on Prophetic Visions in the Book of Daniel.* Edinburgh: Bagster, 1883.

Walton, J. H. "The Four Kingdoms of Daniel." *JETS* 29 (1986): 25-36.

Walvoord, John F. *Daniel: The Key to Prophetic Revelation.* Chicago: Moody, 1971.

Whitcomb, John C. *Darius the Mede.* Grand Rapids: Eerdmans, 1959.

Wilson, R. D. *Studies in the Book of Daniel.* Grand Rapids: Baker, 1972.

Wiseman, Donald J. *Chronicles of Chaldaean Kings*. London: The Trustees of the British Museum, 1956.

____. *Nebuchadnezzar and Babylon*. London: Oxford Press, n.d.

____. *Notes on some Problems in the Book of Daniel*. London: The Tyndale Press, 1965.

Wood, Leon. *A Commentary on Daniel*. Grand Rapids: Zondervan, 1973.

Wood, L. *Daniel* in EBC, Grand Rapids: Zondervan, 1985.

Young, Edward J. *The Messianic Prophecies of Daniel*. Grand Rapids: Eerdmans, 1955.

____. *The Prophecy of Daniel*. Grand Rapids: Eerdmans, 1949.

Minor Prophets

Allen, Leslie C. *The Books of Joel, Obadiah, Jonah, and Micah*. NICOT. Grand Rapids: Eerdmans, 1976.

Anderson, F. I. and D. N. Freedman. *Hosea* in Anchor Bible. Garden City, NY: Doubleday and Company, 1980.

____. *Amos*. Same publication data.

Baldwin, Joyce. *Haggai, Zechariah, and Malachi*. Tyndale Old Testament Commentaries. Downers Grove, IL: Inter-Varsity Press, 1972.

Cheyne, T. K. *Hosea, with Notes and Introduction*. Cambridge: University Press, 1899.

____. *Micah, with Notes and Introduction*. Cambridge: University Press, 1902.

Chisholm, Robert. *Interpreting the Minor Prophets*. Grand Rapids: Zondervan, 1991.

_____. Joel in *BKC*. J. Walvoord and R. Zuck, eds. Wheaton: Victor Books, 1985.

Cohen, A. *The Twelve Prophets*. London: Soncino, 1948.

Cohen, Simon. "The Political Background of the Words of Amos." *HUCA* 36 (1965): 153-160, 319-329.

Cripps, Richard S. *A Critical and Exegetical Commentary on the Book of Amos*. London: SPCK, 1929. Reprint ed., 1969.

Davidson, A. B. *Nahum, Habakkuk, and Zephaniah*. Cambridge: University Press, 1896.

Driver, S. R. *The Books of Joel and Amos*. Cambridge: University Press, 1897.

Ellison, H. L. *Men Spake from God*. Grand Rapids: Eerdmans, 1952.

____. *The Prophets of Israel*. Grand Rapids: Eerdmans, 1969.

Farr, G. "The Concept of Grace in the Book of Hosea." *ZAW* 70 (1958): 98-107.

Feinberg, Charles L. *The Minor Prophets*. Chicago: Moody, 1976.

Freedman and Anderson, "Harmon in Amos 4:3," *BASOR* 198 (1970):41

Freeman, Hobart O. *Nahum, Zephaniah, and Habakkuk*. Chicago: Moody, 1973.

Frick, F. S. "Rain" in ABD.

Gaebelein, Arno C. *The Prophet Joel*. New York: Our Hope, 1909.

Garrett, D. A. "The Structure of Joel." *JETS* 28 (1985): 289-297.

_____. *Hosea* in The New American Commentary. Nashville: Broadman and Holman, 1997.

Hall, H. R. "The Ethiopians and Assyrians in Egypt," *CAH* Vol. 3.

Hanson, P. "Jewish Apocalyptic against Its Near Eastern Environment," *RB* 78 (1971): 31-58.

Haran, M. "Observations on the Historical Background of Amos 1:2—2:6." *IEJ* 18 (1968): 201-212.

Heater, H. *Zechariah* in Bible Studies Commentary. Grand Rapids: Zondervan, 1987.

_____. *Amos* in *The Case for Premillennialism*, ed. Campbell and Thompson. Chicago: Moody, 1992.

_____. "Matthew 2:6 and Its Old Testament Sources." *JETS* 26 (1983) 395-397.

Hiers, Richard H. *Day of Yahweh*. ABD.

Honeycutt, Roy L. *Amos and His Message*. Nashville: Broadman, 1963.

____. *Hosea and His Message*. Nashville: Broadman, 1975.

Hubbard, David Allan. *With Bands of Love.* Grand Rapids: Eerdmans, 1968.

Keil, C. F. *The Twelve Minor Prophets.* 2 vols. Grand Rapids: Eerdmans, 1954.

Kobayashi, Y. "Elkosh" in *ABD*.

Laetsch, Theodore. *The Minor Prophets.* St. Louis: Concordia, 1945.

Lamarche, P. *Zacharie IX-XIV, Structure Littérarie et Messianisme.* Paris: Gabalda, 1961.

Lanchester, H. C. O. *Obadiah and Jonah.* Cambridge: University Press, 1918.

Lewis, Jack P. *The Minor Prophets.* Grand Rapids: Baker, 1966.

Longenecker, R. N. *Acts* in *EBC*. Grand Rapids: Zondervan, 1995.

Maier, Walter A. *The Book of Nahum: A Commentary*. St. Louis: Concordia, 1959.

Mays, James L. *Amos: A Commentary*. Philadelphia: Westminster, 1969.

____. *Hosea: A Commentary*. Philadelphia: Westminster, 1969.

Mays, James L. *Micah: A Commentary*. Philadelphia: Westminster, 1976.

McComiskey, T. E. *Amos*, in *EBC*. Grand Rapids: Zondervan, 1985.

____. *Micah*, in *EBC*. Grand Rapids: Zondervan, 1985.

Motyer, J. A. *The Day of the Lion*. Downers Grove, IL: Inter-Varsity, 1974.

Patterson, Richard D. *Joel,* in *EBC*. Grand Rapids: Zondervan, 1985.

Price, Walter K. *The Prophet Joel and the Day of the Lord*. 2 vols. Chicago: Moody, 1976.

Pusey, Edward B. *The Minor Prophets*. 2 vols. Reprint ed. Grand Rapids: Baker, 1950.

Rowley, H. H. "The Marriage of Hosea." *BJRL* 39 (1956-57): 220-33.

Rudolph, W. *Haggai—Sacharja 1-8—Sacharja 9-14—Maleachi* in Kommentar zum Alten Testament, XIII. Gütersloh : Gütersloher Verlagshaus Gerd Mohn , 1981.

Sasson, Jack. *Jonah* in AB. NY: Doubleday, 1990.

Scott, Jack B. *The Book of Hosea*. Grand Rapids: Baker, 1971.

Smith, Ralph L. "Micah-Malachi" in *Word Biblical Commentary*. Waco, TX: Word, 1984

Smith, B. K., and Frank Page. *Amos, Obadiah, and Jonah in* The New American Commentary. Nashville: B&H Publishing Group, 1995.

Stuart, Douglas. *Hosea through Jonah* in Word Biblical Commentary. Vol 31. Word Books: Waco, TX., 1987.

Verhoef, P. A. *The Books of Haggai and Malachi* in NICOT. Grand Rapids: Eerdmans, 1987

Von Orelli. *The Twelve Minor Prophets*. Trans. by J. S. Banks. 1897. Reprint ed. Minneapolis: Klock & Klock Christian Publishers, 1977.

Watts, John D. W. *Obadiah: A Critical Exegetical Commentary.* Grand Rapids: Eerdmans, 1969.

Weiss, Meir. "The Origin of the 'Day of the Lord' Reconsidered." *HUCA* 37 (1966): 29-71.

Wolff, Hans W. *Hosea: A Commentary on the Book of the Prophet Hosea.* Hermeneia. Philadelphia: Fortress, 1974.

____. *Joel and Amos.* Hermeneia. Philadelphia: Fortress, 1977.

Wood, Leon. *Hosea* in EBC. Grand Rapids: Zondervan, 1995.

Made in the USA
Columbia, SC
13 August 2018